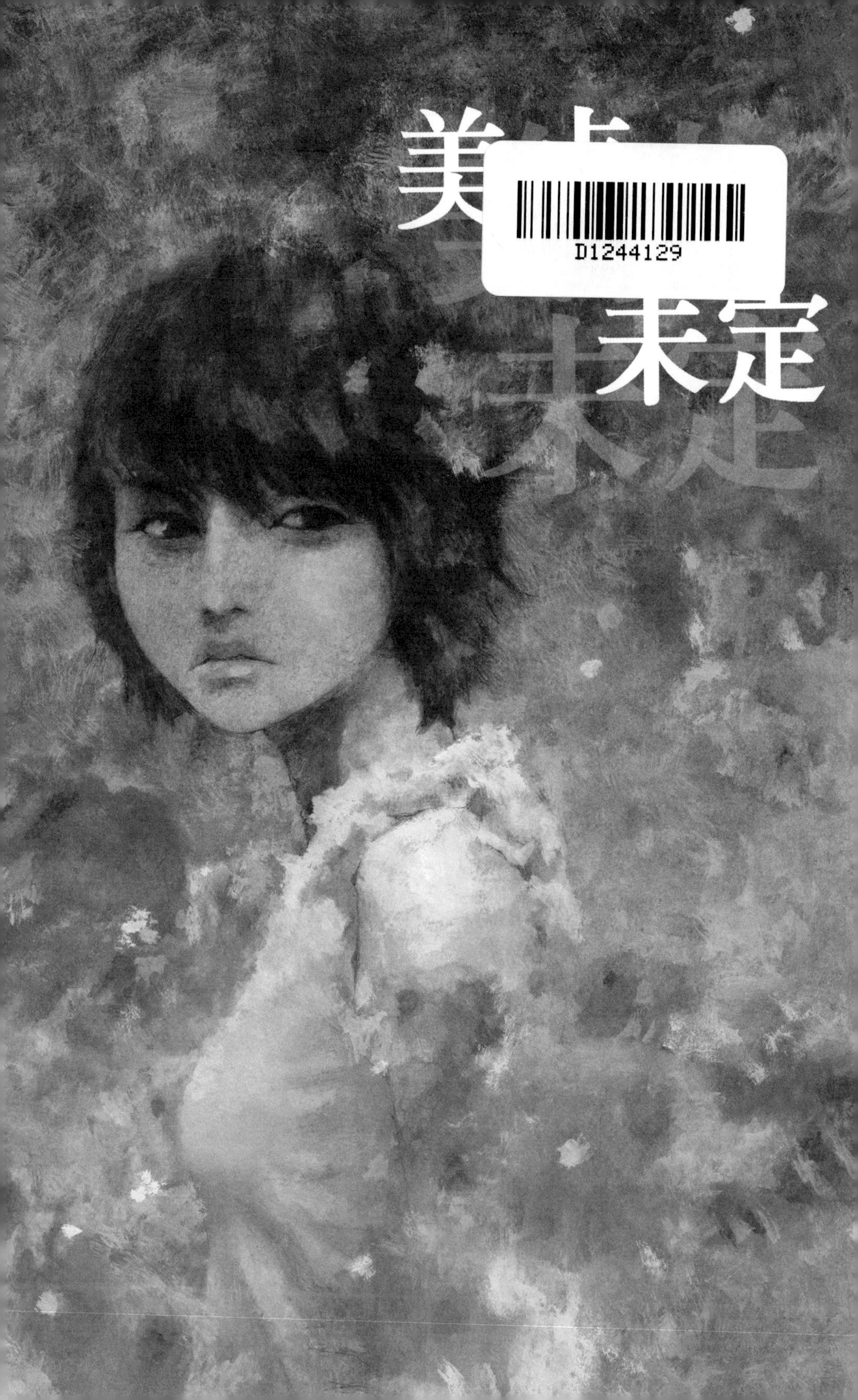
美
未定

READER REVIEW

What did you think of this book? Let other readers know your opinion

_____

_____

_____

_____

_____

_____

_____

_____

_____

_____

_____

_____

_____

ISBN 13: 978-1-56163-554-2
ISBN 10: 1-56163-554-5
© 2003 Byun Byung-Jun
All rights reserved
First published in Korea in 2003 by Imageframe Co. Ltd.
English translation rights arranged with Imageframe Co. Ltd.
through Orange Agency
© 2009 NBM for the English translation
Translation by Joe Johnson
Lettering by Ortho
Printed in Hong Kong

3   2   1

ComicsLit is an imprint
and trademark of

NANTIER · BEALL · MINOUSTCHINE
Publishing inc.
new york

CONTENTS

What one artist thinks

The monochromatic esthetic of Byun Byung Jun's manwha leaves no room for despair. His technopolistical fantasies set against a background of rough cement and blue-toned asphalt draw you in. Thought, hypnotized by the line, freezes at the lost look of a young girl who seems to conceal all the secrets of the world.

Kim Hyeong-Bae,

Since 1999, the Seoul Animation Center has been organizing competitions to encourage the creation of manhwas. It was because of these efforts that Kim Sung Jun's **Cosmos** and Byun Byung Jun's **Mijeong** (Prize for Excellence in Short or Long Stories) came to be published in Korea.

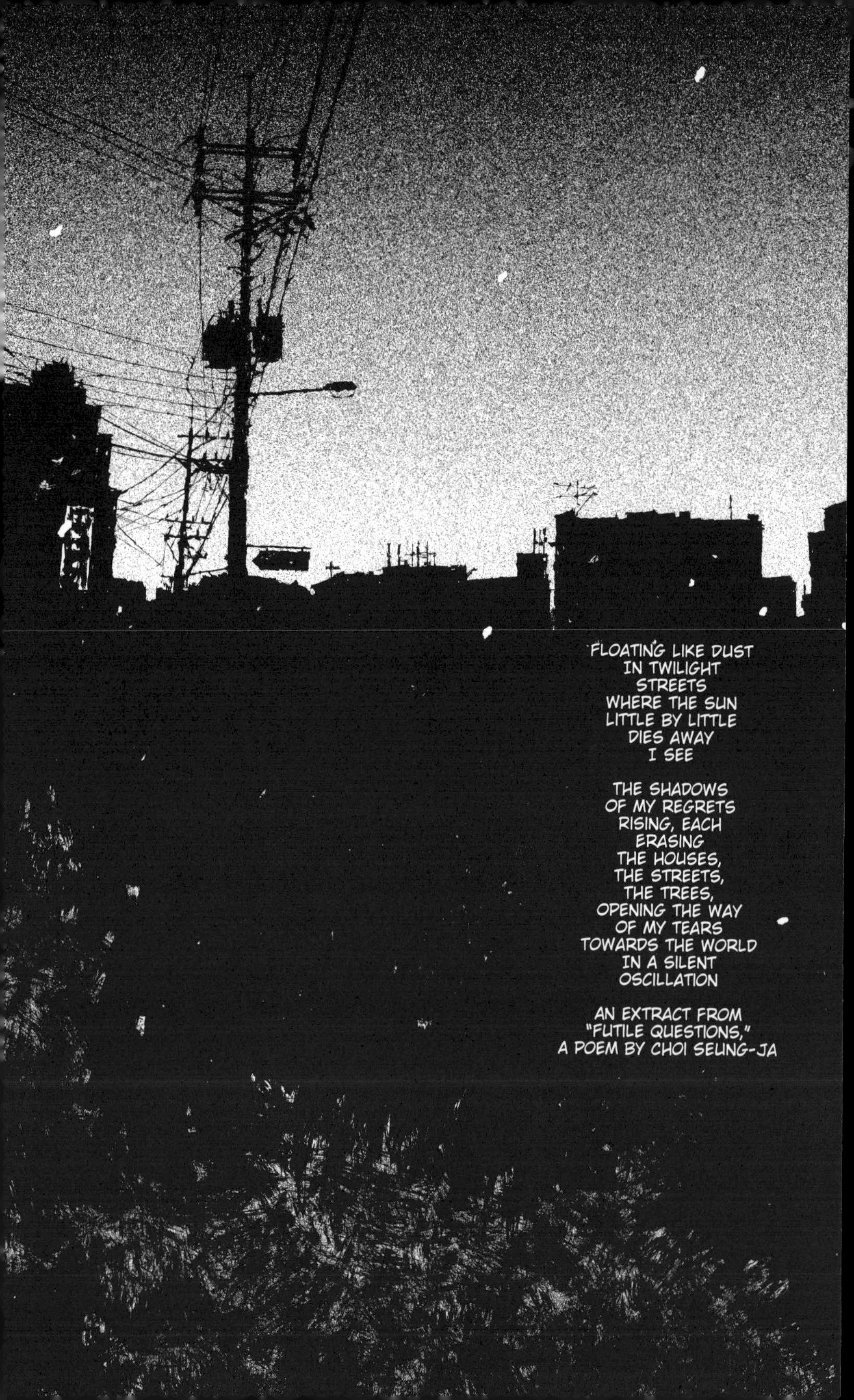
FLOATING LIKE DUST
IN TWILIGHT
STREETS
WHERE THE SUN
LITTLE BY LITTLE
DIES AWAY
I SEE

THE SHADOWS
OF MY REGRETS
RISING, EACH
ERASING
THE HOUSES,
THE STREETS,
THE TREES,
OPENING THE WAY
OF MY TEARS
TOWARDS THE WORLD
IN A SILENT
OSCILLATION

AN EXTRACT FROM
"FUTILE QUESTIONS,"
A POEM BY CHOI SEUNG-JA

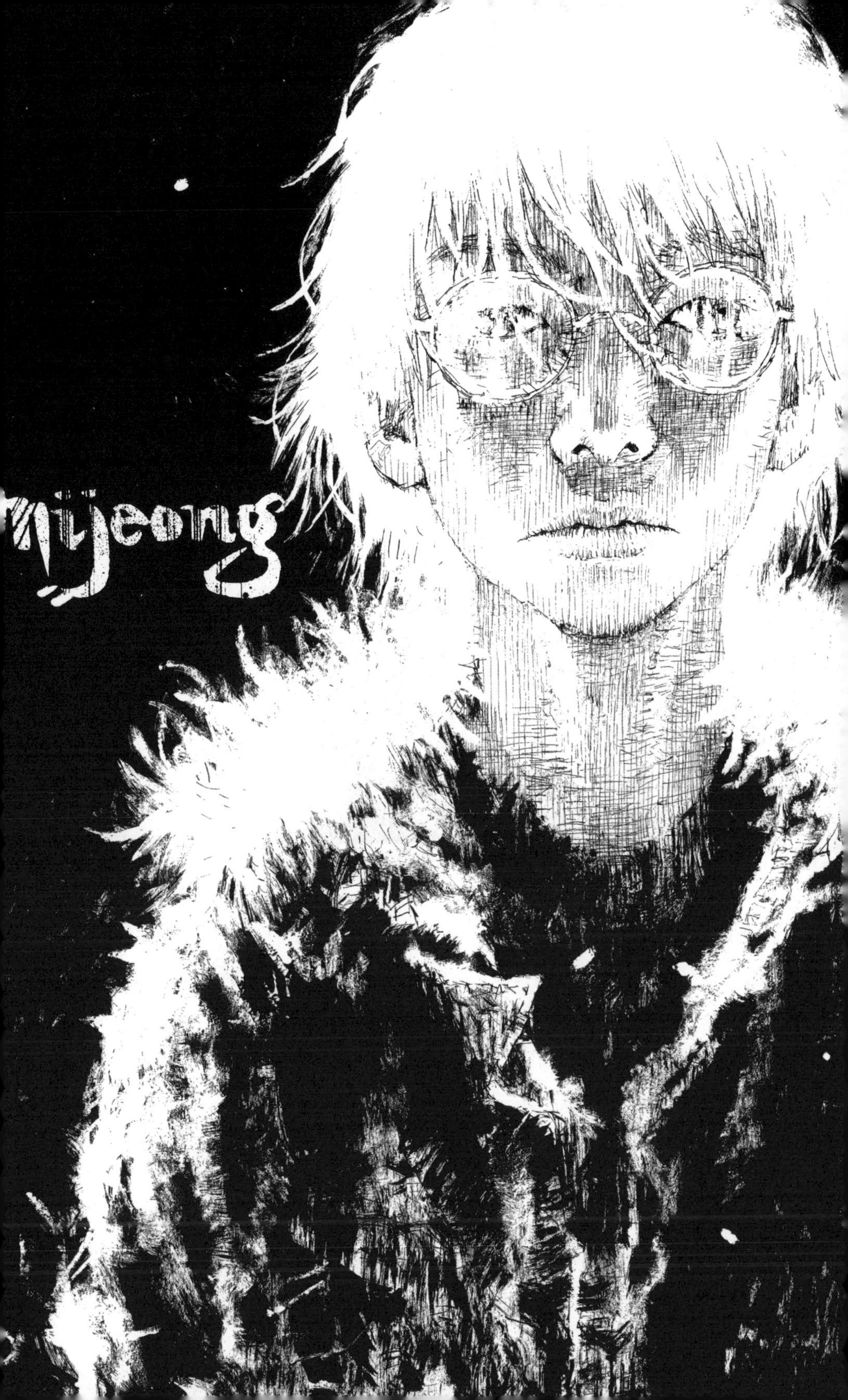
ijeong

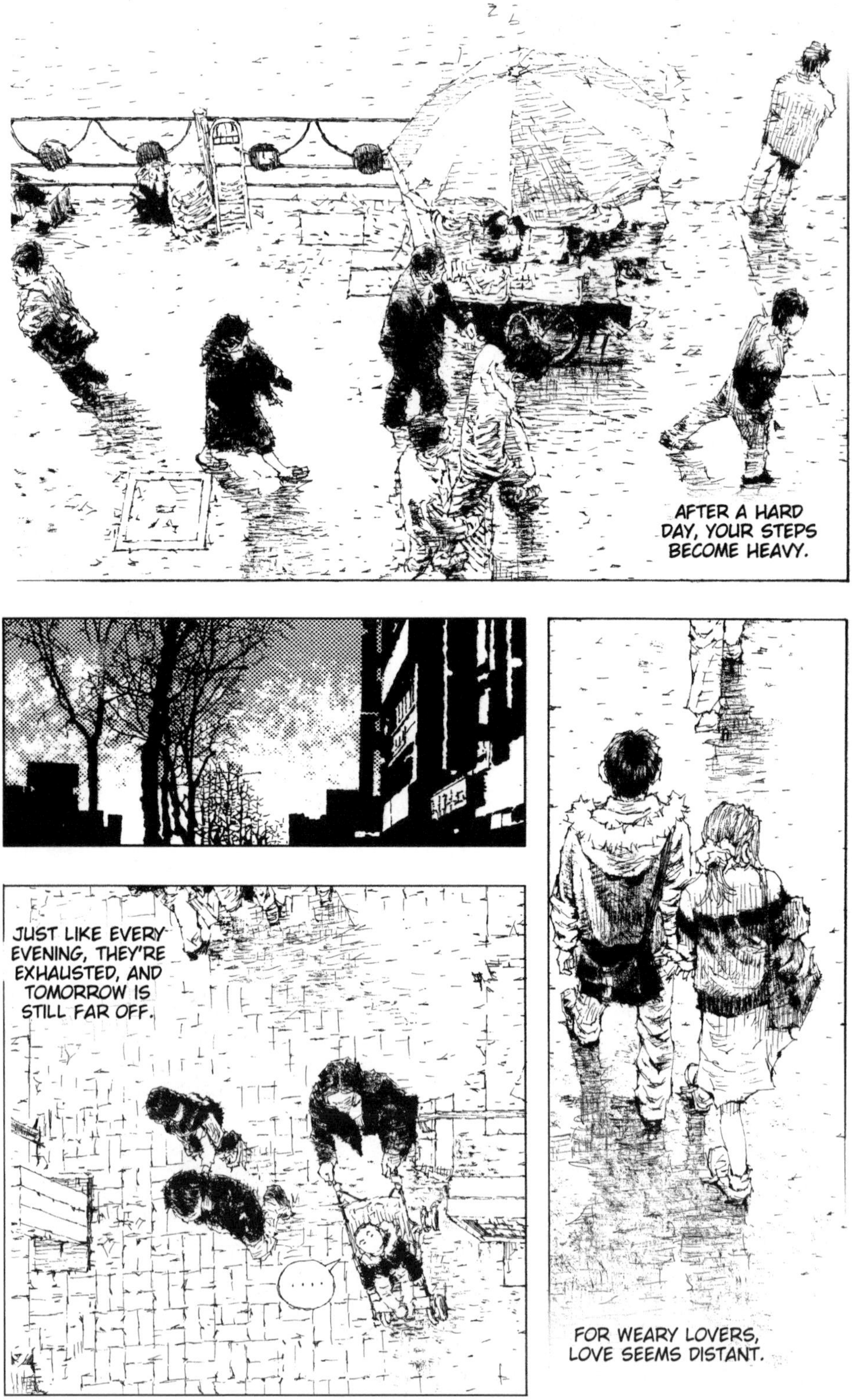
AFTER A HARD DAY, YOUR STEPS BECOME HEAVY.
JUST LIKE EVERY EVENING, THEY'RE EXHAUSTED, AND TOMORROW IS STILL FAR OFF.
....
FOR WEARY LOVERS, LOVE SEEMS DISTANT.

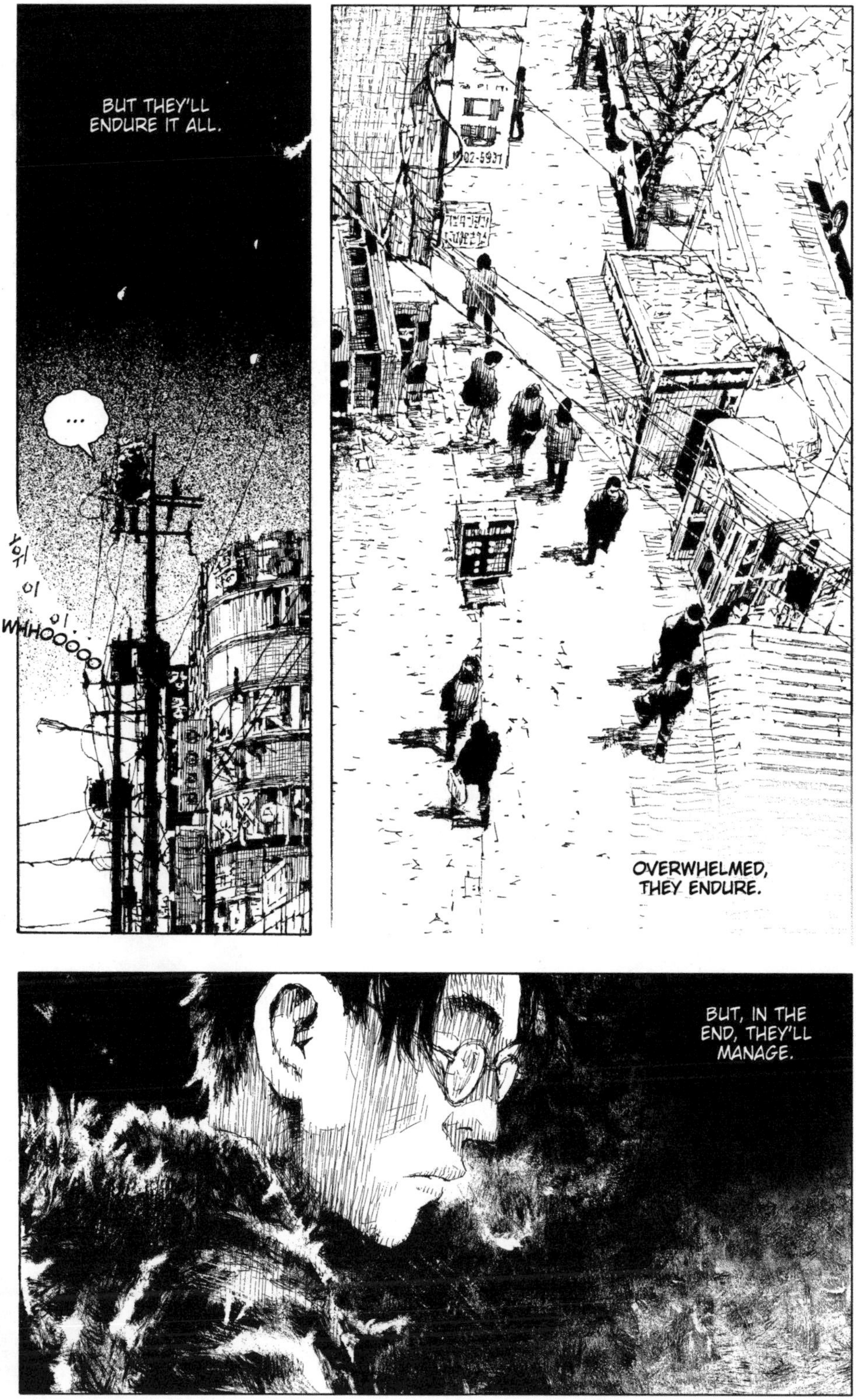
BUT THEY'LL
ENDURE IT ALL.
...
휘
이
이
WHHOOOOO
OVERWHELMED,
THEY ENDURE.
BUT, IN THE
END, THEY'LL
MANAGE.

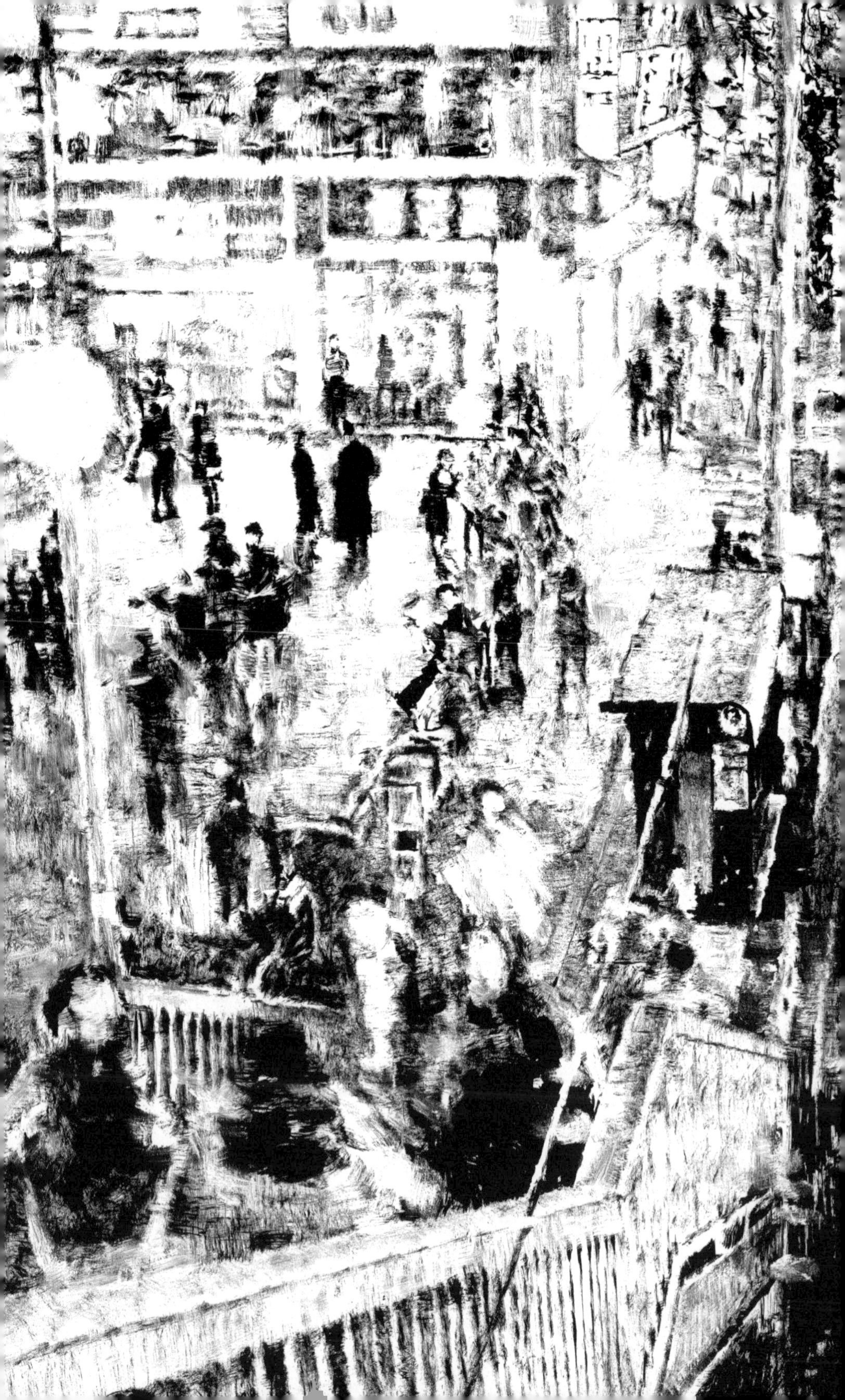

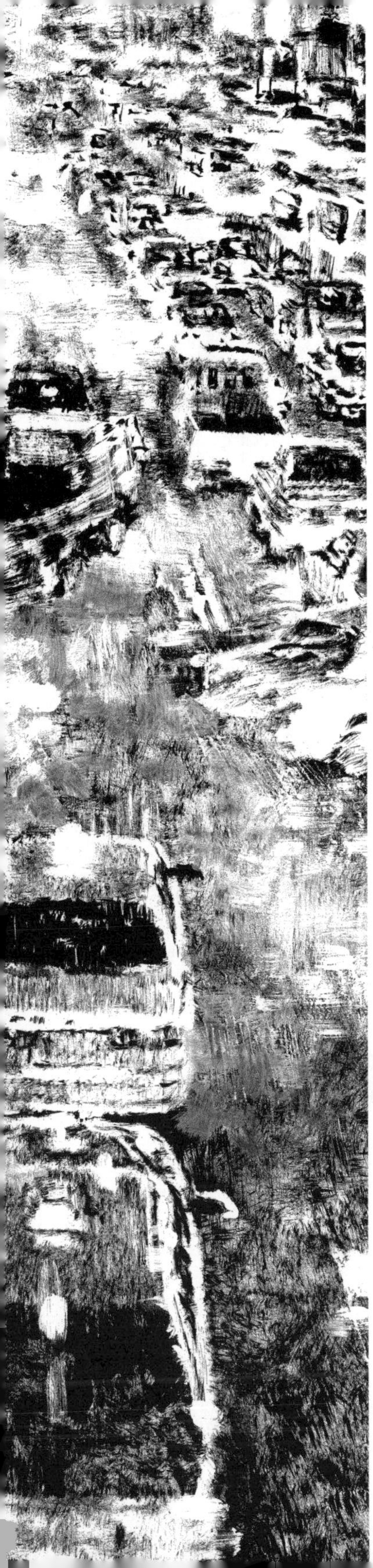

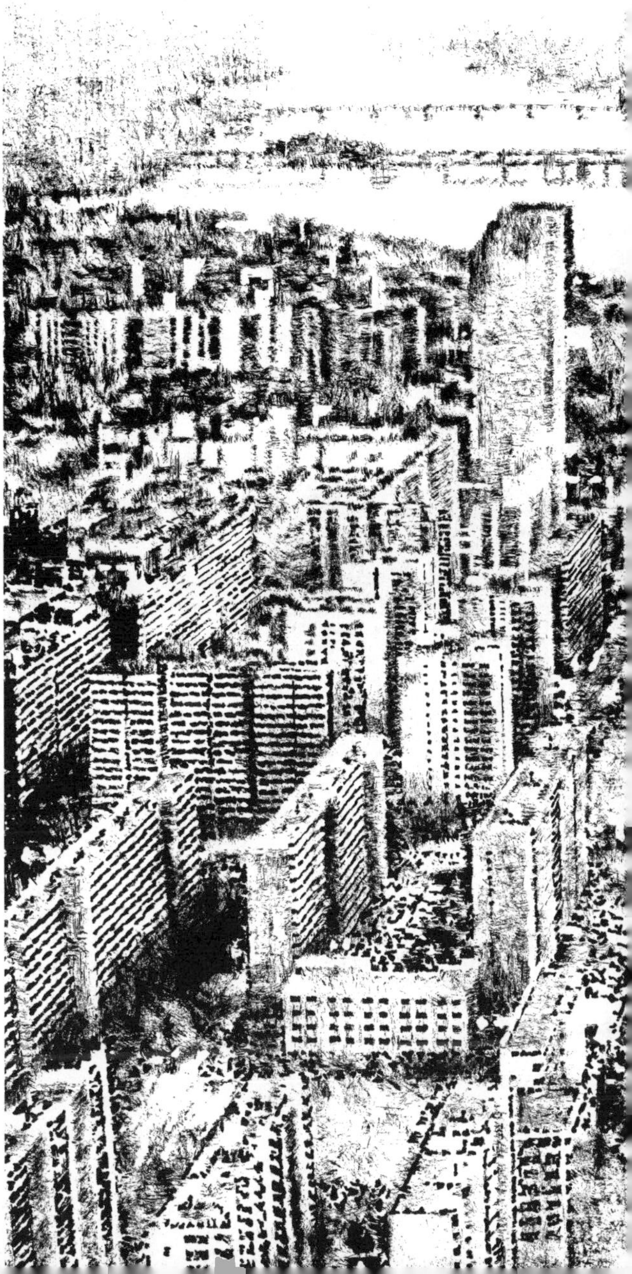

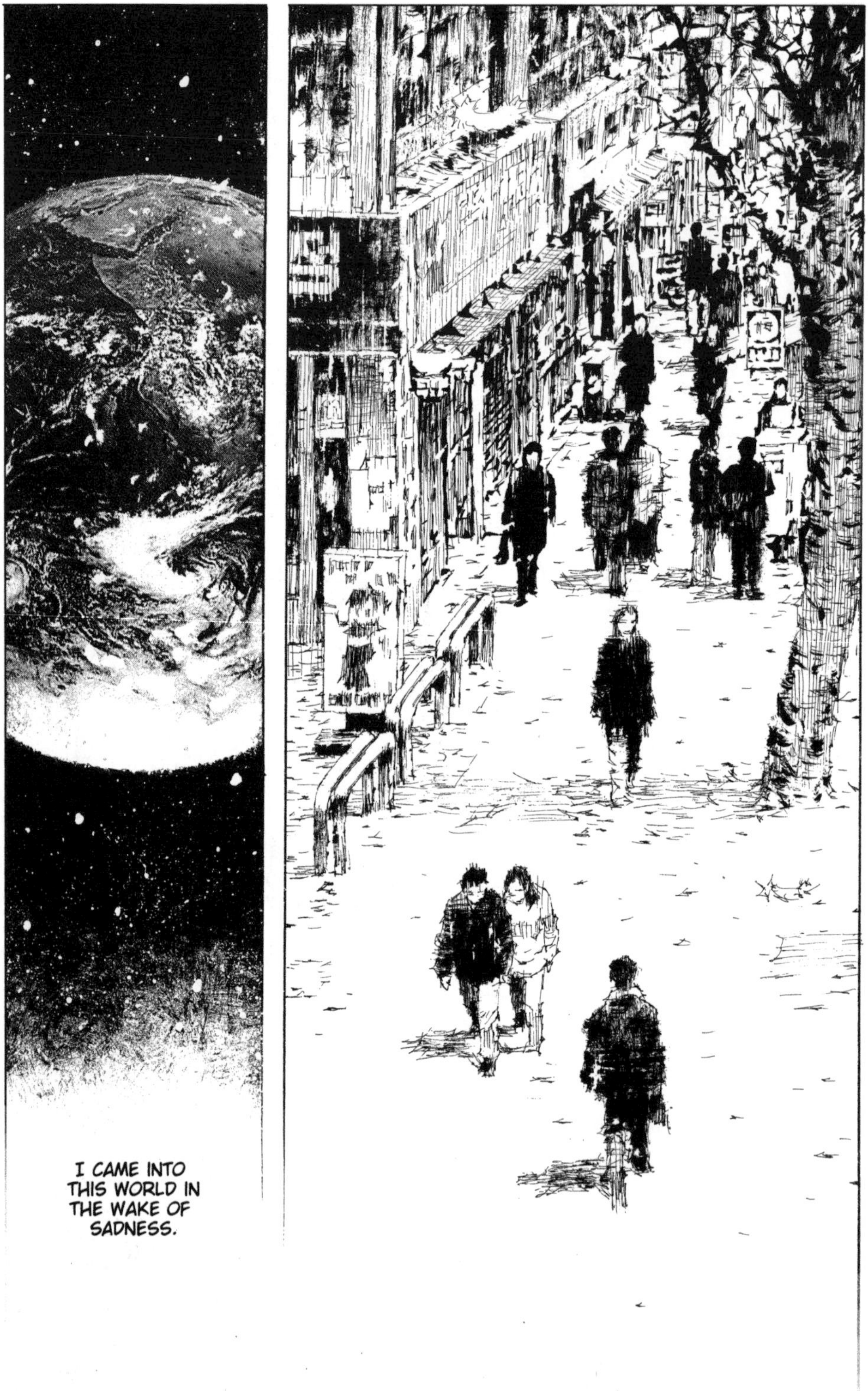
I CAME INTO THIS WORLD IN THE WAKE OF SADNESS.

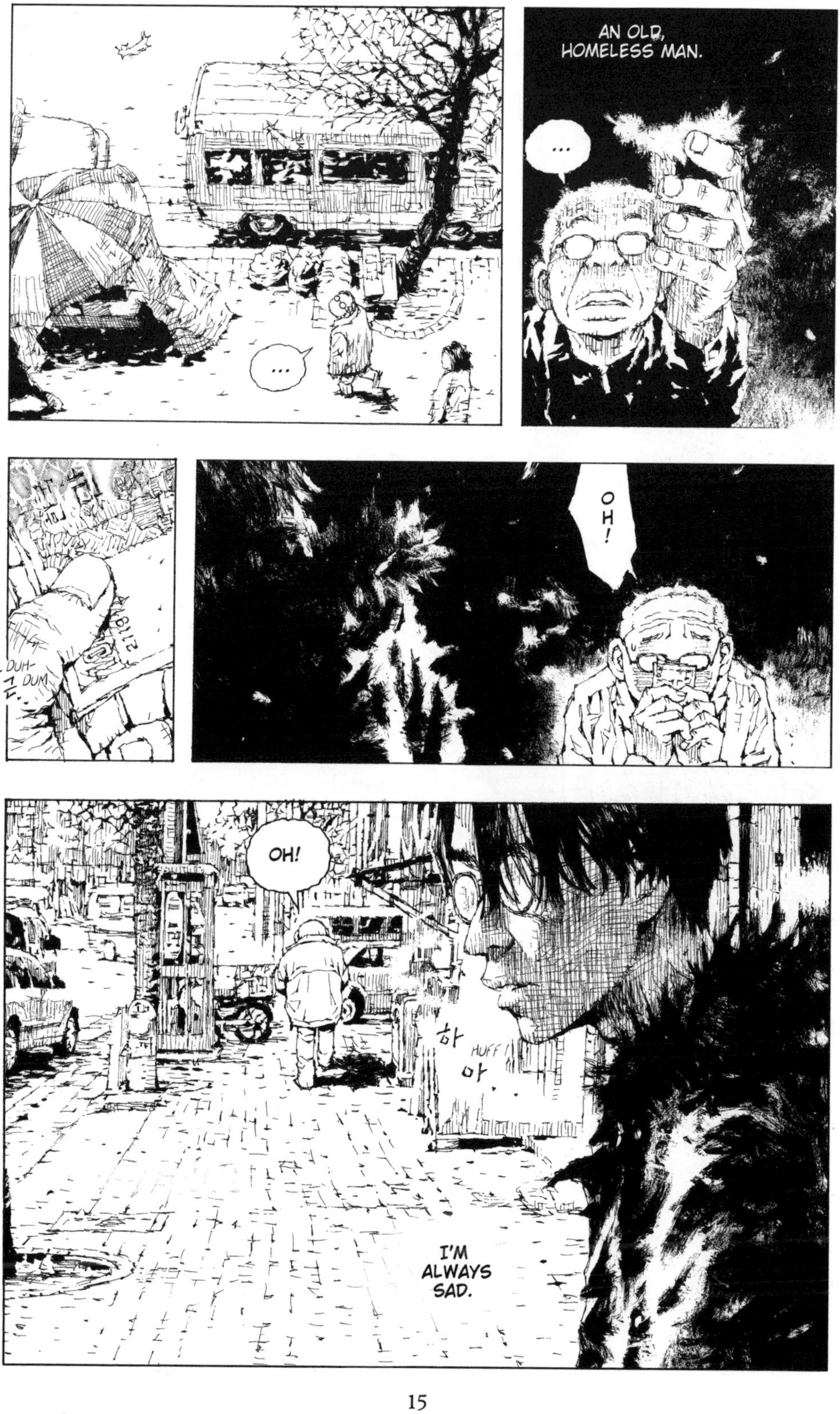
...
AN OLD, HOMELESS MAN.
...
듬
DUH-DUM
OH!
OH!
하아
HUFF
I'M ALWAYS SAD.

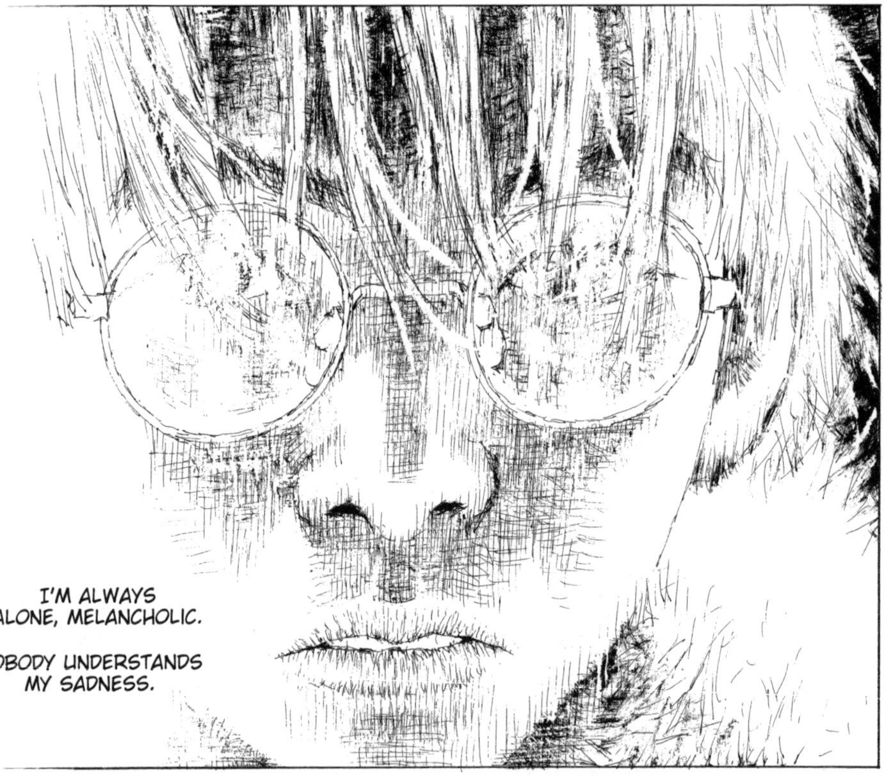
I'M ALWAYS ALONE, MELANCHOLIC.
NOBODY UNDERSTANDS MY SADNESS.

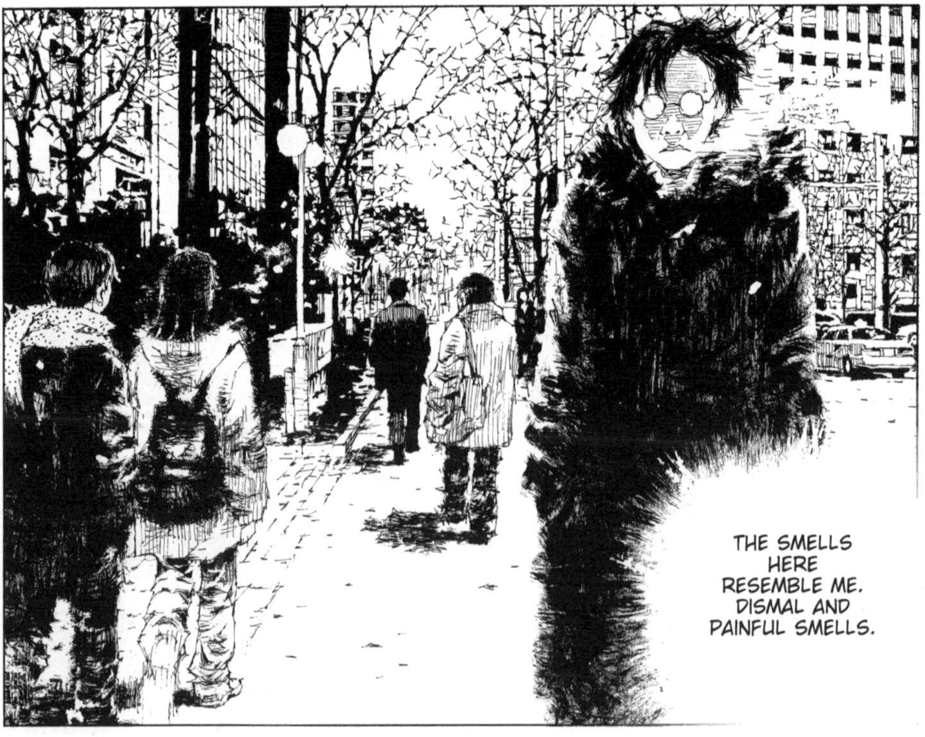
THE SMELLS HERE RESEMBLE ME. DISMAL AND PAINFUL SMELLS.

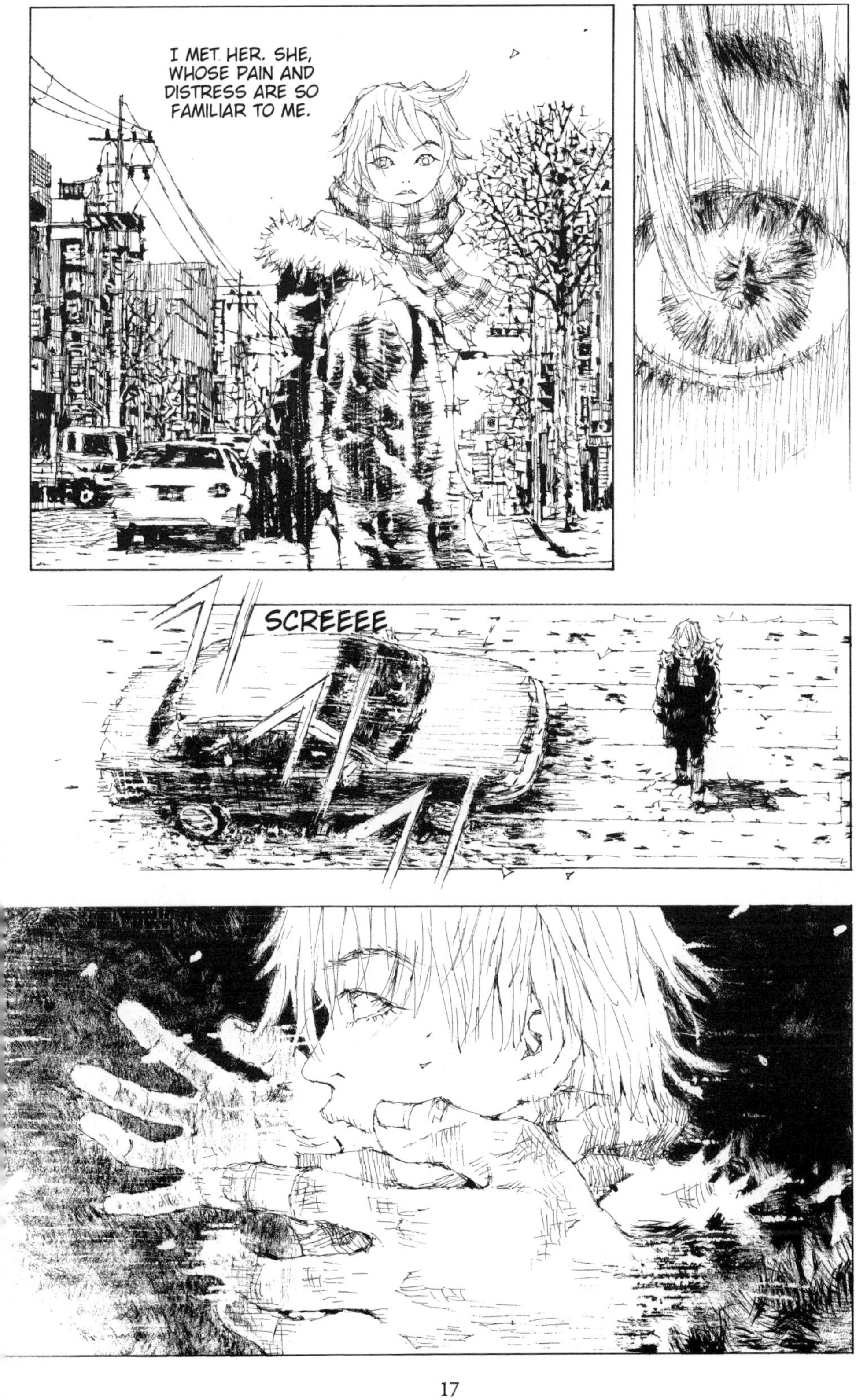
I MET HER. SHE, WHOSE PAIN AND DISTRESS ARE SO FAMILIAR TO ME.
SCREEEE

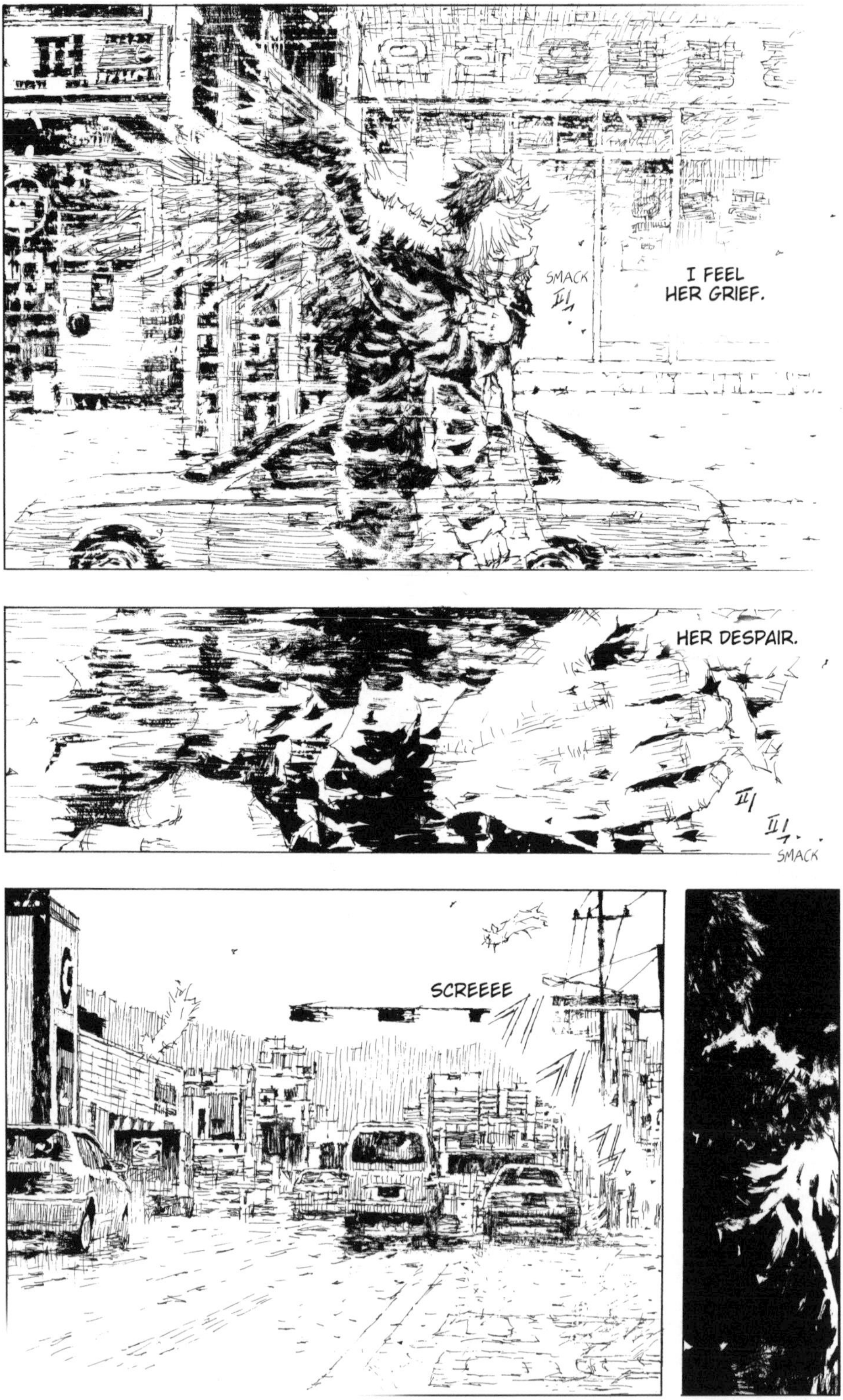
I FEEL HER GRIEF.
SMACK
HER DESPAIR.
SMACK
SCREEEE

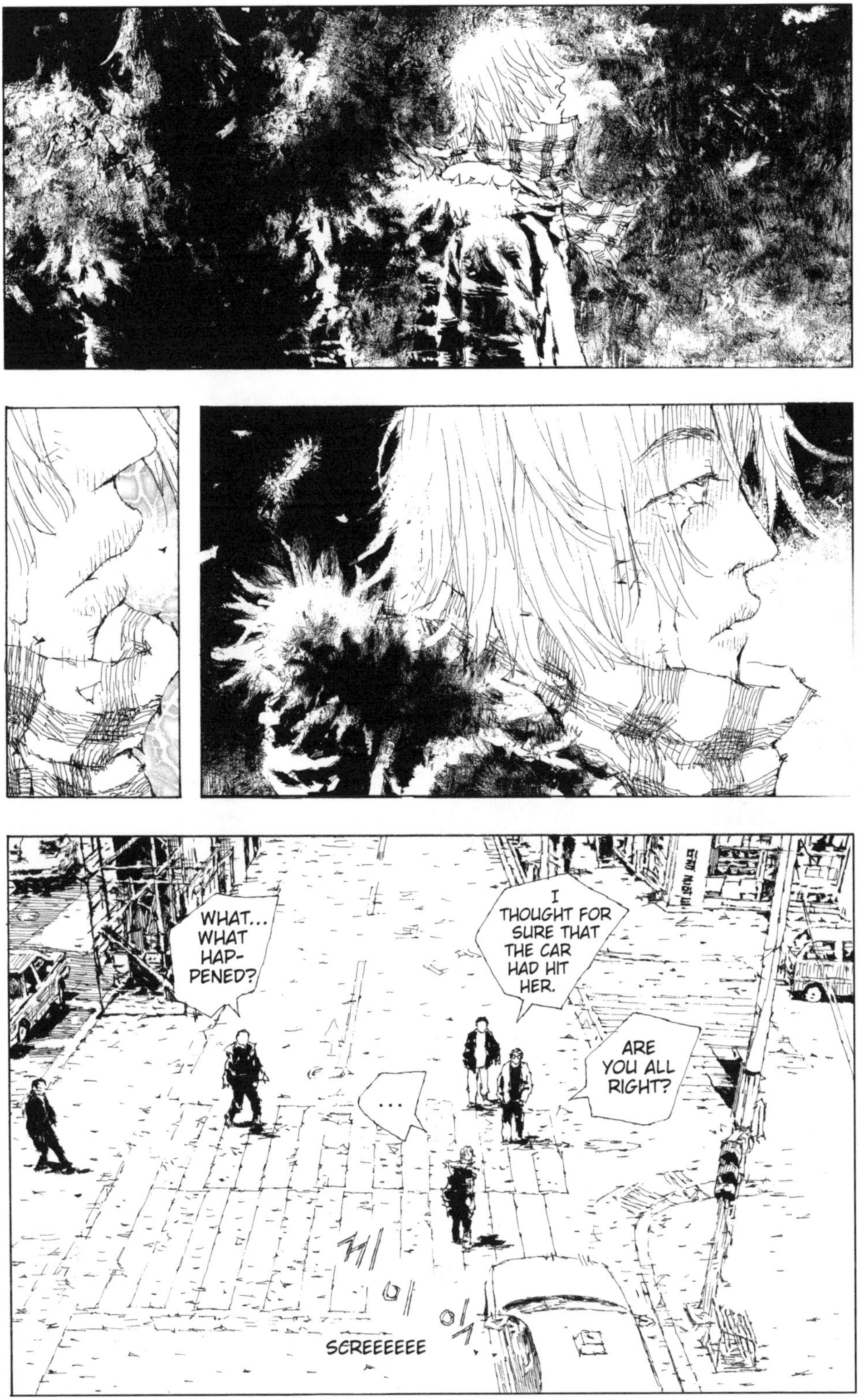
WHAT... WHAT HAP-PENED?
I THOUGHT FOR SURE THAT THE CAR HAD HIT HER.
...
ARE YOU ALL RIGHT?
SCREEEEEEE

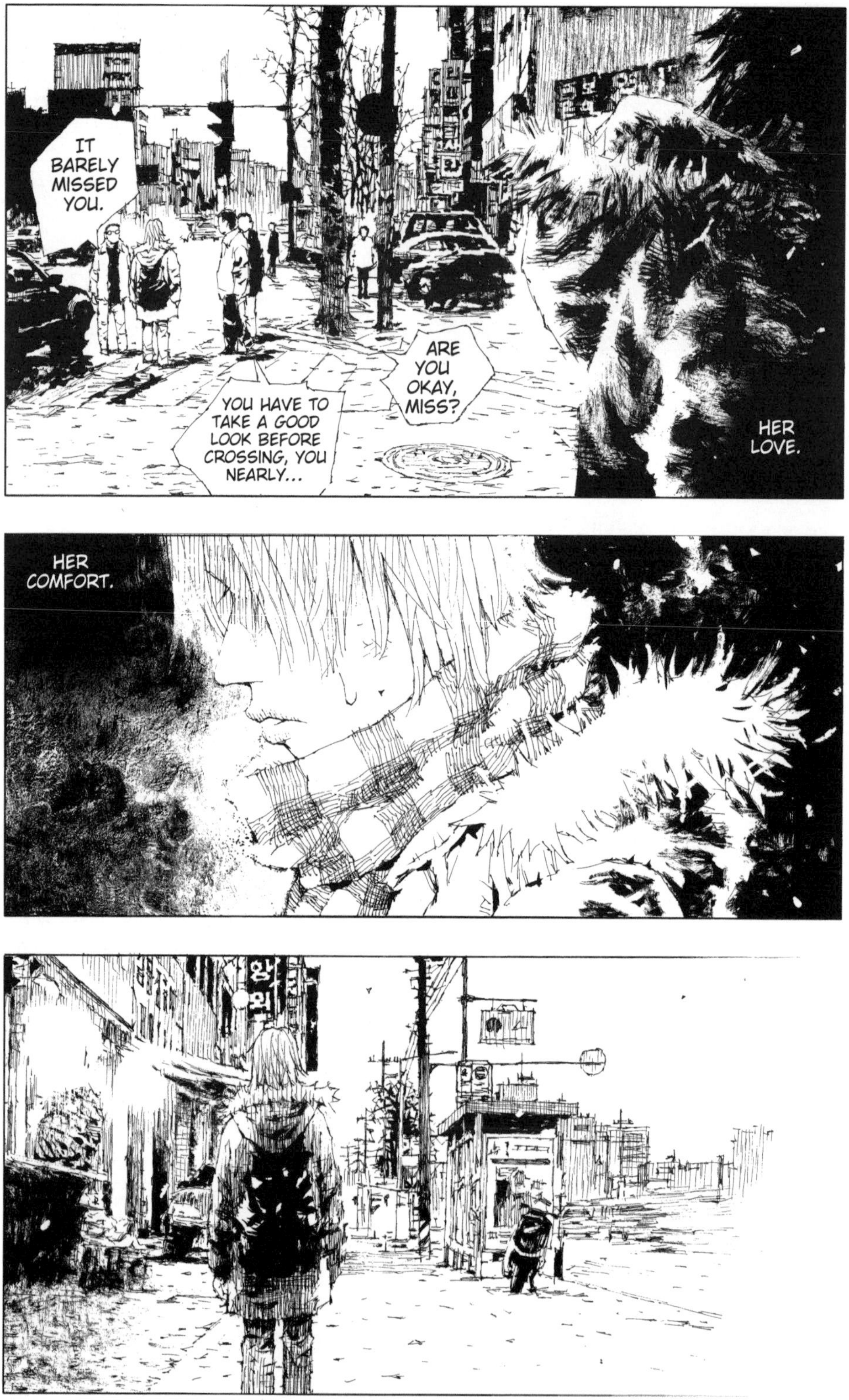
IT BARELY MISSED YOU.
YOU HAVE TO TAKE A GOOD LOOK BEFORE CROSSING, YOU NEARLY...
ARE YOU OKAY, MISS?
HER LOVE.
HER COMFORT.

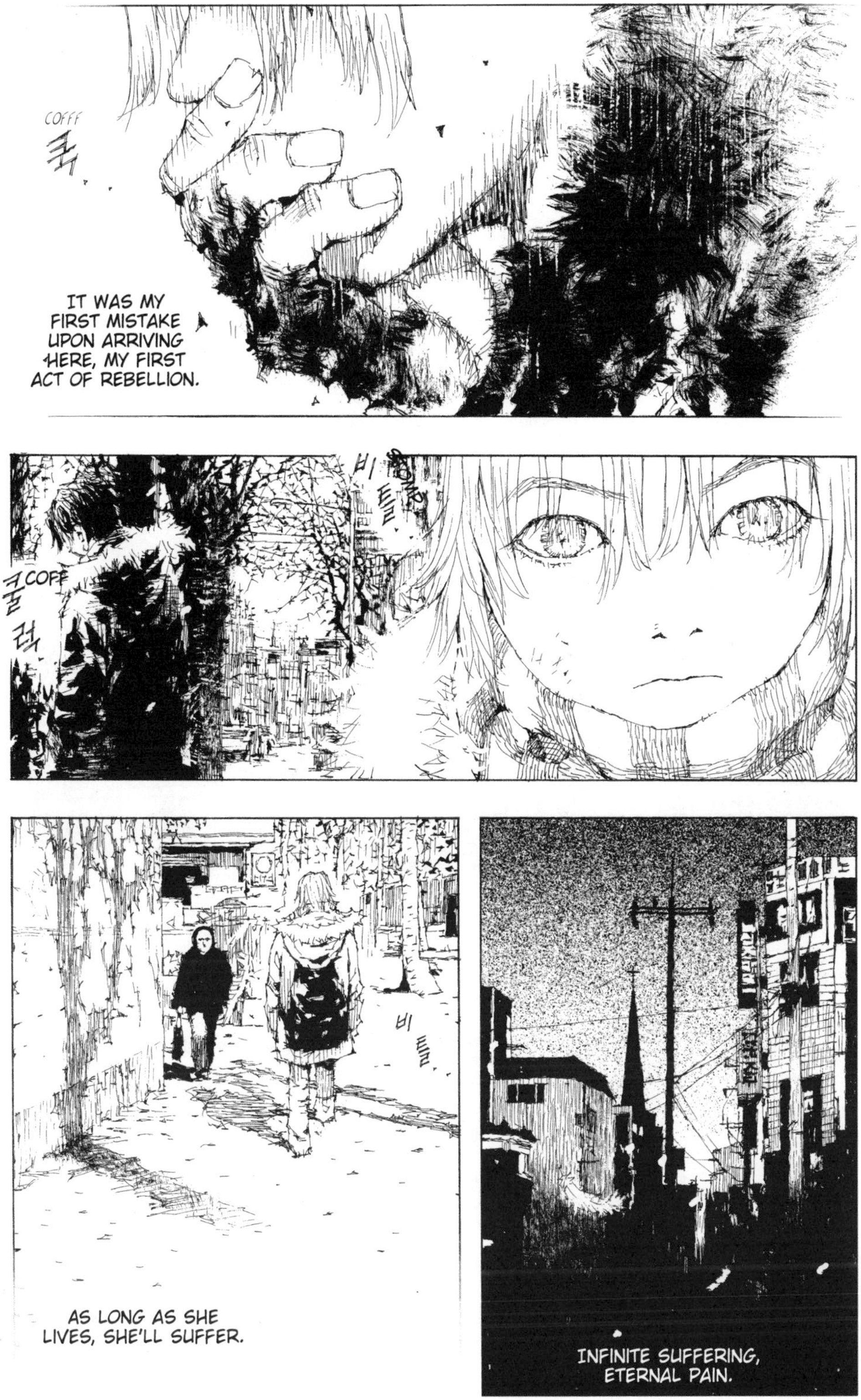
COFFF
IT WAS MY FIRST MISTAKE UPON ARRIVING HERE, MY FIRST ACT OF REBELLION.
비틀
STOMP
COFF
비틀
AS LONG AS SHE LIVES, SHE'LL SUFFER.
INFINITE SUFFERING, ETERNAL PAIN.

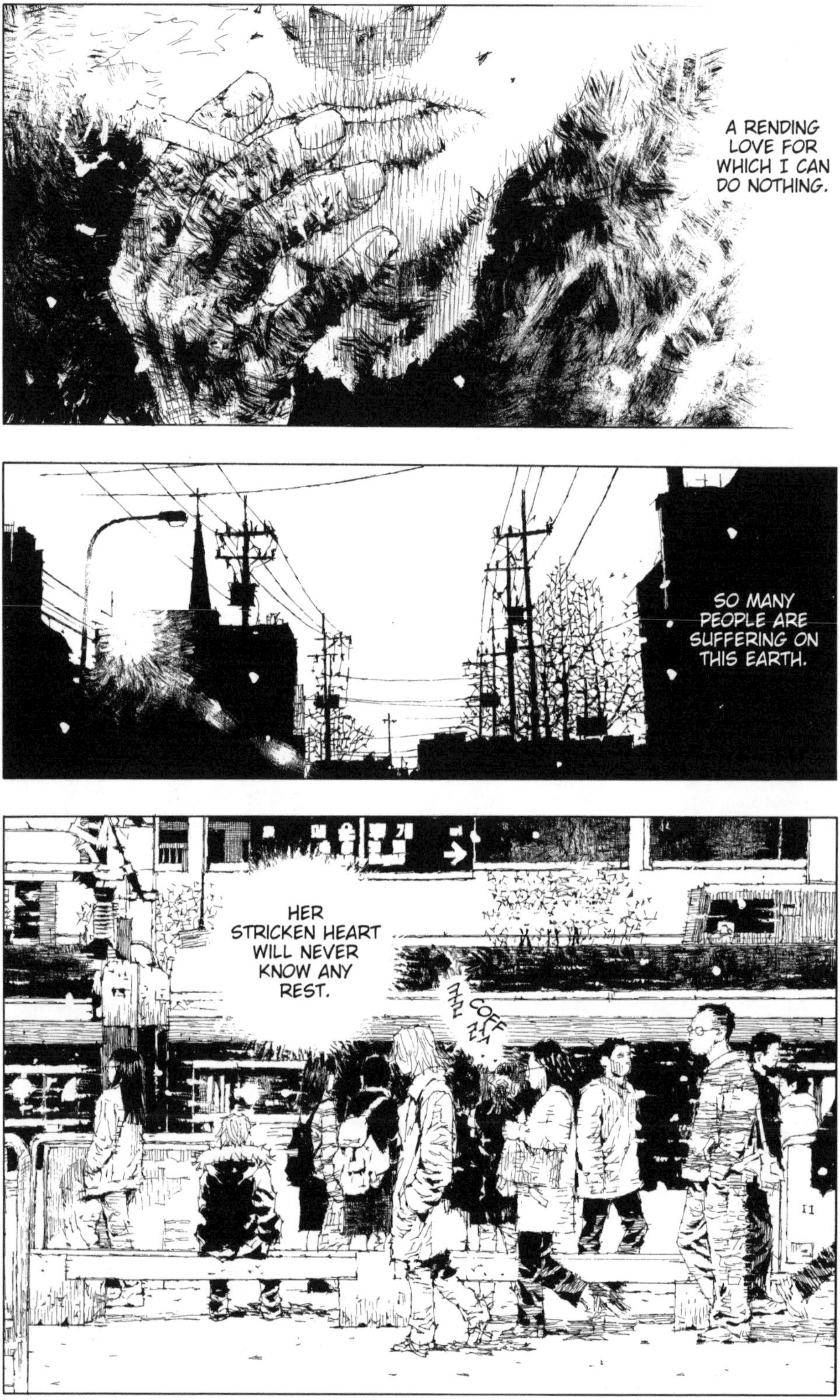
A RENDING LOVE FOR WHICH I CAN DO NOTHING.
SO MANY PEOPLE ARE SUFFERING ON THIS EARTH.
HER STRICKEN HEART WILL NEVER KNOW ANY REST.
COFF

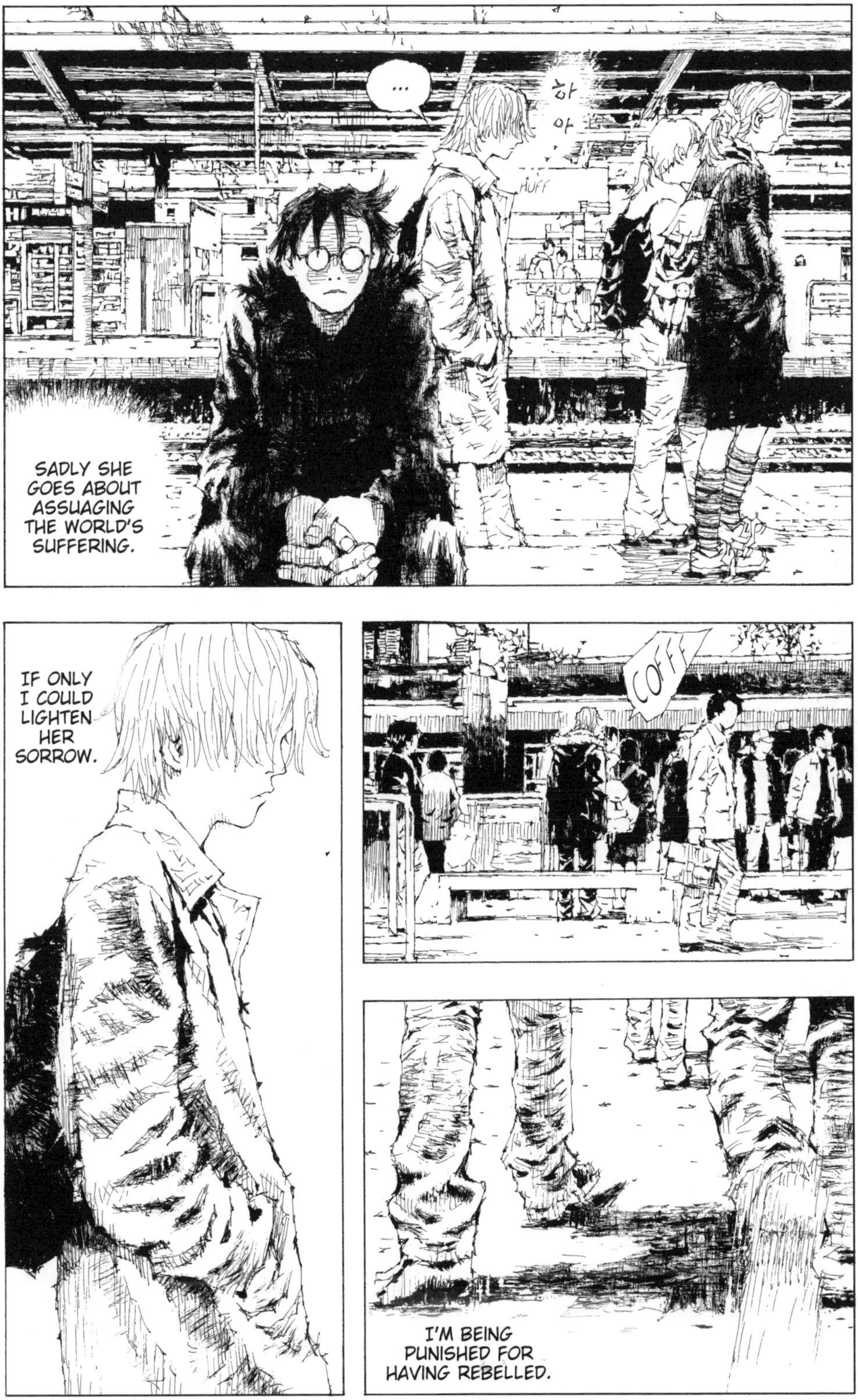
...
하아
HUFF
SADLY SHE GOES ABOUT ASSUAGING THE WORLD'S SUFFERING.
IF ONLY I COULD LIGHTEN HER SORROW.
COFF
I'M BEING PUNISHED FOR HAVING REBELLED.

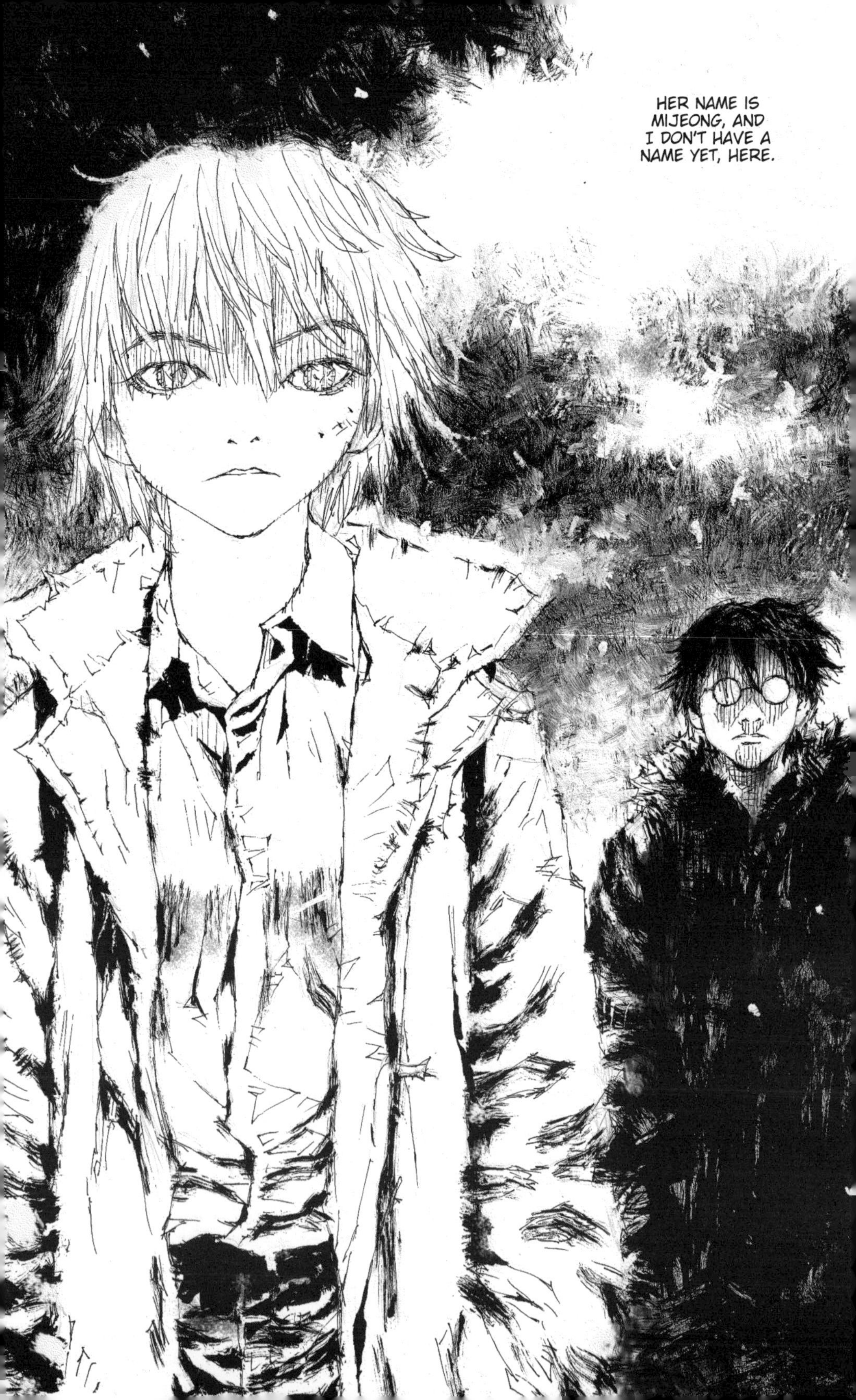
HER NAME IS MIJEONG, AND I DON'T HAVE A NAME YET, HERE.

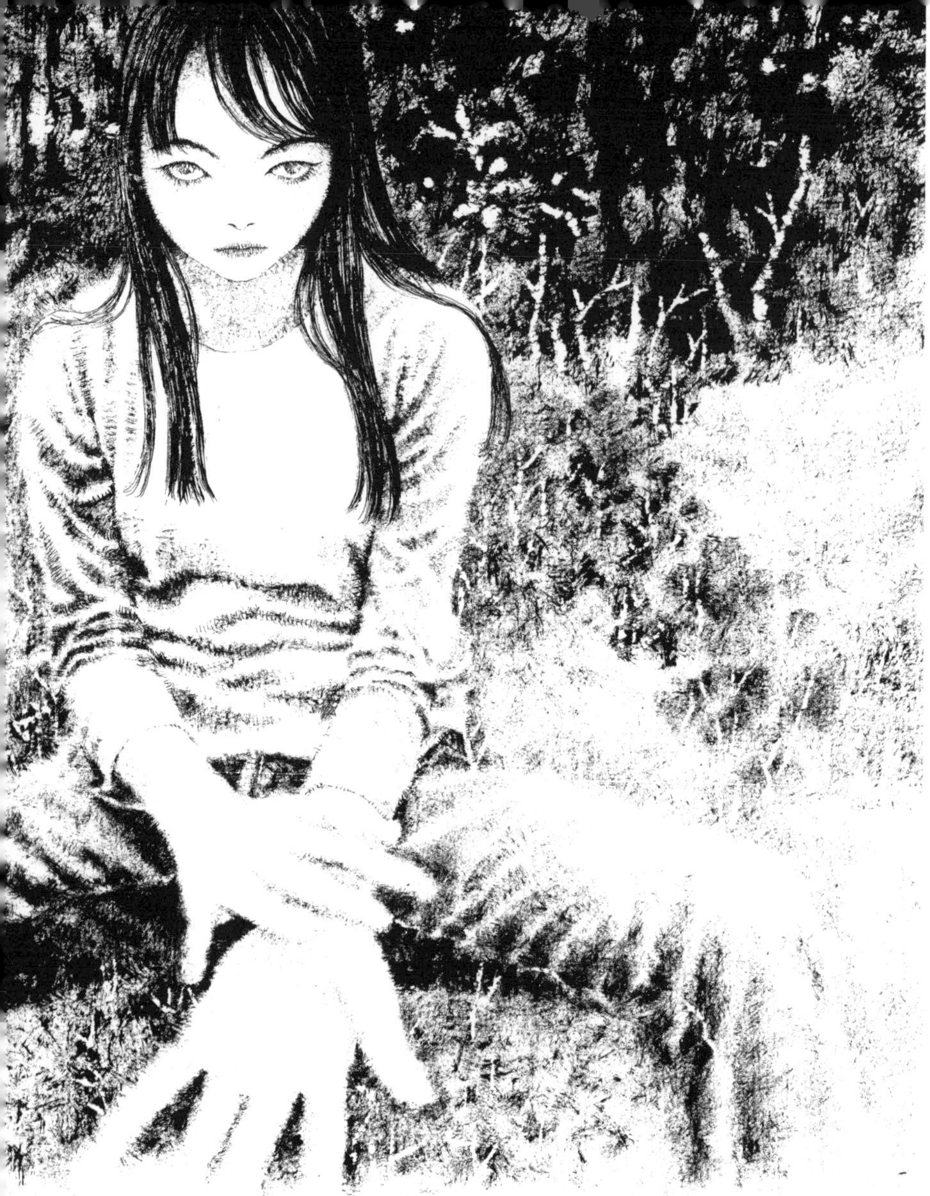

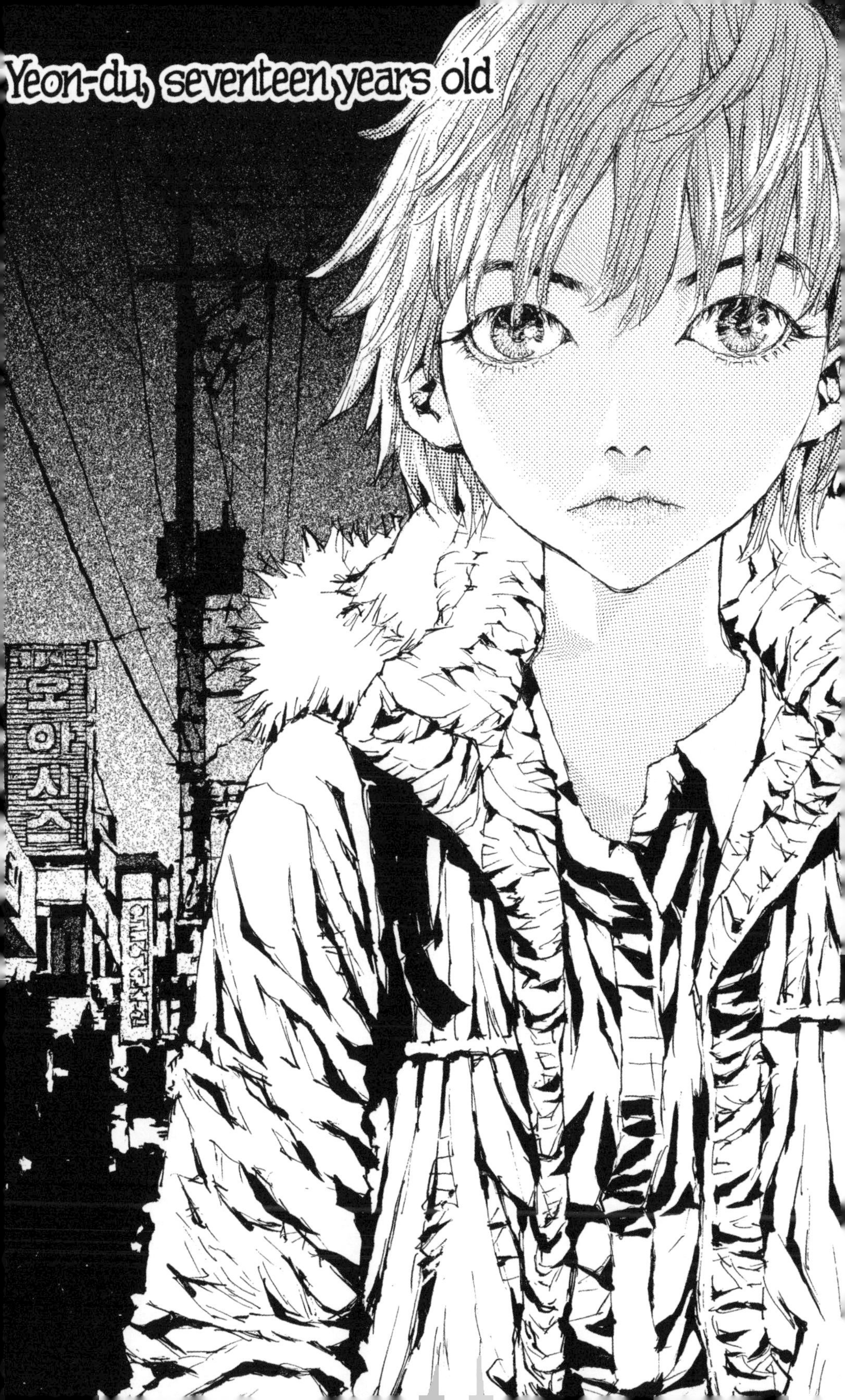
Yeon-du, seventeen years old
오아시스

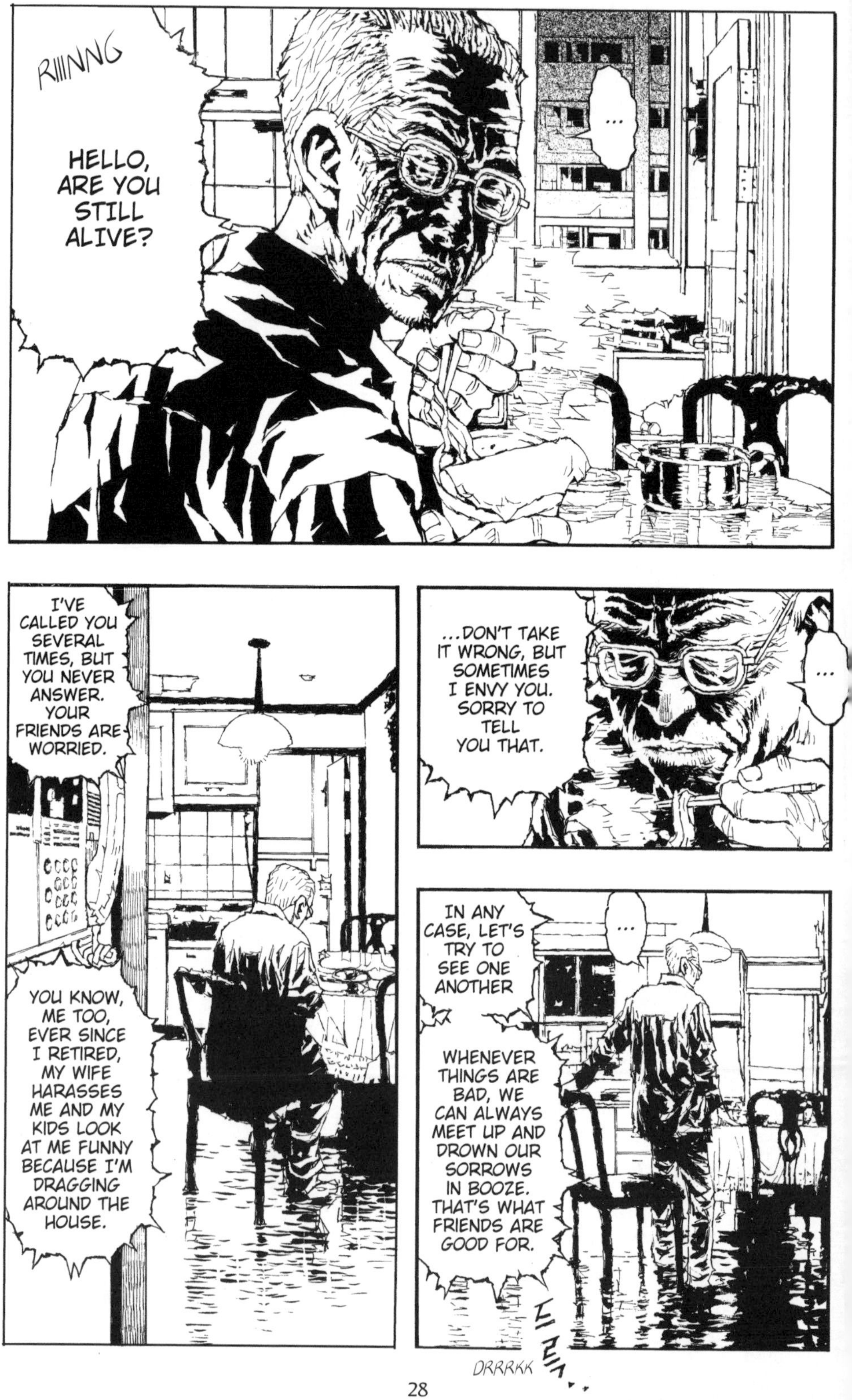

RIIINNG
HELLO, ARE YOU STILL ALIVE?
...
I'VE CALLED YOU SEVERAL TIMES, BUT YOU NEVER ANSWER. YOUR FRIENDS ARE WORRIED.
YOU KNOW, ME TOO, EVER SINCE I RETIRED, MY WIFE HARASSES ME AND MY KIDS LOOK AT ME FUNNY BECAUSE I'M DRAGGING AROUND THE HOUSE.
...DON'T TAKE IT WRONG, BUT SOMETIMES I ENVY YOU. SORRY TO TELL YOU THAT.
...
IN ANY CASE, LET'S TRY TO SEE ONE ANOTHER
...
WHENEVER THINGS ARE BAD, WE CAN ALWAYS MEET UP AND DROWN OUR SORROWS IN BOOZE. THAT'S WHAT FRIENDS ARE GOOD FOR.
DRRRKK

THE WIFE, THE KIDS, THEY'RE ALL USELESS. OKAY, THEN, SEE YOU SOON, EH?

CLICK

SHLOOP

...

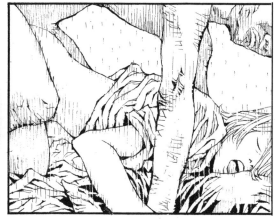

MEOW

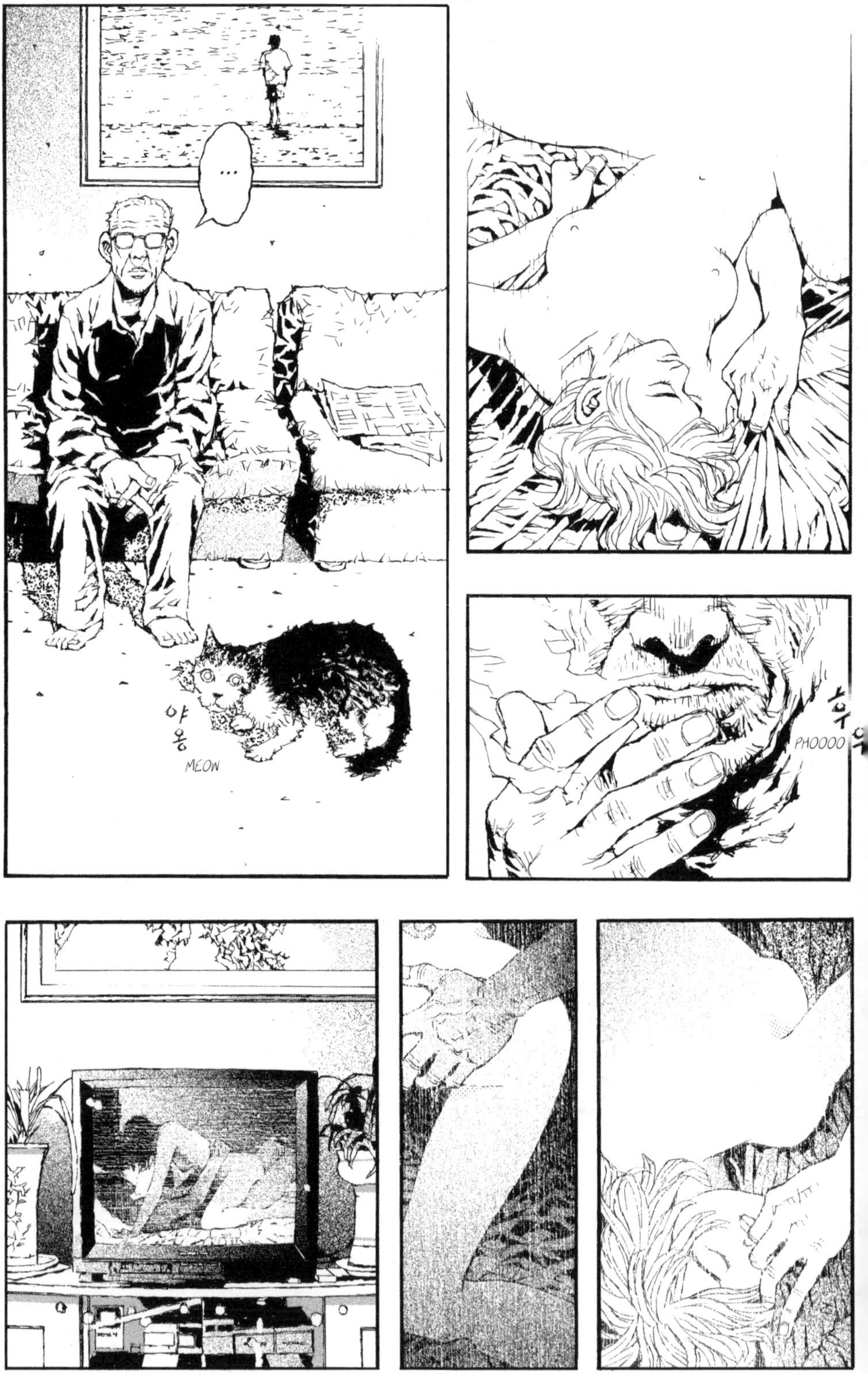
...
야옹
MEOW
PHOOOO

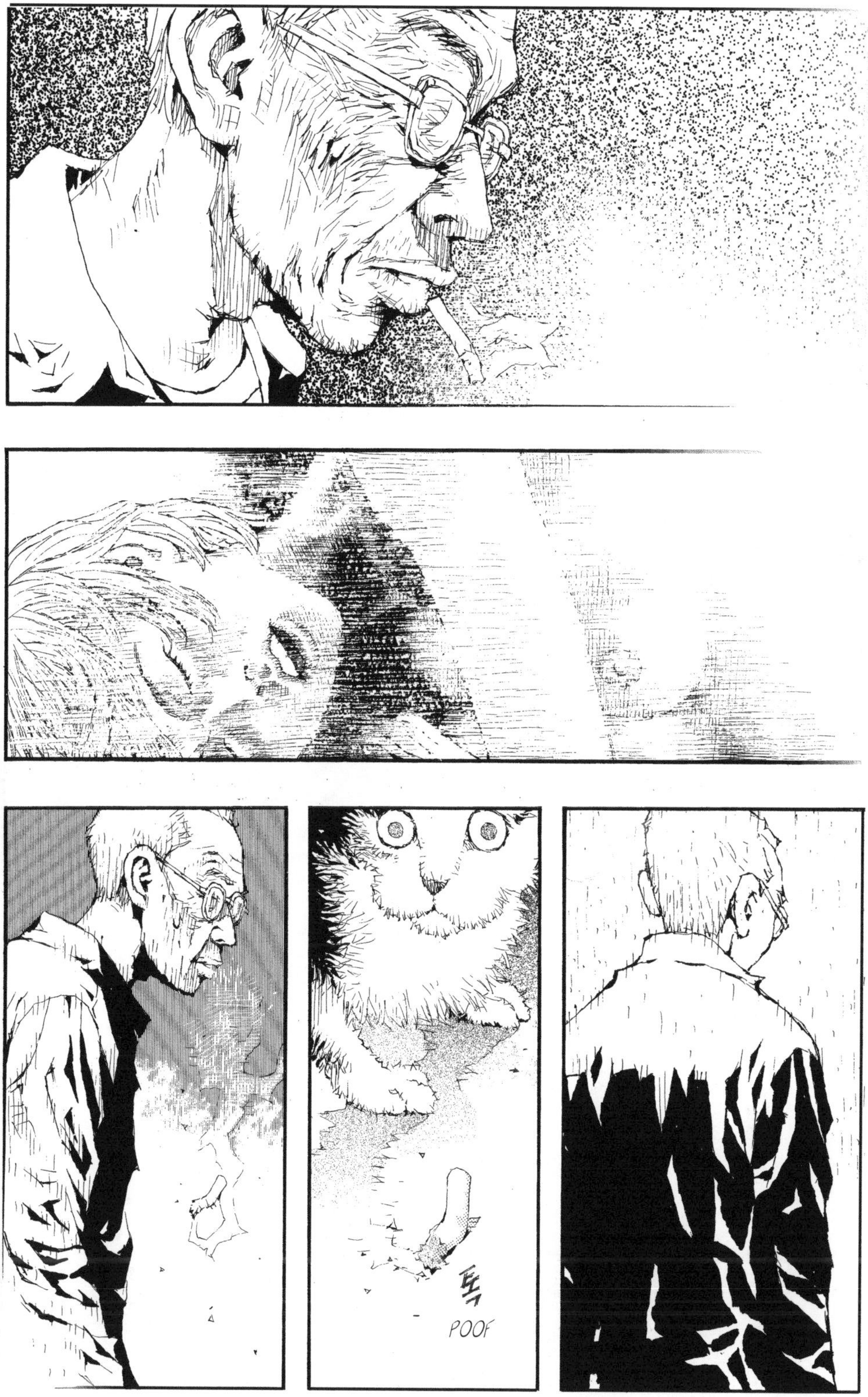
톡
POOF

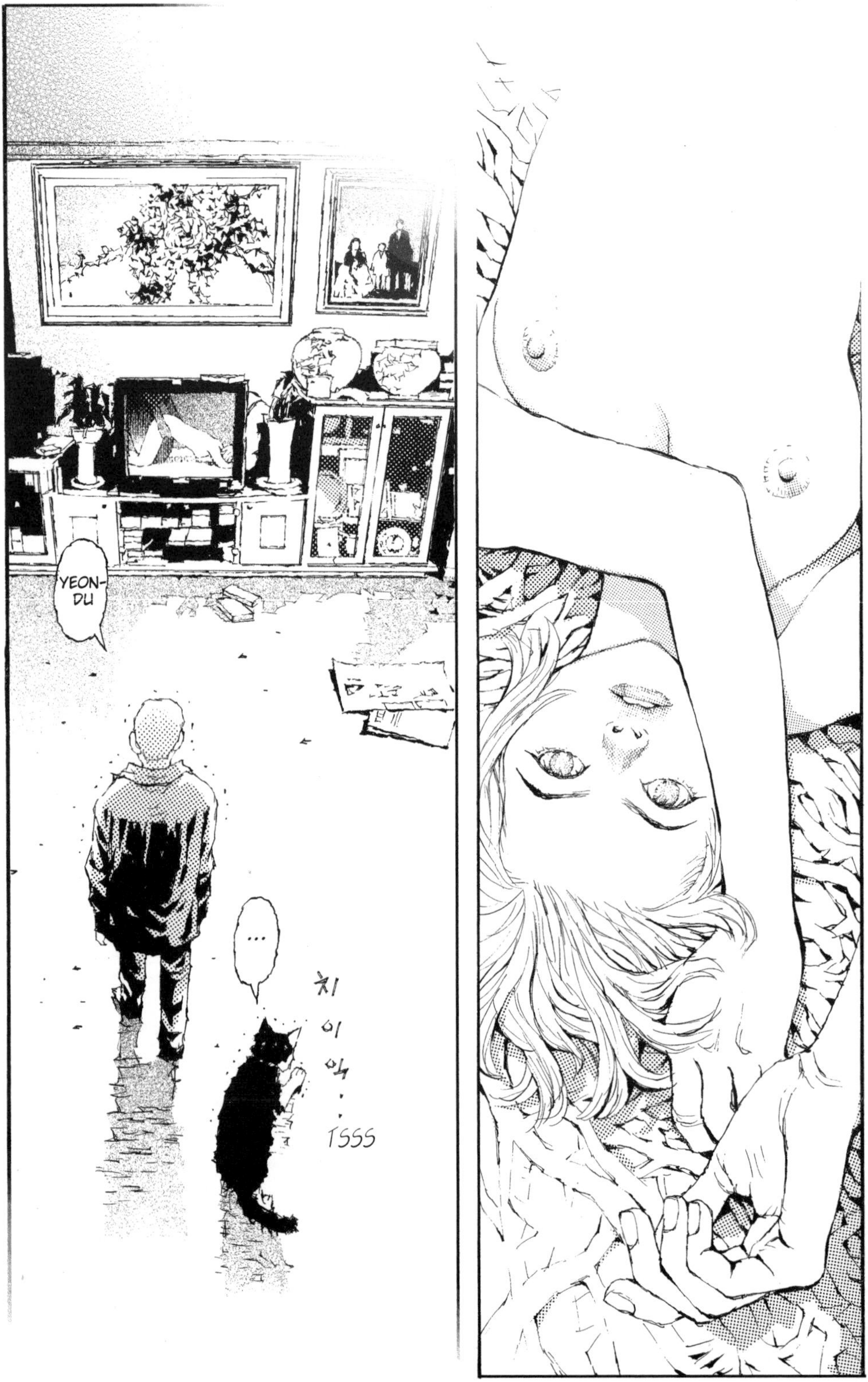

YEON-DU
...
치이악..
TSSS

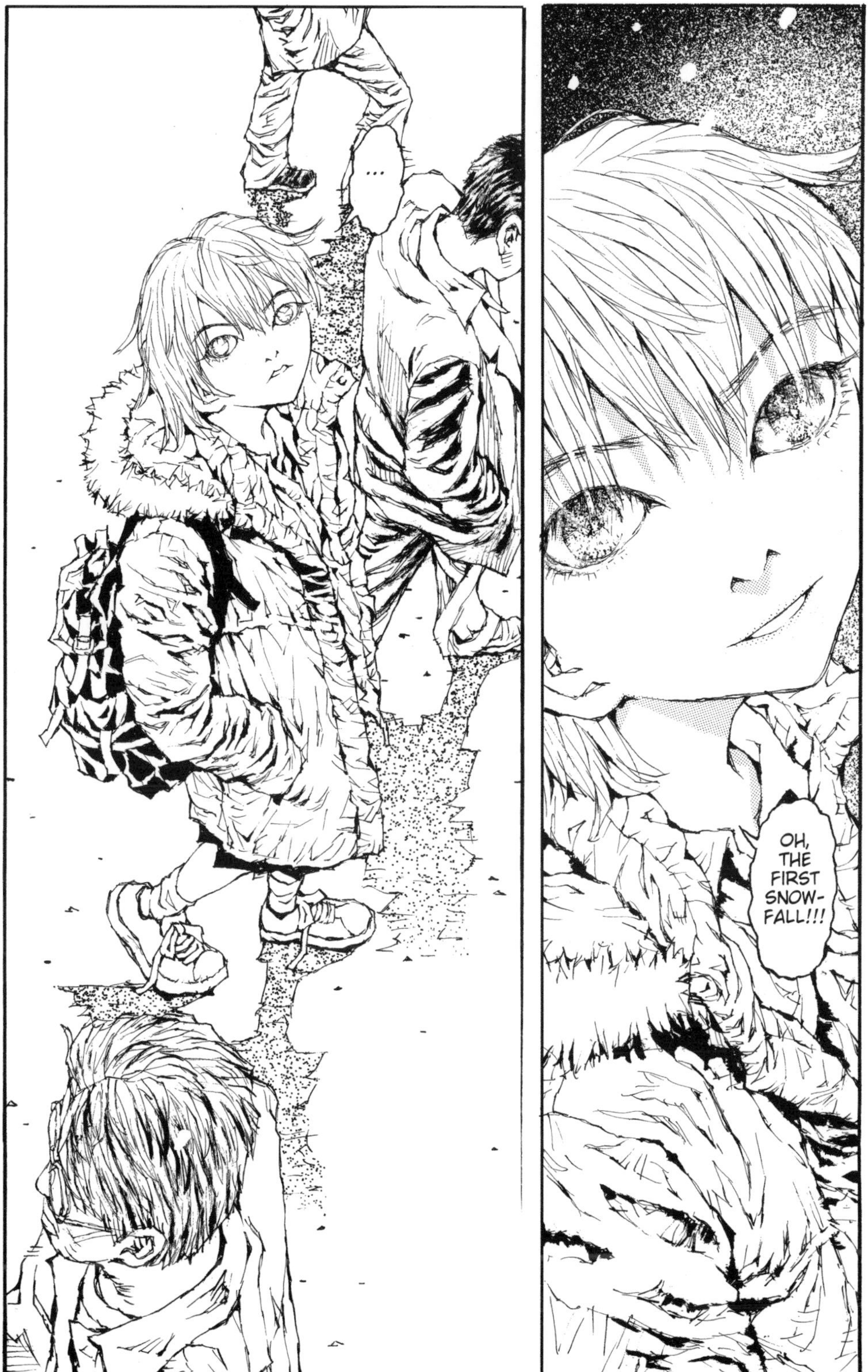
OH, THE FIRST SNOW-FALL!!!
...

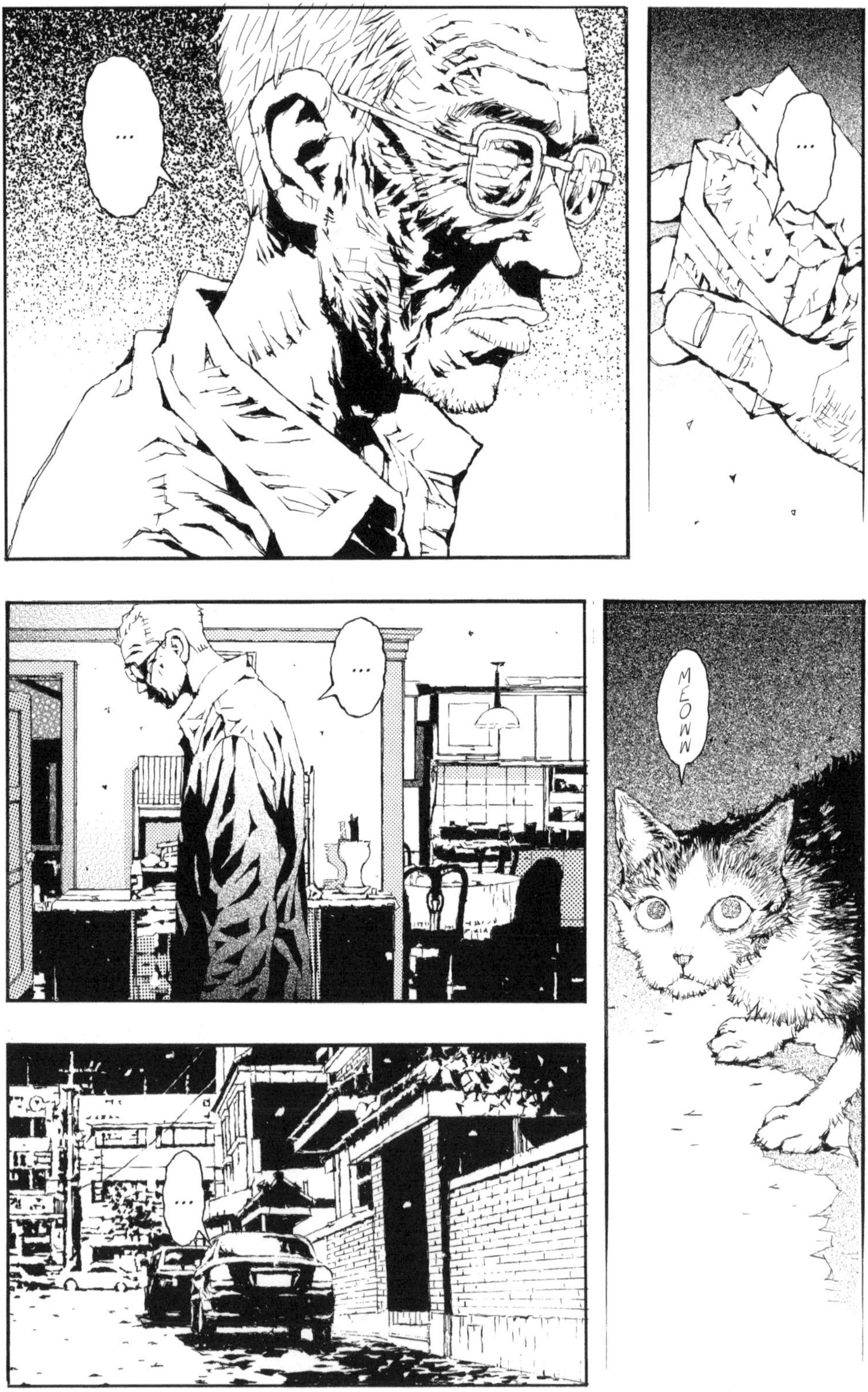
...
...
...
MEOWW
...

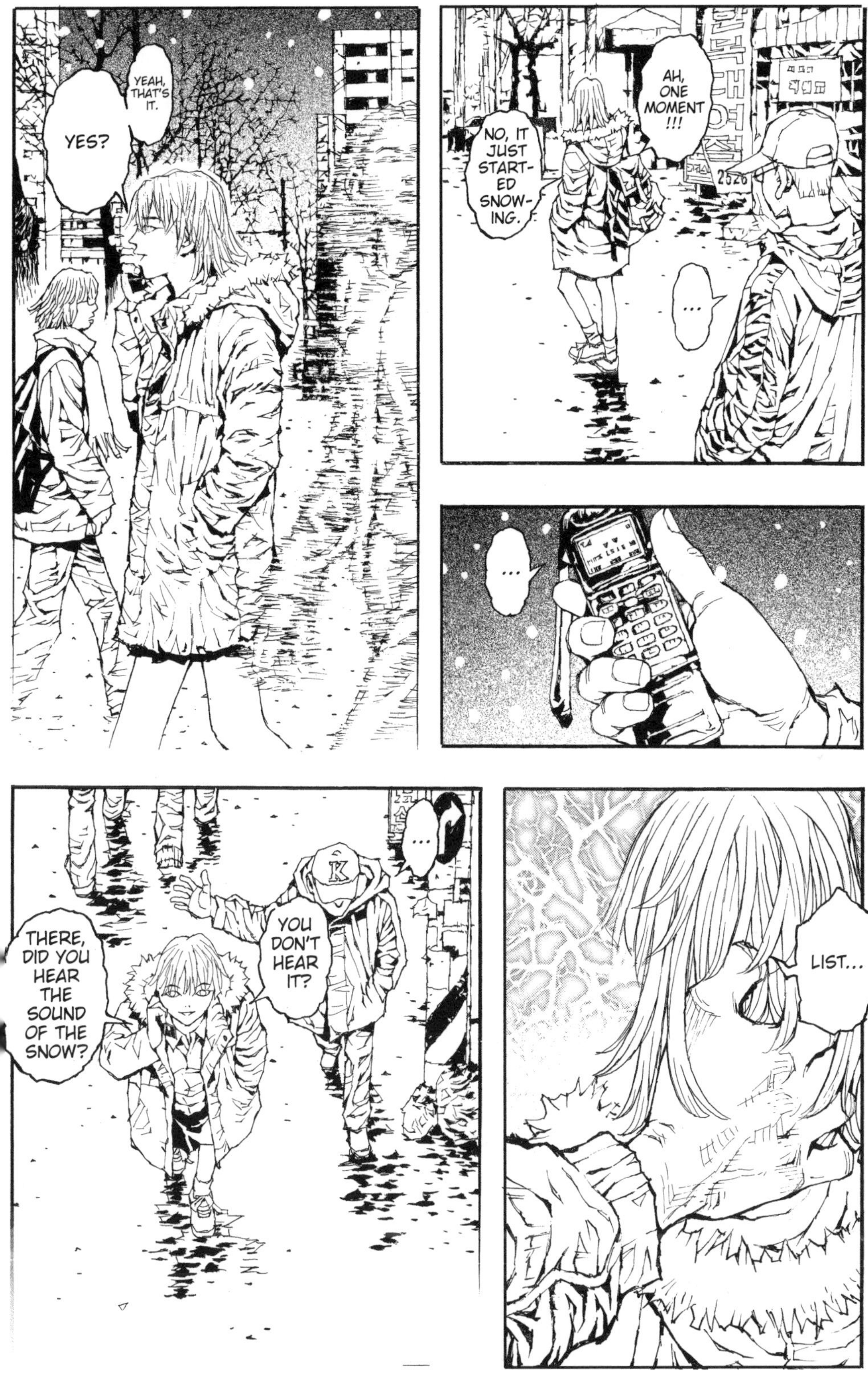
YES?
YEAH, THAT'S IT.
AH, ONE MOMENT !!!
NO, IT JUST START-ED SNOW-ING.
...
...
...
YOU DON'T HEAR IT?
THERE, DID YOU HEAR THE SOUND OF THE SNOW?
LIST...

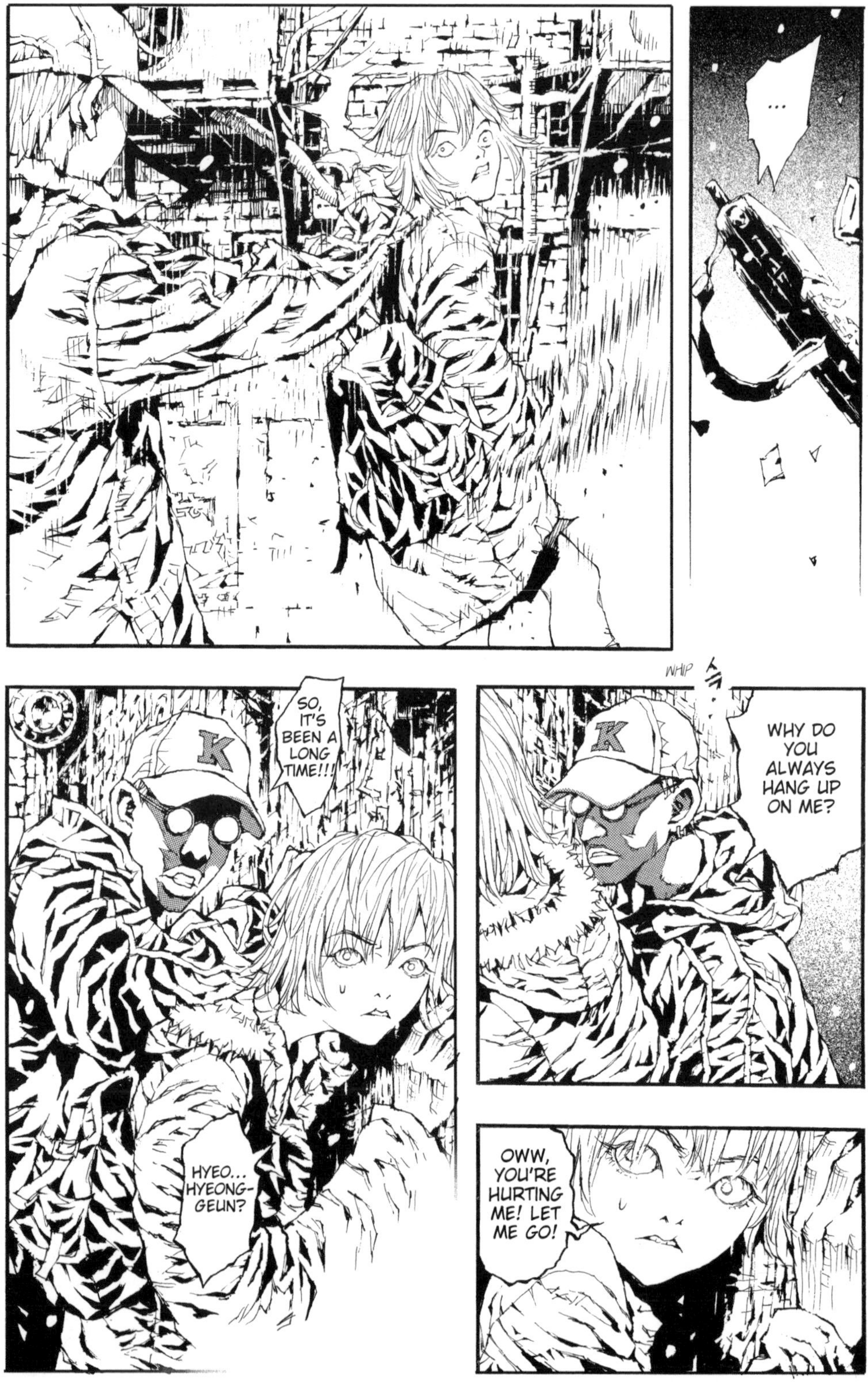
...
SO, IT'S BEEN A LONG TIME!!!
HYEO... HYEONG-GEUN?
WHIP
WHY DO YOU ALWAYS HANG UP ON ME?
OWW, YOU'RE HURTING ME! LET ME GO!

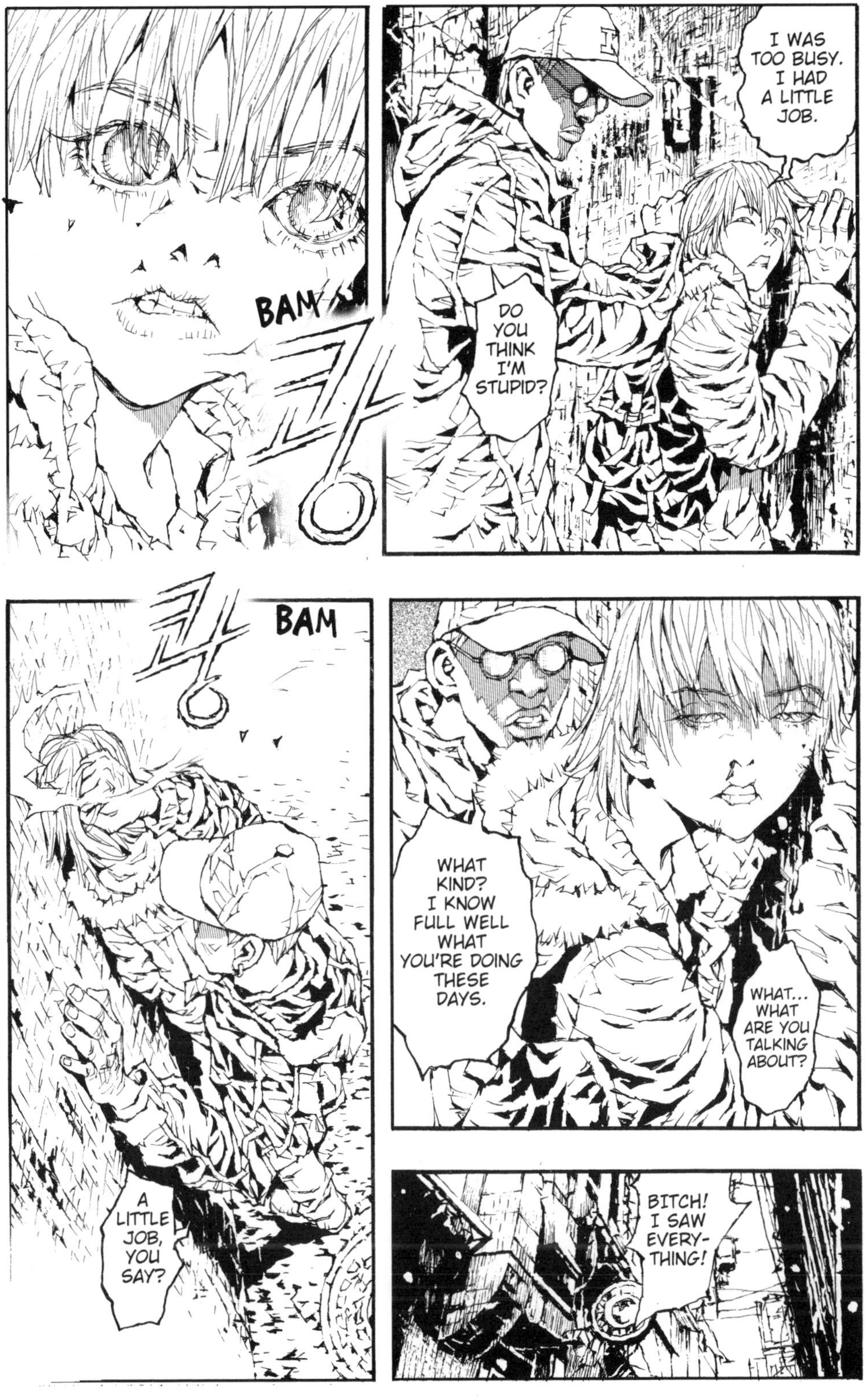
BAM
I WAS TOO BUSY. I HAD A LITTLE JOB.
DO YOU THINK I'M STUPID?
BAM
A LITTLE JOB, YOU SAY?
WHAT KIND? I KNOW FULL WELL WHAT YOU'RE DOING THESE DAYS.
WHAT... WHAT ARE YOU TALKING ABOUT?
BITCH! I SAW EVERYTHING!

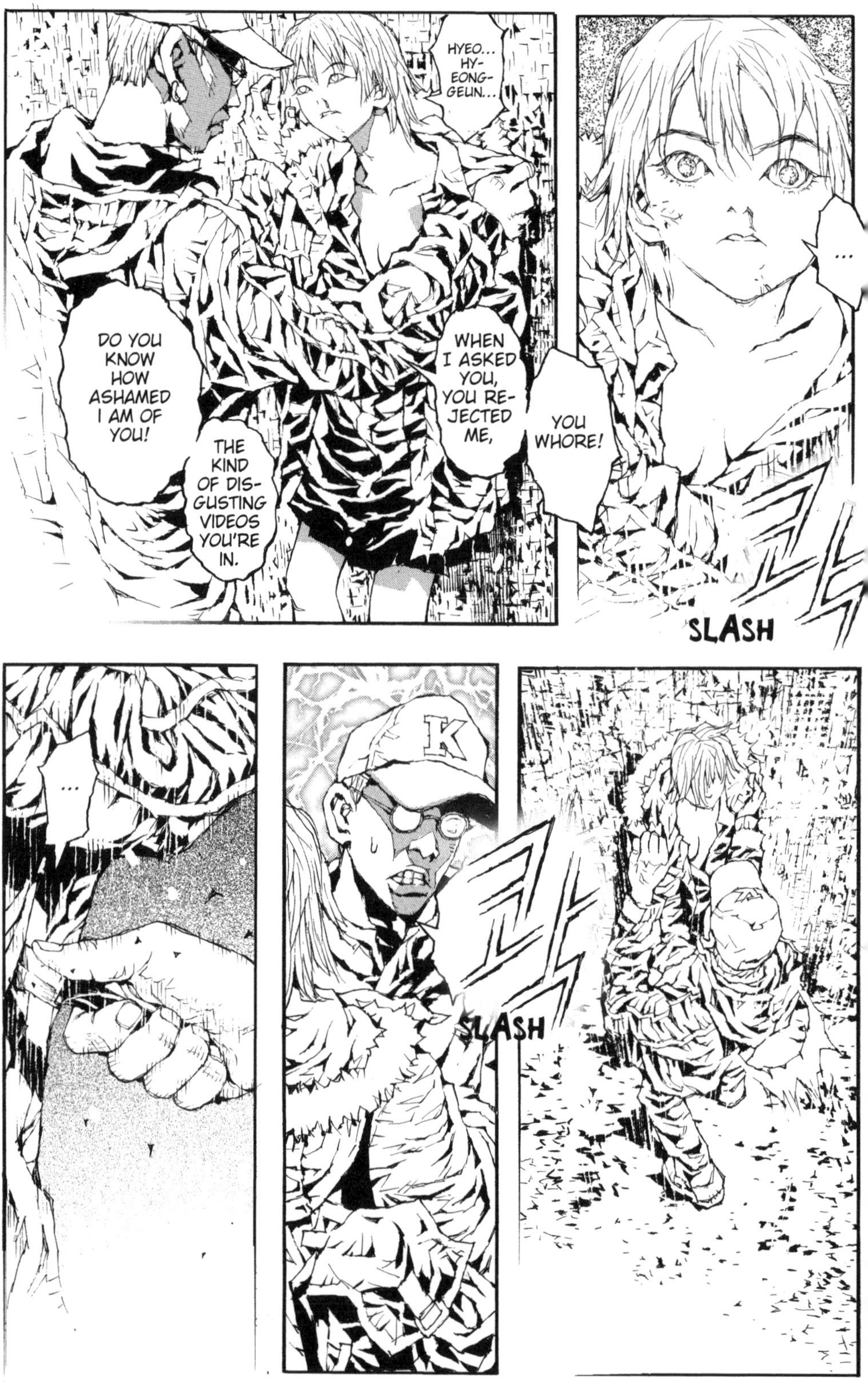
HYEO... HY-EONG-GEUN...
DO YOU KNOW HOW ASHAMED I AM OF YOU!
THE KIND OF DIS-GUSTING VIDEOS YOU'RE IN.
WHEN I ASKED YOU, YOU RE-JECTED ME,
YOU WHORE!
...
SLASH
...
SLASH

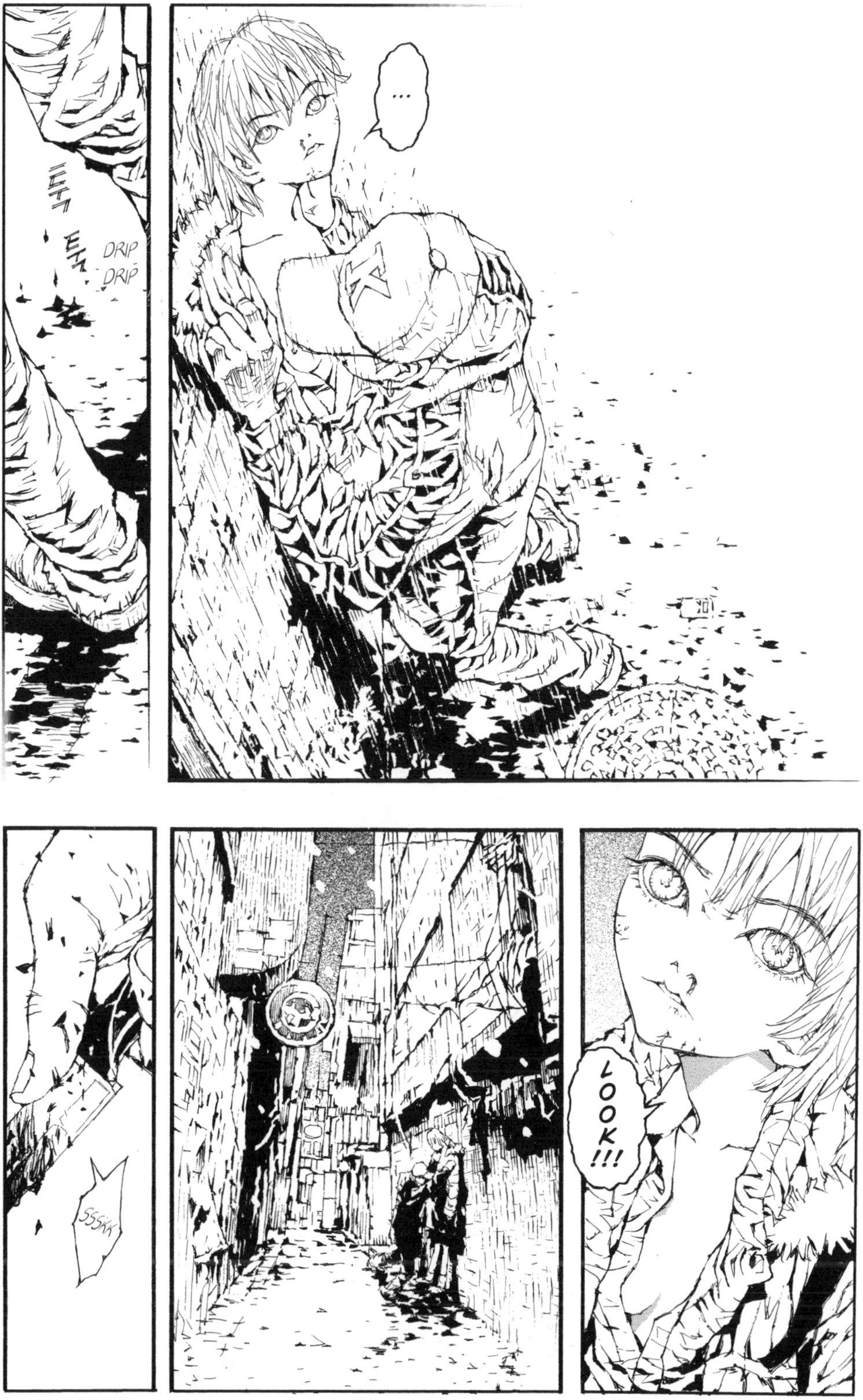
...
DRIP
DRIP
LOOK!!!
SSSKK

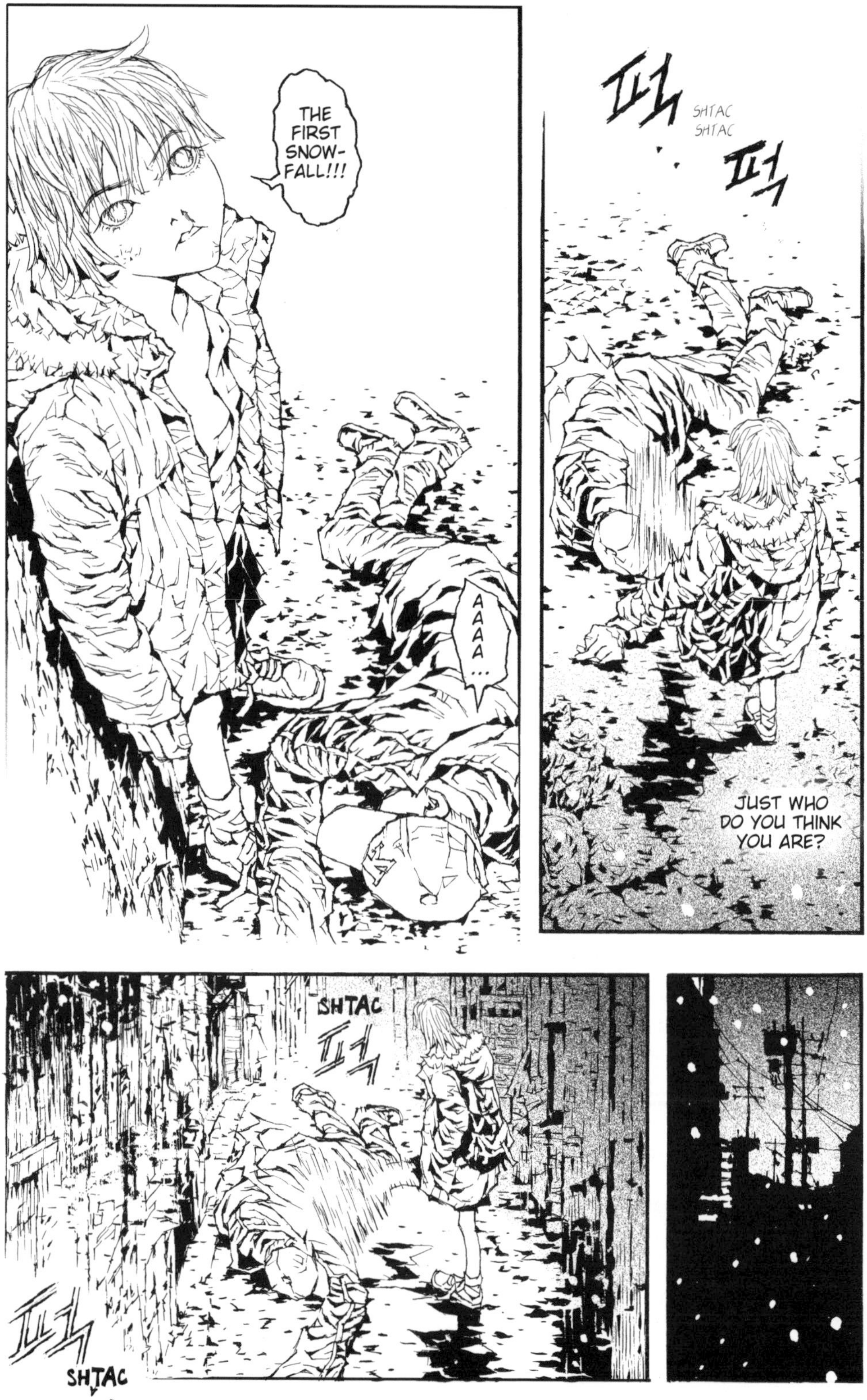
THE FIRST SNOW-FALL!!!
AAAA...
SHTAC
SHTAC
JUST WHO DO YOU THINK YOU ARE?
SHTAC
SHTAC

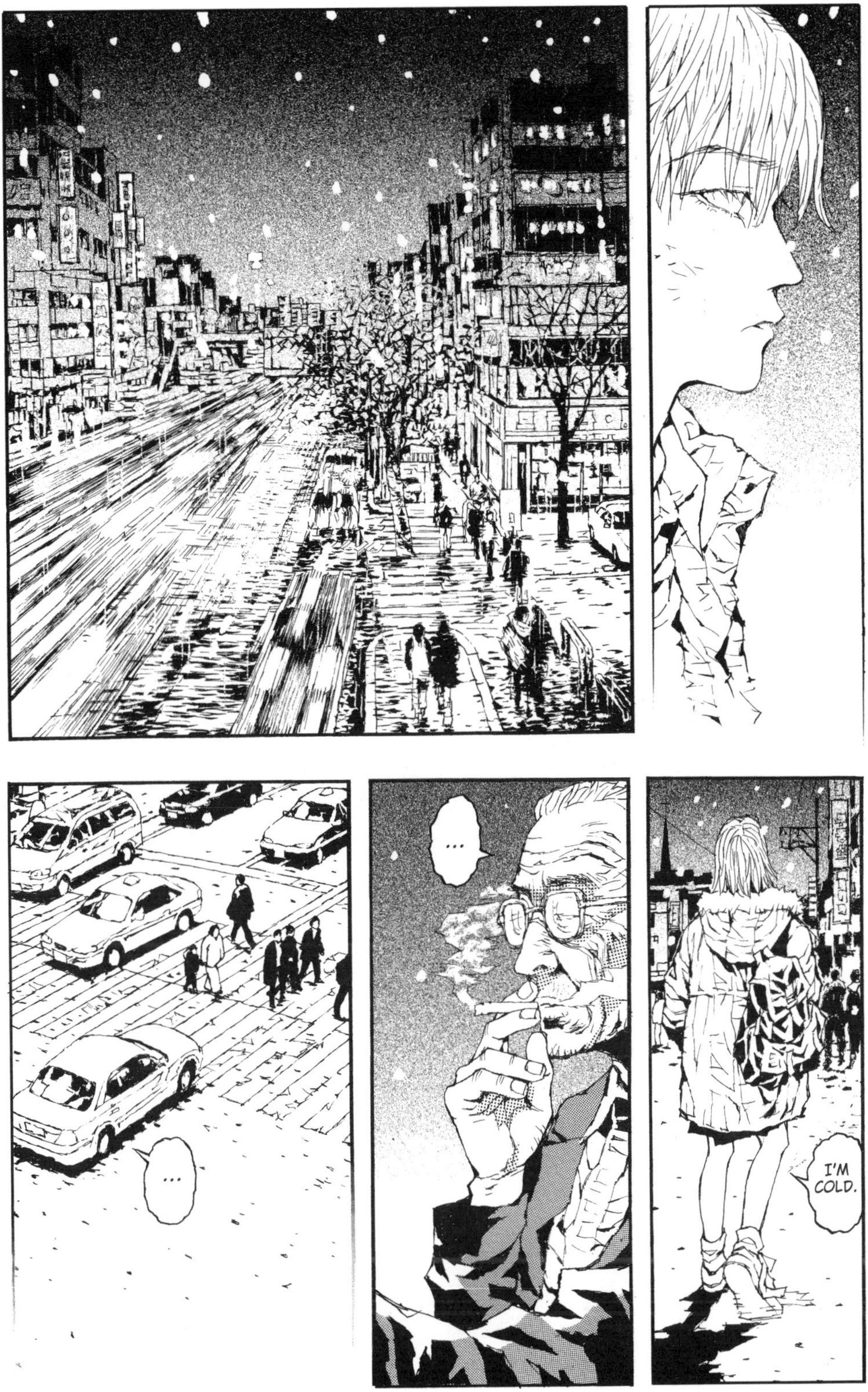
...
...
I'M COLD.

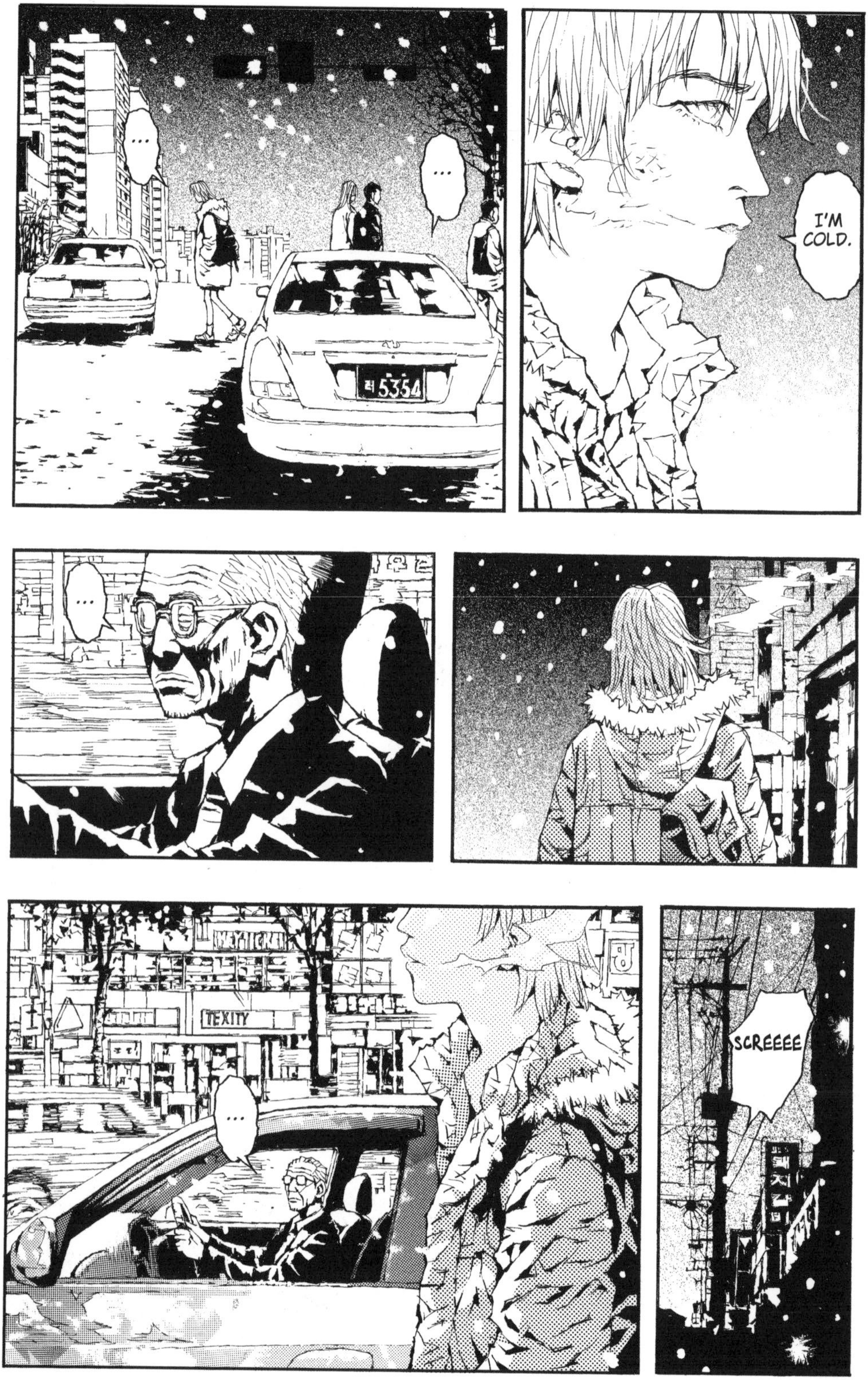
...
...
I'M COLD.
...
TEXITY
...
SCREEEE

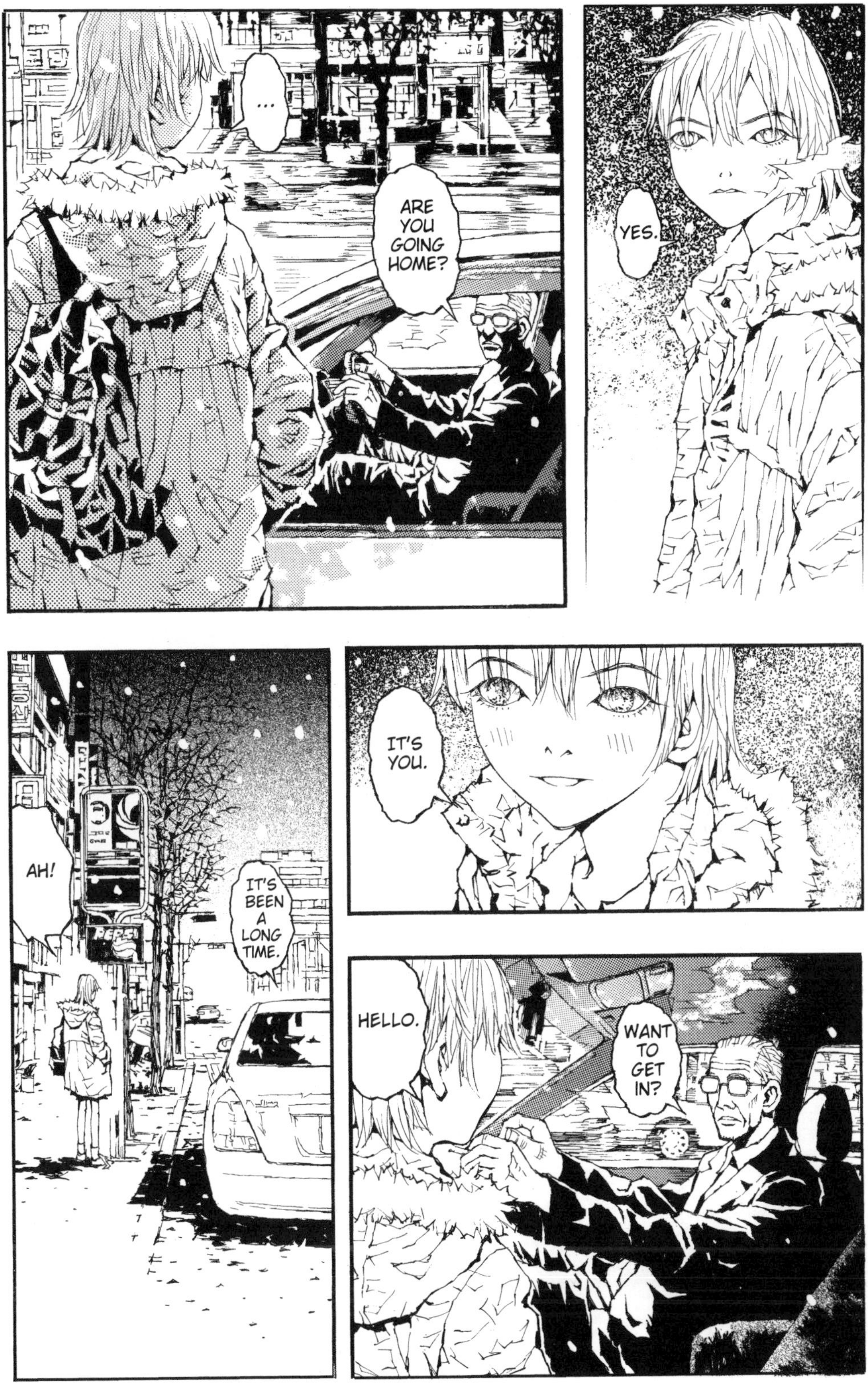
...
ARE YOU GOING HOME?
YES.
AH!
IT'S BEEN A LONG TIME.
IT'S YOU.
HELLO.
WANT TO GET IN?

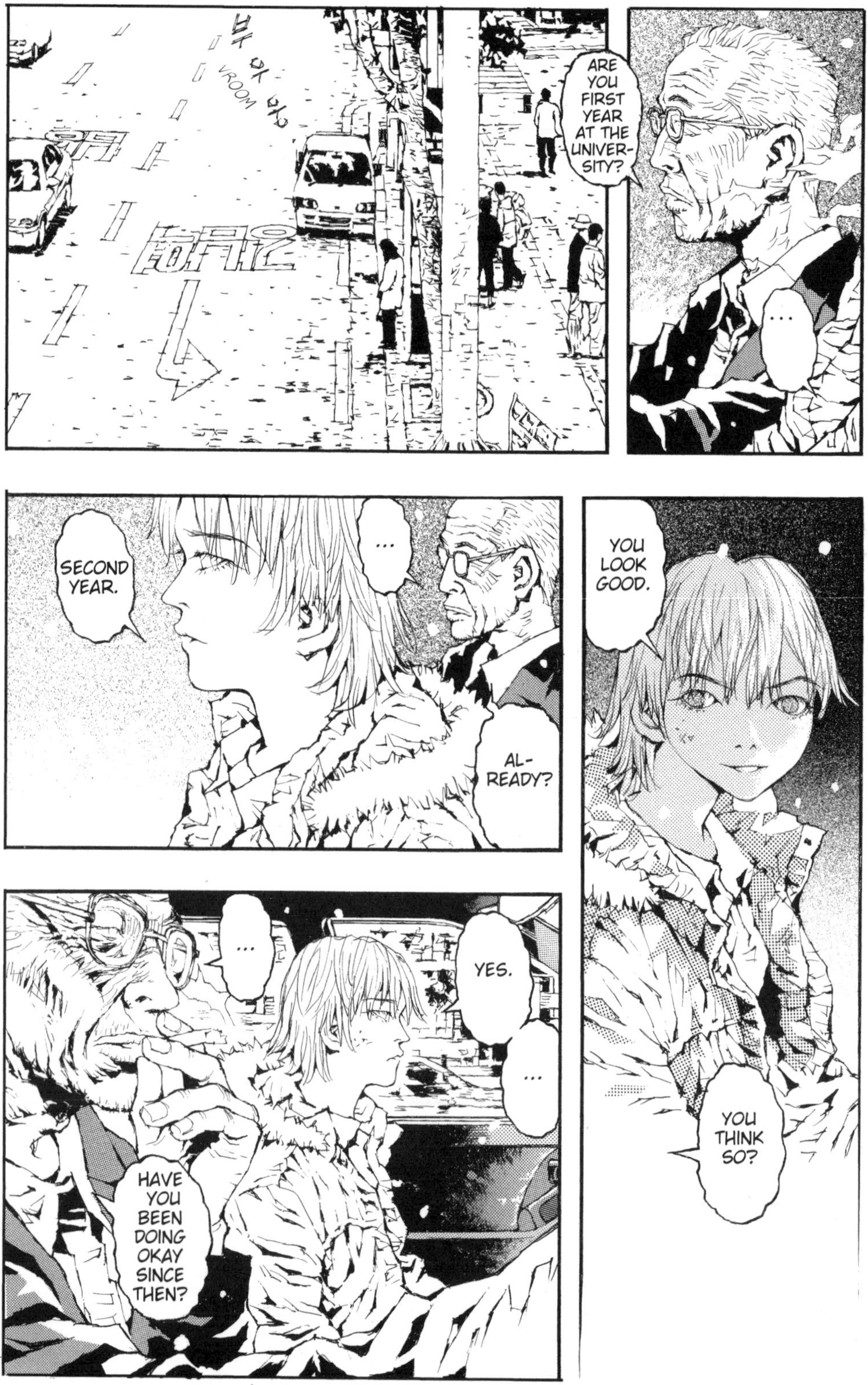
VROOM
ARE YOU FIRST YEAR AT THE UNIVER-SITY?
...
SECOND YEAR.
...
AL-READY?
...
YES.
...
HAVE YOU BEEN DOING OKAY SINCE THEN?
YOU LOOK GOOD.
YOU THINK SO?

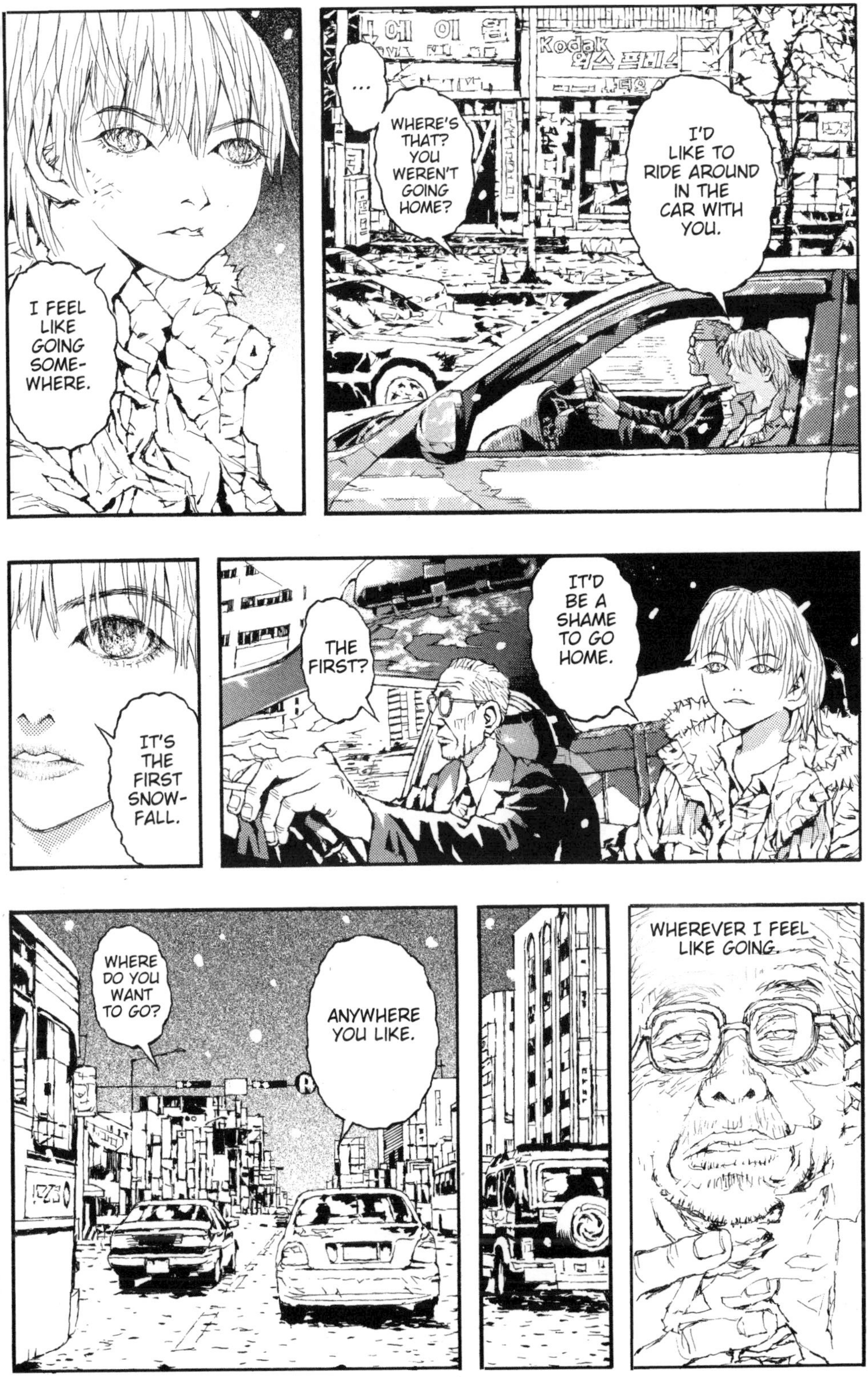
I FEEL LIKE GOING SOME-WHERE.
...
WHERE'S THAT? YOU WEREN'T GOING HOME?
Kodak
I'D LIKE TO RIDE AROUND IN THE CAR WITH YOU.
IT'S THE FIRST SNOW-FALL.
THE FIRST?
IT'D BE A SHAME TO GO HOME.
WHERE DO YOU WANT TO GO?
ANYWHERE YOU LIKE.
WHEREVER I FEEL LIKE GOING.

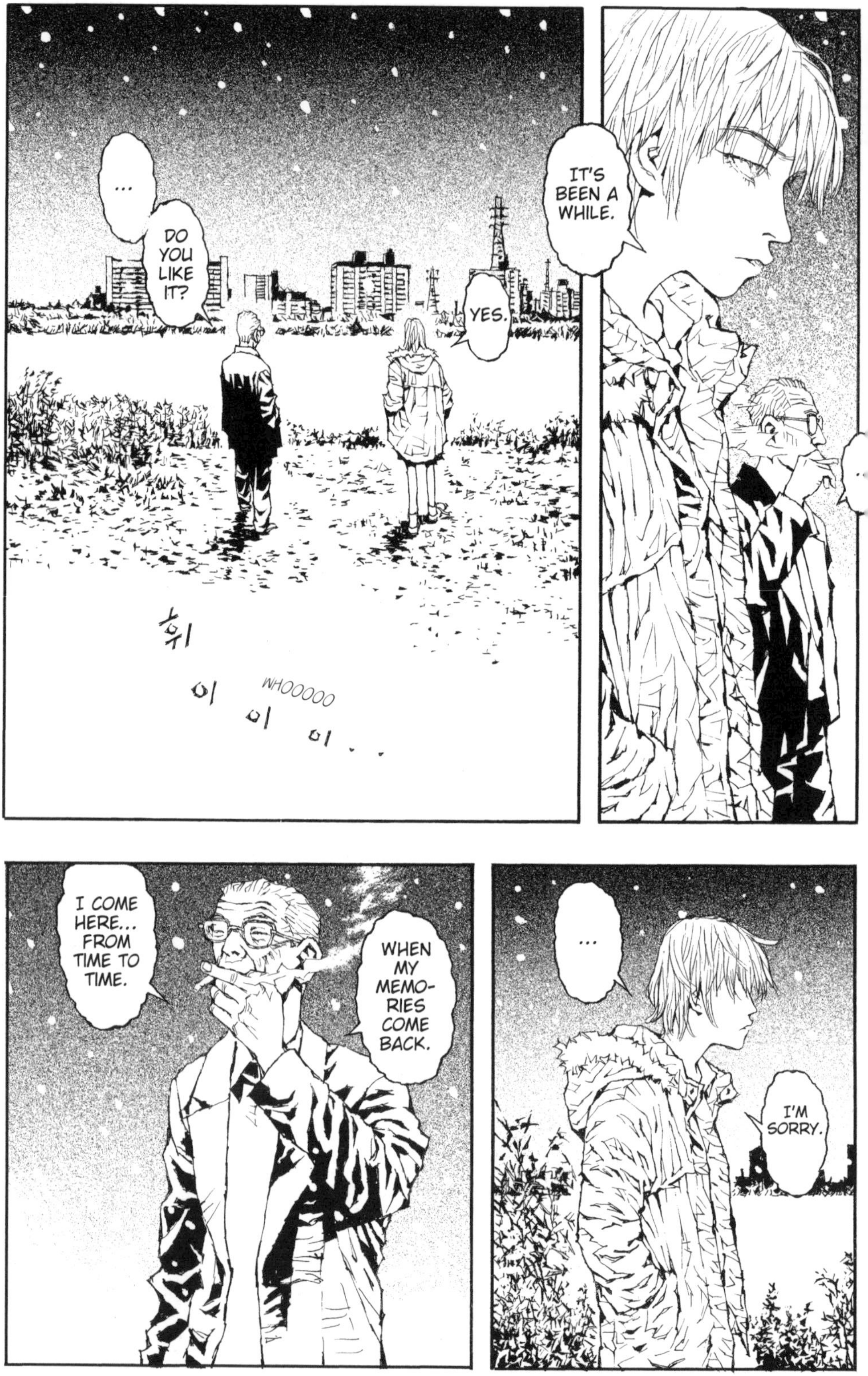
...
DO YOU LIKE IT?
YES.
휘이이이..
WHOOOOO
IT'S BEEN A WHILE.
I COME HERE... FROM TIME TO TIME.
WHEN MY MEMORIES COME BACK.
...
I'M SORRY.

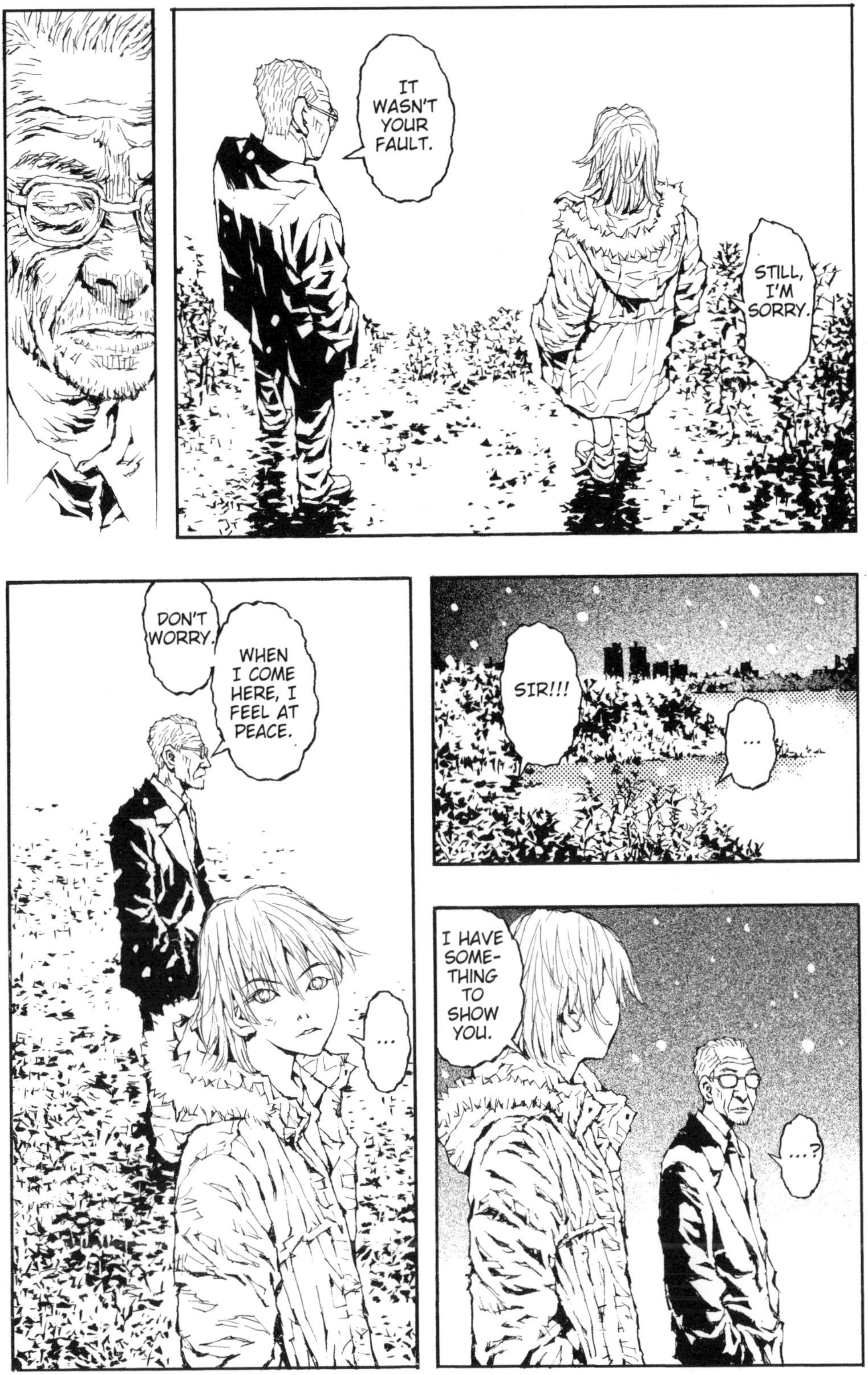
IT WASN'T YOUR FAULT.
STILL, I'M SORRY.
DON'T WORRY.
WHEN I COME HERE, I FEEL AT PEACE.
...
SIR!!!
...
I HAVE SOMETHING TO SHOW YOU.
...?

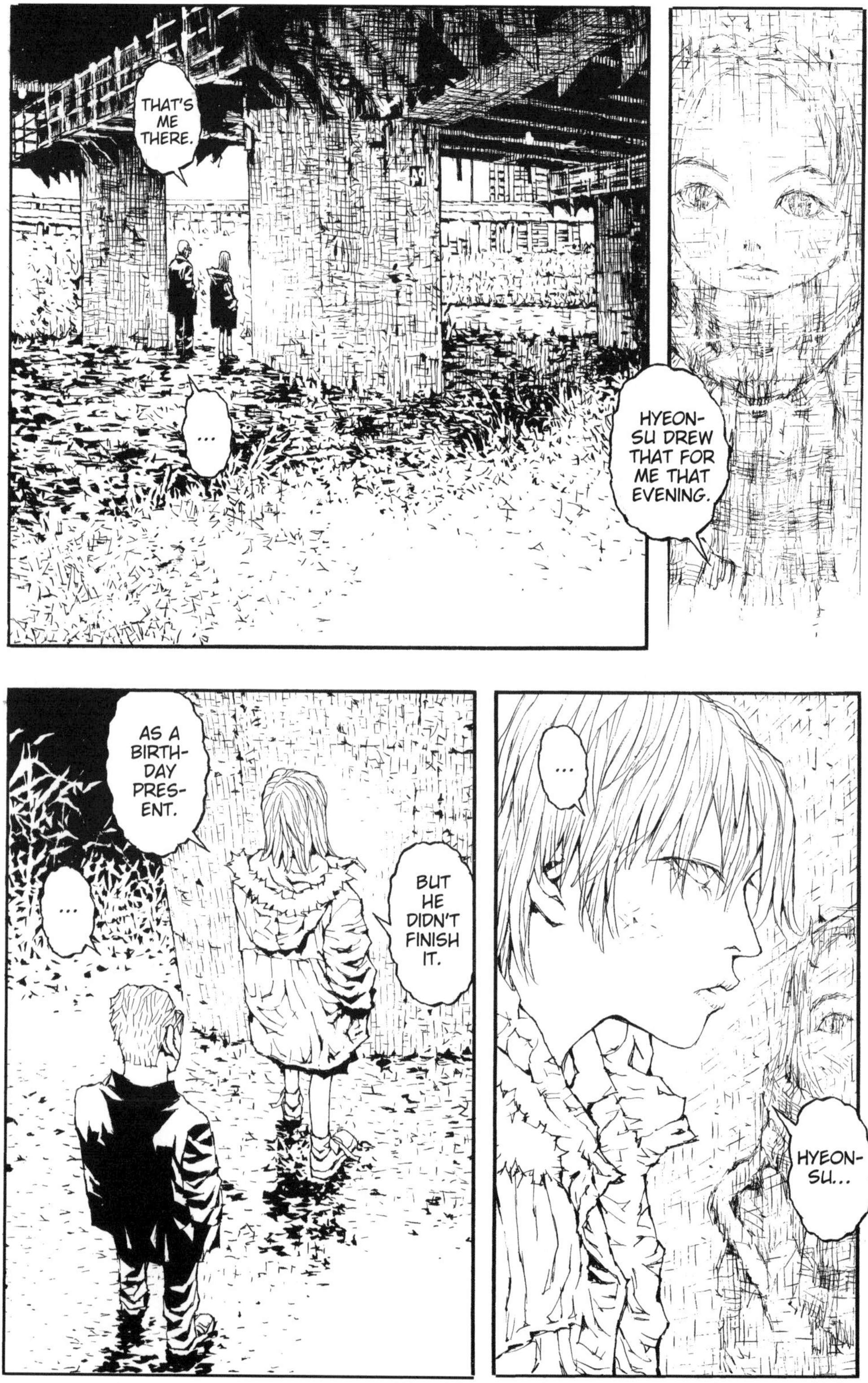
THAT'S ME THERE.
...
HYEON-SU DREW THAT FOR ME THAT EVENING.
AS A BIRTHDAY PRESENT.
...
BUT HE DIDN'T FINISH IT.
...
HYEON-SU...

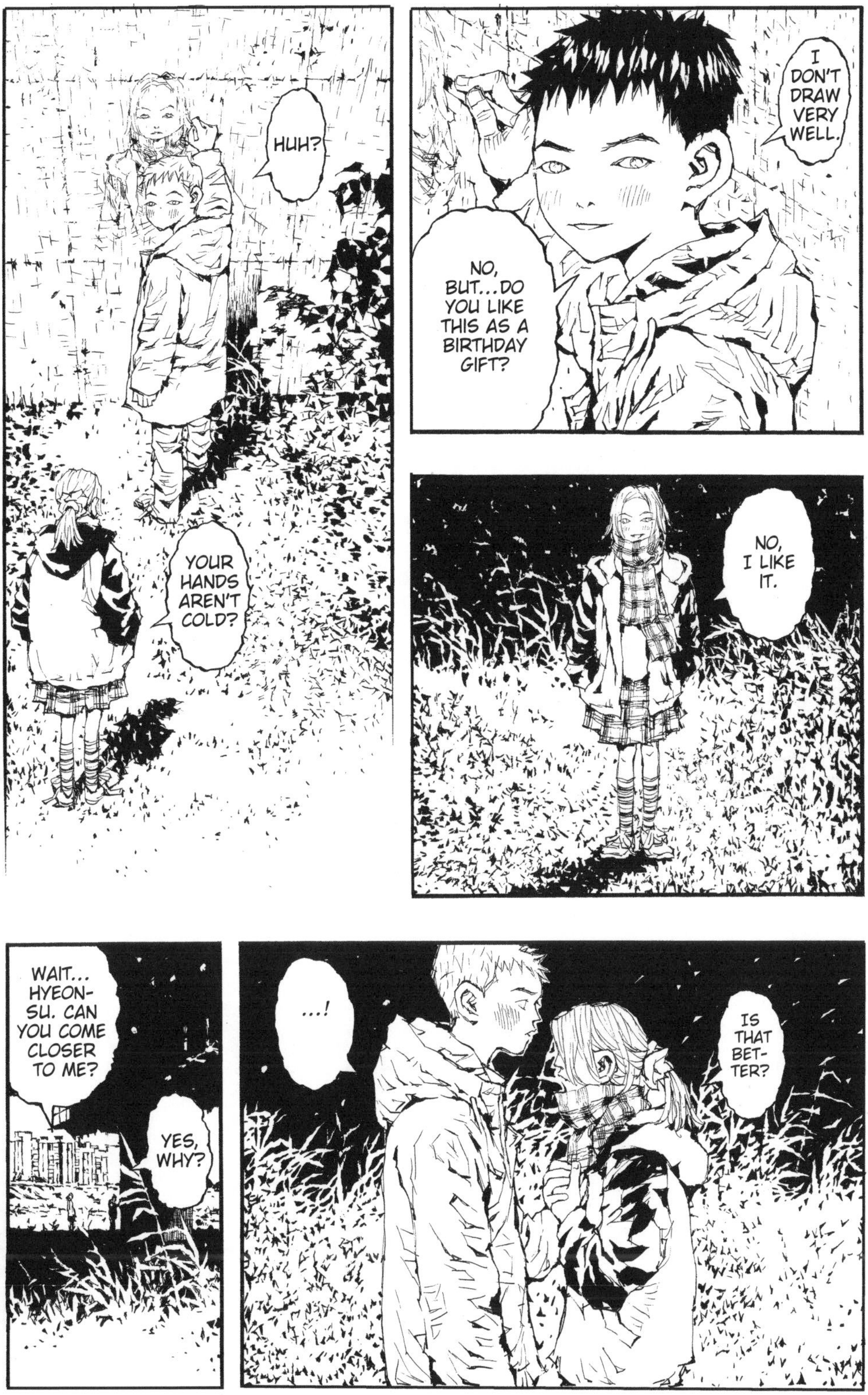
HUH?
I DON'T DRAW VERY WELL.
NO, BUT...DO YOU LIKE THIS AS A BIRTHDAY GIFT?
YOUR HANDS AREN'T COLD?
NO, I LIKE IT.
WAIT... HYEON-SU. CAN YOU COME CLOSER TO ME?
YES, WHY?
...!
IS THAT BET-TER?

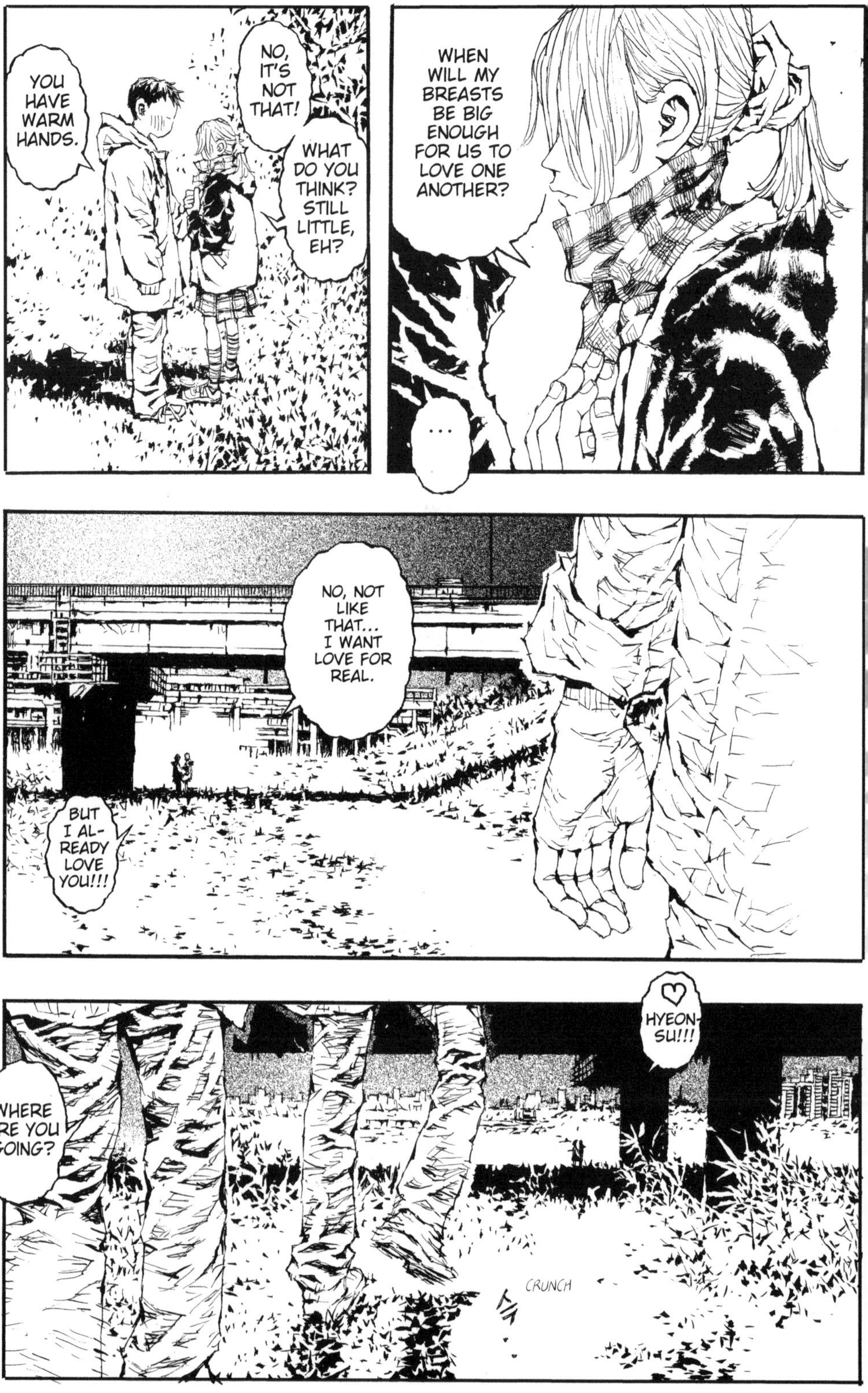
YOU HAVE WARM HANDS.
NO, IT'S NOT THAT!
WHAT DO YOU THINK? STILL LITTLE, EH?
WHEN WILL MY BREASTS BE BIG ENOUGH FOR US TO LOVE ONE ANOTHER?
...
NO, NOT LIKE THAT... I WANT LOVE FOR REAL.
BUT I ALREADY LOVE YOU!!!
WHERE ARE YOU GOING?
♡ HYEON-SU!!!
CRUNCH

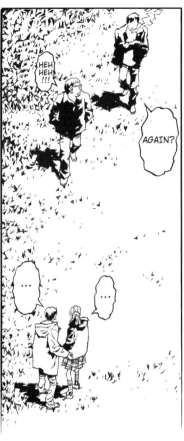

HEH HEH !!!

AGAIN?

...

...

ONCE HE'S HAD A FEW DRINKS.

HEH HEH !!!

...

YEON-DU!

HUF

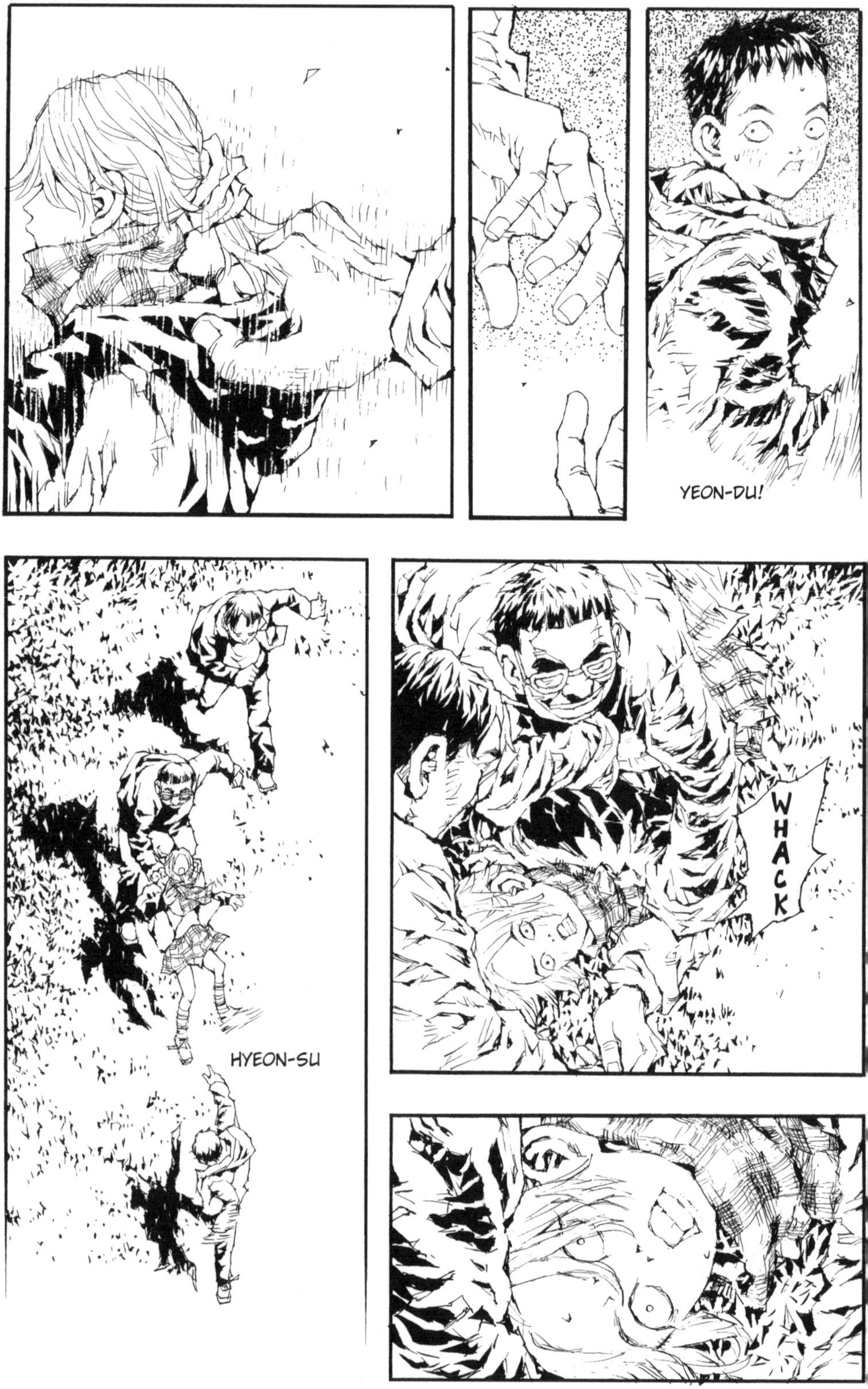
YEON-DU!
HYEON-SU
WHACK

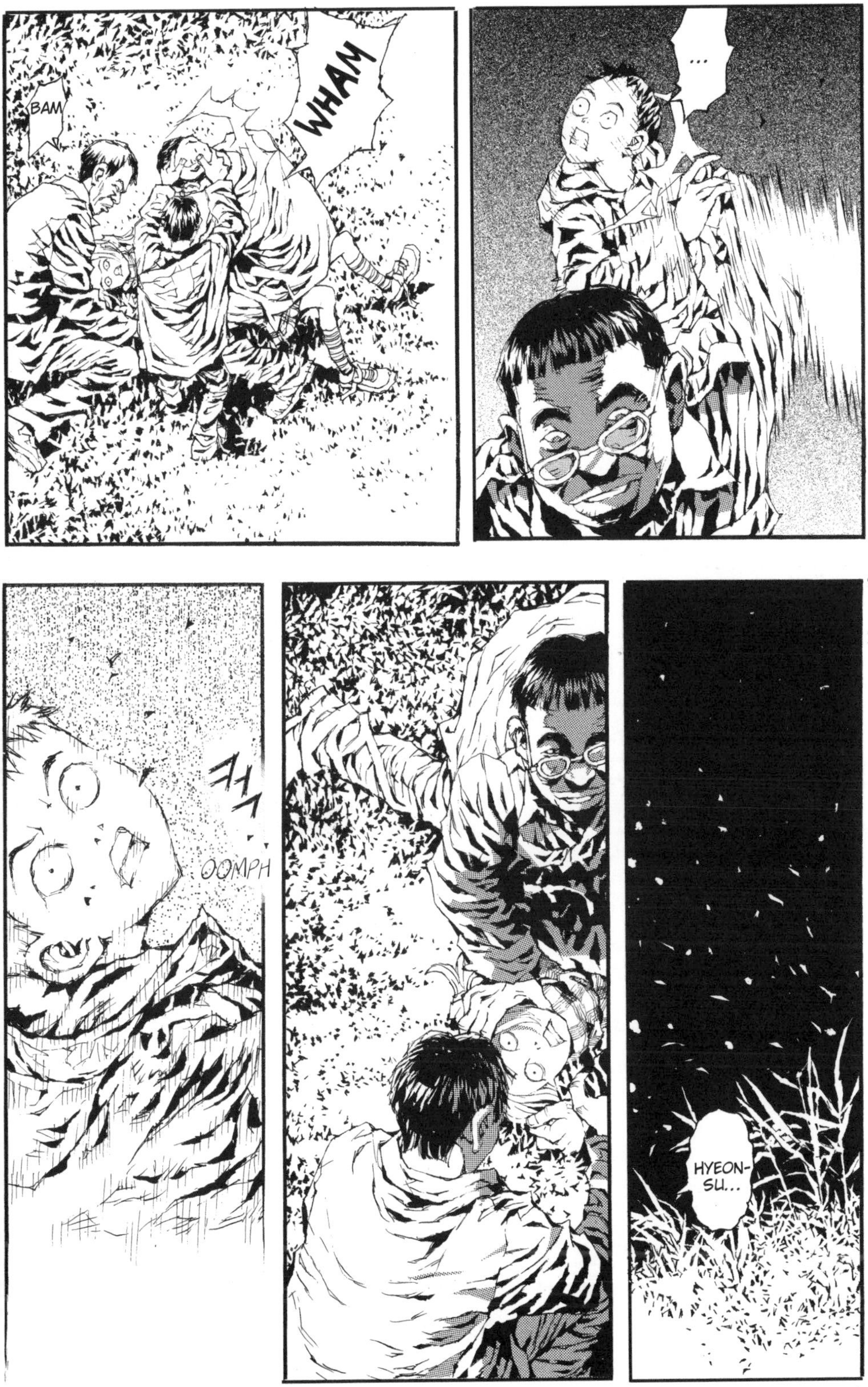
BAM
WHAM
...
OOMPH
HYEON-
SU...

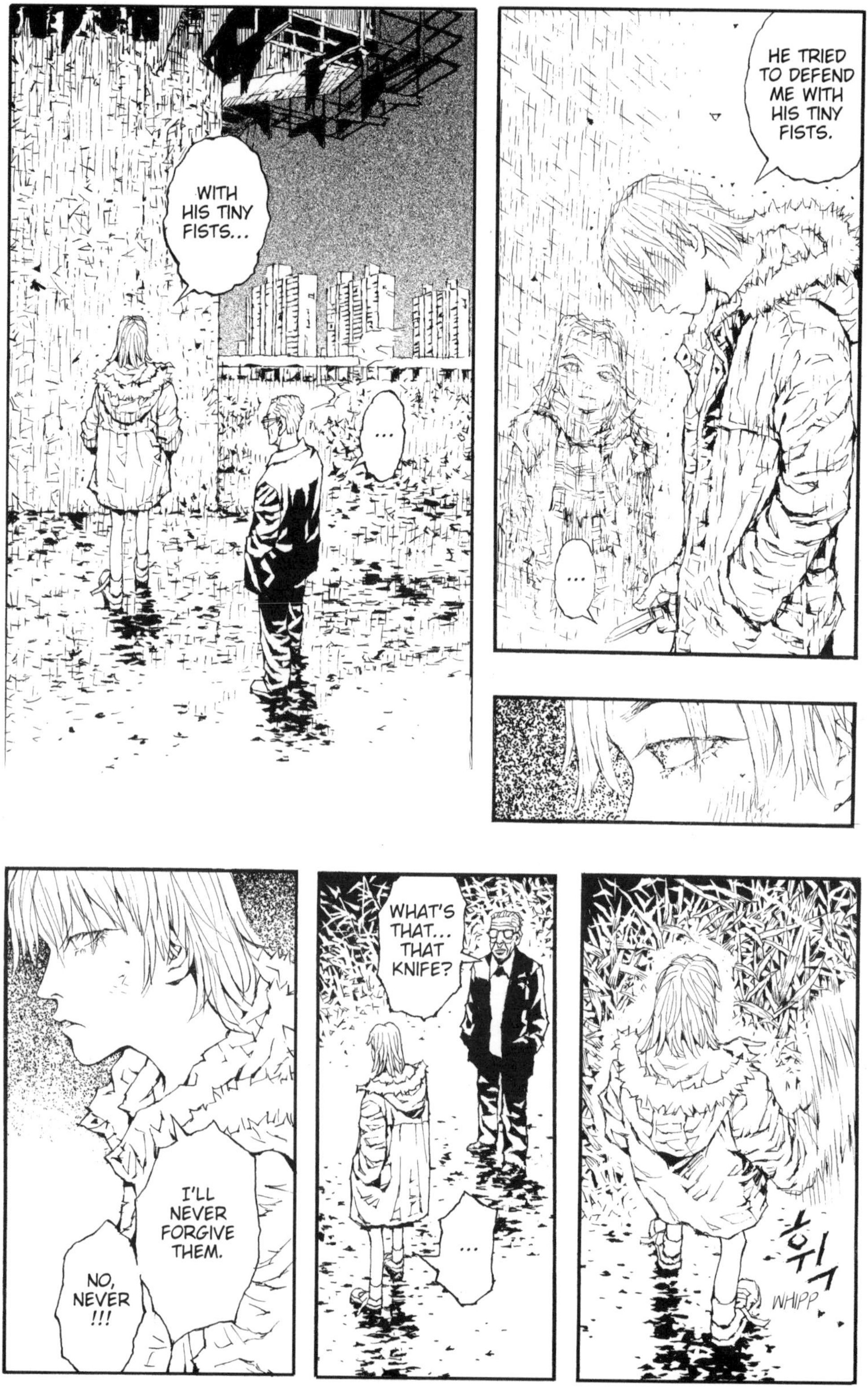
WITH HIS TINY FISTS...
...
HE TRIED TO DEFEND ME WITH HIS TINY FISTS.
...
I'LL NEVER FORGIVE THEM.
NO, NEVER!!!
WHAT'S THAT... THAT KNIFE?
...
WHIPP

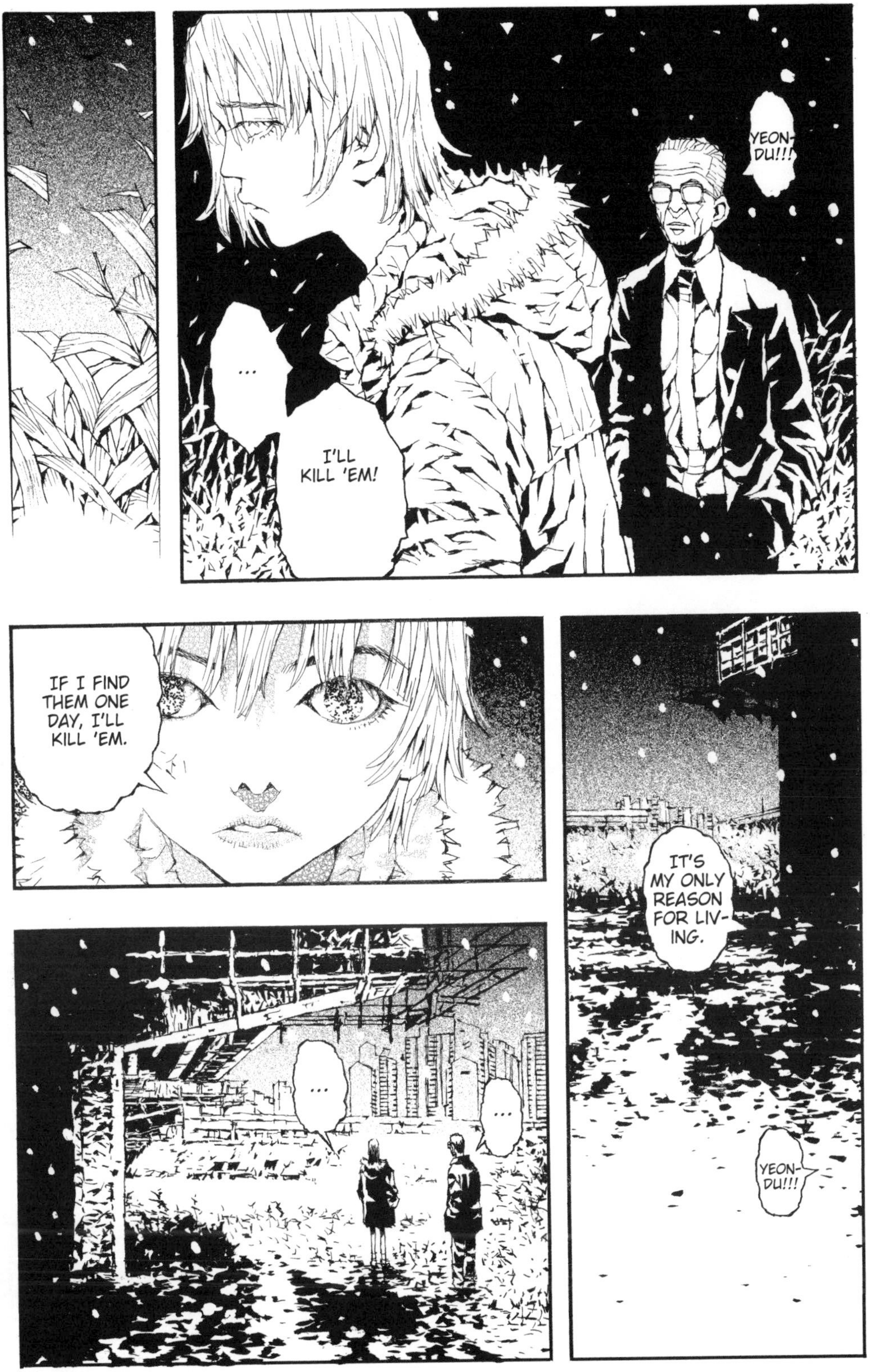
YEON-DU!!!
...
I'LL KILL 'EM!
IF I FIND THEM ONE DAY, I'LL KILL 'EM.
IT'S MY ONLY REASON FOR LIV-ING.
...
...
YEON-DU!!!

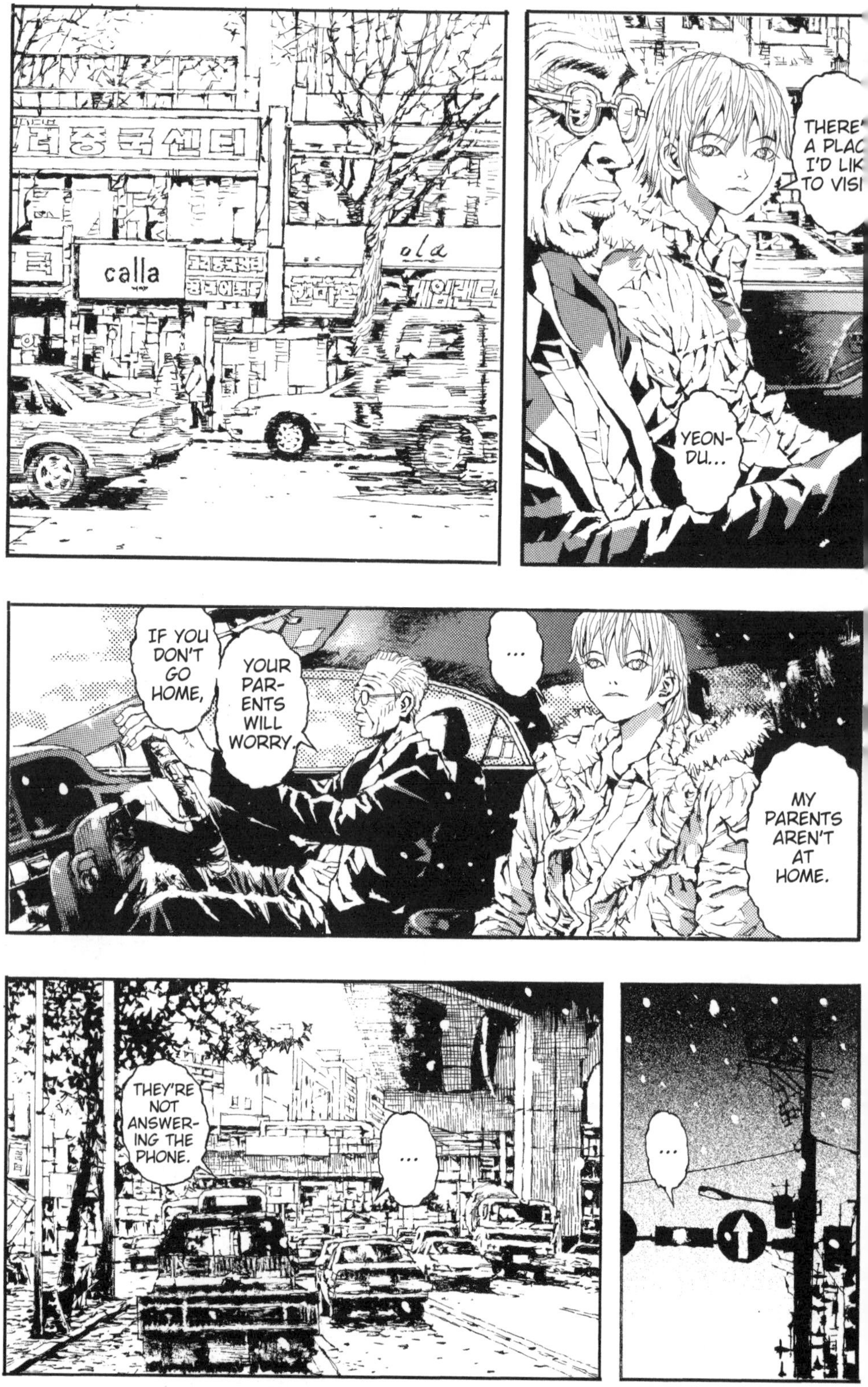
calla
ola
THERE' A PLAC I'D LIK TO VISI
YEON-DU...
IF YOU DON'T GO HOME,
YOUR PAR-ENTS WILL WORRY.
...
MY PARENTS AREN'T AT HOME.
THEY'RE NOT ANSWER-ING THE PHONE.
...
...

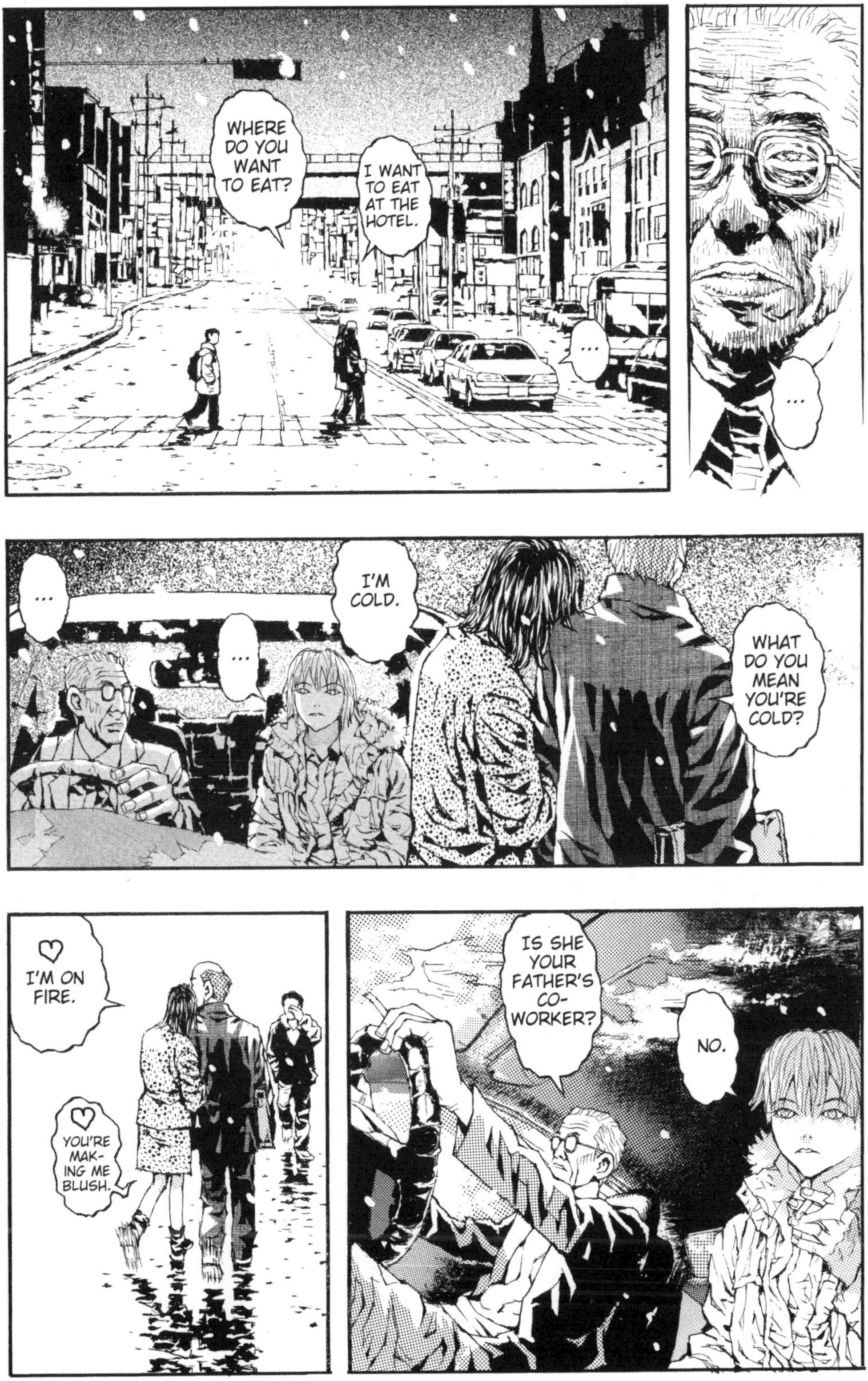
WHERE DO YOU WANT TO EAT?
I WANT TO EAT AT THE HOTEL.
...
...
...
...
I'M COLD.
WHAT DO YOU MEAN YOU'RE COLD?
♡ I'M ON FIRE.
♡ YOU'RE MAK-ING ME BLUSH.
IS SHE YOUR FATHER'S CO-WORKER?
NO.

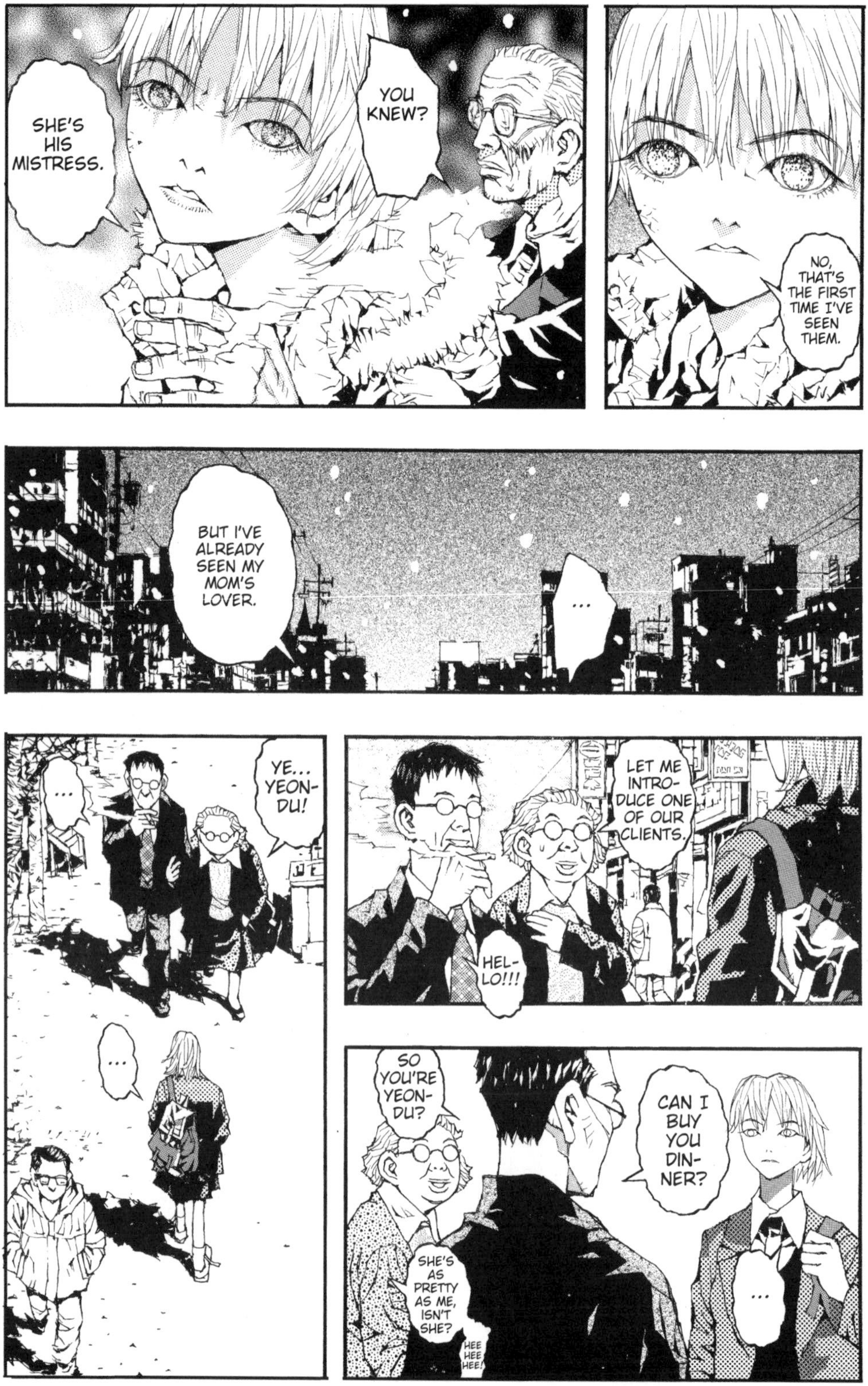
SHE'S HIS MISTRESS.
YOU KNEW?
NO, THAT'S THE FIRST TIME I'VE SEEN THEM.
BUT I'VE ALREADY SEEN MY MOM'S LOVER.
...
...
YE... YEON-DU!
...
LET ME INTRO-DUCE ONE OF OUR CLIENTS.
HEL-LO!!!
SO YOU'RE YEON-DU?
CAN I BUY YOU DIN-NER?
SHE'S AS PRETTY AS ME, ISN'T SHE?
HEE HEE HEE!
...

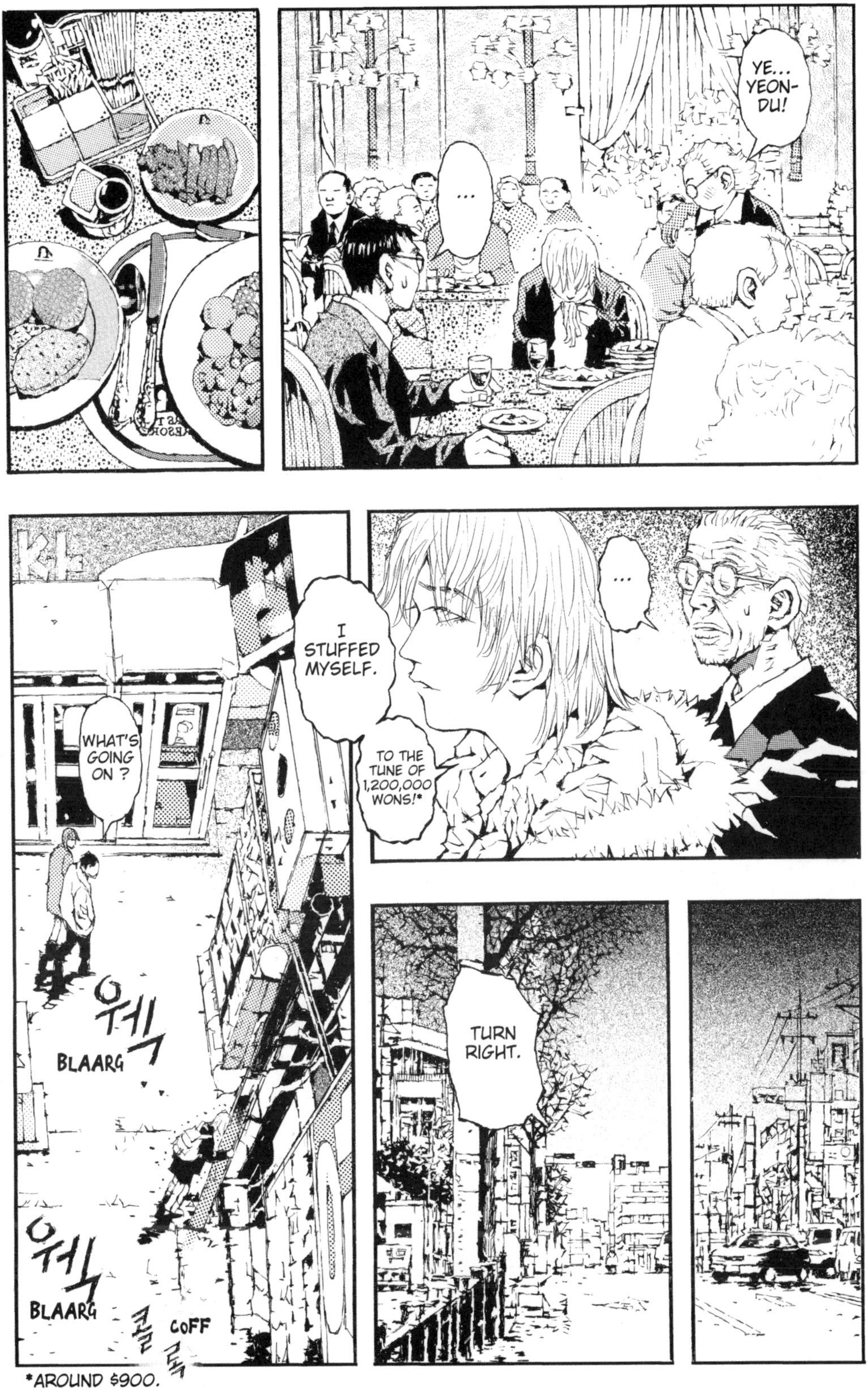
...
YE... YEON-DU!
I STUFFED MYSELF.
TO THE TUNE OF 1,200,000 WONS!*
...
WHAT'S GOING ON ?
우웩
BLAARG
우웩
BLAARG
콜록
COFF
TURN RIGHT.

*AROUND $900.

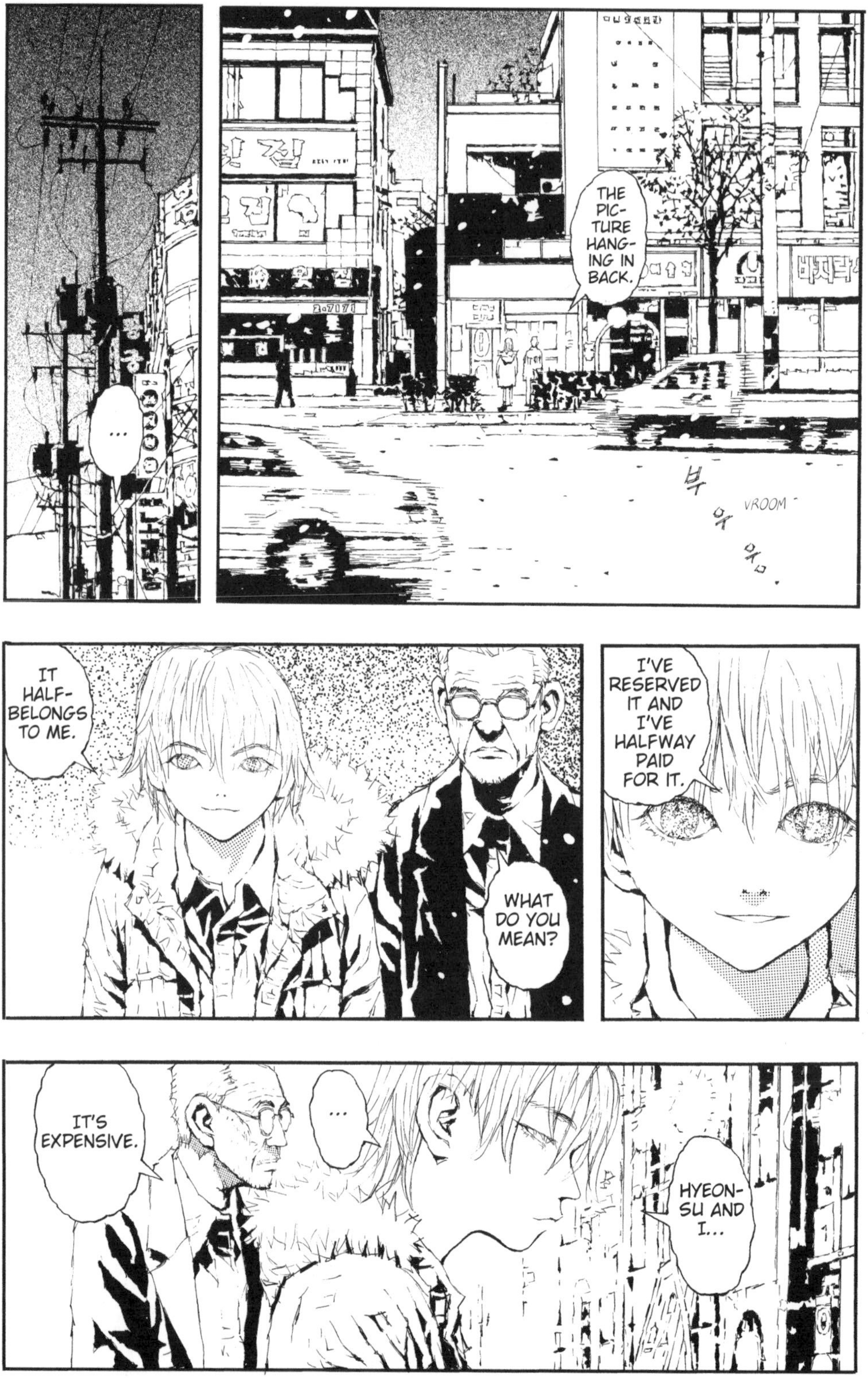
THE PIC-TURE HANG-ING IN BACK.
...
VROOM
IT HALF-BELONGS TO ME.
WHAT DO YOU MEAN?
I'VE RESERVED IT AND I'VE HALFWAY PAID FOR IT.
HYEON-SU AND I...
...
IT'S EXPENSIVE.

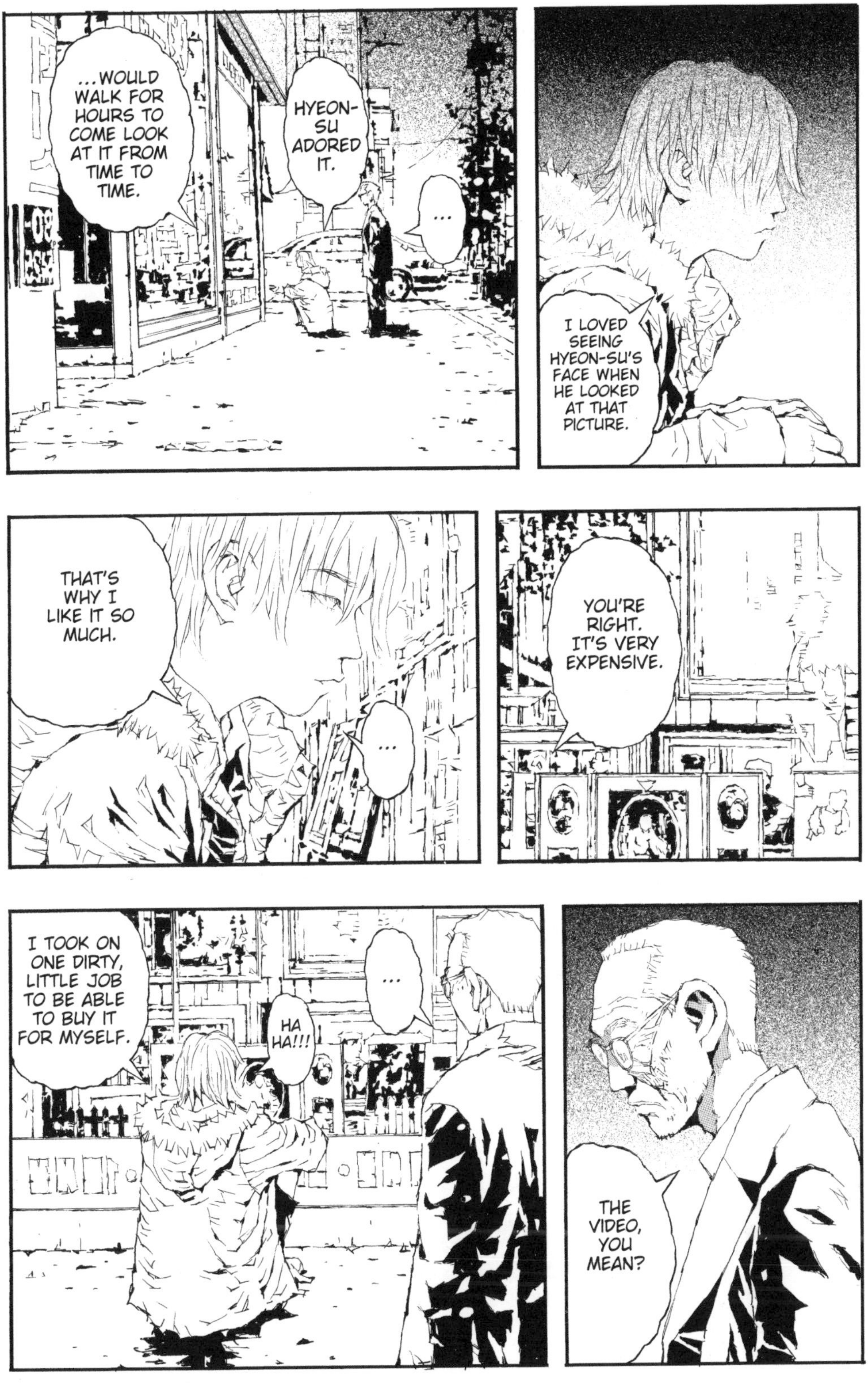
...WOULD WALK FOR HOURS TO COME LOOK AT IT FROM TIME TO TIME.
HYEON-SU ADORED IT.
...
I LOVED SEEING HYEON-SU'S FACE WHEN HE LOOKED AT THAT PICTURE.
THAT'S WHY I LIKE IT SO MUCH.
...
YOU'RE RIGHT. IT'S VERY EXPENSIVE.
I TOOK ON ONE DIRTY, LITTLE JOB TO BE ABLE TO BUY IT FOR MYSELF.
HA HA!!!
...
THE VIDEO, YOU MEAN?

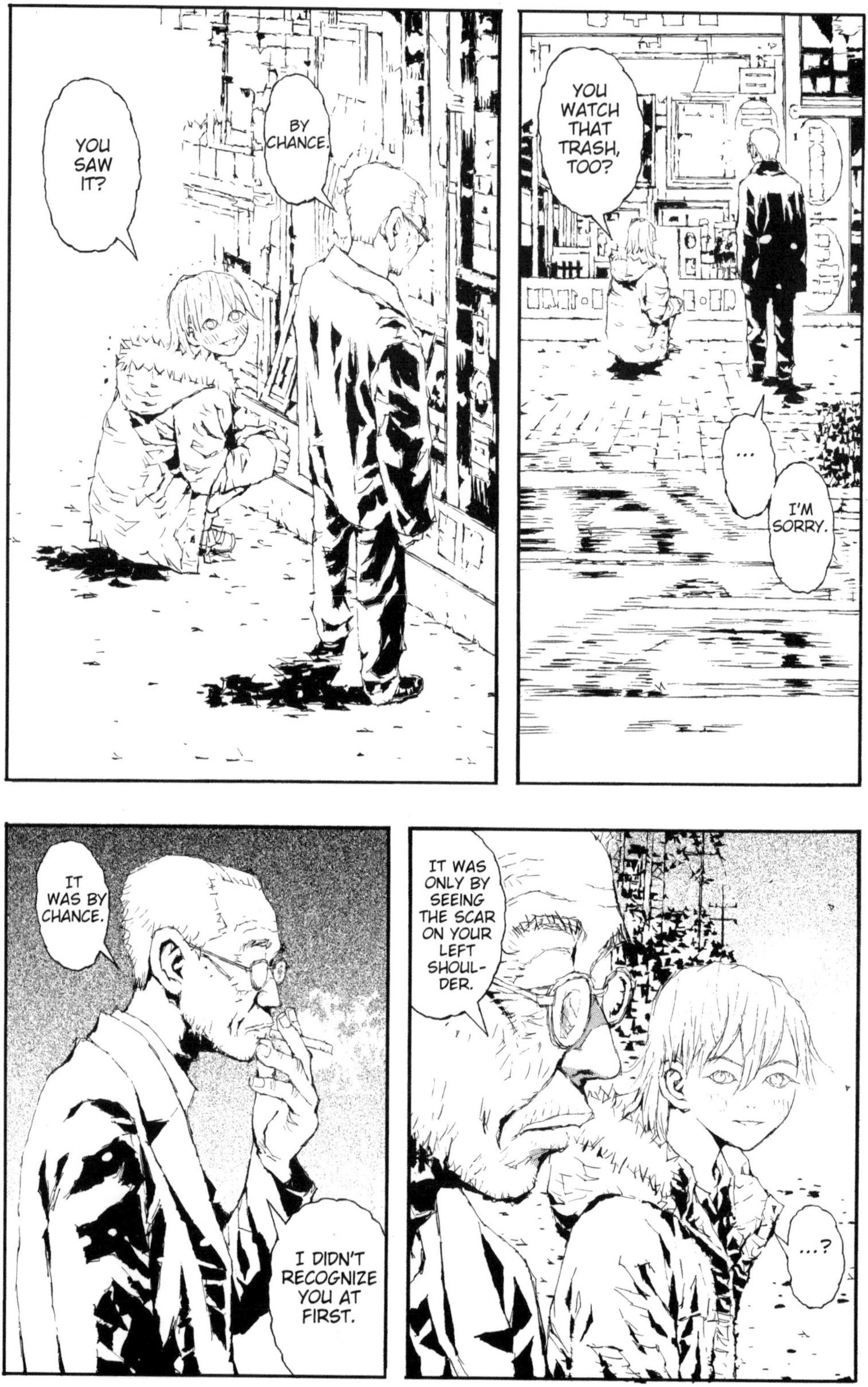
YOU SAW IT?
BY CHANCE.
YOU WATCH THAT TRASH, TOO?
...
I'M SORRY.
IT WAS BY CHANCE.
I DIDN'T RECOGNIZE YOU AT FIRST.
IT WAS ONLY BY SEEING THE SCAR ON YOUR LEFT SHOULDER.
...?

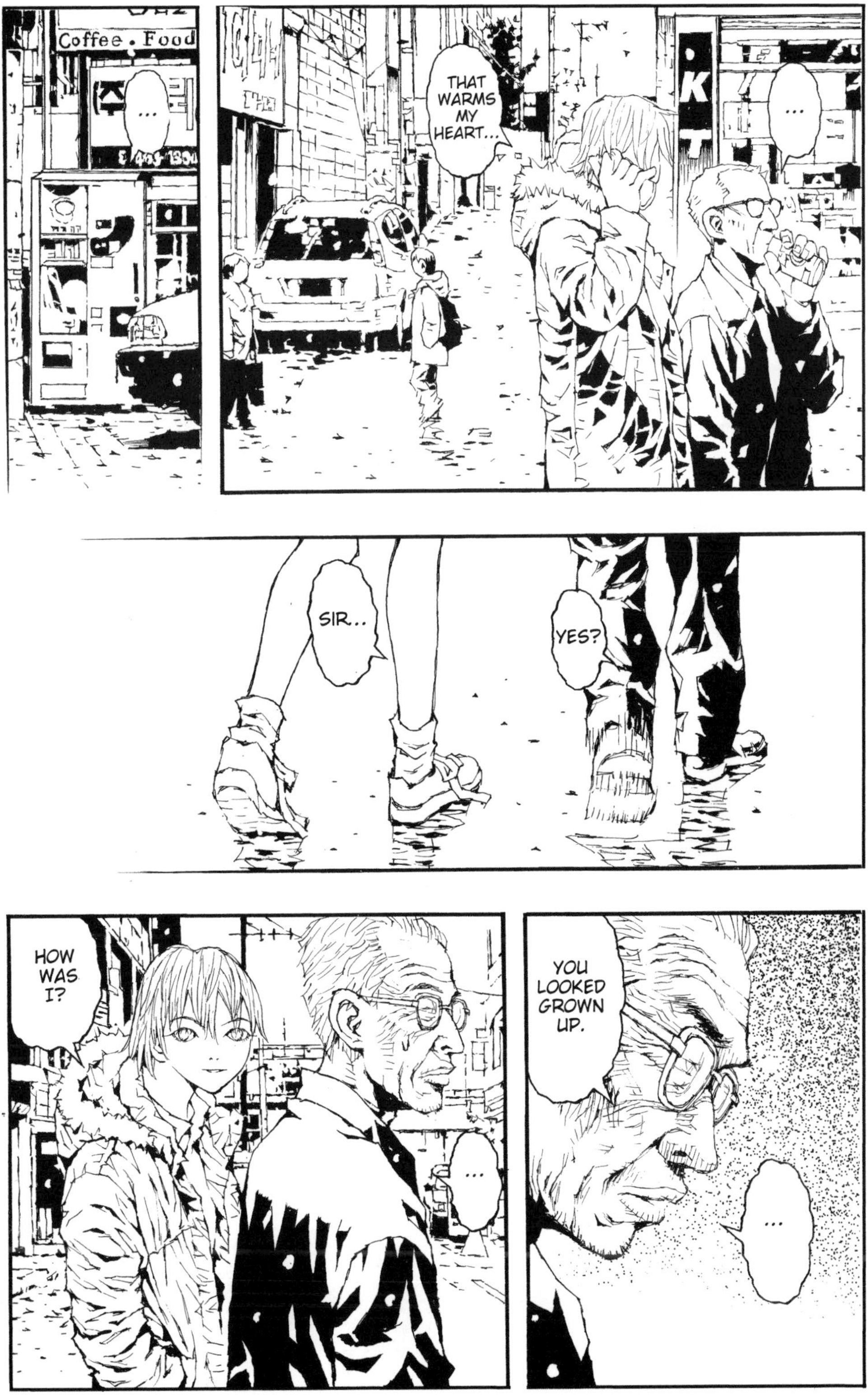

Coffee . Food
...
THAT WARMS MY HEART...
...
SIR...
YES?
HOW WAS I?
...
YOU LOOKED GROWN UP.
...

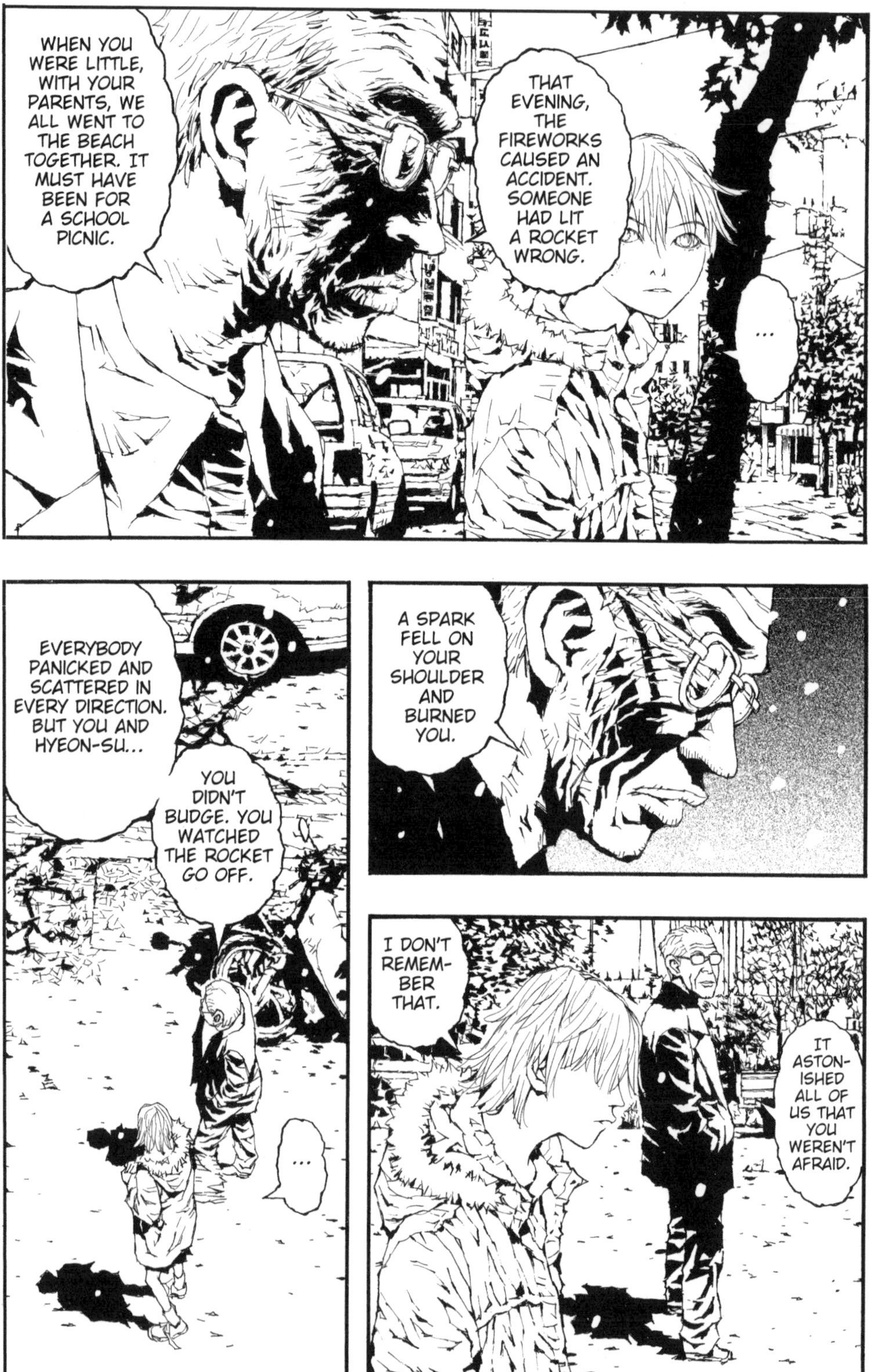
WHEN YOU WERE LITTLE, WITH YOUR PARENTS, WE ALL WENT TO THE BEACH TOGETHER. IT MUST HAVE BEEN FOR A SCHOOL PICNIC.
THAT EVENING, THE FIREWORKS CAUSED AN ACCIDENT. SOMEONE HAD LIT A ROCKET WRONG.
...
EVERYBODY PANICKED AND SCATTERED IN EVERY DIRECTION. BUT YOU AND HYEON-SU...
YOU DIDN'T BUDGE. YOU WATCHED THE ROCKET GO OFF.
...
A SPARK FELL ON YOUR SHOULDER AND BURNED YOU.
I DON'T REMEM-BER THAT.
IT ASTON-ISHED ALL OF US THAT YOU WEREN'T AFRAID.

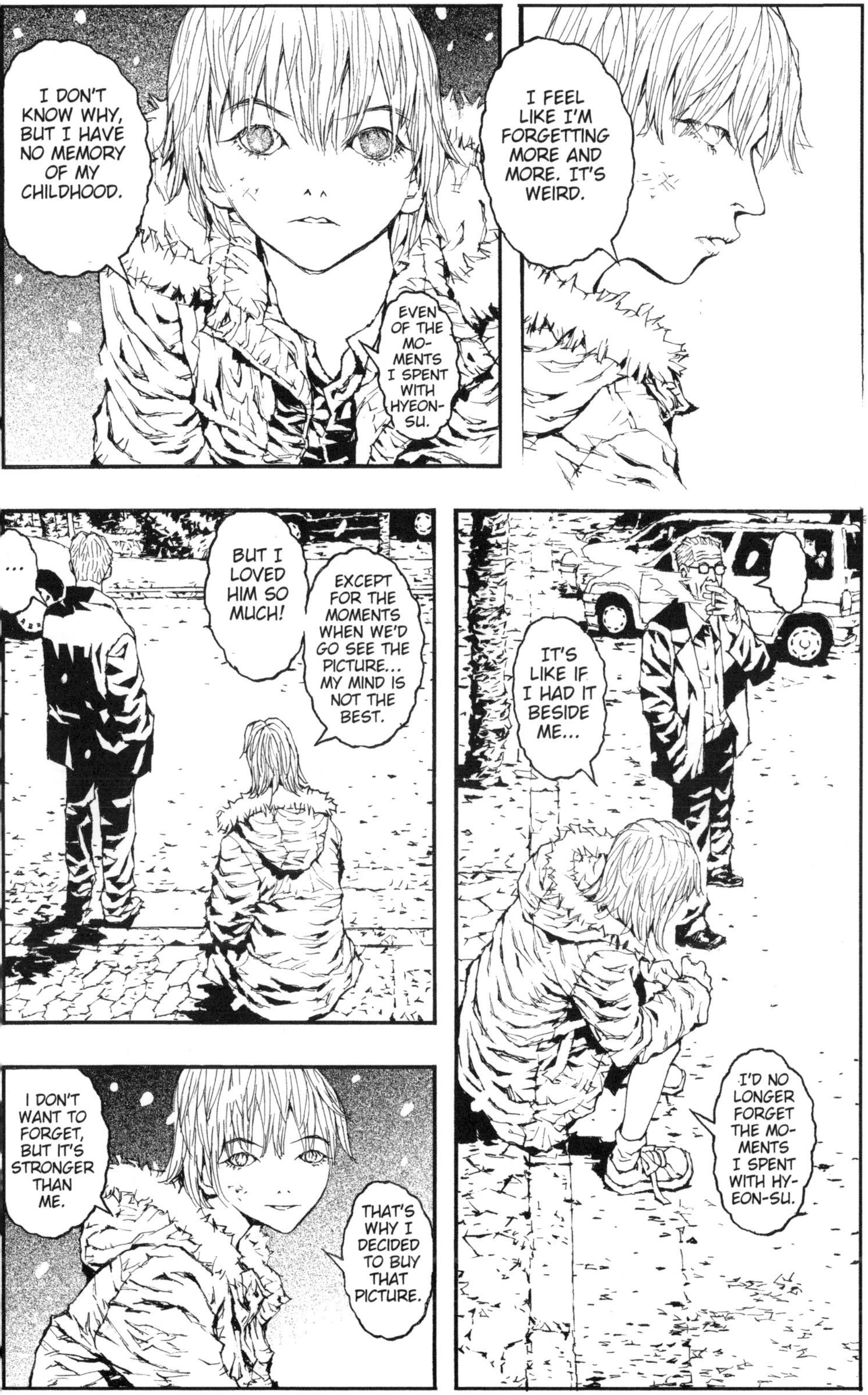
I DON'T KNOW WHY, BUT I HAVE NO MEMORY OF MY CHILDHOOD.
EVEN OF THE MO-MENTS I SPENT WITH HYEON-SU.
I FEEL LIKE I'M FORGETTING MORE AND MORE. IT'S WEIRD.
...
BUT I LOVED HIM SO MUCH!
EXCEPT FOR THE MOMENTS WHEN WE'D GO SEE THE PICTURE... MY MIND IS NOT THE BEST.
I DON'T WANT TO FORGET, BUT IT'S STRONGER THAN ME.
THAT'S WHY I DECIDED TO BUY THAT PICTURE.
IT'S LIKE IF I HAD IT BESIDE ME...
I'D NO LONGER FORGET THE MO-MENTS I SPENT WITH HY-EON-SU.

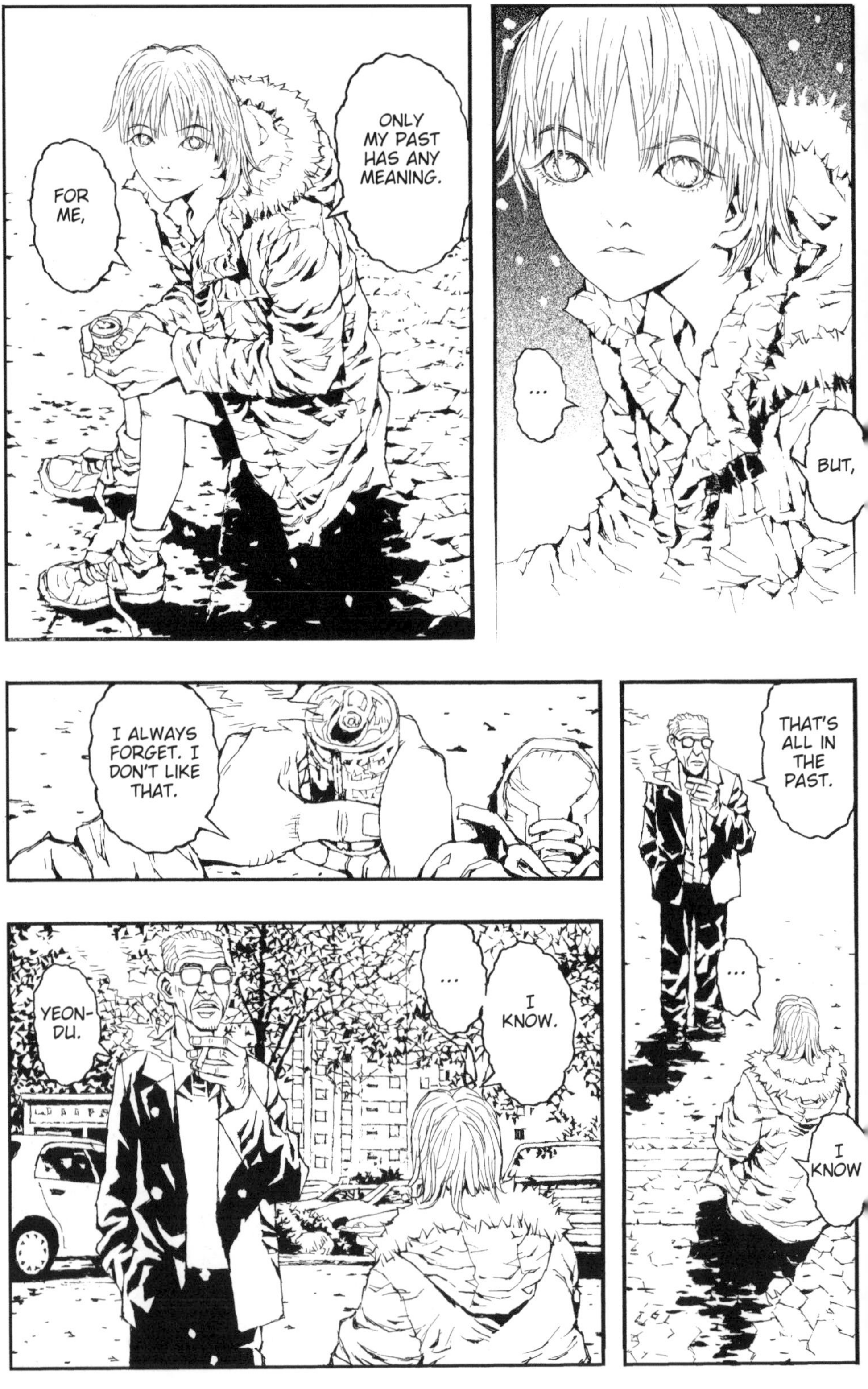
FOR ME,
ONLY MY PAST HAS ANY MEANING.
...
BUT,
I ALWAYS FORGET. I DON'T LIKE THAT.
THAT'S ALL IN THE PAST.
YEON-DU.
...
I KNOW.
...
I KNOW

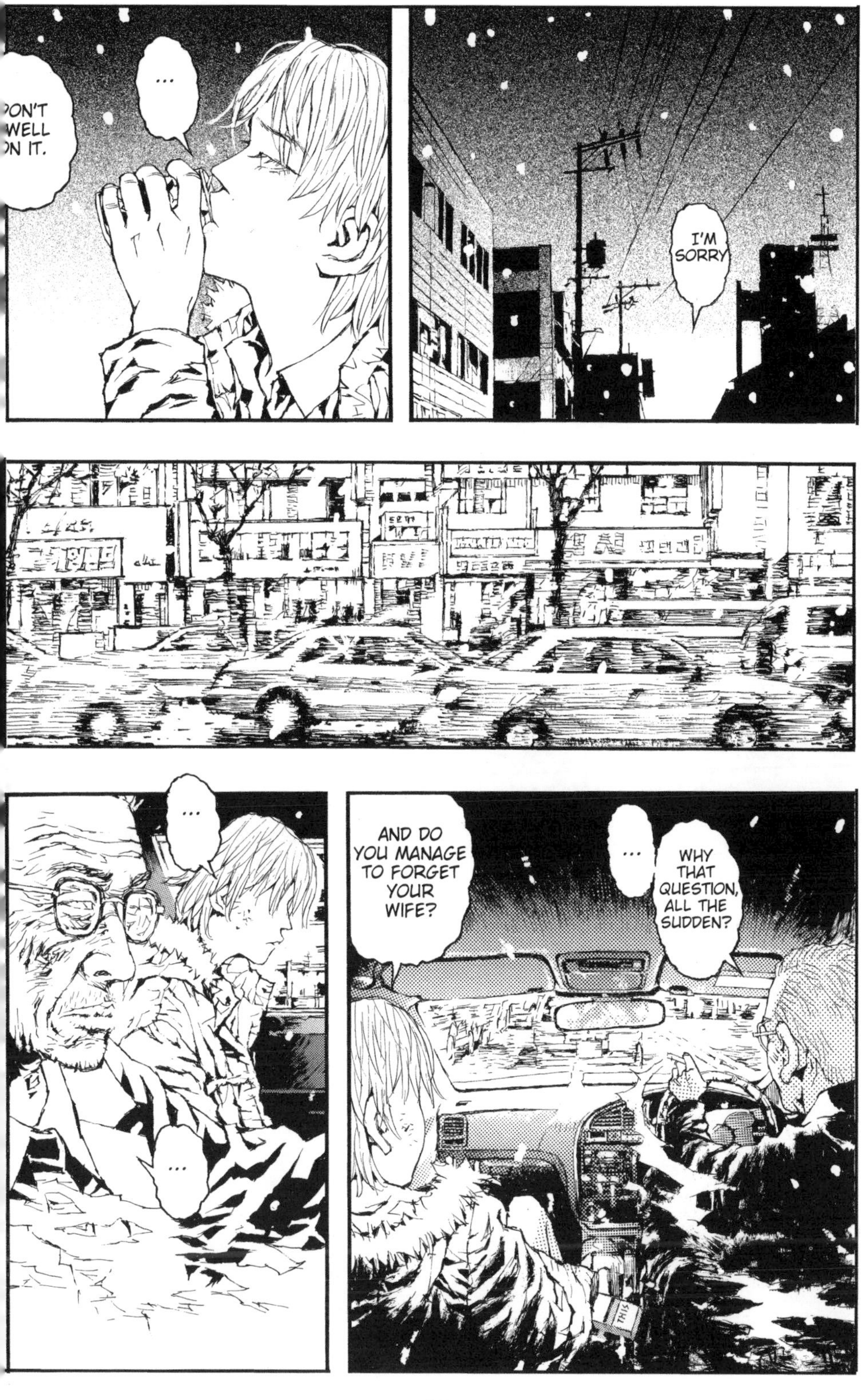
ON'T WELL ON IT.
...
I'M SORRY
...
...
AND DO YOU MANAGE TO FORGET YOUR WIFE?
...
WHY THAT QUESTION, ALL THE SUDDEN?
THIS

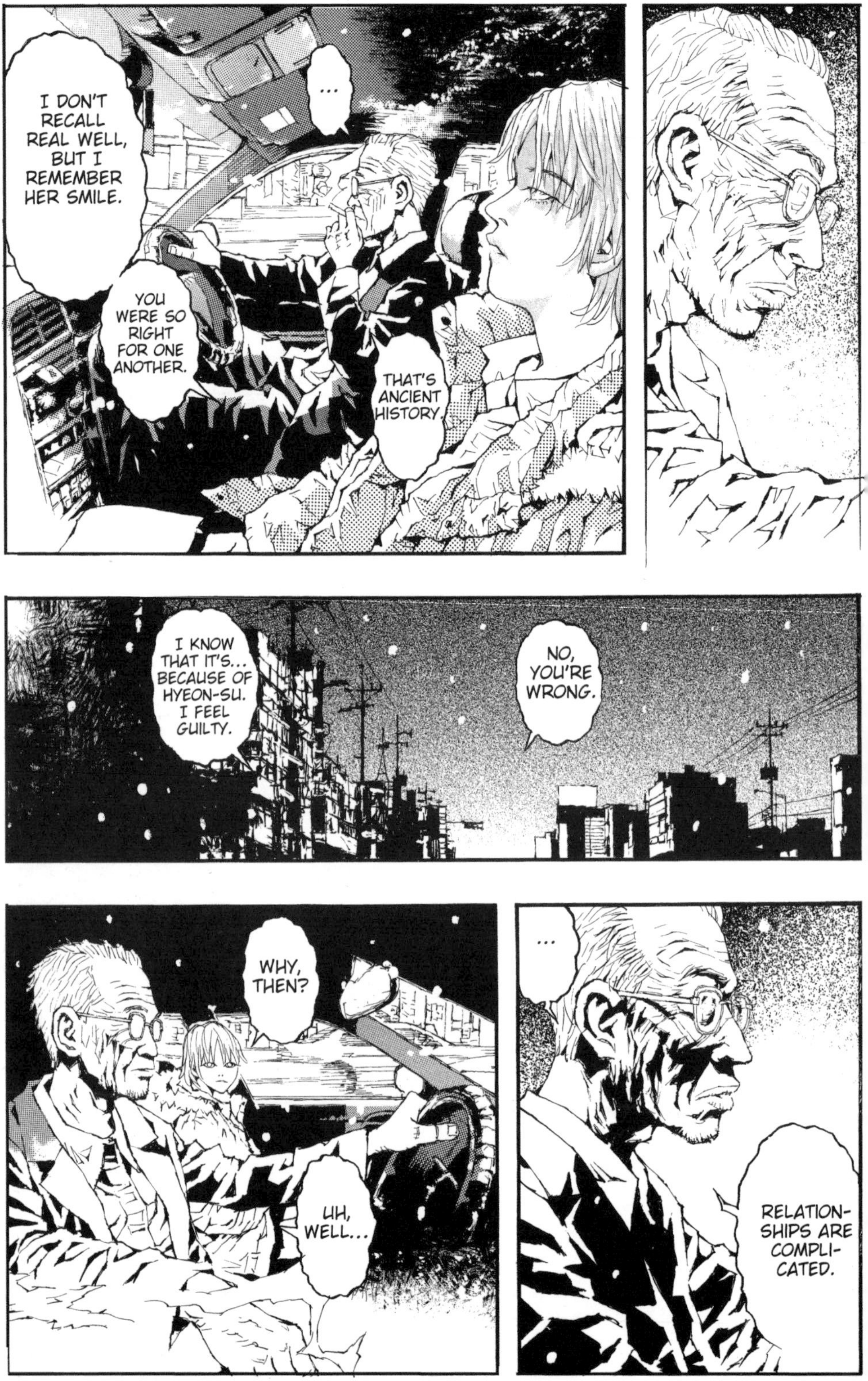
...
I DON'T RECALL REAL WELL, BUT I REMEMBER HER SMILE.
YOU WERE SO RIGHT FOR ONE ANOTHER.
THAT'S ANCIENT HISTORY.
NO, YOU'RE WRONG.
I KNOW THAT IT'S... BECAUSE OF HYEON-SU. I FEEL GUILTY.
WHY, THEN?
UH, WELL...
...
RELATION-SHIPS ARE COMPLI-CATED.

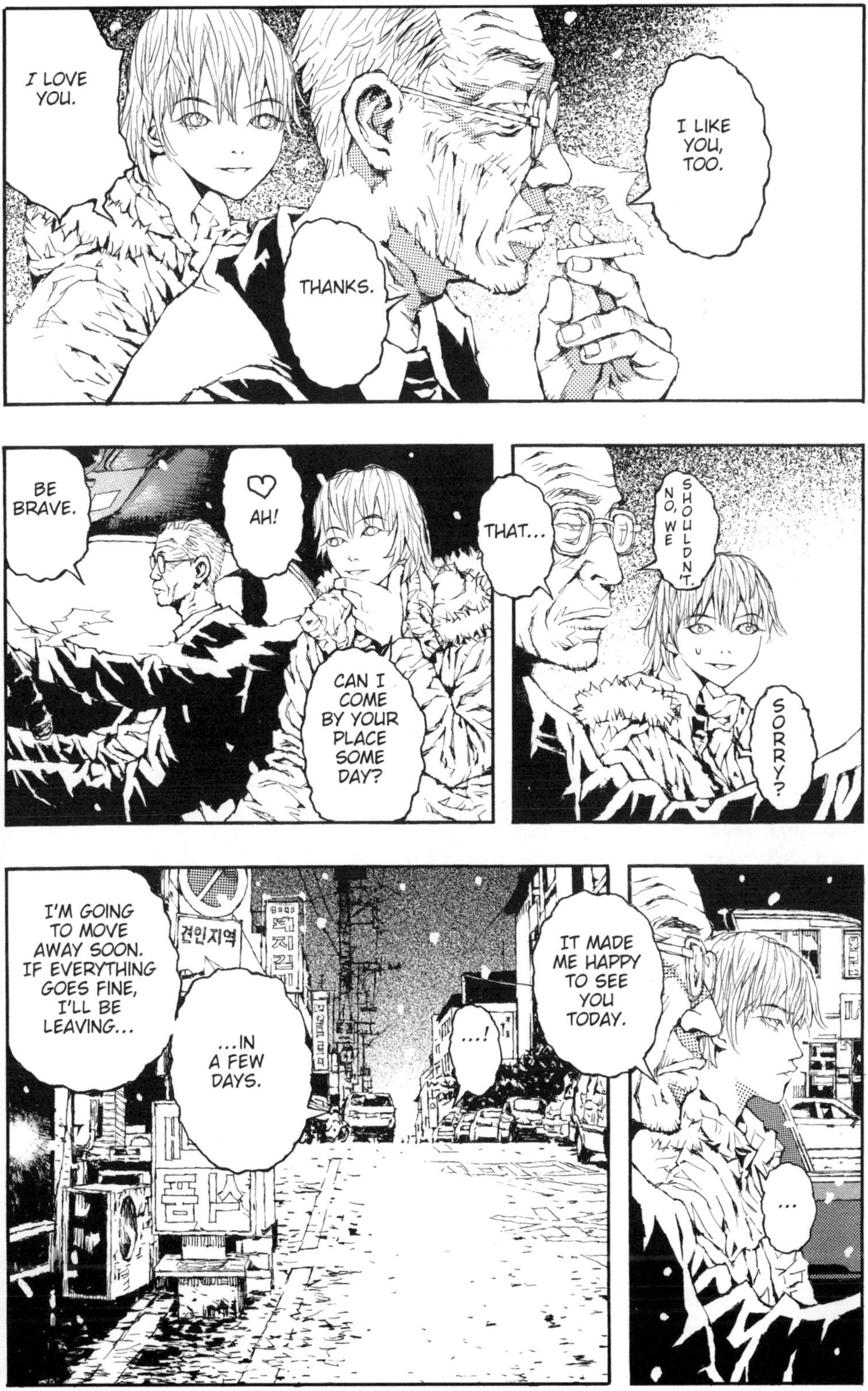
I LOVE YOU.
THANKS.
I LIKE YOU, TOO.
BE BRAVE.
♡ AH!
CAN I COME BY YOUR PLACE SOME DAY?
THAT...
NO, WE SHOULDN'T.
SORRY?
I'M GOING TO MOVE AWAY SOON. IF EVERYTHING GOES FINE, I'LL BE LEAVING...
...IN A FEW DAYS.
견인지역
...!
IT MADE ME HAPPY TO SEE YOU TODAY.
...

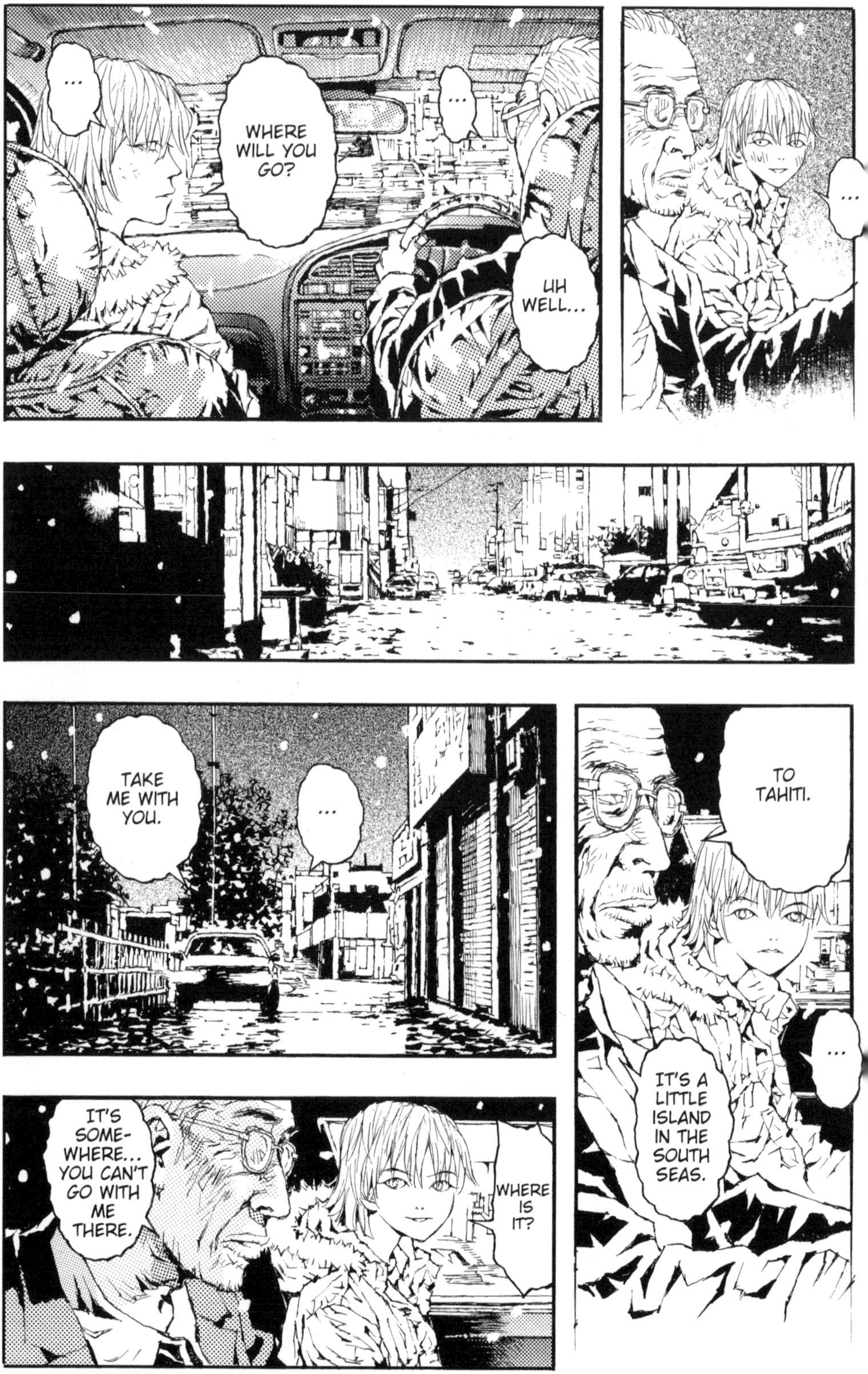
...
WHERE WILL YOU GO?
...
UH WELL...
...
TAKE ME WITH YOU.
...
TO TAHITI.
...
IT'S A LITTLE ISLAND IN THE SOUTH SEAS.
IT'S SOME-WHERE... YOU CAN'T GO WITH ME THERE.
WHERE IS IT?

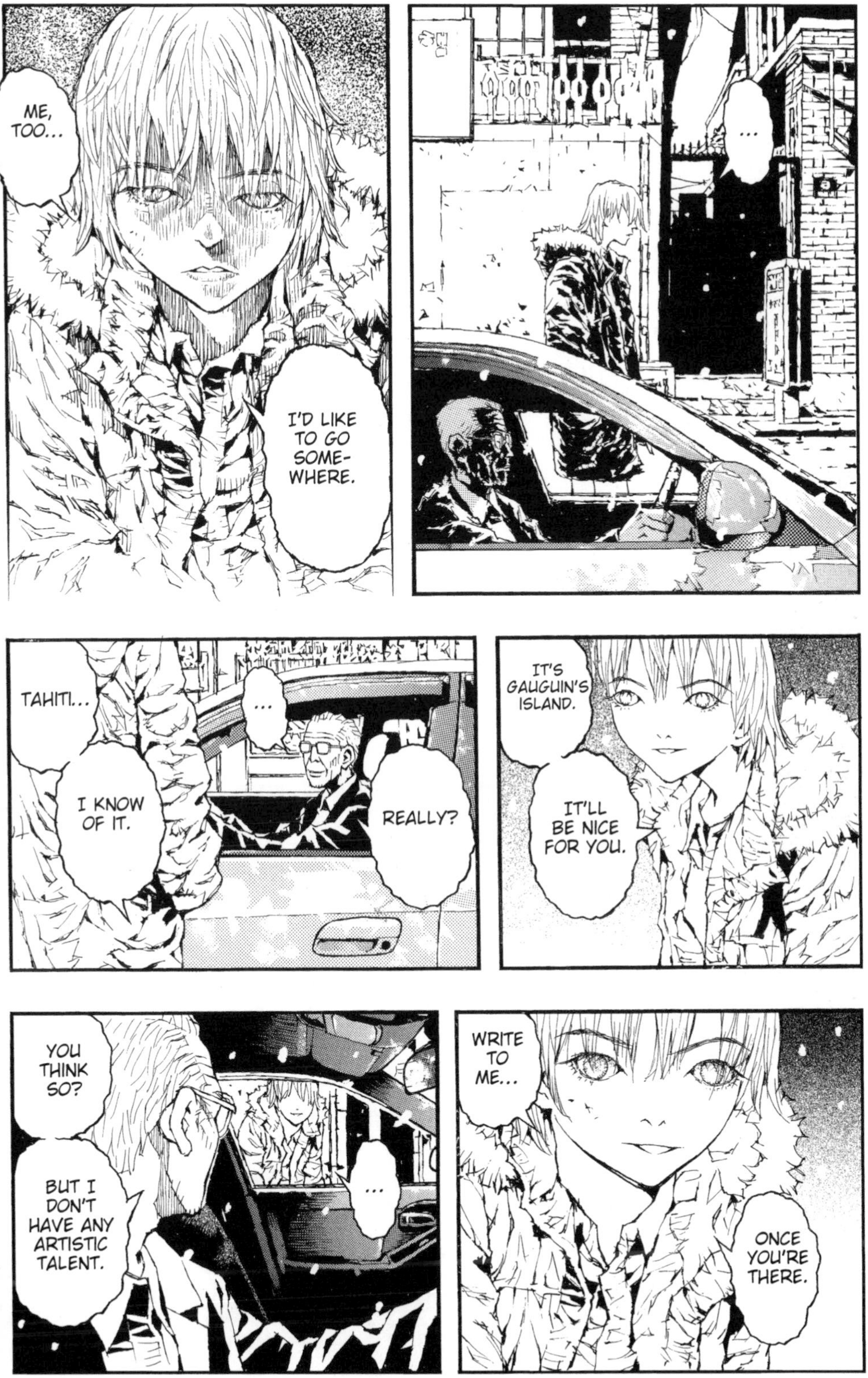
ME, TOO...
I'D LIKE TO GO SOME-WHERE.
...
TAHITI...
I KNOW OF IT.
...
REALLY?
IT'S GAUGUIN'S ISLAND.
IT'LL BE NICE FOR YOU.
YOU THINK SO?
BUT I DON'T HAVE ANY ARTISTIC TALENT.
...
WRITE TO ME...
ONCE YOU'RE THERE.

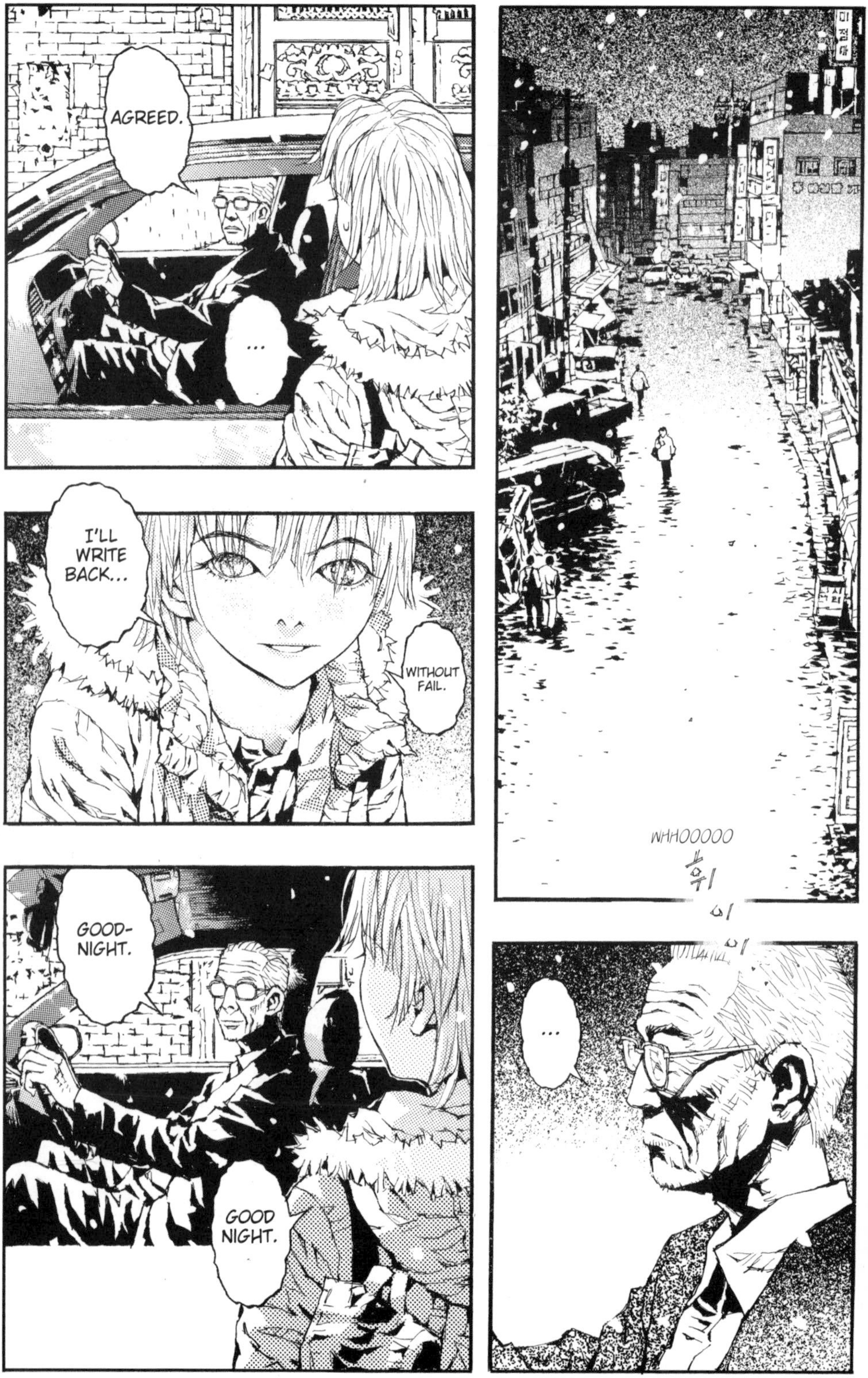
AGREED.
...
I'LL WRITE BACK...
WITHOUT FAIL.
GOOD-NIGHT.
GOOD NIGHT.
WHHOOOOO
...

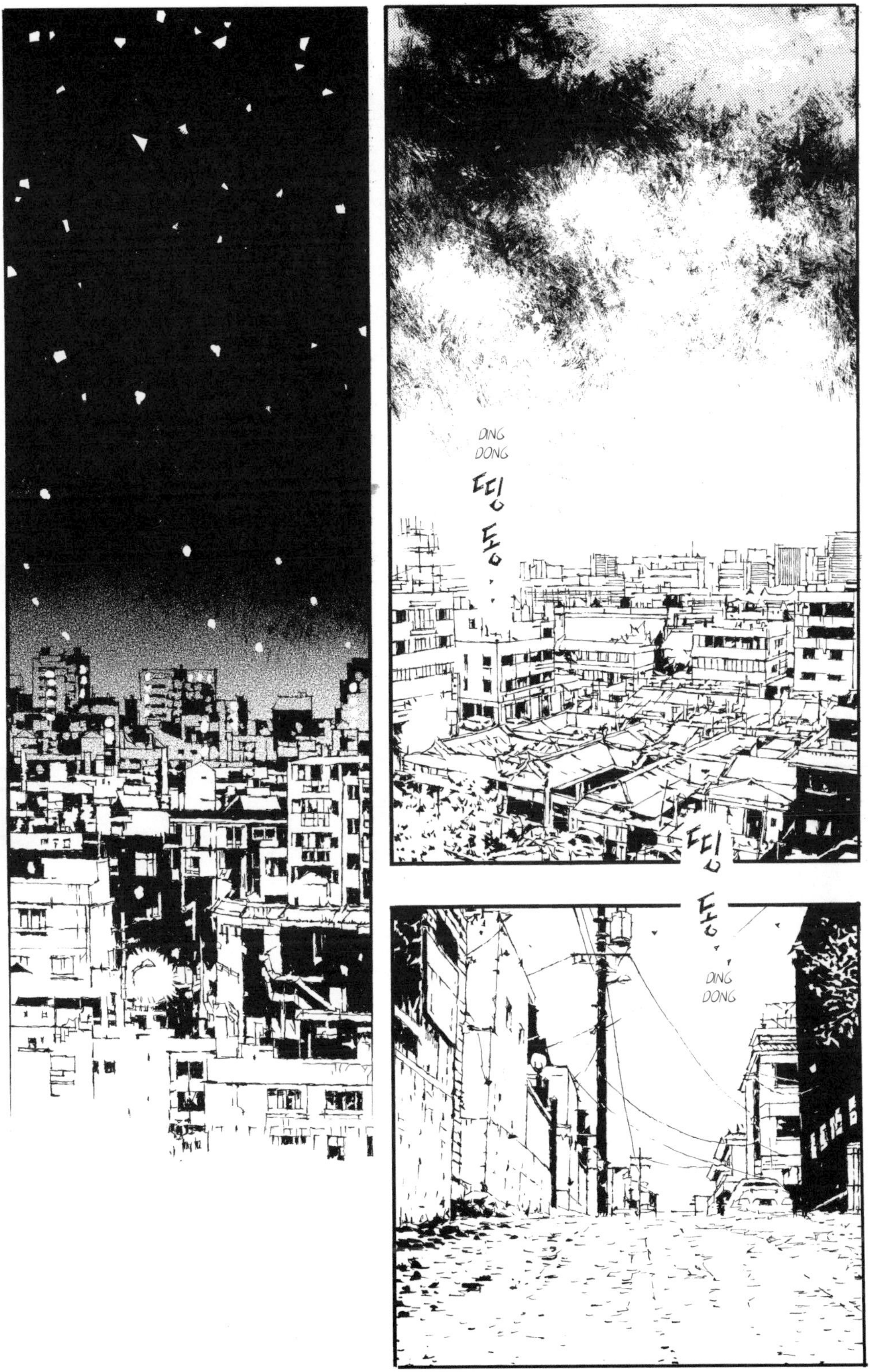
DING DONG
띵 동
띵 동
DING DONG

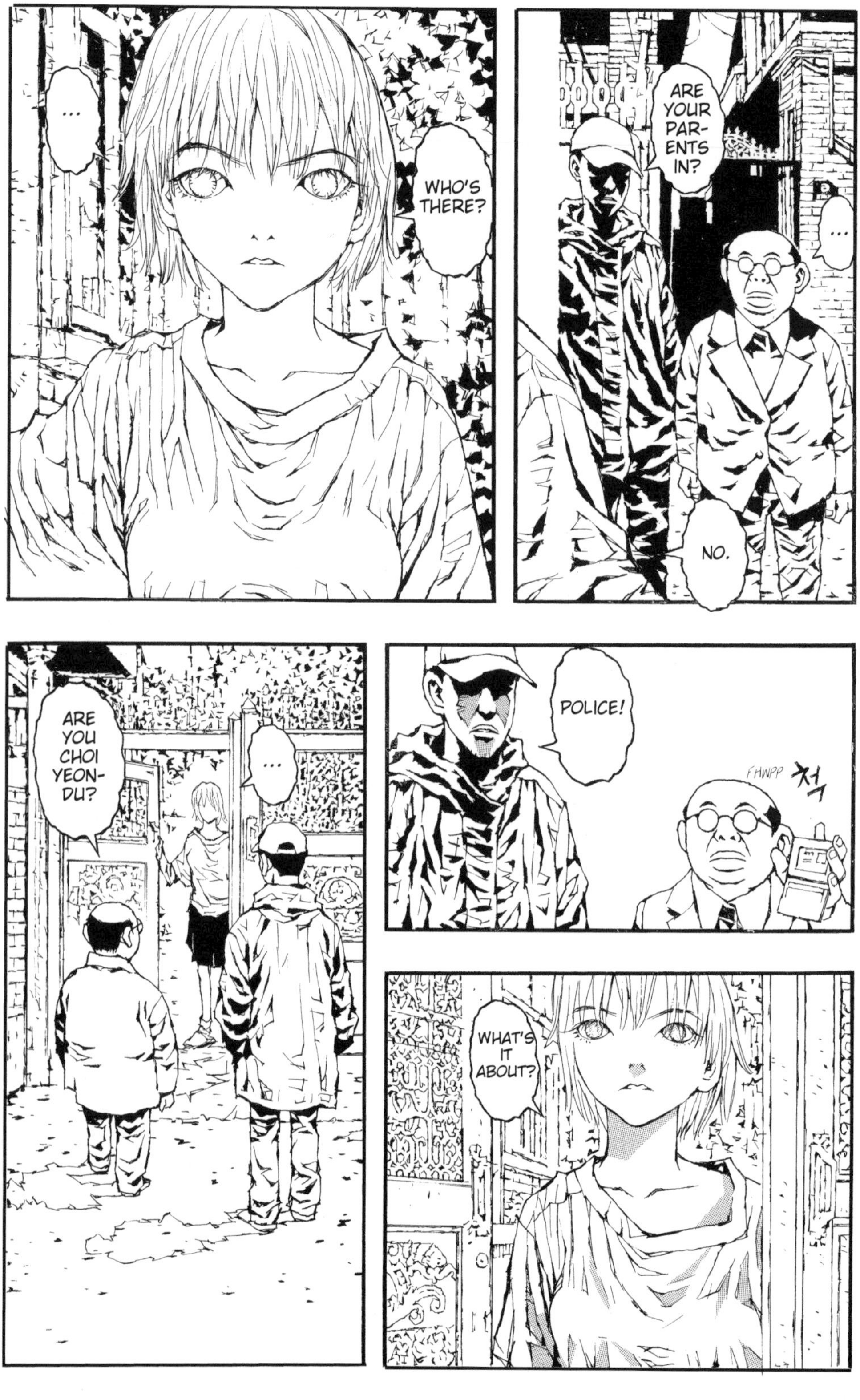
...
WHO'S THERE?
ARE YOUR PAR-ENTS IN?
...
NO.
ARE YOU CHOI YEON-DU?
...
POLICE!
FHWPP 척
WHAT'S IT ABOUT?

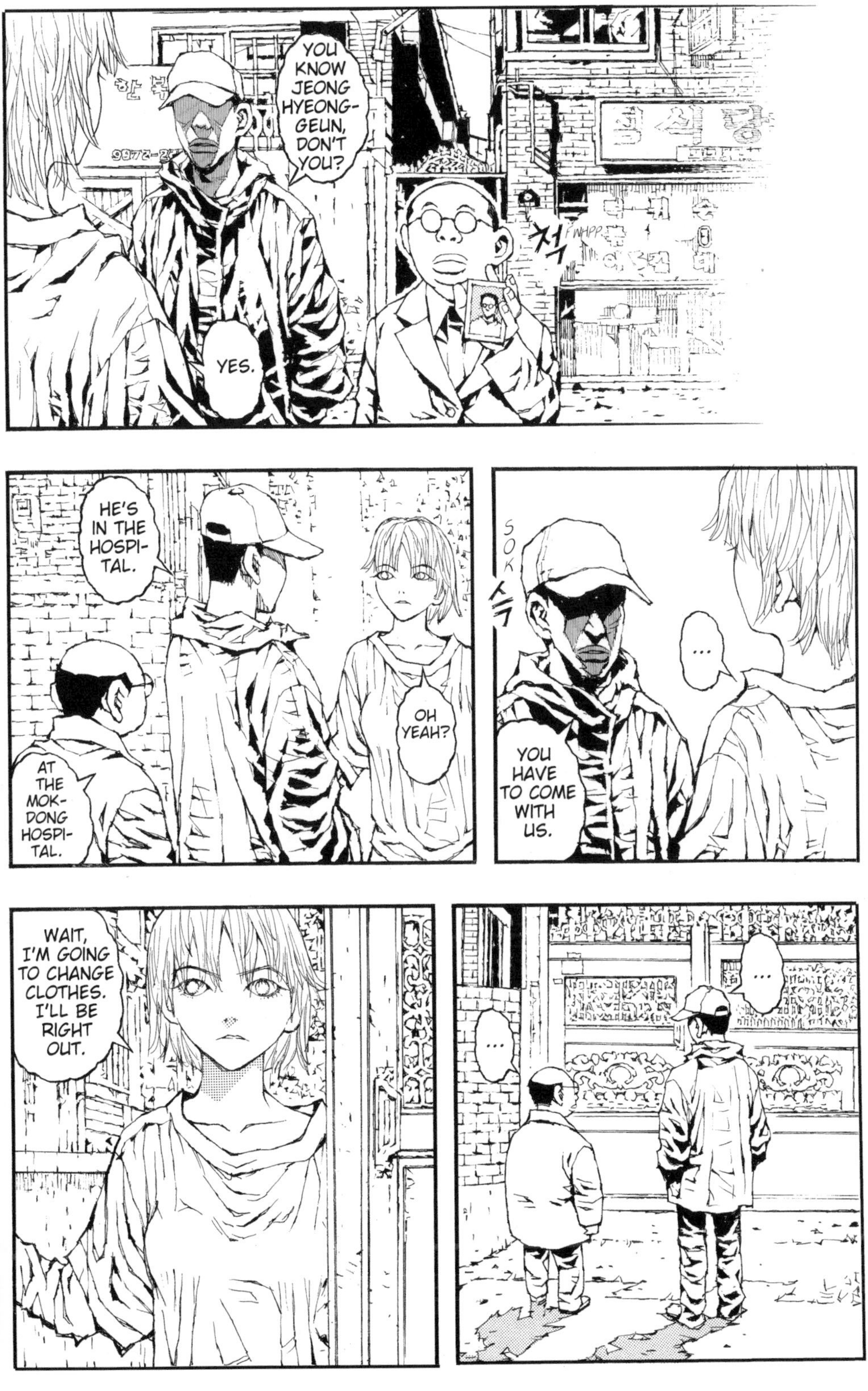
YOU KNOW JEONG HYEONG-GEUN, DON'T YOU?
FWHPP
YES.
HE'S IN THE HOSPITAL.
OH YEAH?
AT THE MOK-DONG HOSPITAL.
SOK
...
YOU HAVE TO COME WITH US.
WAIT, I'M GOING TO CHANGE CLOTHES. I'LL BE RIGHT OUT.
...
...

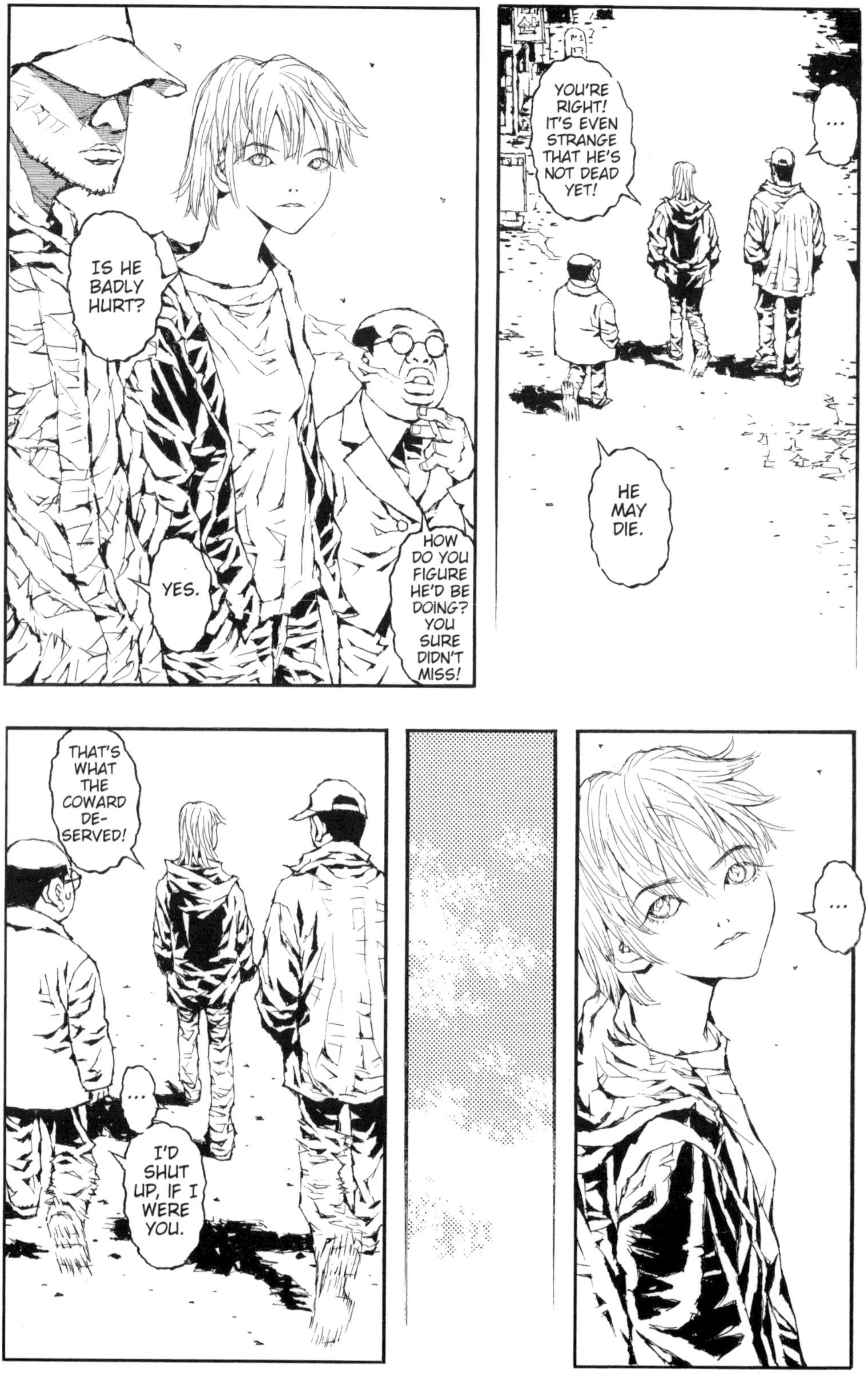
IS HE BADLY HURT?
YES.
HOW DO YOU FIGURE HE'D BE DOING? YOU SURE DIDN'T MISS!
YOU'RE RIGHT! IT'S EVEN STRANGE THAT HE'S NOT DEAD YET!
...
HE MAY DIE.
THAT'S WHAT THE COWARD DE-SERVED!
...
I'D SHUT UP, IF I WERE YOU.
...

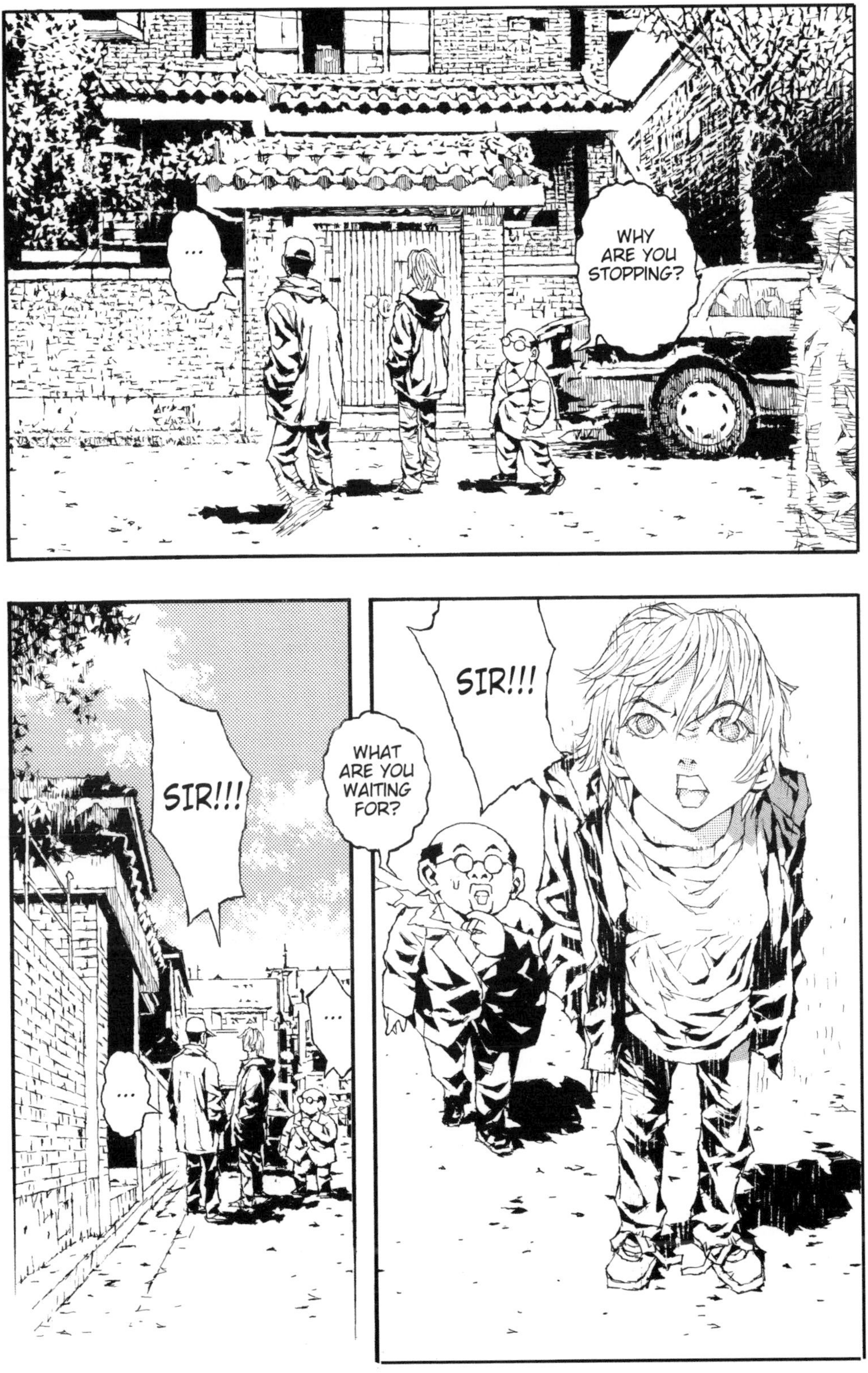
...
WHY ARE YOU STOPPING?
SIR!!!
...
...
SIR!!!
WHAT ARE YOU WAITING FOR?

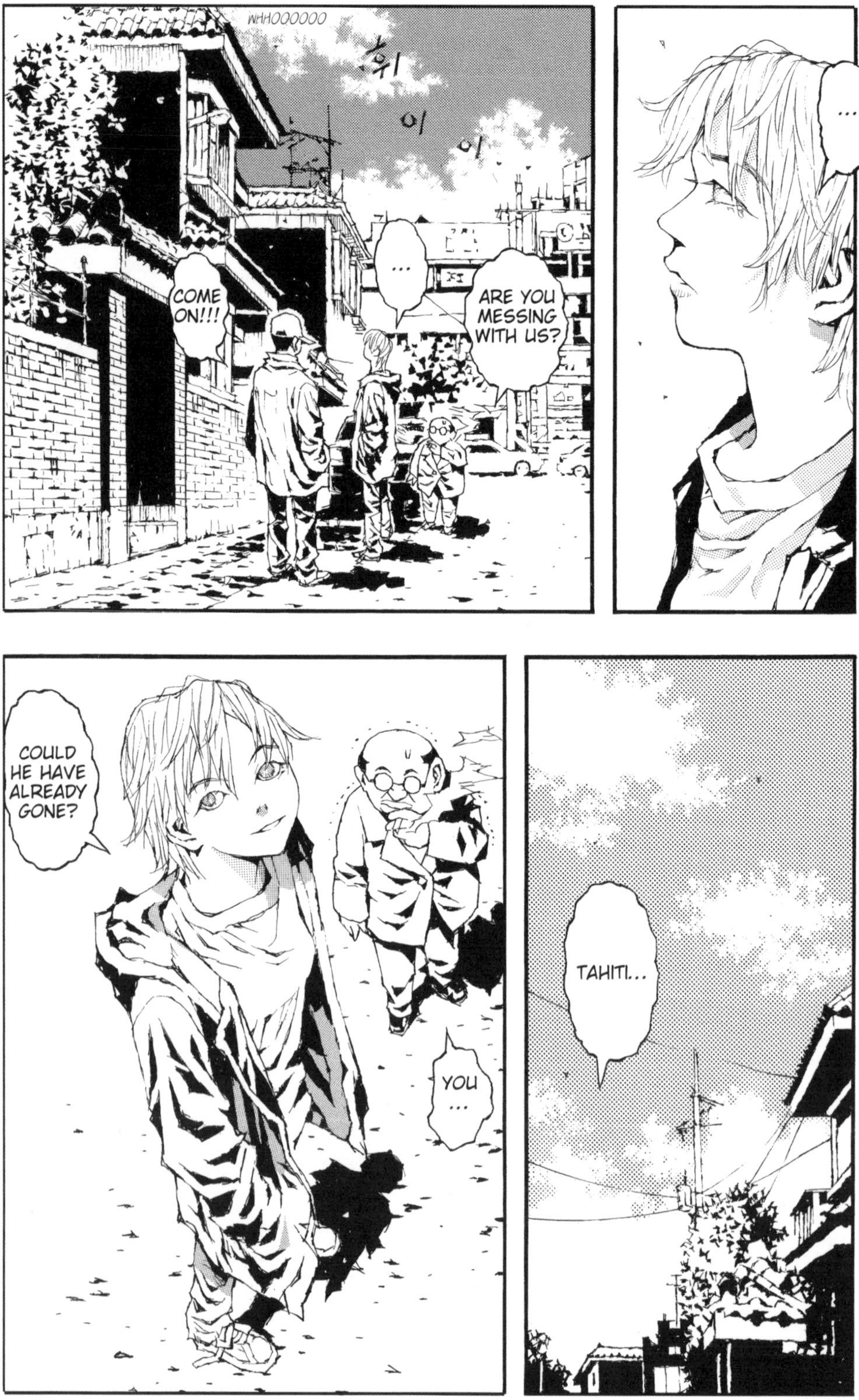
WHHOOOOOO
휘
이
이
COME ON!!!
...
ARE YOU MESSING WITH US?
...
COULD HE HAVE ALREADY GONE?
YOU ...
TAHITI...

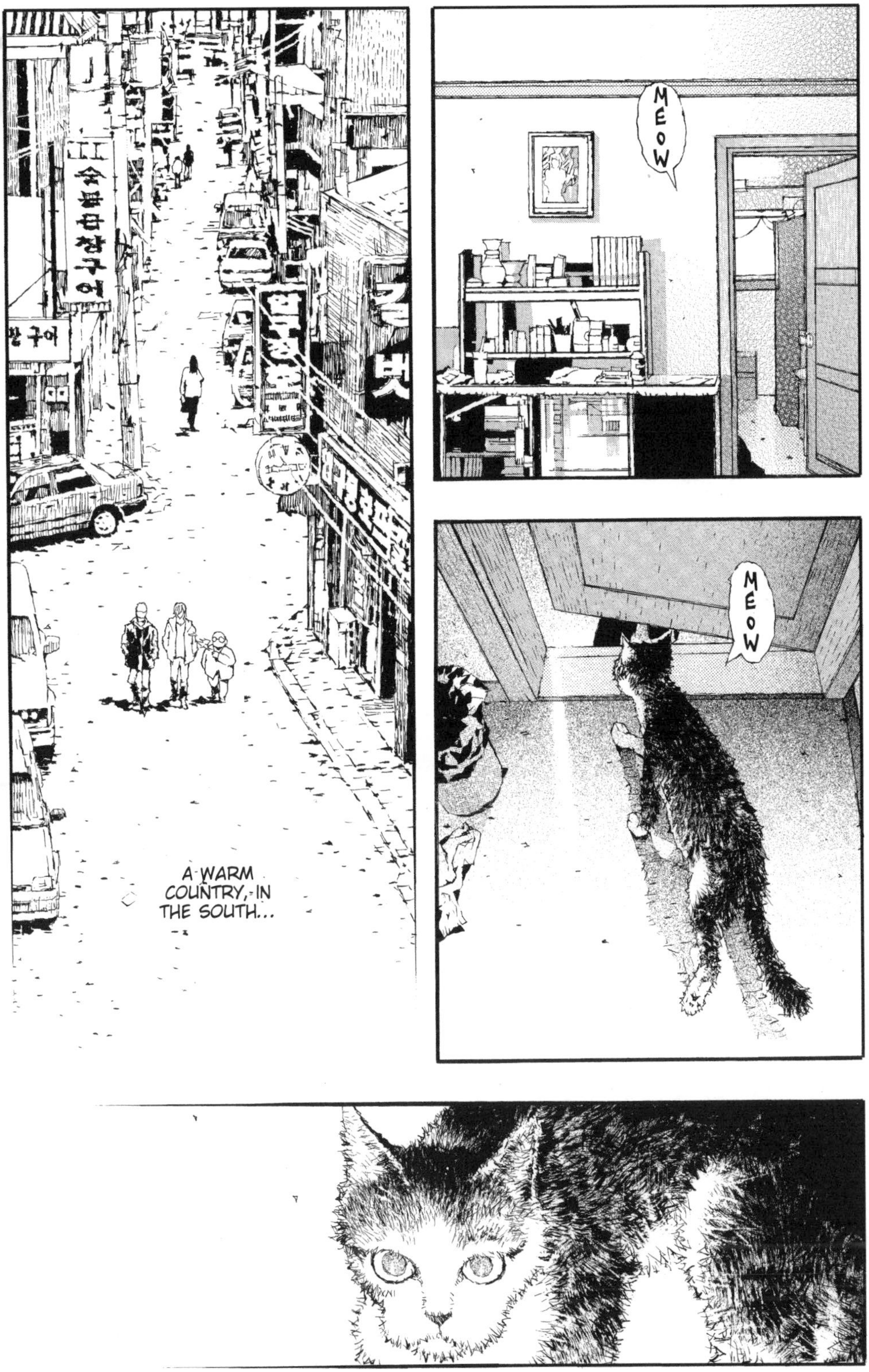
A WARM COUNTRY, IN THE SOUTH...
MEOW
MEOW

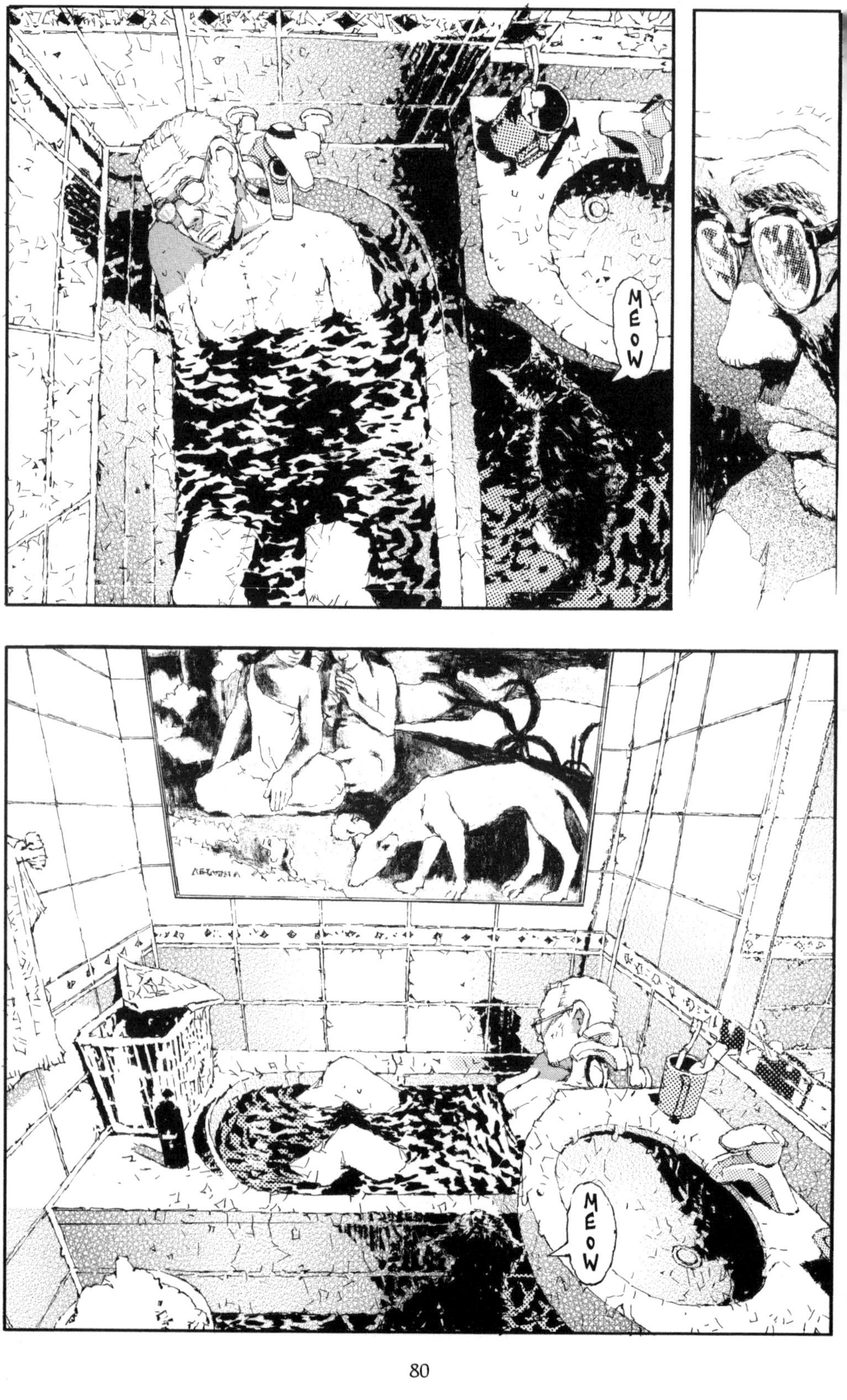
MEOW
MEOW

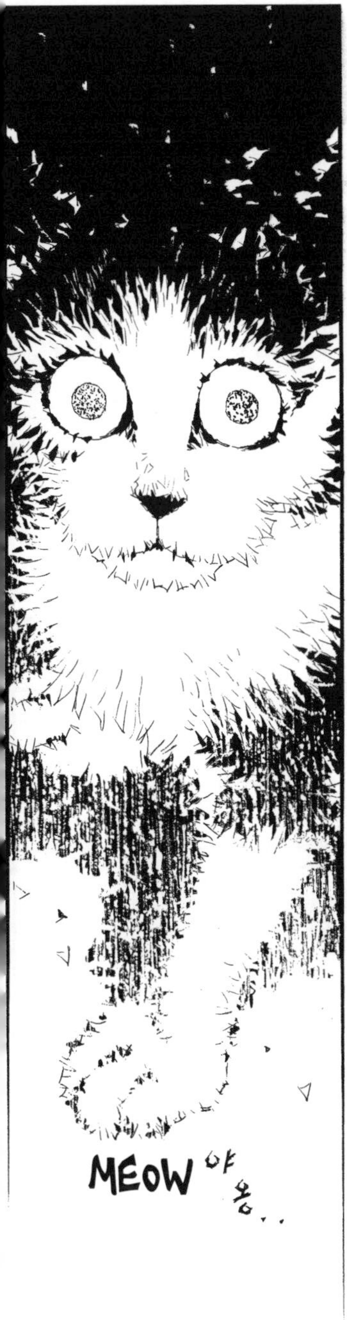
MEOW

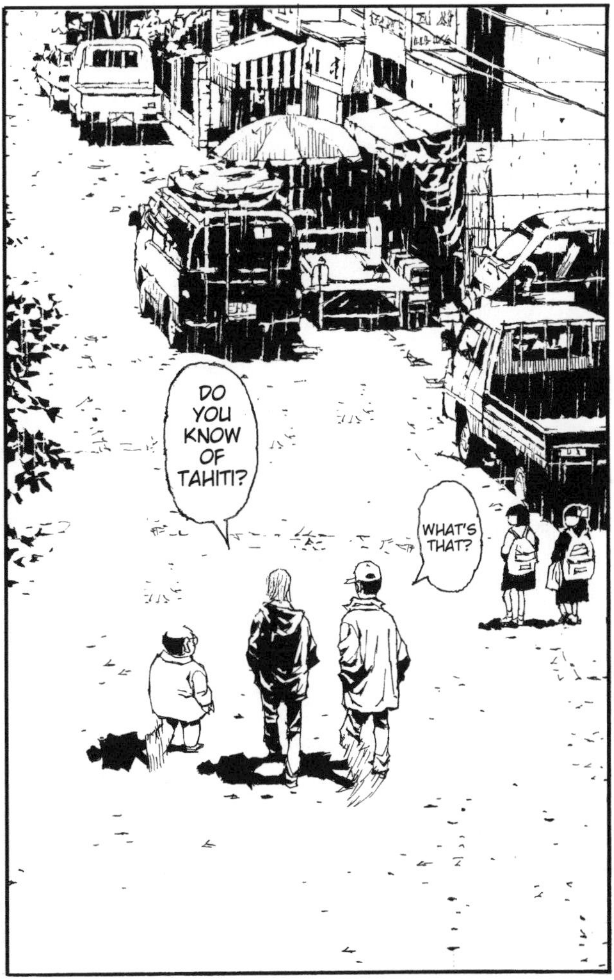
DO YOU KNOW OF TAHITI?
WHAT'S THAT?

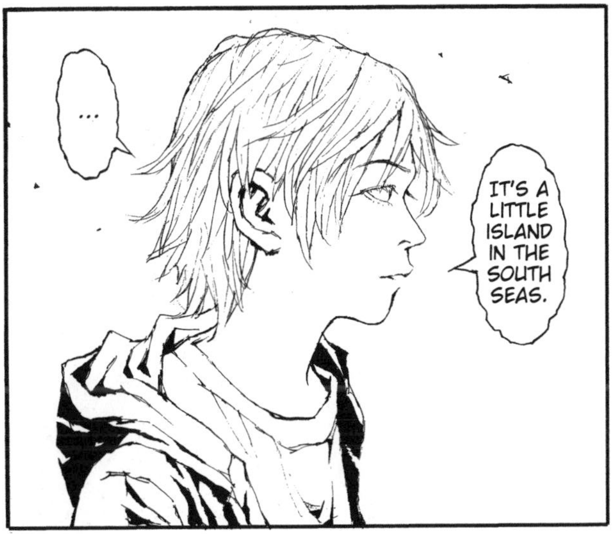
...
IT'S A LITTLE ISLAND IN THE SOUTH SEAS.

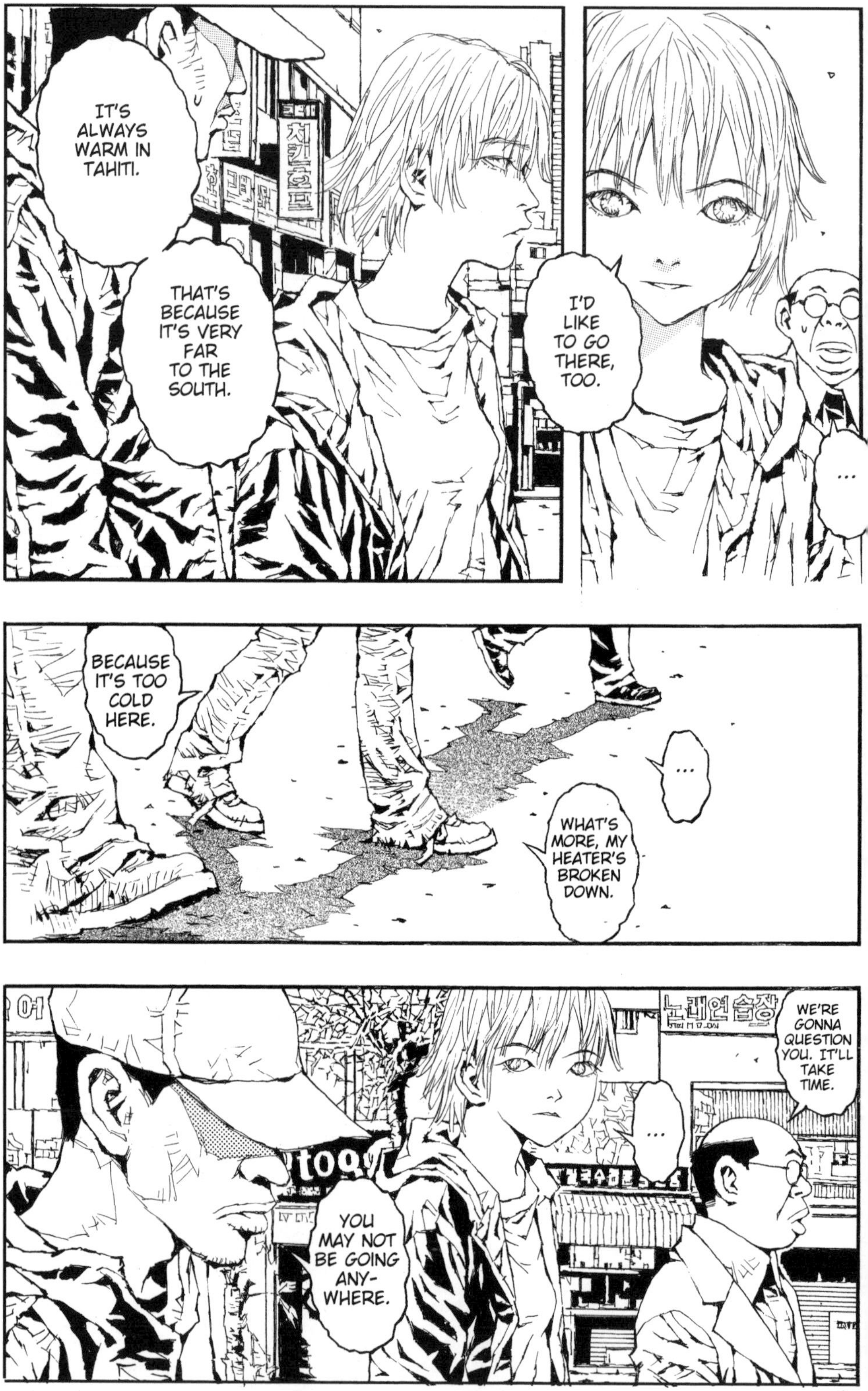
IT'S ALWAYS WARM IN TAHITI.
THAT'S BECAUSE IT'S VERY FAR TO THE SOUTH.
I'D LIKE TO GO THERE, TOO.
...
BECAUSE IT'S TOO COLD HERE.
...
WHAT'S MORE, MY HEATER'S BROKEN DOWN.
WE'RE GONNA QUESTION YOU. IT'LL TAKE TIME.
...
YOU MAY NOT BE GOING ANY-WHERE.

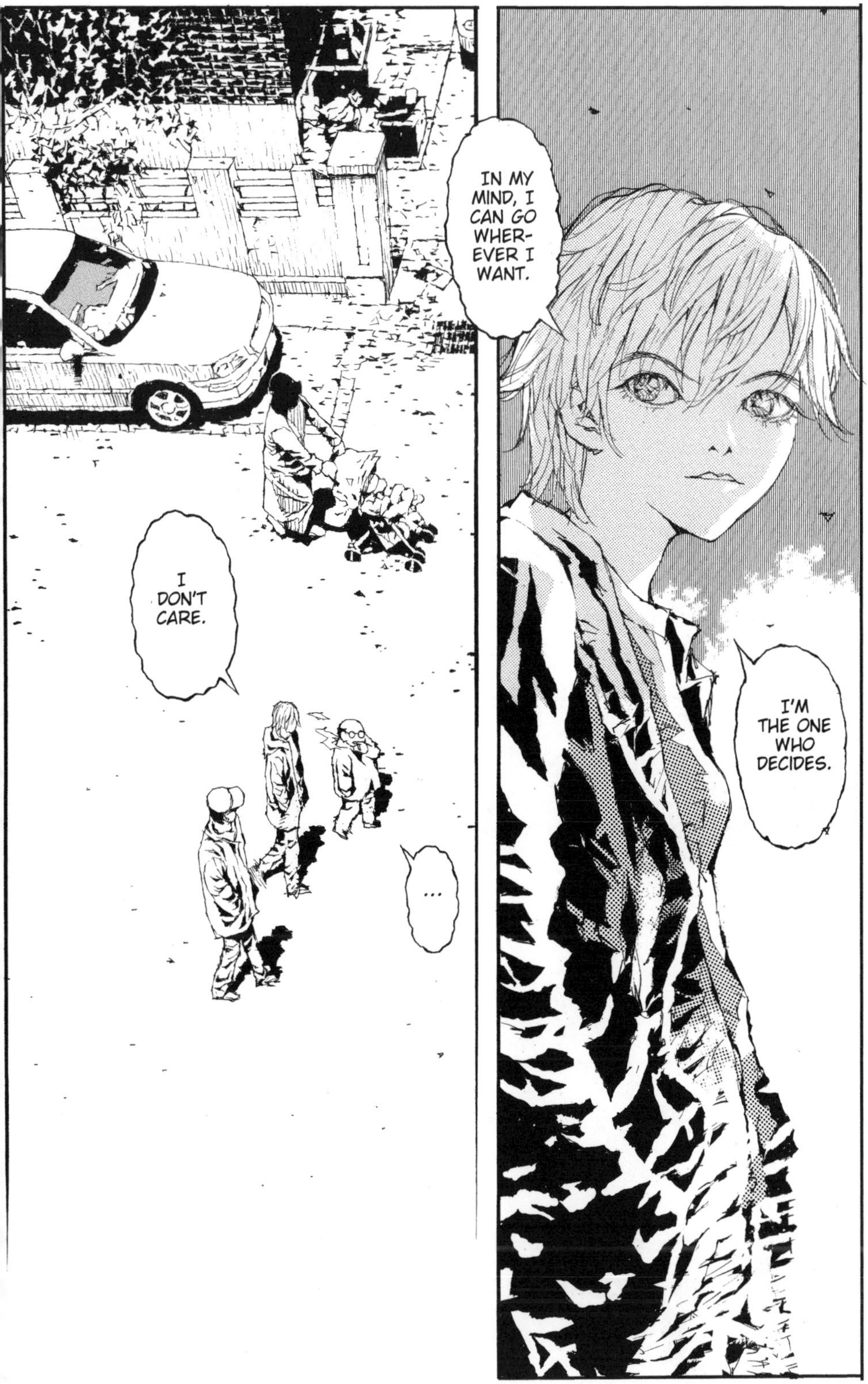
IN MY MIND, I CAN GO WHEREVER I WANT.
I'M THE ONE WHO DECIDES.
I DON'T CARE.
...

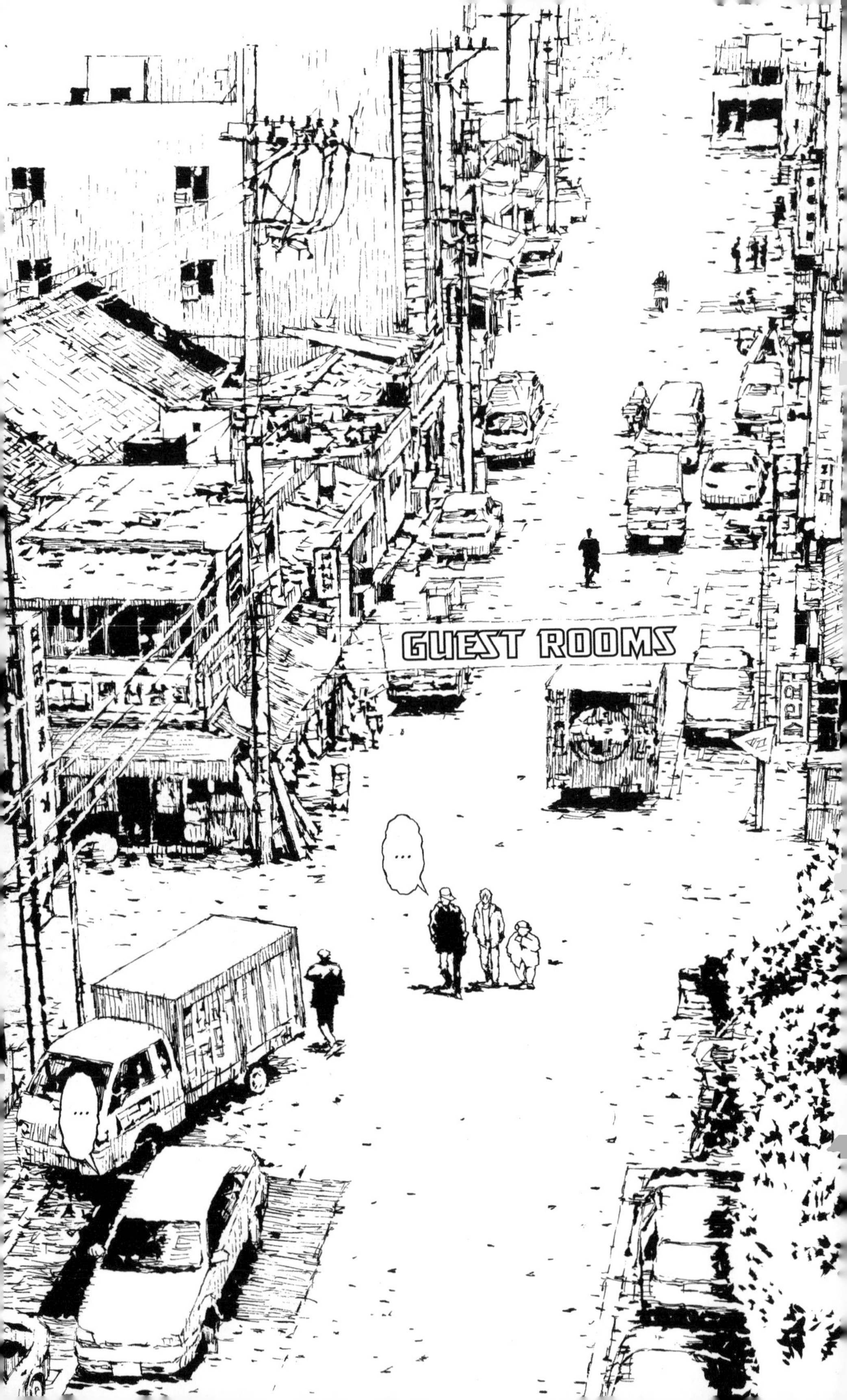
GUEST ROOMS
...
...

I CAN MAKE UP MY OWN MIND, GO WHERE I WANT...
ELSEWHERE, ANYWHERE.

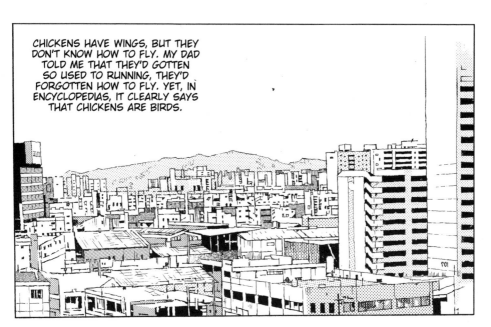

CHICKENS HAVE WINGS, BUT THEY DON'T KNOW HOW TO FLY. MY DAD TOLD ME THAT THEY'D GOTTEN SO USED TO RUNNING, THEY'D FORGOTTEN HOW TO FLY. YET, IN ENCYCLOPEDIAS, IT CLEARLY SAYS THAT CHICKENS ARE BIRDS.

WHAT A SHAMEFUL REGRESSION FOR A BIRD, THROUGH NEGLIGENCE, TO FORGET HOW TO FLY.

MAYBE THEY COULD FLY IF I TAUGHT THEM HOW TO DO SO WHILE THEY'RE STILL CHICKS.

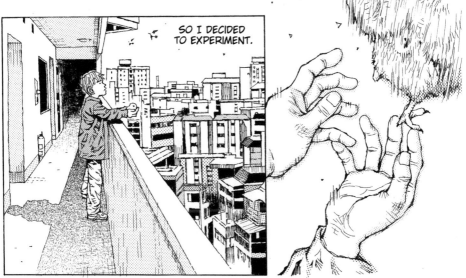

SO I DECIDED TO EXPERIMENT.

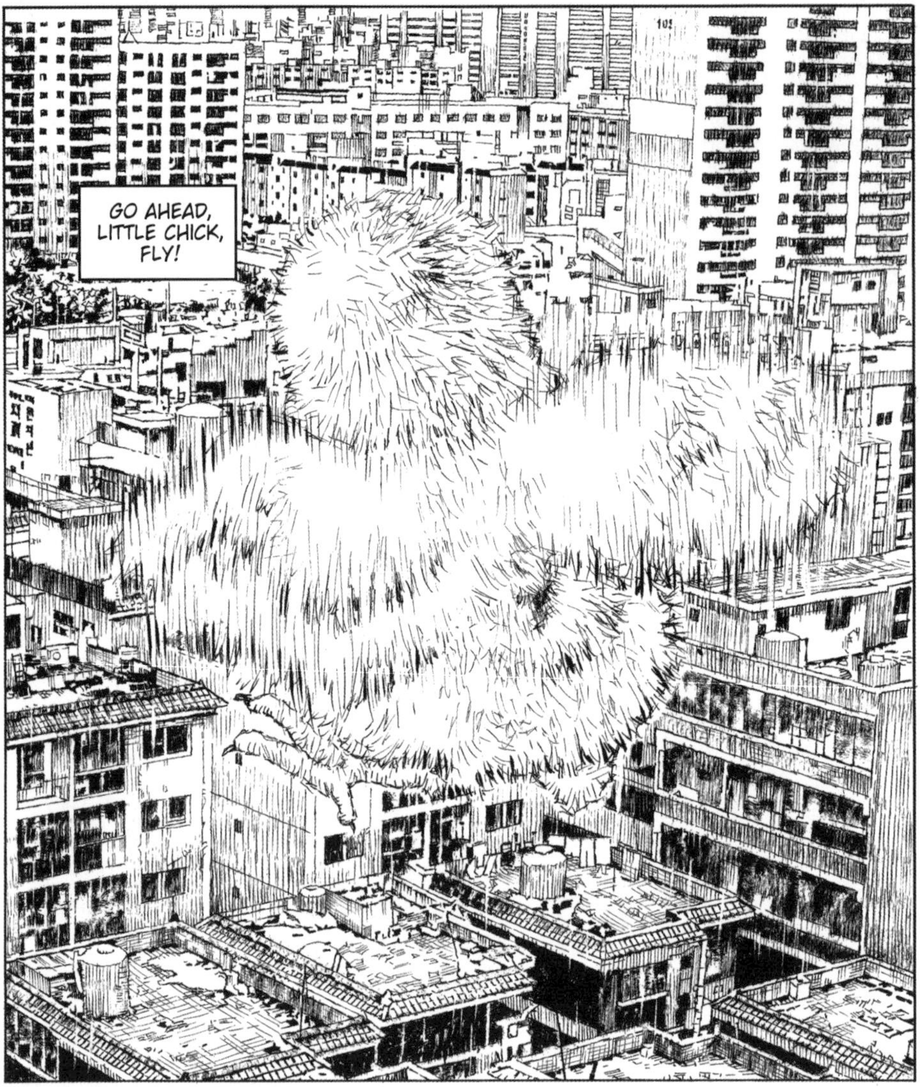
GO AHEAD, LITTLE CHICK, FLY!

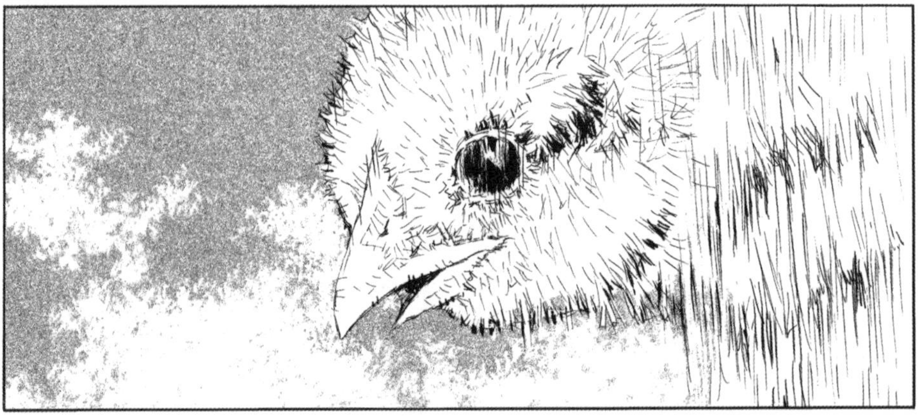

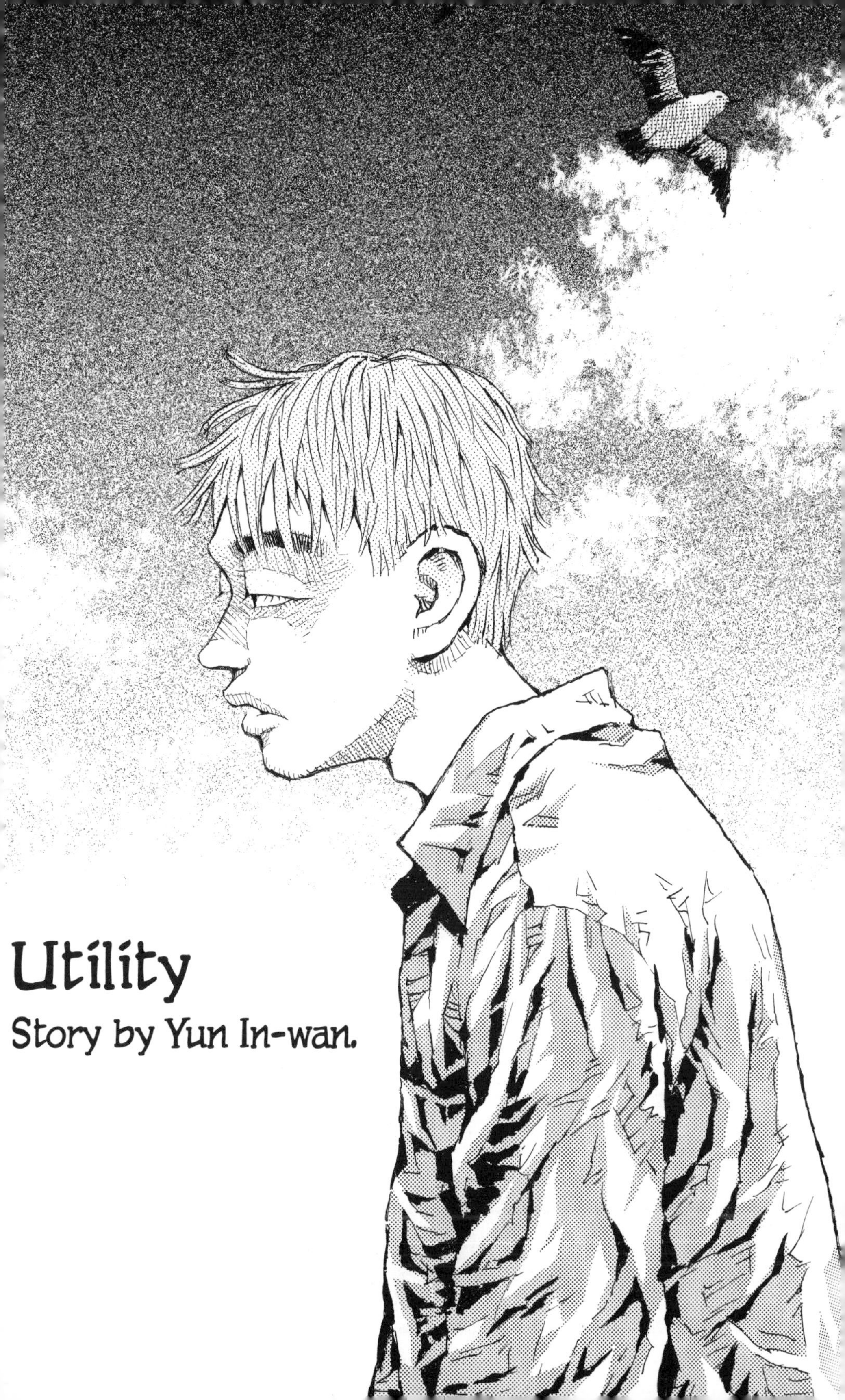

Utility

Story by Yun In-wan.

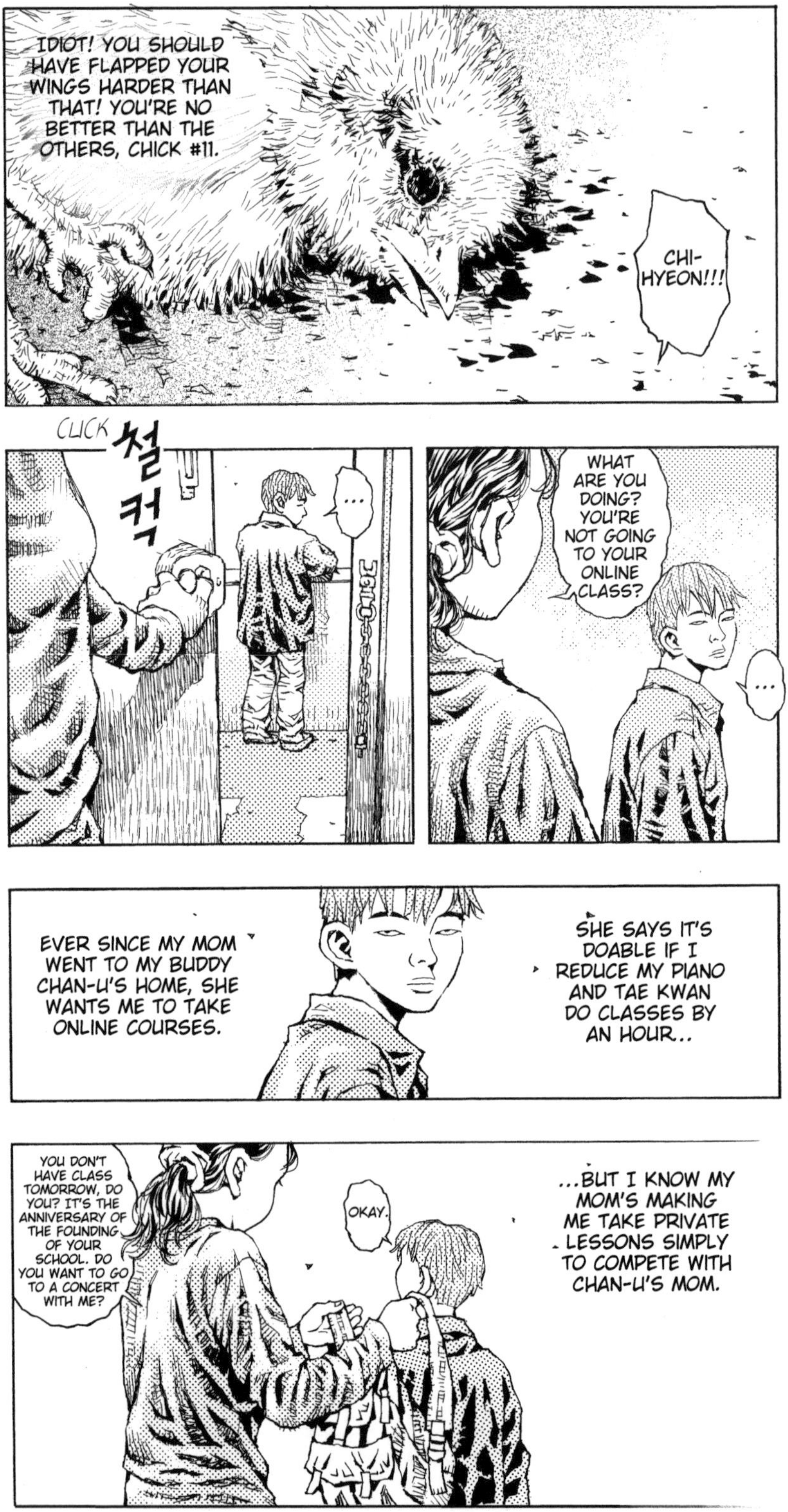
IDIOT! YOU SHOULD HAVE FLAPPED YOUR WINGS HARDER THAN THAT! YOU'RE NO BETTER THAN THE OTHERS, CHICK #11.
CHI-HYEON!!!
CLICK
철컥
...
WHAT ARE YOU DOING? YOU'RE NOT GOING TO YOUR ONLINE CLASS?
...
EVER SINCE MY MOM WENT TO MY BUDDY CHAN-U'S HOME, SHE WANTS ME TO TAKE ONLINE COURSES.
SHE SAYS IT'S DOABLE IF I REDUCE MY PIANO AND TAE KWAN DO CLASSES BY AN HOUR...
YOU DON'T HAVE CLASS TOMORROW, DO YOU? IT'S THE ANNIVERSARY OF THE FOUNDING OF YOUR SCHOOL. DO YOU WANT TO GO TO A CONCERT WITH ME?
OKAY.
...BUT I KNOW MY MOM'S MAKING ME TAKE PRIVATE LESSONS SIMPLY TO COMPETE WITH CHAN-U'S MOM.

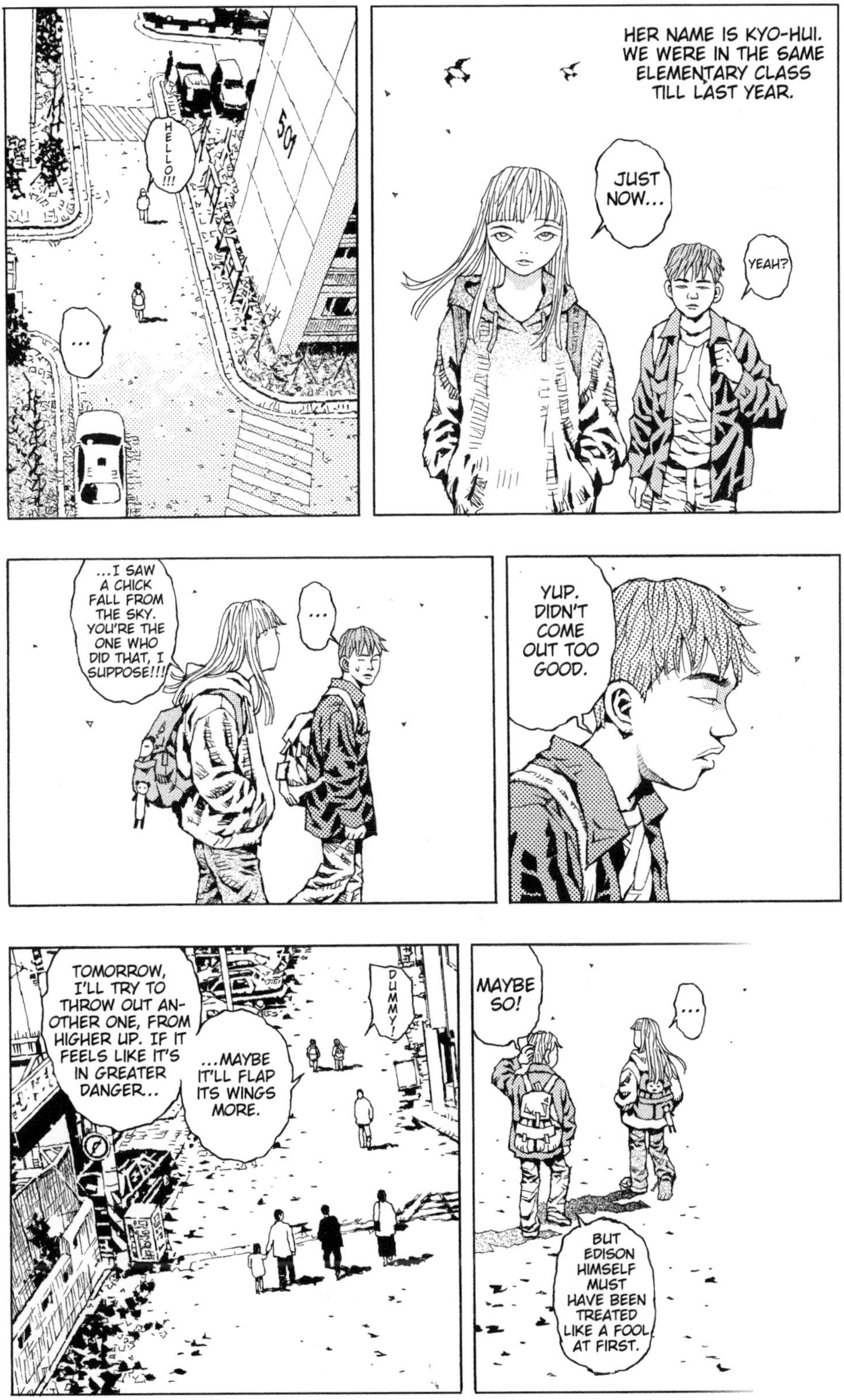
HELLO!!!
...
HER NAME IS KYO-HUI. WE WERE IN THE SAME ELEMENTARY CLASS TILL LAST YEAR.
JUST NOW...
YEAH?
...I SAW A CHICK FALL FROM THE SKY. YOU'RE THE ONE WHO DID THAT, I SUPPOSE!!!
...
YUP. DIDN'T COME OUT TOO GOOD.
TOMORROW, I'LL TRY TO THROW OUT AN-OTHER ONE, FROM HIGHER UP. IF IT FEELS LIKE IT'S IN GREATER DANGER...
...MAYBE IT'LL FLAP ITS WINGS MORE.
DUMMY!
MAYBE SO!
...
BUT EDISON HIMSELF MUST HAVE BEEN TREATED LIKE A FOOL AT FIRST.

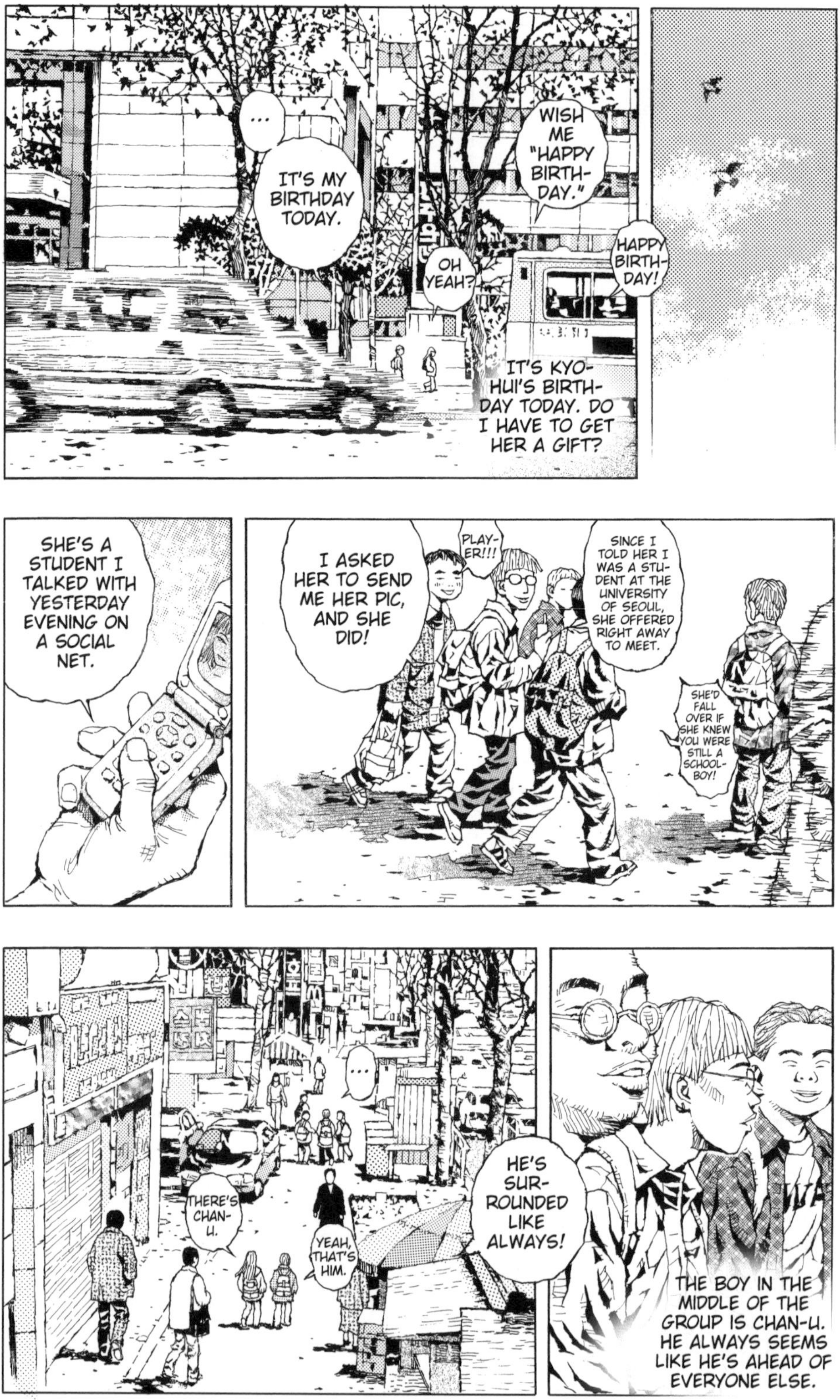
...
IT'S MY BIRTHDAY TODAY.
OH YEAH?
WISH ME "HAPPY BIRTH-DAY."
HAPPY BIRTH-DAY!
IT'S KYO-HUI'S BIRTH-DAY TODAY. DO I HAVE TO GET HER A GIFT?
SHE'S A STUDENT I TALKED WITH YESTERDAY EVENING ON A SOCIAL NET.
I ASKED HER TO SEND ME HER PIC, AND SHE DID!
PLAY-ER!!!
SINCE I TOLD HER I WAS A STU-DENT AT THE UNIVERSITY OF SEOUL, SHE OFFERED RIGHT AWAY TO MEET.
SHE'D FALL OVER IF SHE KNEW YOU WERE STILL A SCHOOL-BOY!
...
THERE'S CHAN-U.
YEAH, THAT'S HIM.
HE'S SUR-ROUNDED LIKE ALWAYS!
THE BOY IN THE MIDDLE OF THE GROUP IS CHAN-U. HE ALWAYS SEEMS LIKE HE'S AHEAD OF EVERYONE ELSE.

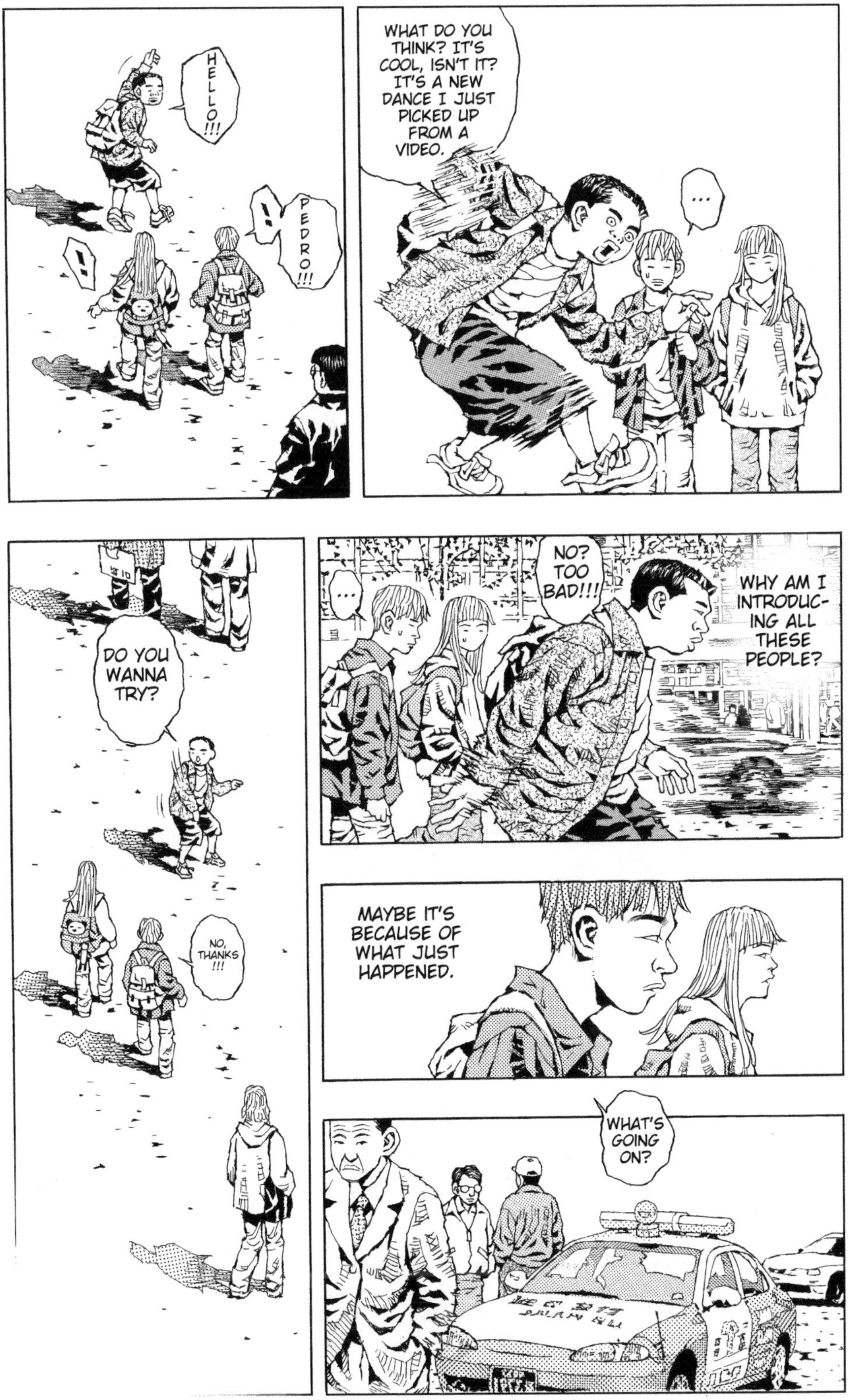
HELLO!!!
!
!
PEDRO!!!
WHAT DO YOU THINK? IT'S COOL, ISN'T IT? IT'S A NEW DANCE I JUST PICKED UP FROM A VIDEO.
...
DO YOU WANNA TRY?
NO, THANKS!!!
...
NO? TOO BAD!!!
WHY AM I INTRODUCING ALL THESE PEOPLE?
MAYBE IT'S BECAUSE OF WHAT JUST HAPPENED.
WHAT'S GOING ON?

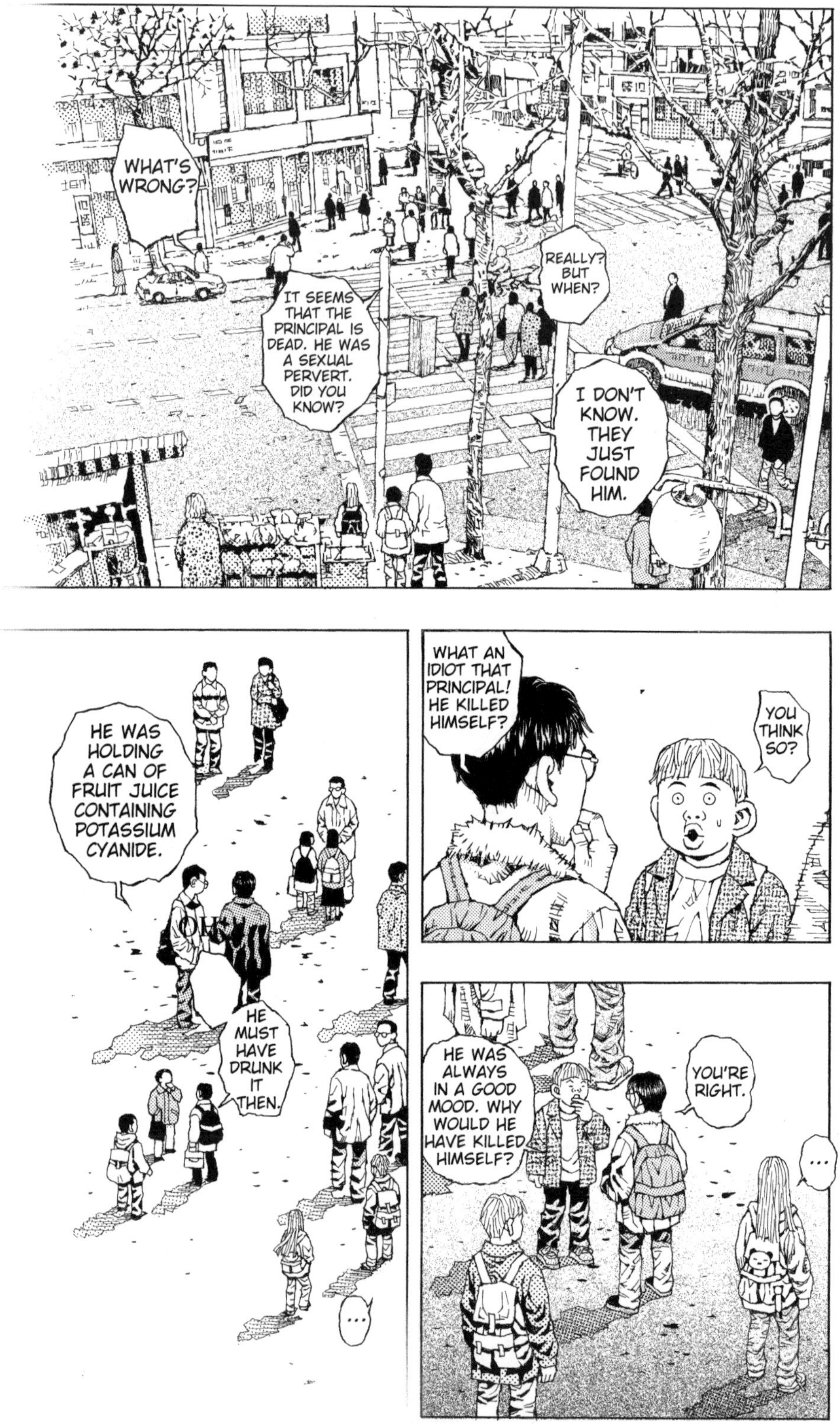
WHAT'S WRONG?
IT SEEMS THAT THE PRINCIPAL IS DEAD. HE WAS A SEXUAL PERVERT. DID YOU KNOW?
REALLY? BUT WHEN?
I DON'T KNOW. THEY JUST FOUND HIM.
HE WAS HOLDING A CAN OF FRUIT JUICE CONTAINING POTASSIUM CYANIDE.
HE MUST HAVE DRUNK IT THEN.
...
WHAT AN IDIOT THAT PRINCIPAL! HE KILLED HIMSELF?
YOU THINK SO?
HE WAS ALWAYS IN A GOOD MOOD. WHY WOULD HE HAVE KILLED HIMSELF?
YOU'RE RIGHT.
...

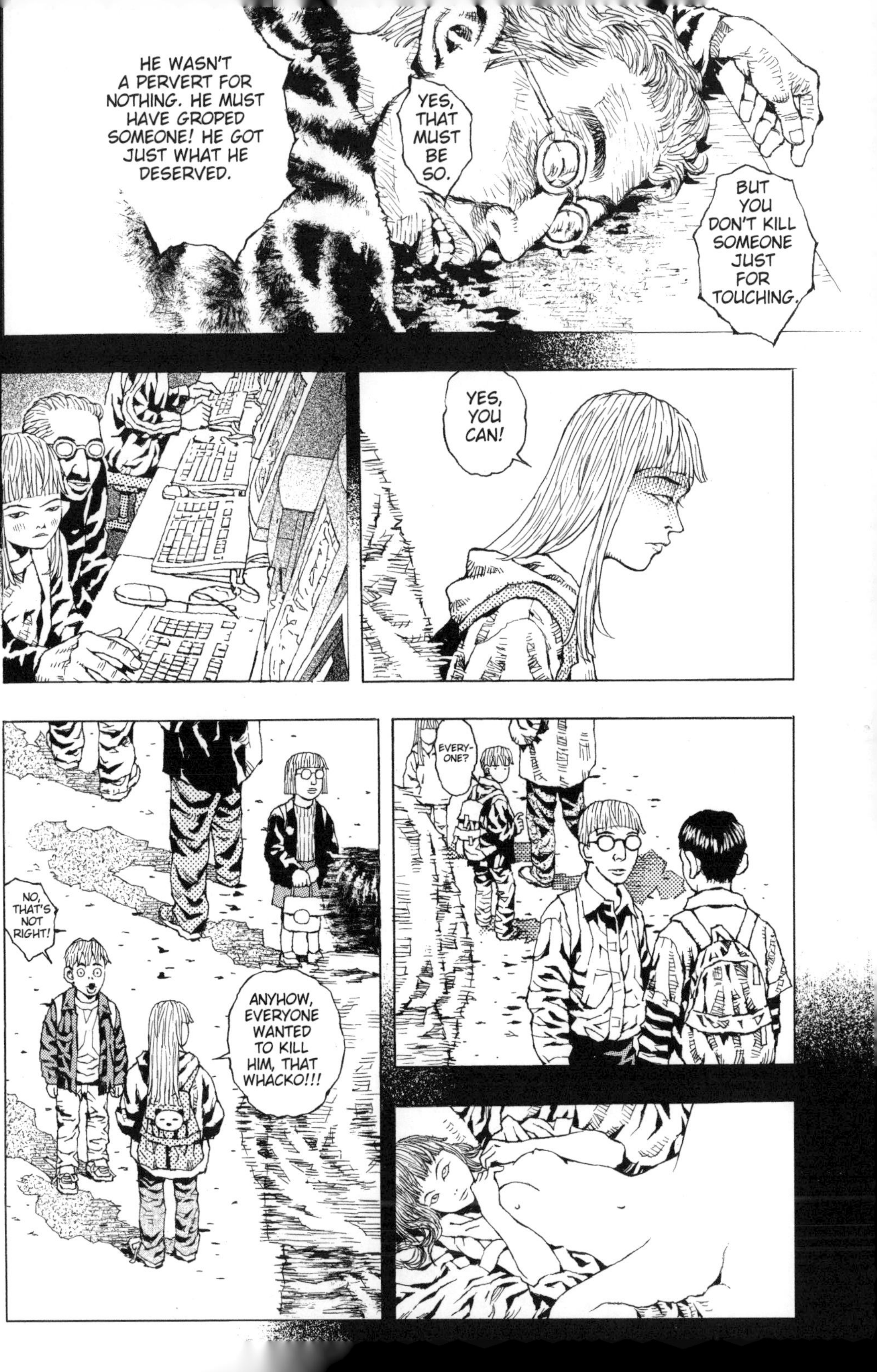
HE WASN'T A PERVERT FOR NOTHING. HE MUST HAVE GROPED SOMEONE! HE GOT JUST WHAT HE DESERVED.
YES, THAT MUST BE SO.
BUT YOU DON'T KILL SOMEONE JUST FOR TOUCHING.
YES, YOU CAN!
NO, THAT'S NOT RIGHT!
ANYHOW, EVERYONE WANTED TO KILL HIM, THAT WHACKO!!!
EVERY-ONE?

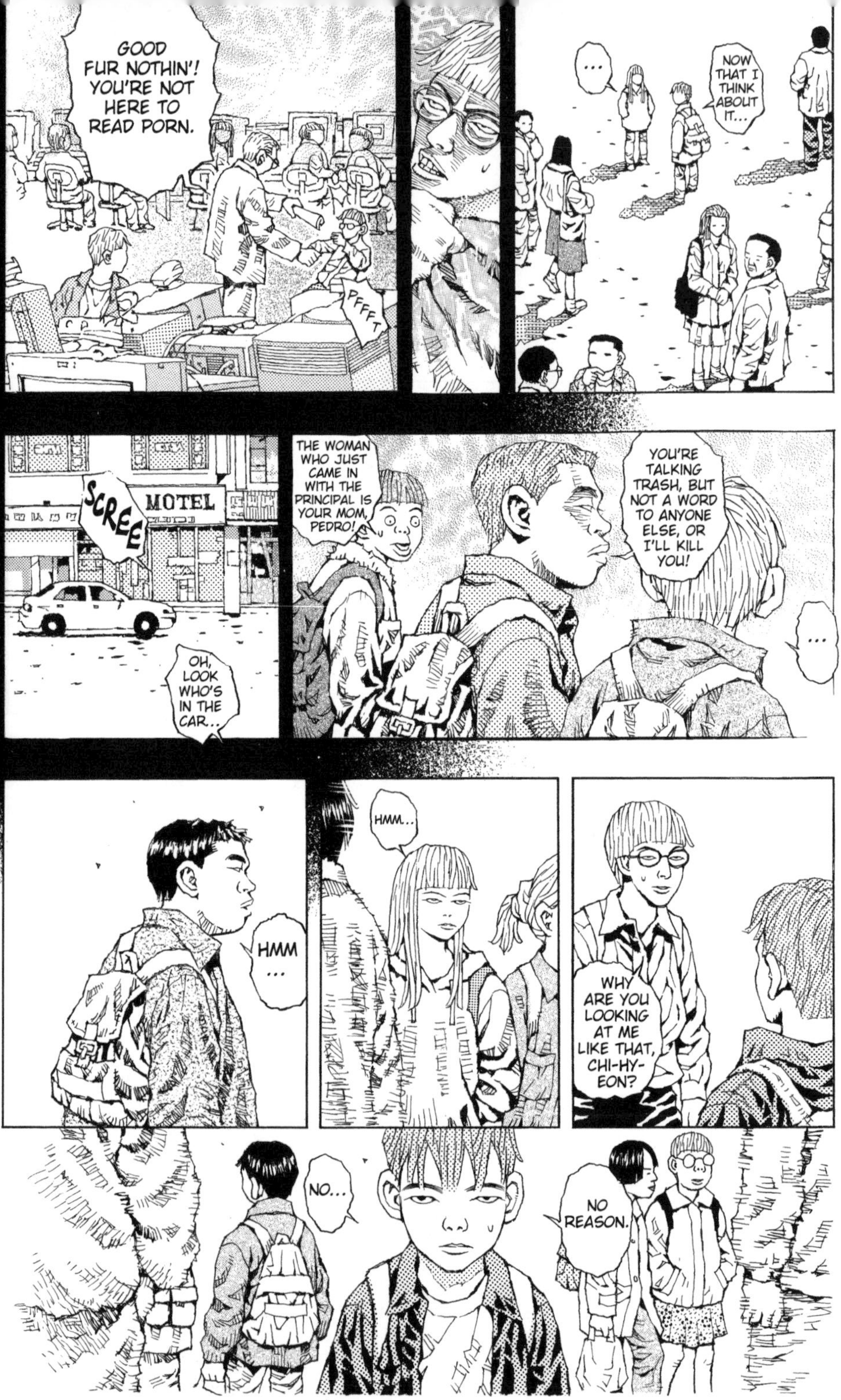
GOOD FUR NOTHIN'! YOU'RE NOT HERE TO READ PORN.
PFFFT
...
NOW THAT I THINK ABOUT IT...
SCREE
MOTEL
OH, LOOK WHO'S IN THE CAR...
THE WOMAN WHO JUST CAME IN WITH THE PRINCIPAL IS YOUR MOM, PEDRO!
YOU'RE TALKING TRASH, BUT NOT A WORD TO ANYONE ELSE, OR I'LL KILL YOU!
...
HMM...
HMM...
WHY ARE YOU LOOKING AT ME LIKE THAT, CHI-HYEON?
NO...
NO REASON.

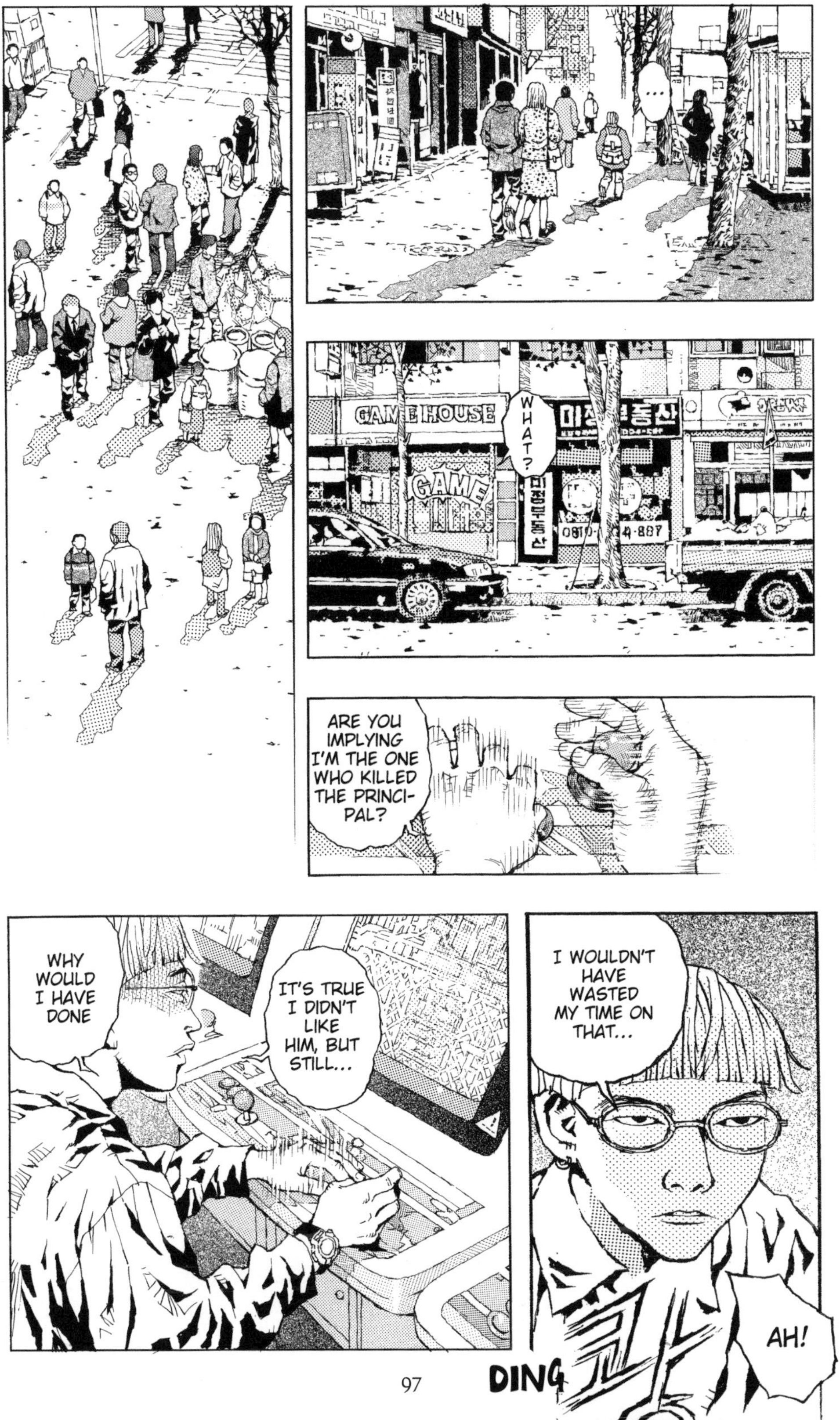
...
GAME HOUSE
WHAT?
GAME
미정부동산
ARE YOU IMPLYING I'M THE ONE WHO KILLED THE PRINCIPAL?
WHY WOULD I HAVE DONE
IT'S TRUE I DIDN'T LIKE HIM, BUT STILL...
I WOULDN'T HAVE WASTED MY TIME ON THAT...
DING
AH!

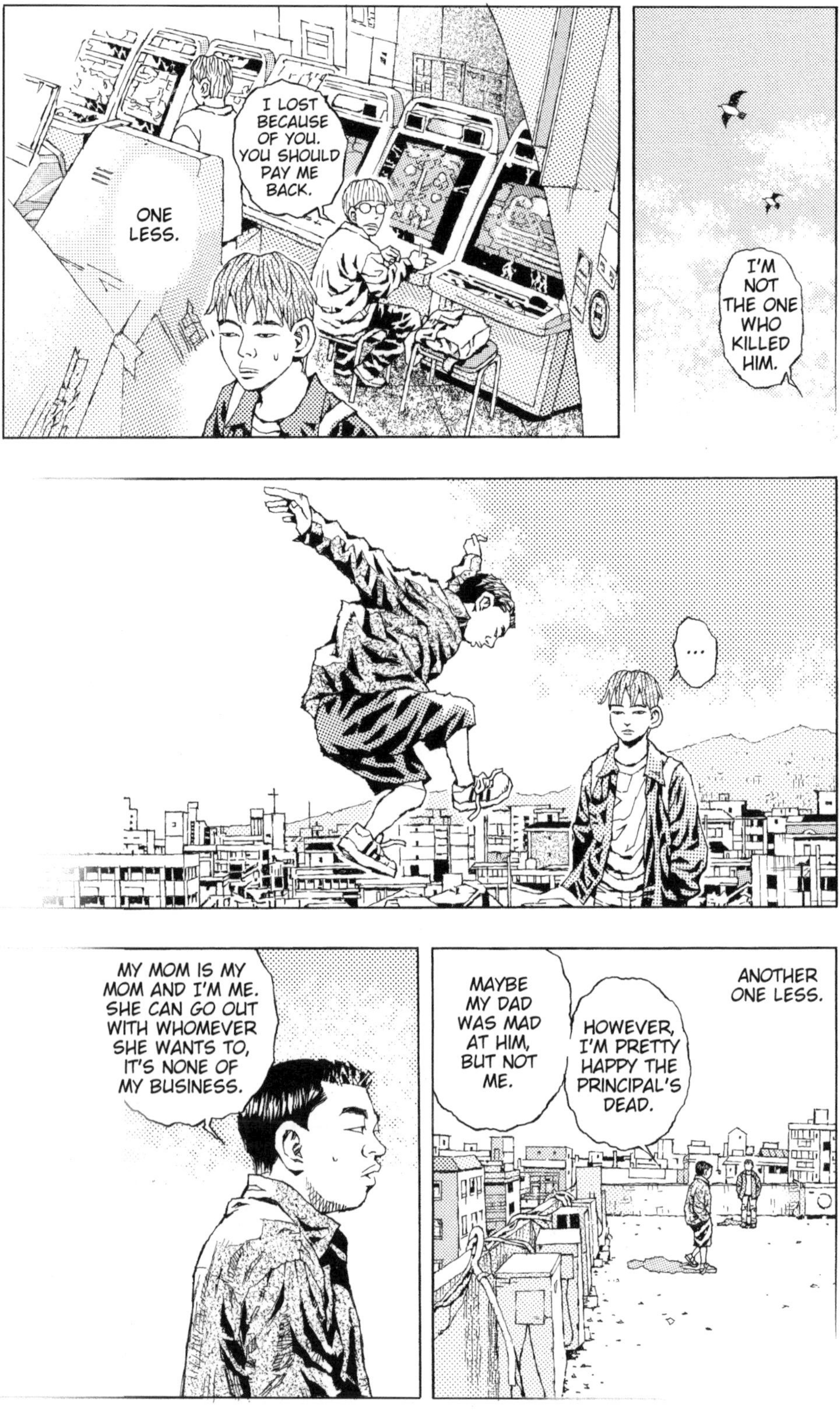
I LOST BECAUSE OF YOU. YOU SHOULD PAY ME BACK.
ONE LESS.
I'M NOT THE ONE WHO KILLED HIM.
...
MY MOM IS MY MOM AND I'M ME. SHE CAN GO OUT WITH WHOMEVER SHE WANTS TO, IT'S NONE OF MY BUSINESS.
MAYBE MY DAD WAS MAD AT HIM, BUT NOT ME.
HOWEVER, I'M PRETTY HAPPY THE PRINCIPAL'S DEAD.
ANOTHER ONE LESS.

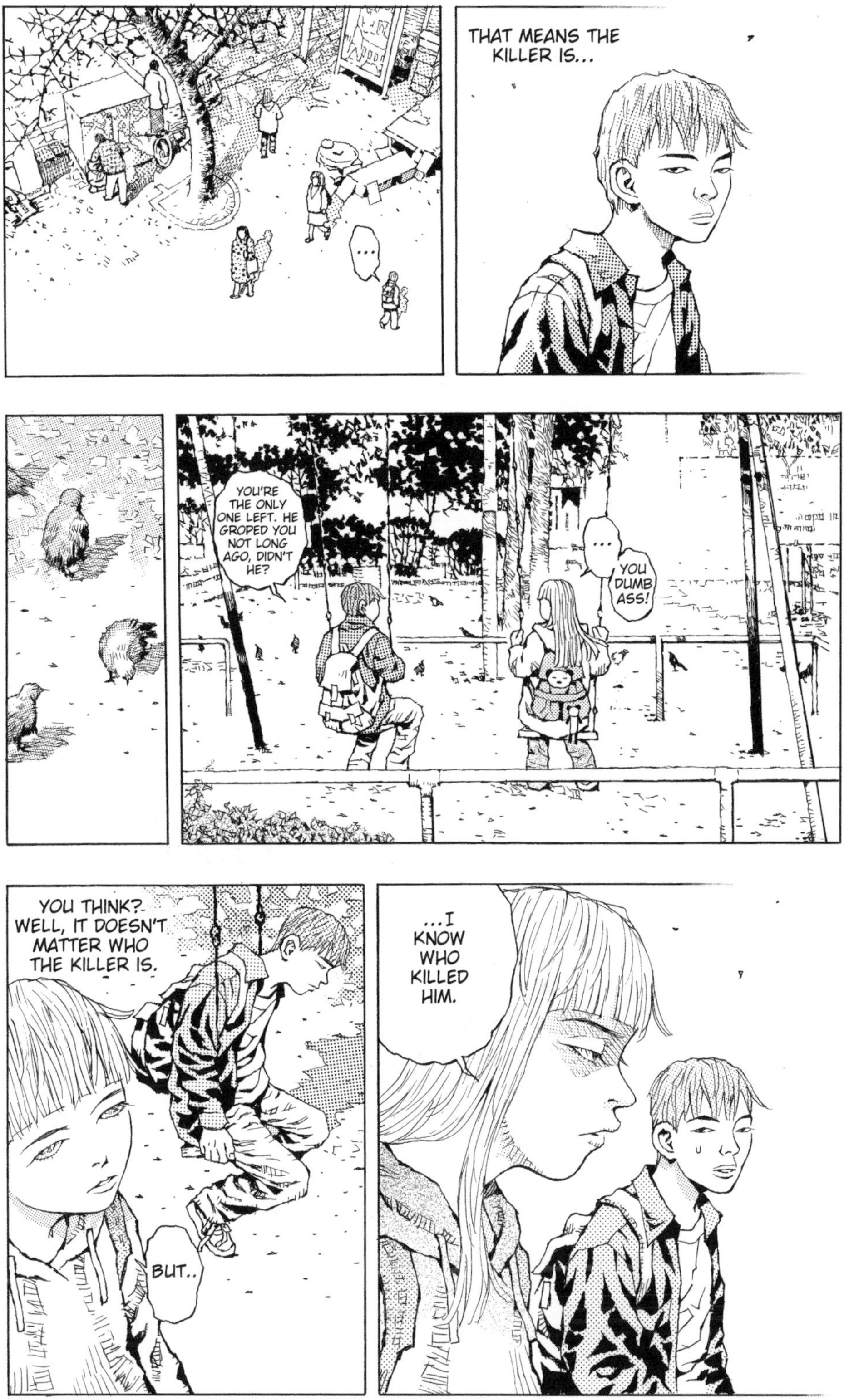
...
THAT MEANS THE KILLER IS...
YOU'RE THE ONLY ONE LEFT. HE GROPED YOU NOT LONG AGO, DIDN'T HE?
...
YOU DUMB ASS!
YOU THINK? WELL, IT DOESN'T MATTER WHO THE KILLER IS.
BUT..
...I KNOW WHO KILLED HIM.

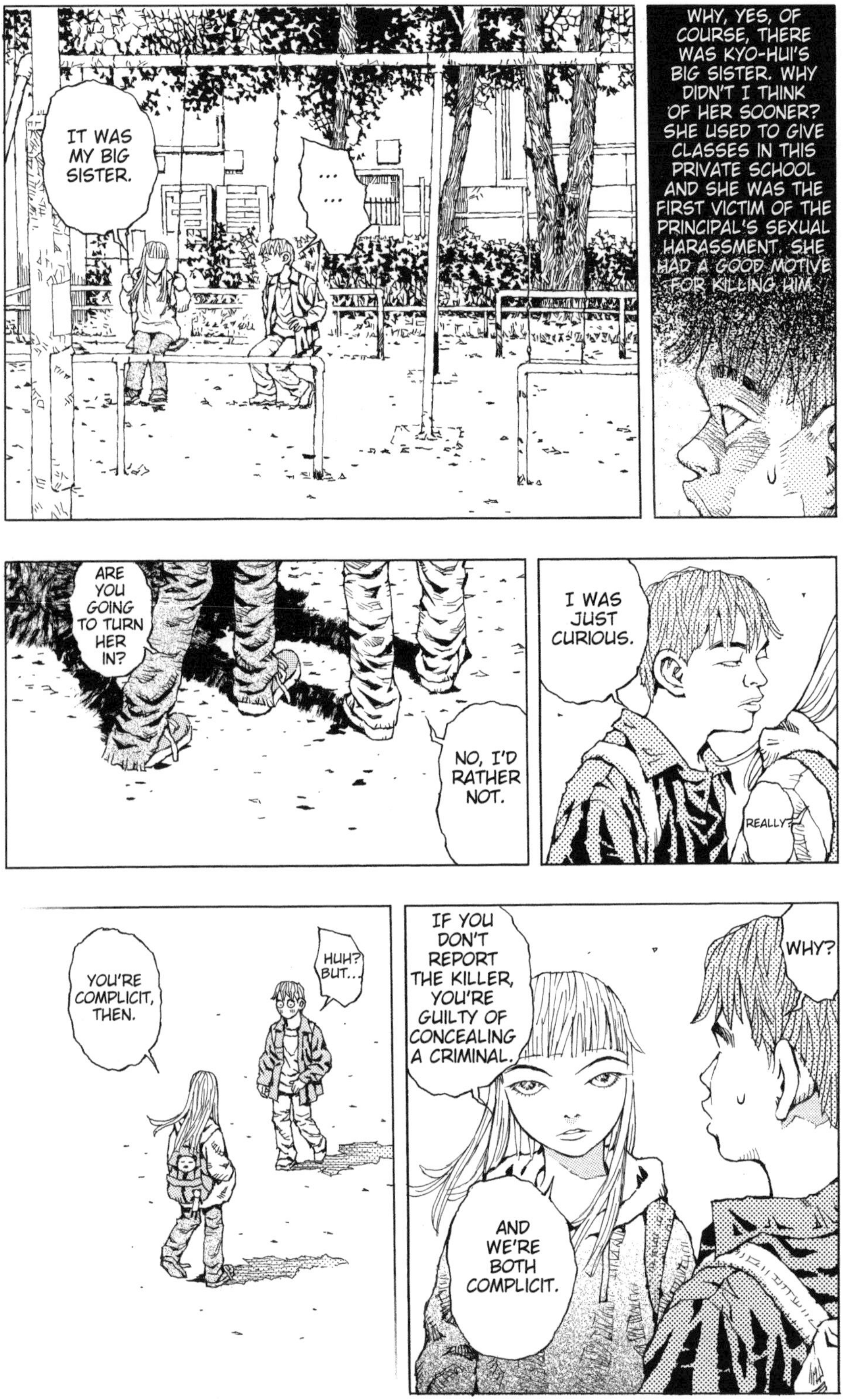
IT WAS MY BIG SISTER.
... ...
WHY, YES, OF COURSE, THERE WAS KYO-HUI'S BIG SISTER. WHY DIDN'T I THINK OF HER SOONER? SHE USED TO GIVE CLASSES IN THIS PRIVATE SCHOOL AND SHE WAS THE FIRST VICTIM OF THE PRINCIPAL'S SEXUAL HARASSMENT. SHE HAD A GOOD MOTIVE FOR KILLING HIM.
ARE YOU GOING TO TURN HER IN?
NO, I'D RATHER NOT.
I WAS JUST CURIOUS.
REALLY?
YOU'RE COMPLICIT, THEN.
HUH? BUT...
IF YOU DON'T REPORT THE KILLER, YOU'RE GUILTY OF CONCEALING A CRIMINAL.
WHY?
AND WE'RE BOTH COMPLICIT.

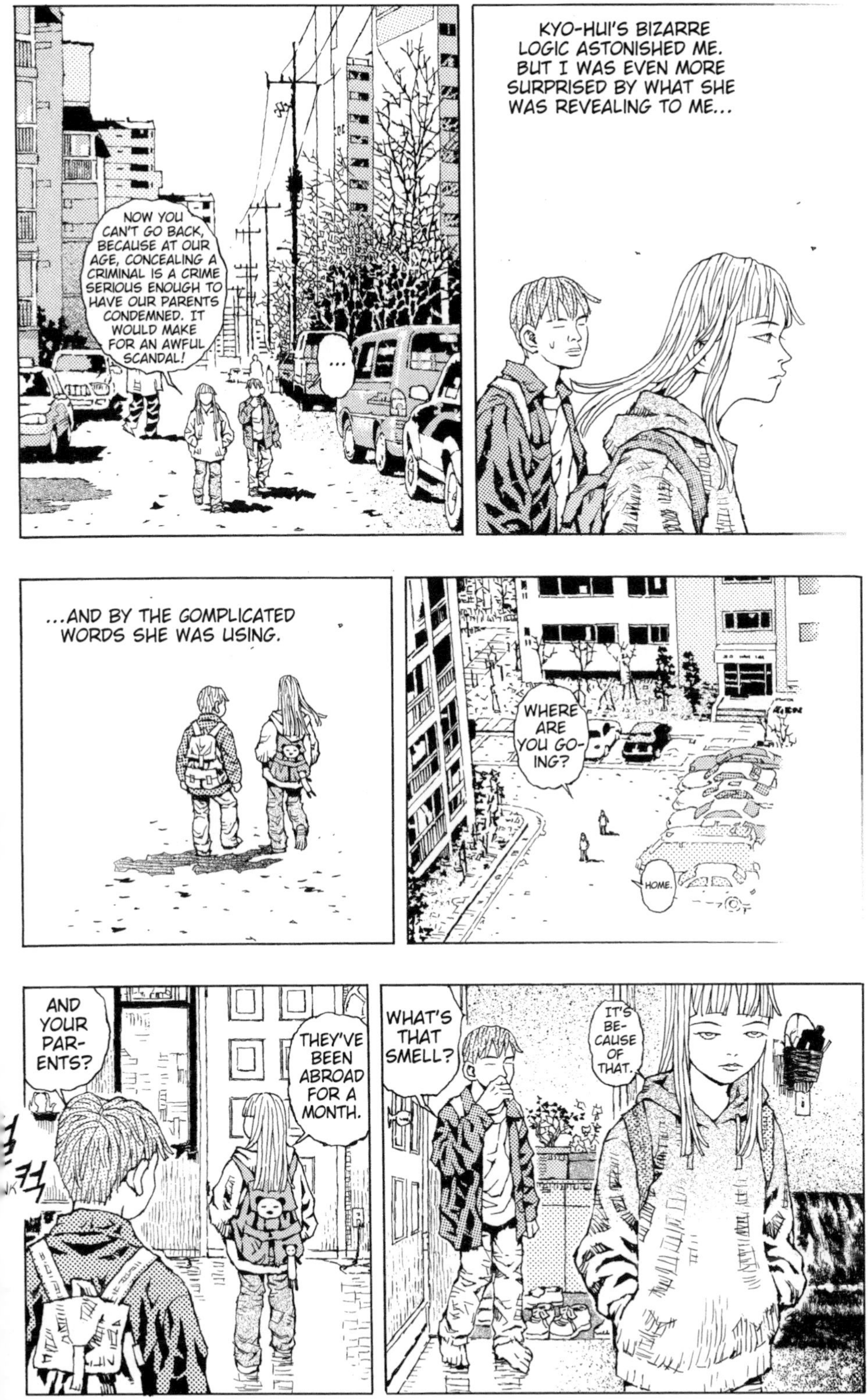
NOW YOU CAN'T GO BACK, BECAUSE AT OUR AGE, CONCEALING A CRIMINAL IS A CRIME SERIOUS ENOUGH TO HAVE OUR PARENTS CONDEMNED. IT WOULD MAKE FOR AN AWFUL SCANDAL!
...
KYO-HUI'S BIZARRE LOGIC ASTONISHED ME. BUT I WAS EVEN MORE SURPRISED BY WHAT SHE WAS REVEALING TO ME...
...AND BY THE COMPLICATED WORDS SHE WAS USING.
WHERE ARE YOU GO-ING?
HOME.
AND YOUR PAR-ENTS?
THEY'VE BEEN ABROAD FOR A MONTH.
WHAT'S THAT SMELL?
IT'S BE-CAUSE OF THAT.

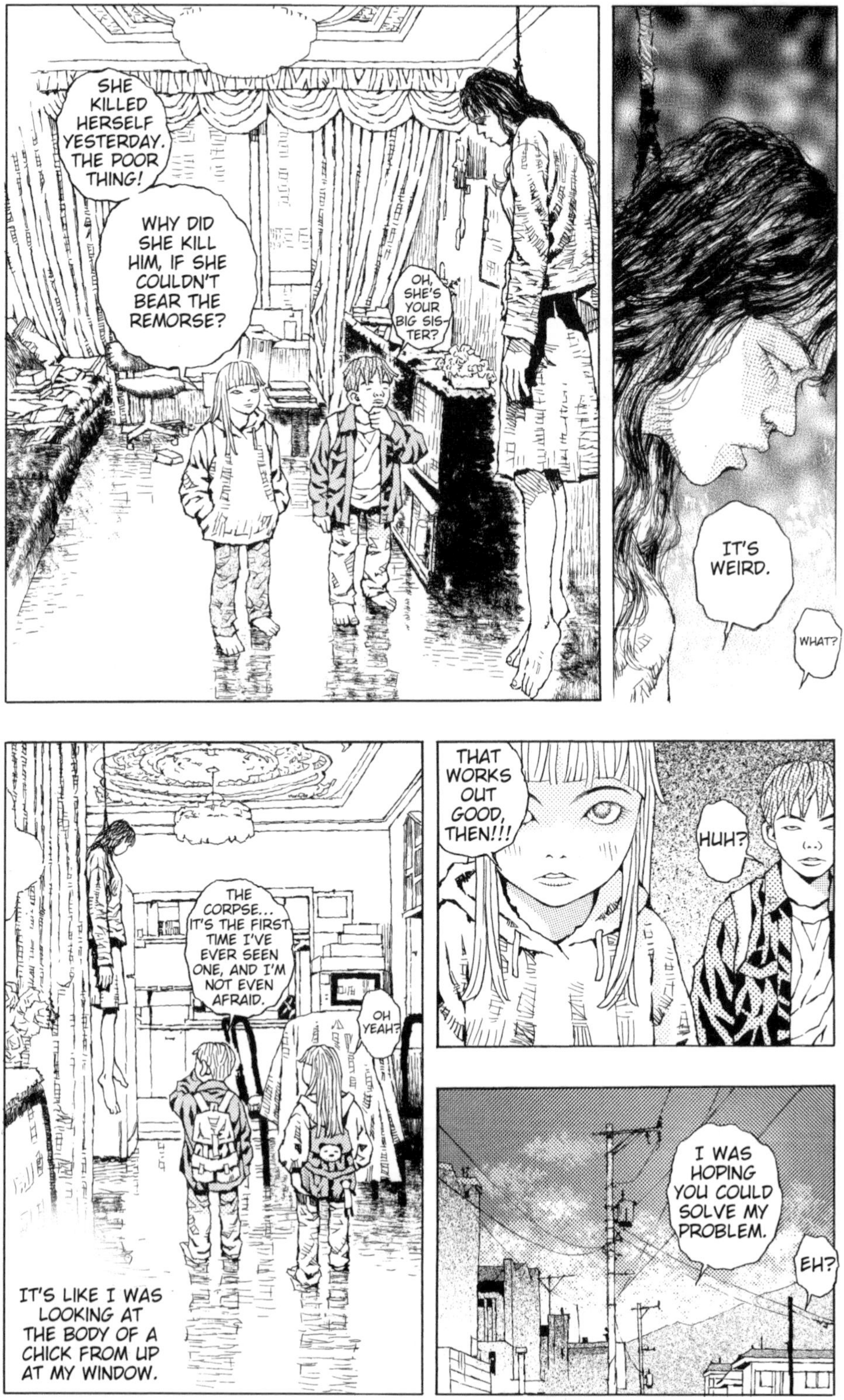
SHE KILLED HERSELF YESTERDAY. THE POOR THING!
WHY DID SHE KILL HIM, IF SHE COULDN'T BEAR THE REMORSE?
OH, SHE'S YOUR BIG SIS-TER?
IT'S WEIRD.
WHAT?
THE CORPSE... IT'S THE FIRST TIME I'VE EVER SEEN ONE, AND I'M NOT EVEN AFRAID.
OH YEAH?
IT'S LIKE I WAS LOOKING AT THE BODY OF A CHICK FROM UP AT MY WINDOW.
THAT WORKS OUT GOOD, THEN!!!
HUH?
I WAS HOPING YOU COULD SOLVE MY PROBLEM.
EH?

IF YOU GO TO THE POLICE, THEY'LL FIND OUT MY BIG SISTER KILLED THE PRINCIPAL.

...

AND THEN I'LL BE AN OUTCAST FROM SOCIETY FOR THE REST OF MY LIFE. I'LL BE CONSIDERED THE LITTLE SISTER OF A MURDERER AND BE FOREVER MARKED.

I HAVE TO MAKE THE CORPSE DISAPPEAR.

...

THAT'S IT! LIKE ALL WOMEN, SHE'S CALCULATING. SHE THINKS OF HERSELF FIRST INSTEAD OF THINKING OF HER SISTER.

DO YOU THINK WE CAN DO THIS TOGETHER?

...

HELLO? CHAN-U?

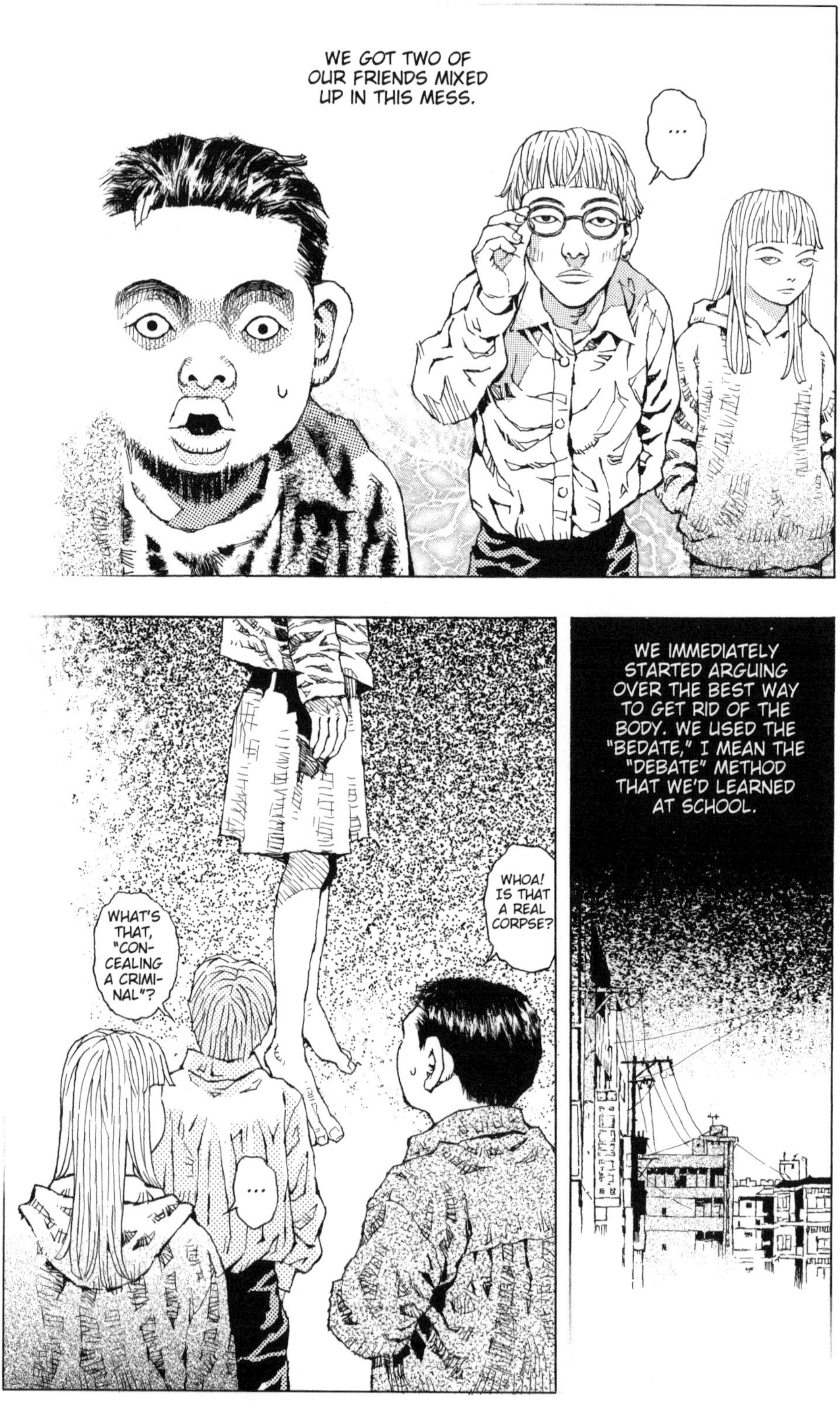
WE GOT TWO OF OUR FRIENDS MIXED UP IN THIS MESS.
...
WHAT'S THAT, "CON-CEALING A CRIMI-NAL"?
WHOA! IS THAT A REAL CORPSE?
...
WE IMMEDIATELY STARTED ARGUING OVER THE BEST WAY TO GET RID OF THE BODY. WE USED THE "BEDATE," I MEAN THE "DEBATE" METHOD THAT WE'D LEARNED AT SCHOOL.

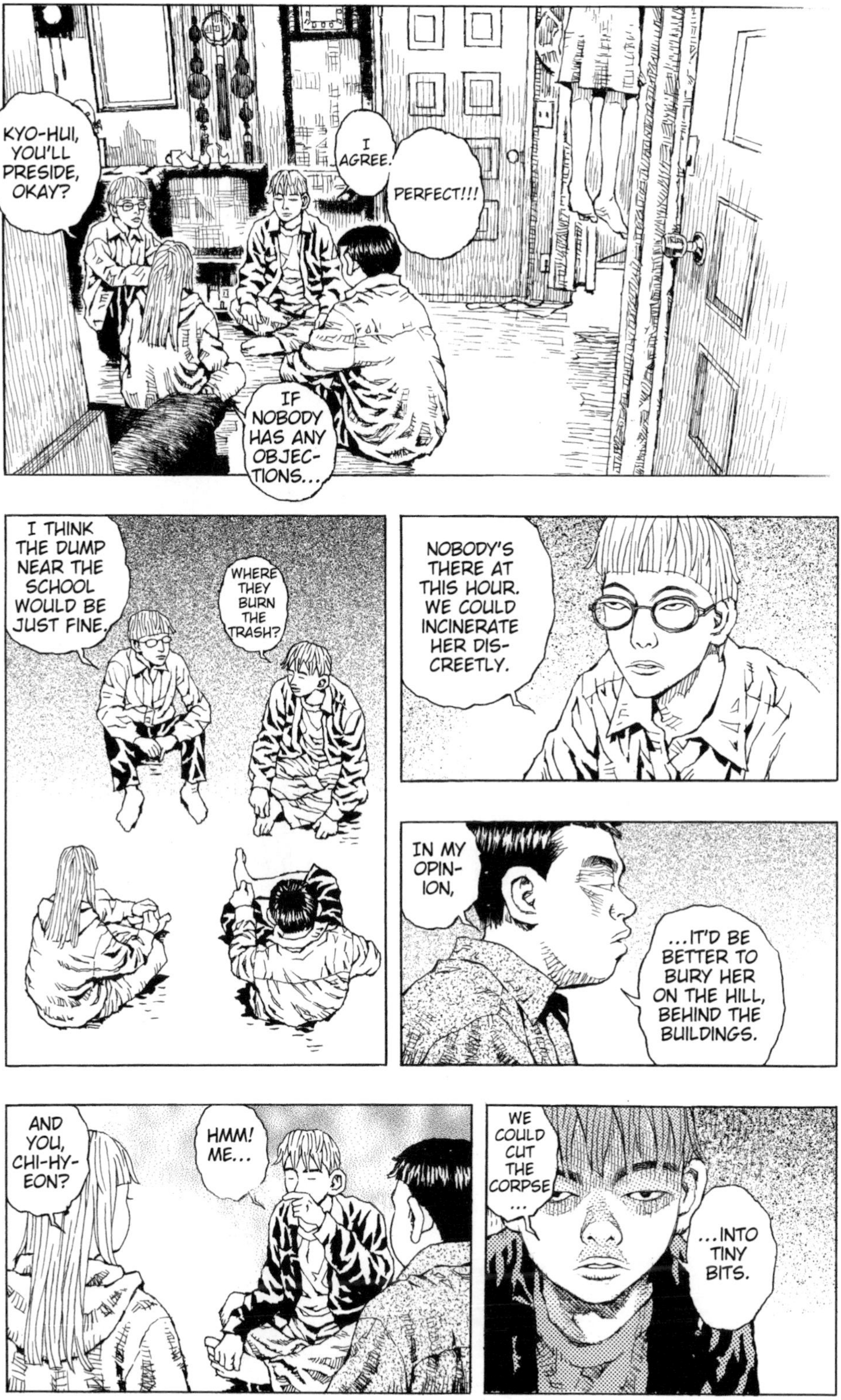
KYO-HUI, YOU'LL PRESIDE, OKAY?
I AGREE.
PERFECT!!!
IF NOBODY HAS ANY OBJEC- TIONS...
I THINK THE DUMP NEAR THE SCHOOL WOULD BE JUST FINE.
WHERE THEY BURN THE TRASH?
NOBODY'S THERE AT THIS HOUR. WE COULD INCINERATE HER DIS- CREETLY.
IN MY OPIN- ION,
...IT'D BE BETTER TO BURY HER ON THE HILL, BEHIND THE BUILDINGS.
AND YOU, CHI-HY- EON?
HMM! ME...
WE COULD CUT THE CORPSE...
...INTO TINY BITS.

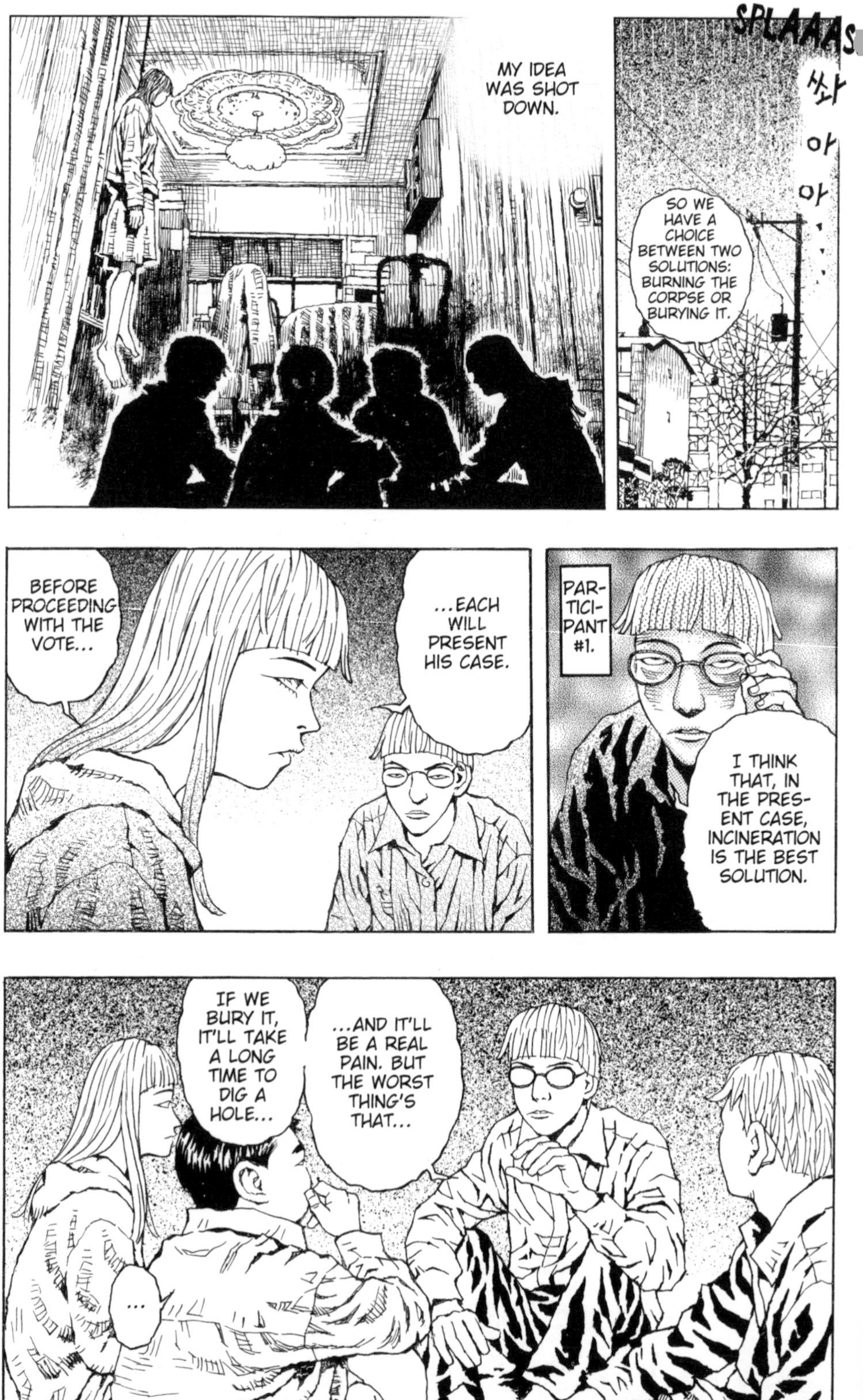
MY IDEA WAS SHOT DOWN.
SPLAAAS
쏴아아...
SO WE HAVE A CHOICE BETWEEN TWO SOLUTIONS: BURNING THE CORPSE OR BURYING IT.
BEFORE PROCEEDING WITH THE VOTE...
...EACH WILL PRESENT HIS CASE.
PAR-TICI-PANT #1.
I THINK THAT, IN THE PRES-ENT CASE, INCINERATION IS THE BEST SOLUTION.
IF WE BURY IT, IT'LL TAKE A LONG TIME TO DIG A HOLE...
...AND IT'LL BE A REAL PAIN. BUT THE WORST THING'S THAT...
...

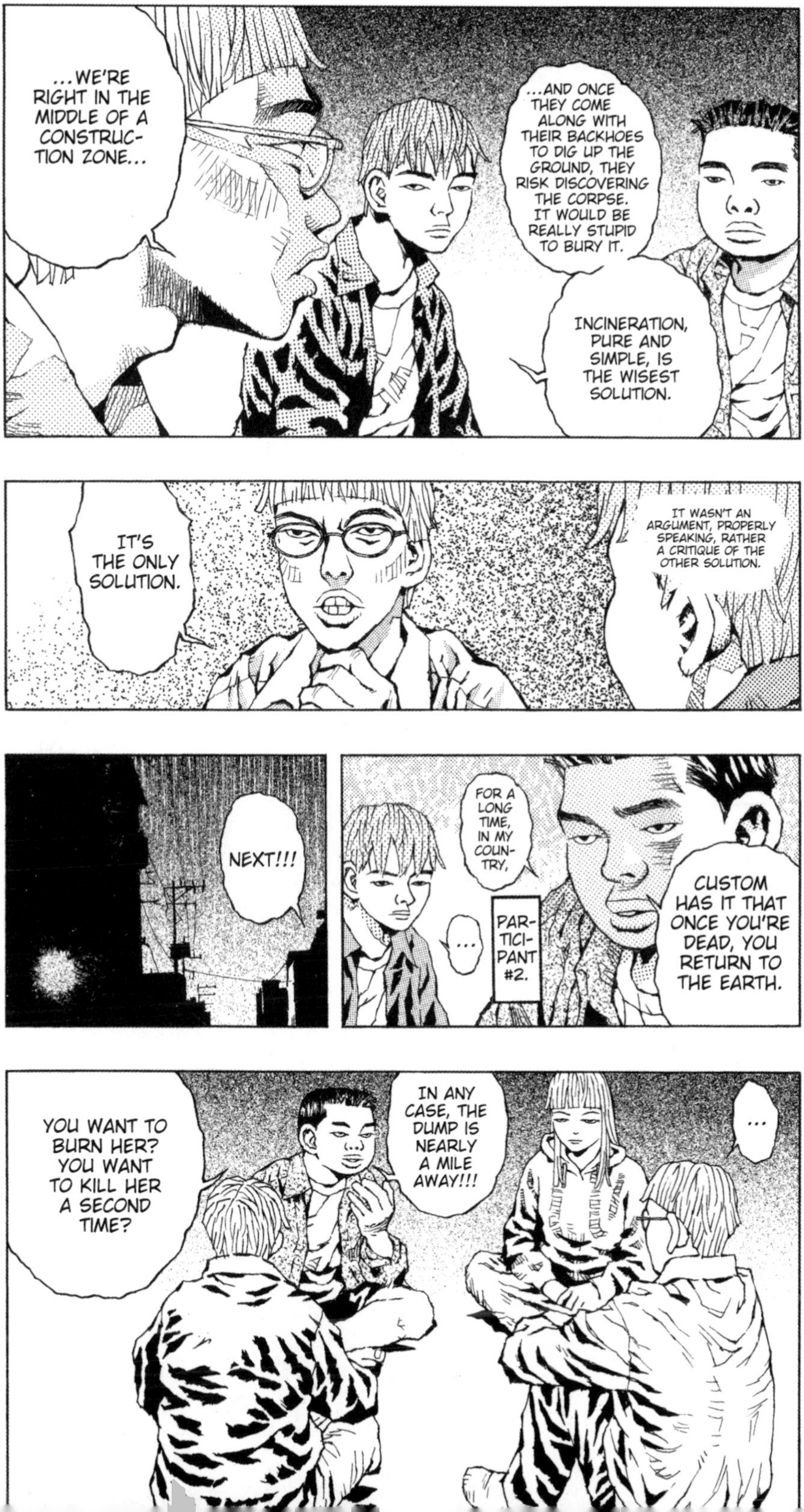
...WE'RE RIGHT IN THE MIDDLE OF A CONSTRUCTION ZONE...
...AND ONCE THEY COME ALONG WITH THEIR BACKHOES TO DIG UP THE GROUND, THEY RISK DISCOVERING THE CORPSE. IT WOULD BE REALLY STUPID TO BURY IT.
INCINERATION, PURE AND SIMPLE, IS THE WISEST SOLUTION.
IT'S THE ONLY SOLUTION.
IT WASN'T AN ARGUMENT, PROPERLY SPEAKING, RATHER A CRITIQUE OF THE OTHER SOLUTION.
NEXT!!!
FOR A LONG TIME, IN MY COUNTRY,
...
PARTICIPANT #2.
CUSTOM HAS IT THAT ONCE YOU'RE DEAD, YOU RETURN TO THE EARTH.
YOU WANT TO BURN HER? YOU WANT TO KILL HER A SECOND TIME?
IN ANY CASE, THE DUMP IS NEARLY A MILE AWAY!!!
...

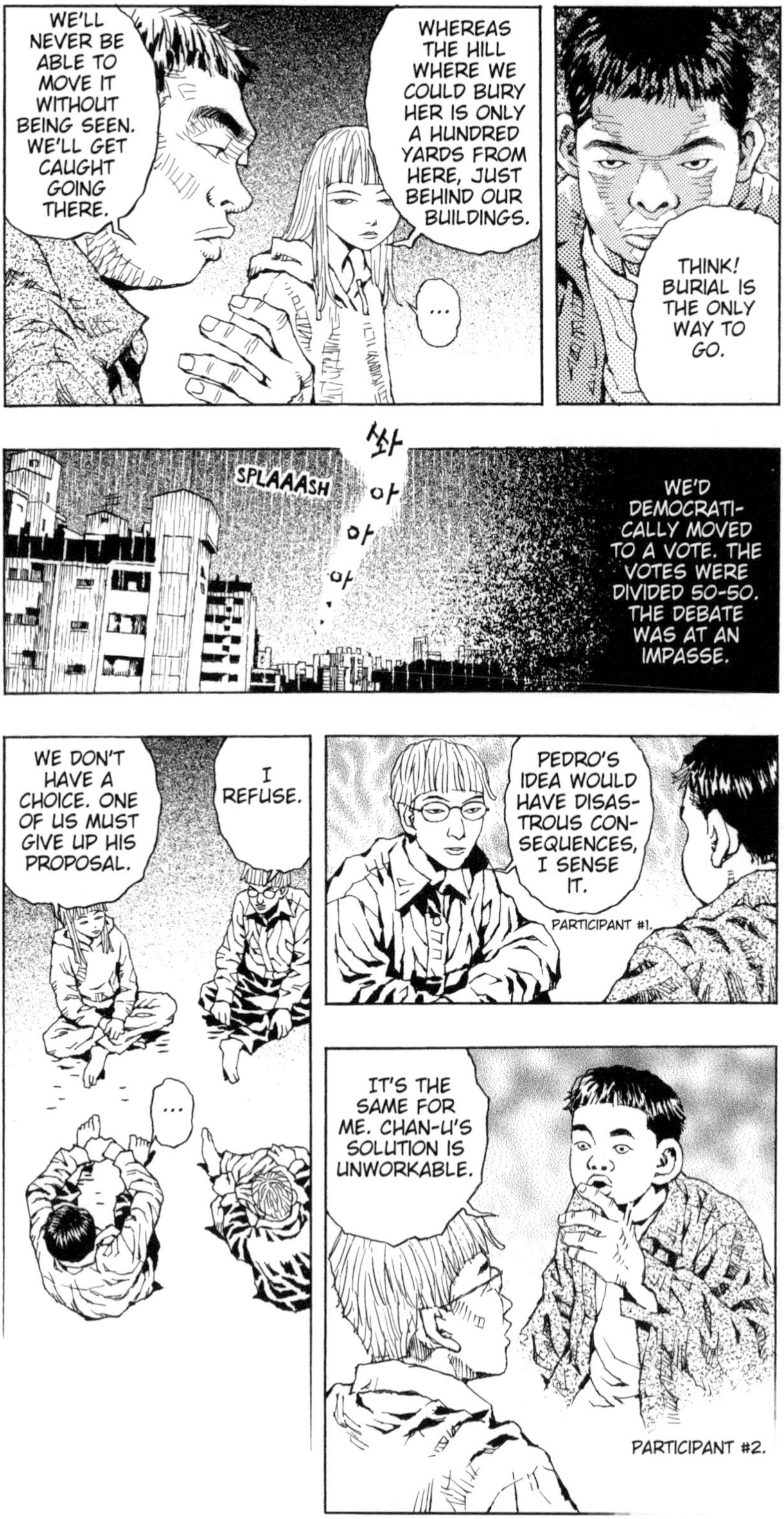
WE'LL NEVER BE ABLE TO MOVE IT WITHOUT BEING SEEN. WE'LL GET CAUGHT GOING THERE.
WHEREAS THE HILL WHERE WE COULD BURY HER IS ONLY A HUNDRED YARDS FROM HERE, JUST BEHIND OUR BUILDINGS.
...
THINK! BURIAL IS THE ONLY WAY TO GO.
쏴
아
아
아
SPLAAAASH
WE'D DEMOCRATI-CALLY MOVED TO A VOTE. THE VOTES WERE DIVIDED 50-50. THE DEBATE WAS AT AN IMPASSE.
WE DON'T HAVE A CHOICE. ONE OF US MUST GIVE UP HIS PROPOSAL.
I REFUSE.
...
PEDRO'S IDEA WOULD HAVE DISAS-TROUS CON-SEQUENCES, I SENSE IT.
PARTICIPANT #1.
IT'S THE SAME FOR ME. CHAN-U'S SOLUTION IS UNWORKABLE.
PARTICIPANT #2.

WHEN I SEE THE TWO OF YOU LIKE THIS...

THAT'S THE MOMENT WHEN...

IT REMINDS ME OF THE CLASS ELECTIONS.

...KYO-HUI POURED OIL ON THE FIRE.

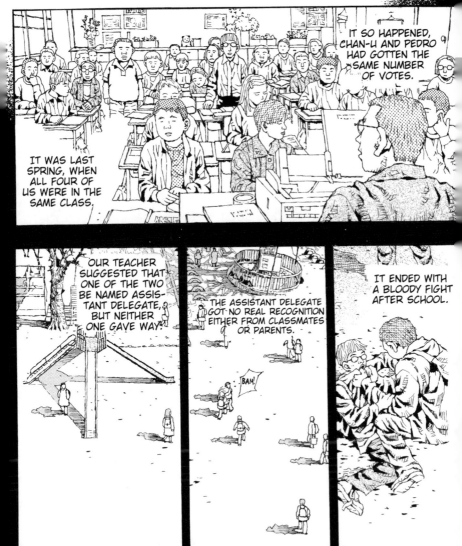

IT SO HAPPENED, CHAN-U AND PEDRO HAD GOTTEN THE SAME NUMBER OF VOTES.

IT WAS LAST SPRING, WHEN ALL FOUR OF US WERE IN THE SAME CLASS.

OUR TEACHER SUGGESTED THAT ONE OF THE TWO BE NAMED ASSISTANT DELEGATE, BUT NEITHER ONE GAVE WAY.

THE ASSISTANT DELEGATE GOT NO REAL RECOGNITION EITHER FROM CLASSMATES OR PARENTS.

BAN!

IT ENDED WITH A BLOODY FIGHT AFTER SCHOOL.

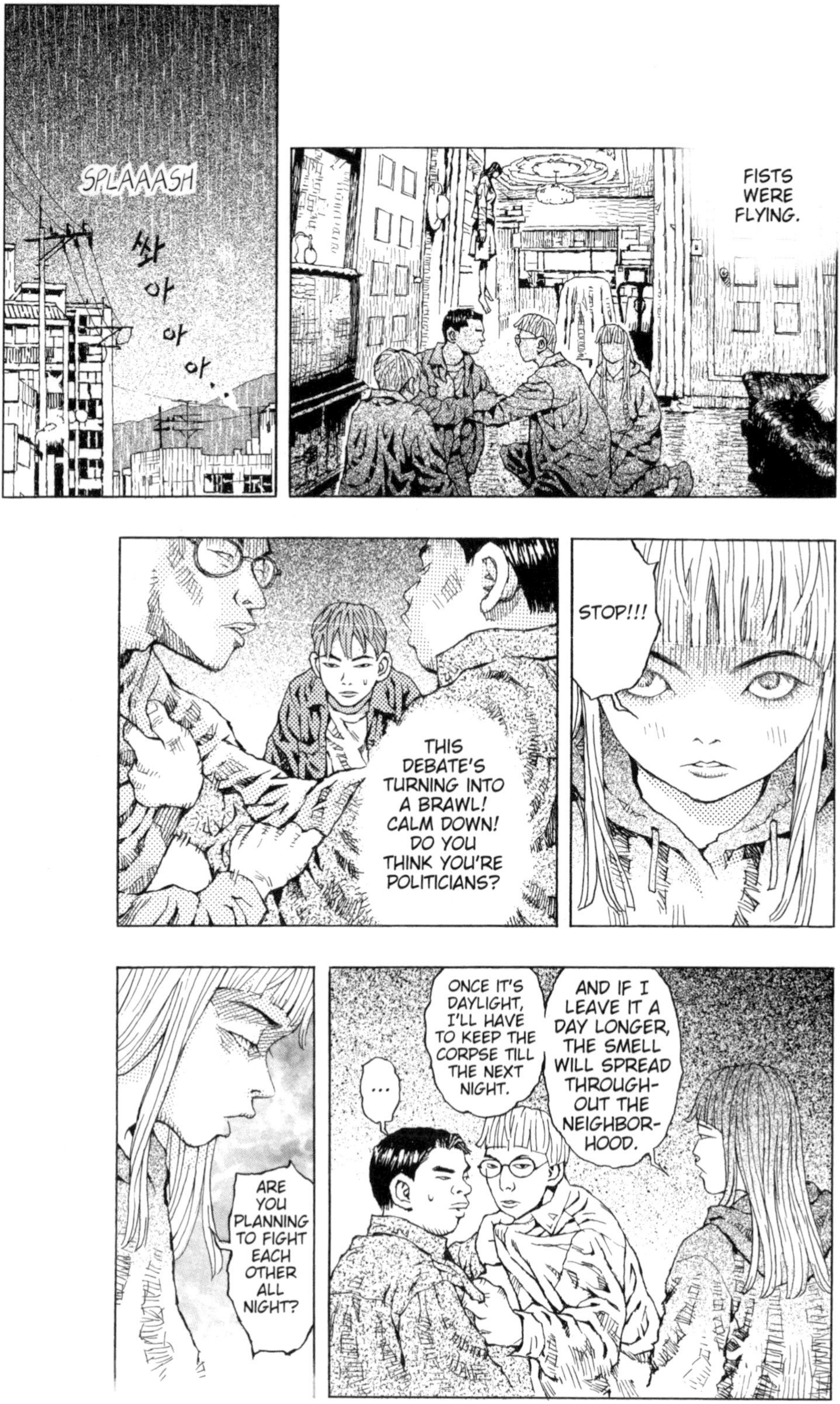

SPLAAASH
쏴
아
아
아...
FISTS WERE FLYING.
THIS DEBATE'S TURNING INTO A BRAWL! CALM DOWN! DO YOU THINK YOU'RE POLITICIANS?
STOP!!!
ARE YOU PLANNING TO FIGHT EACH OTHER ALL NIGHT?
...
ONCE IT'S DAYLIGHT, I'LL HAVE TO KEEP THE CORPSE TILL THE NEXT NIGHT.
AND IF I LEAVE IT A DAY LONGER, THE SMELL WILL SPREAD THROUGH-OUT THE NEIGHBOR-HOOD.

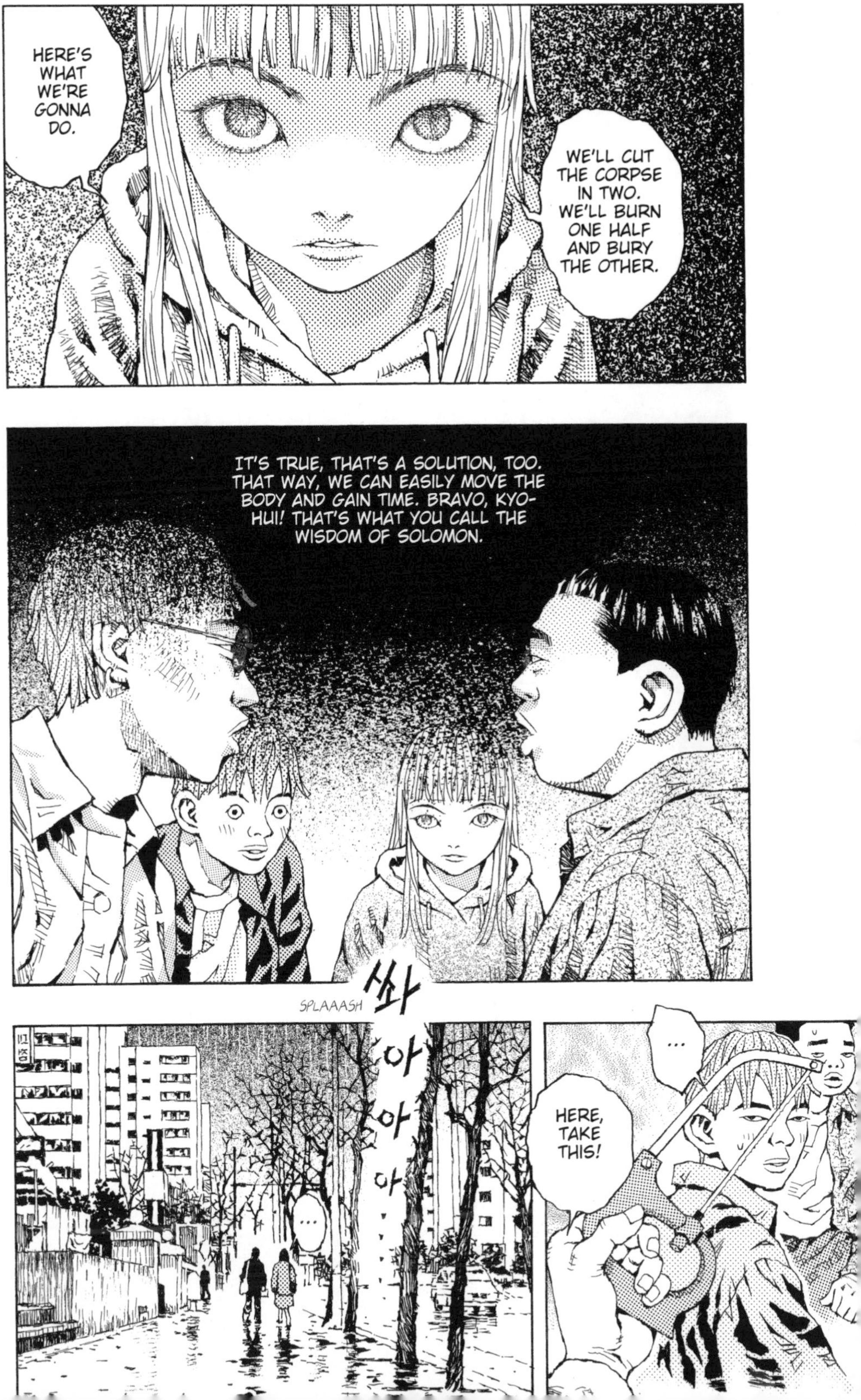
HERE'S WHAT WE'RE GONNA DO.
WE'LL CUT THE CORPSE IN TWO. WE'LL BURN ONE HALF AND BURY THE OTHER.
IT'S TRUE, THAT'S A SOLUTION, TOO. THAT WAY, WE CAN EASILY MOVE THE BODY AND GAIN TIME. BRAVO, KYO-HUI! THAT'S WHAT YOU CALL THE WISDOM OF SOLOMON.
SPLAAASH
쏴아아아아
...
...
HERE, TAKE THIS!

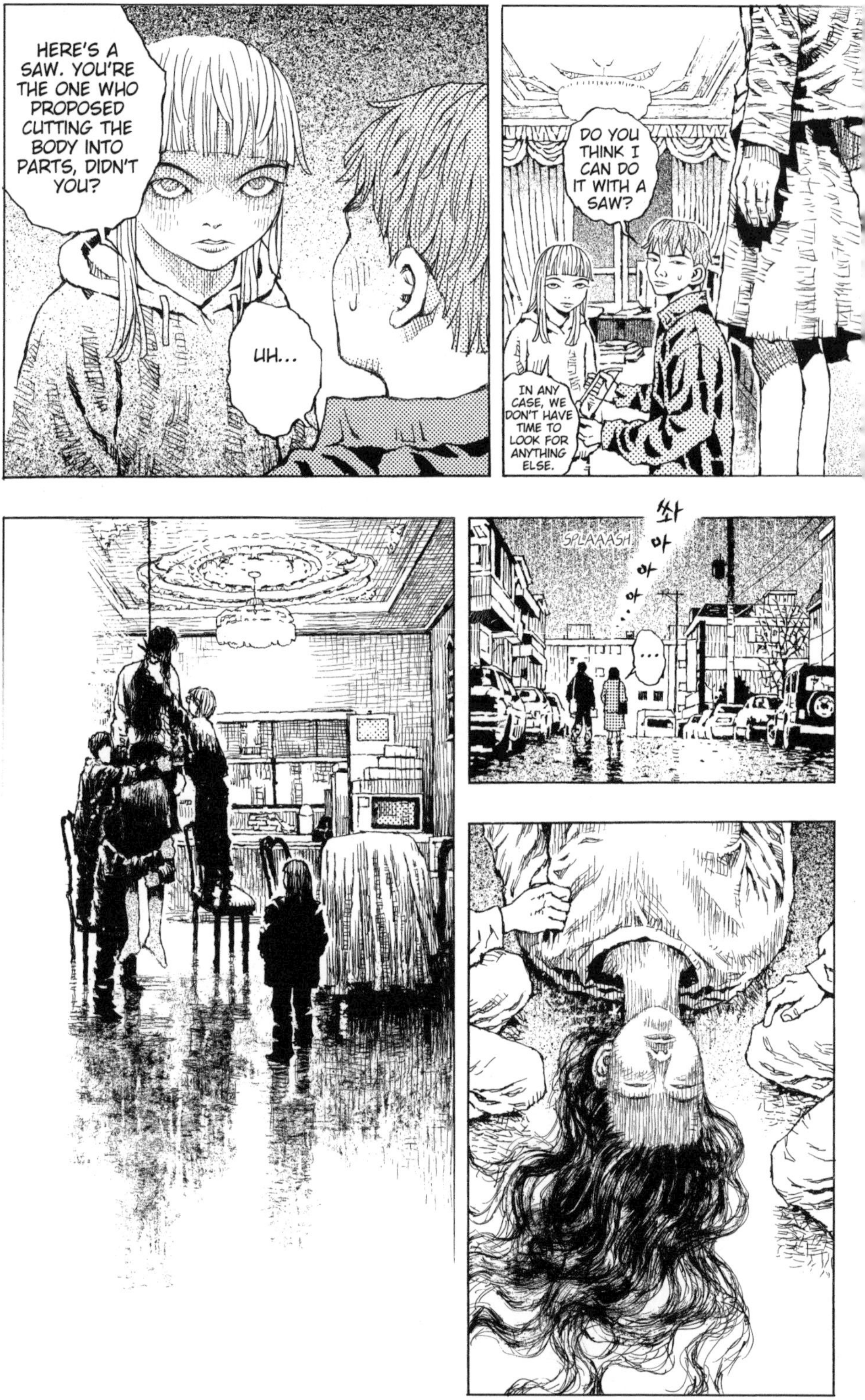
HERE'S A SAW. YOU'RE THE ONE WHO PROPOSED CUTTING THE BODY INTO PARTS, DIDN'T YOU?
UH...
DO YOU THINK I CAN DO IT WITH A SAW?
IN ANY CASE, WE DON'T HAVE TIME TO LOOK FOR ANYTHING ELSE.
쏴아아아...
SPLAAASH
...

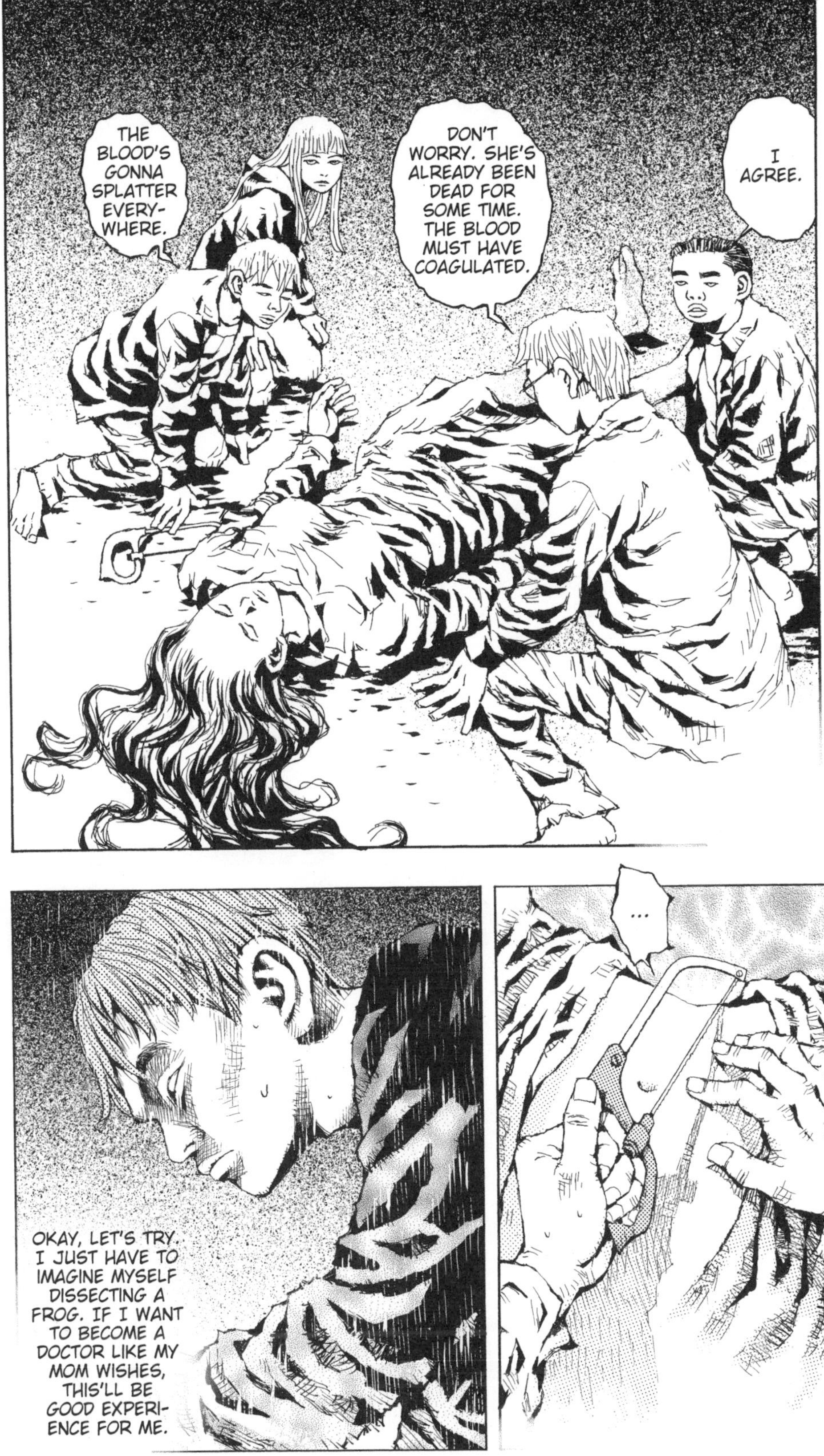
I AGREE.
DON'T WORRY. SHE'S ALREADY BEEN DEAD FOR SOME TIME. THE BLOOD MUST HAVE COAGULATED.
THE BLOOD'S GONNA SPLATTER EVERY-WHERE.
...
OKAY, LET'S TRY. I JUST HAVE TO IMAGINE MYSELF DISSECTING A FROG. IF I WANT TO BECOME A DOCTOR LIKE MY MOM WISHES, THIS'LL BE GOOD EXPERI-ENCE FOR ME.

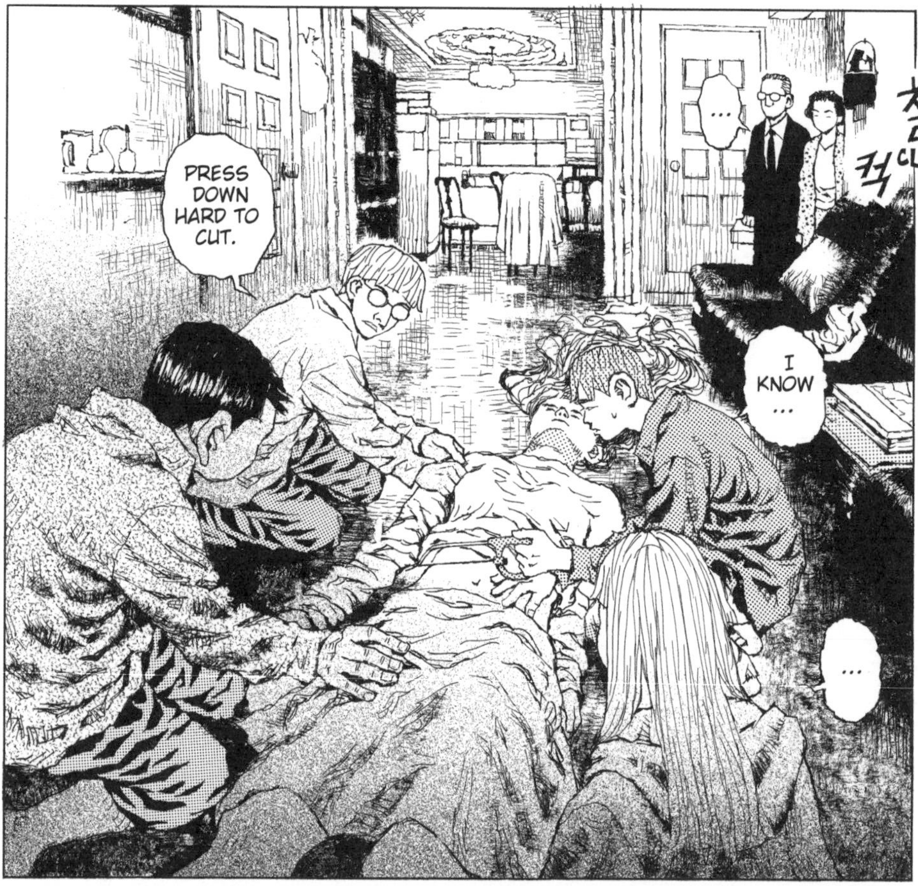
PRESS DOWN HARD TO CUT.
...
철컥 CLIN
I KNOW ...
...

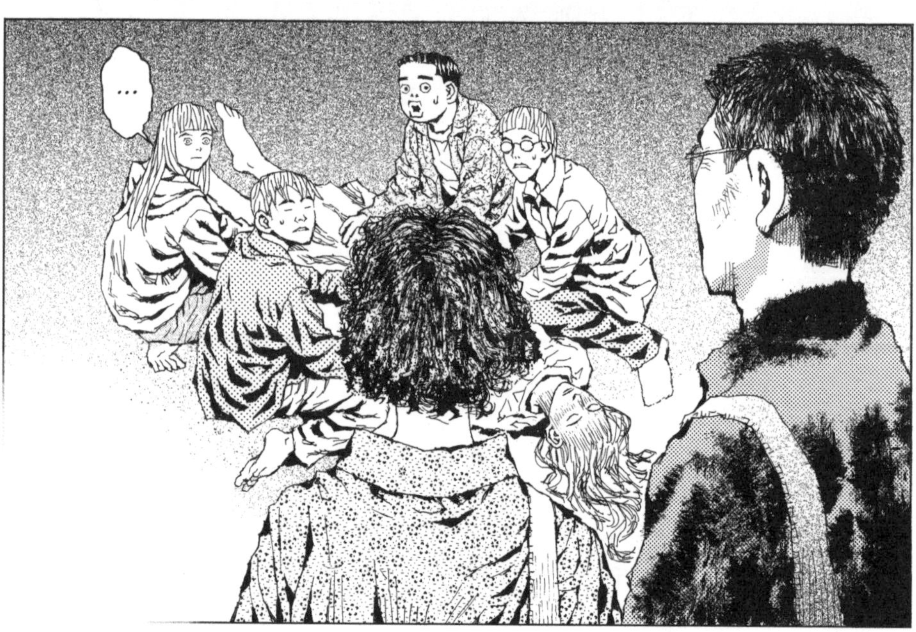
...

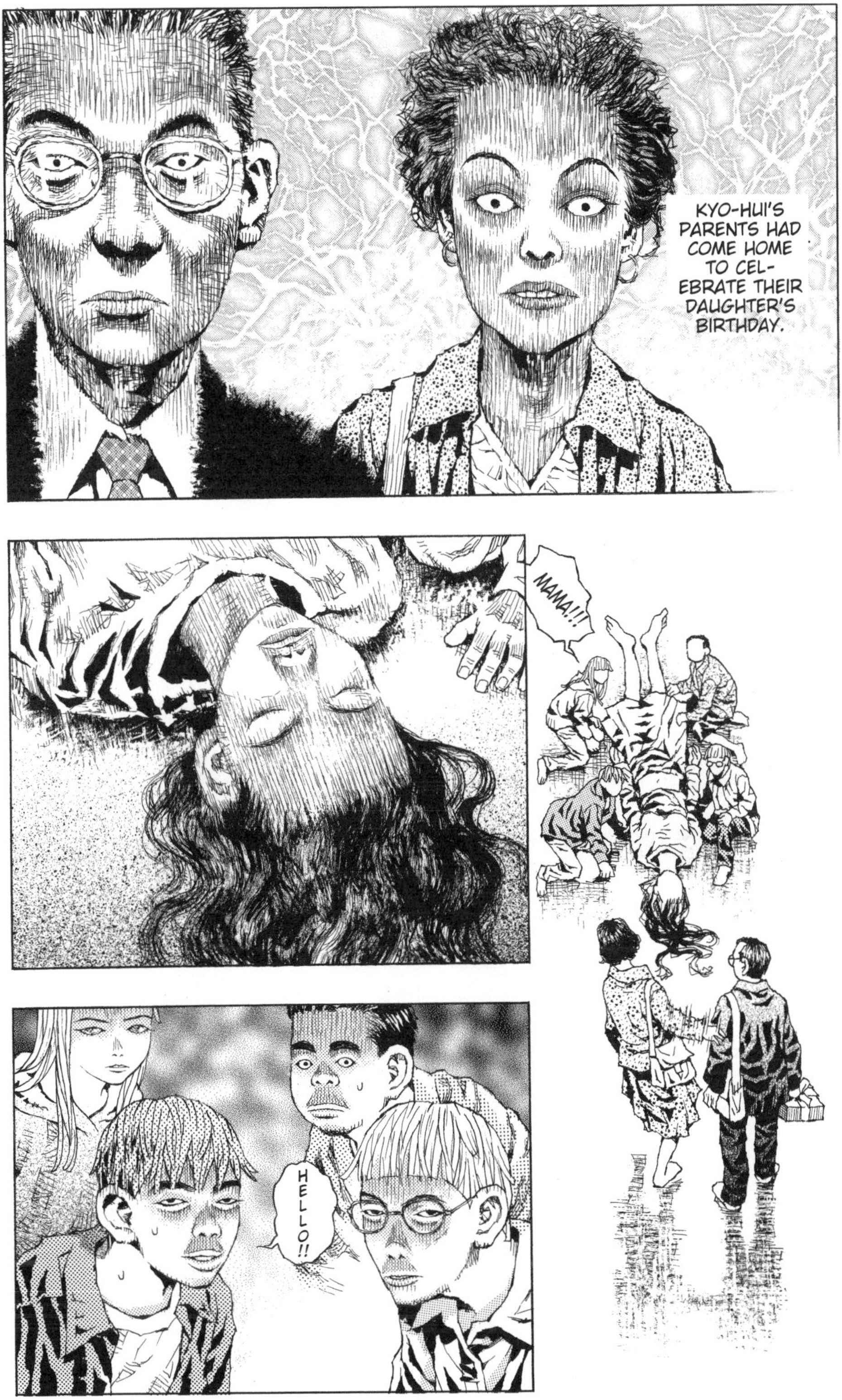
KYO-HUI'S PARENTS HAD COME HOME TO CEL-EBRATE THEIR DAUGHTER'S BIRTHDAY.
MAMA!!!
HELLO!!

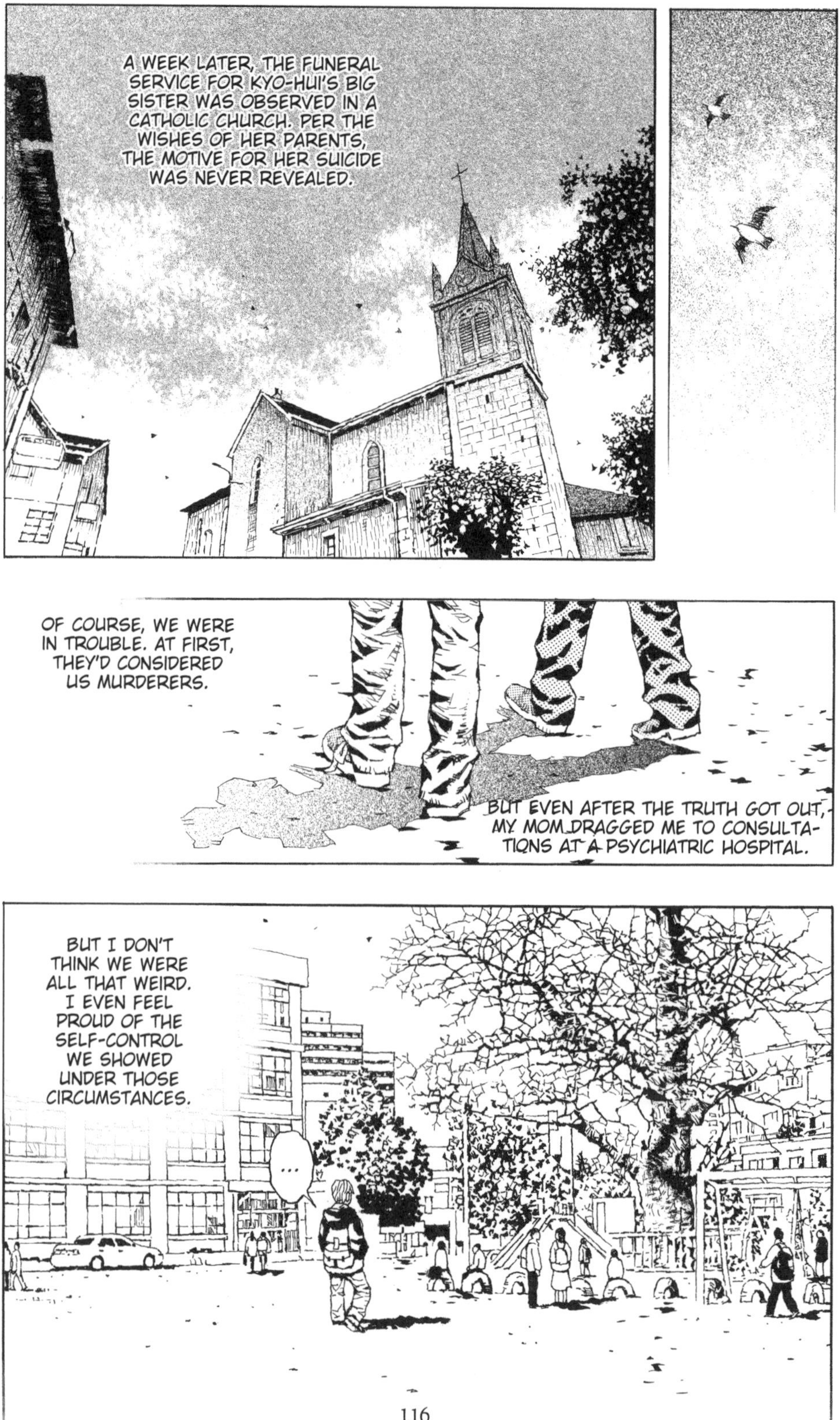
A WEEK LATER, THE FUNERAL SERVICE FOR KYO-HUI'S BIG SISTER WAS OBSERVED IN A CATHOLIC CHURCH. PER THE WISHES OF HER PARENTS, THE MOTIVE FOR HER SUICIDE WAS NEVER REVEALED.
OF COURSE, WE WERE IN TROUBLE. AT FIRST, THEY'D CONSIDERED US MURDERERS.
BUT EVEN AFTER THE TRUTH GOT OUT, MY MOM DRAGGED ME TO CONSULTATIONS AT A PSYCHIATRIC HOSPITAL.
BUT I DON'T THINK WE WERE ALL THAT WEIRD. I EVEN FEEL PROUD OF THE SELF-CONTROL WE SHOWED UNDER THOSE CIRCUMSTANCES.
...

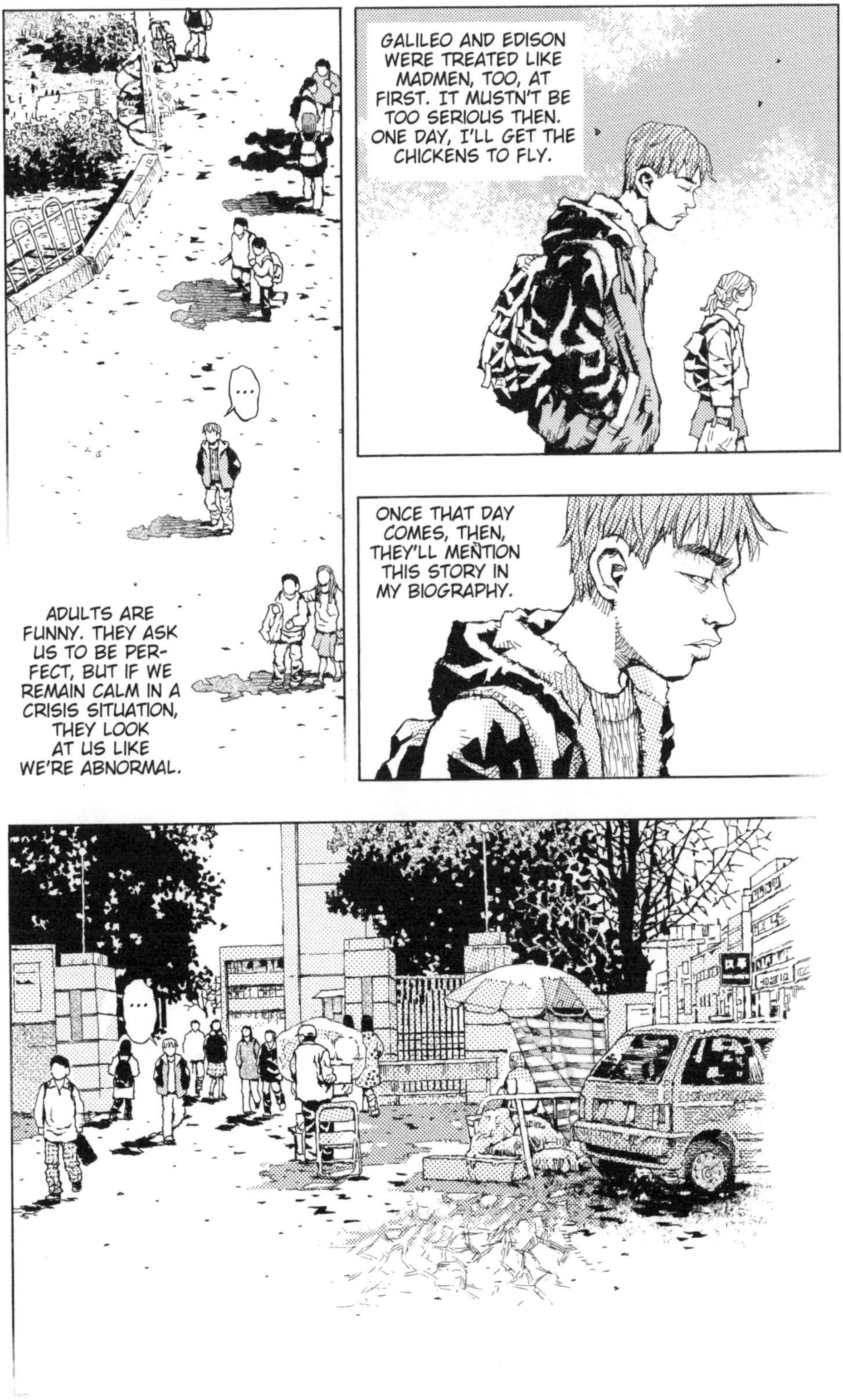

...
ADULTS ARE FUNNY. THEY ASK US TO BE PER- FECT, BUT IF WE REMAIN CALM IN A CRISIS SITUATION, THEY LOOK AT US LIKE WE'RE ABNORMAL.
GALILEO AND EDISON WERE TREATED LIKE MADMEN, TOO, AT FIRST. IT MUSTN'T BE TOO SERIOUS THEN. ONE DAY, I'LL GET THE CHICKENS TO FLY.
ONCE THAT DAY COMES, THEN, THEY'LL MENTION THIS STORY IN MY BIOGRAPHY.
...

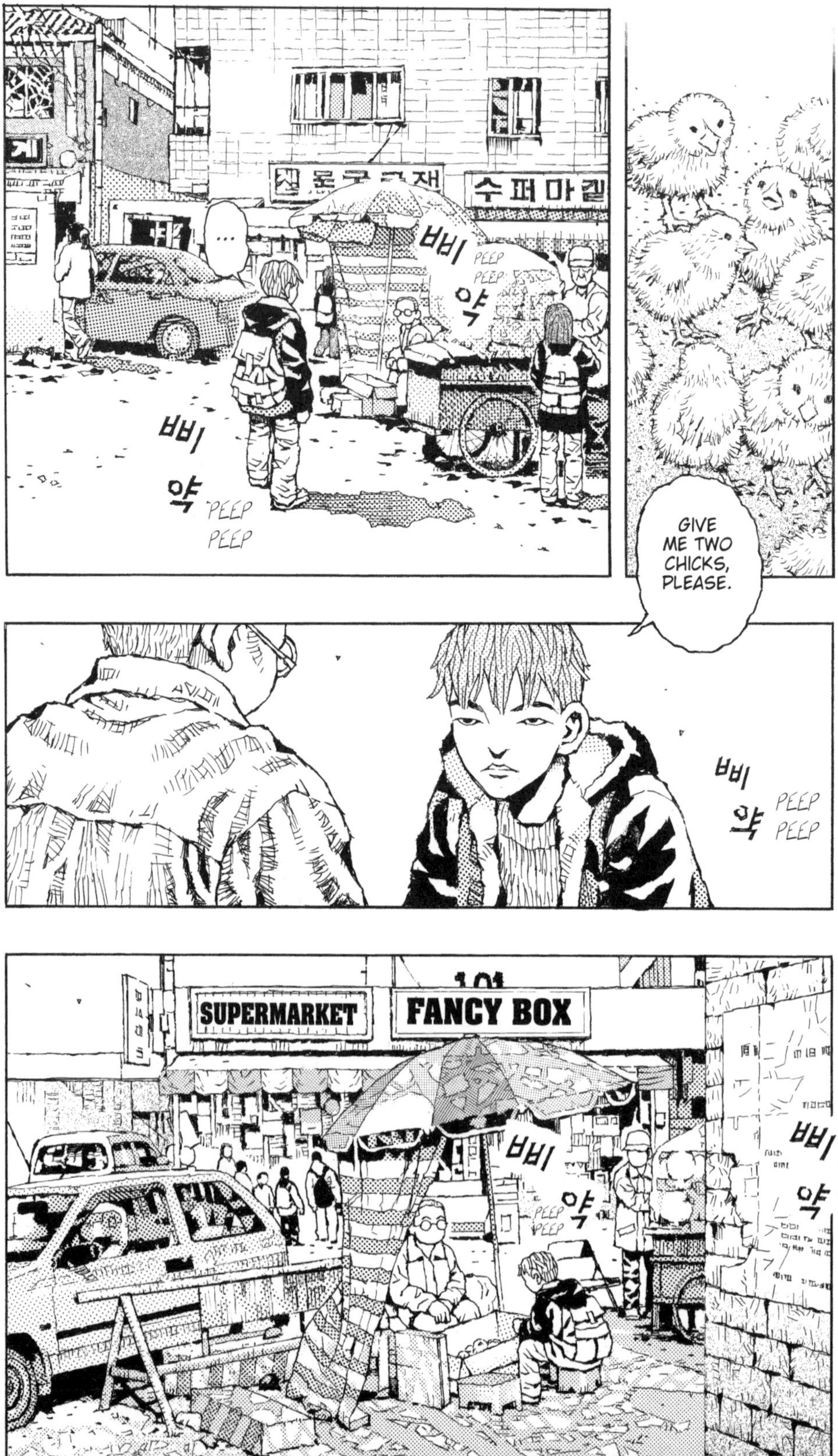

...
삐 약
PEEP PEEP
삐 약
PEEP PEEP
GIVE ME TWO CHICKS, PLEASE.
삐 약
PEEP PEEP
SUPERMARKET
FANCY BOX
삐 약
PEEP PEEP

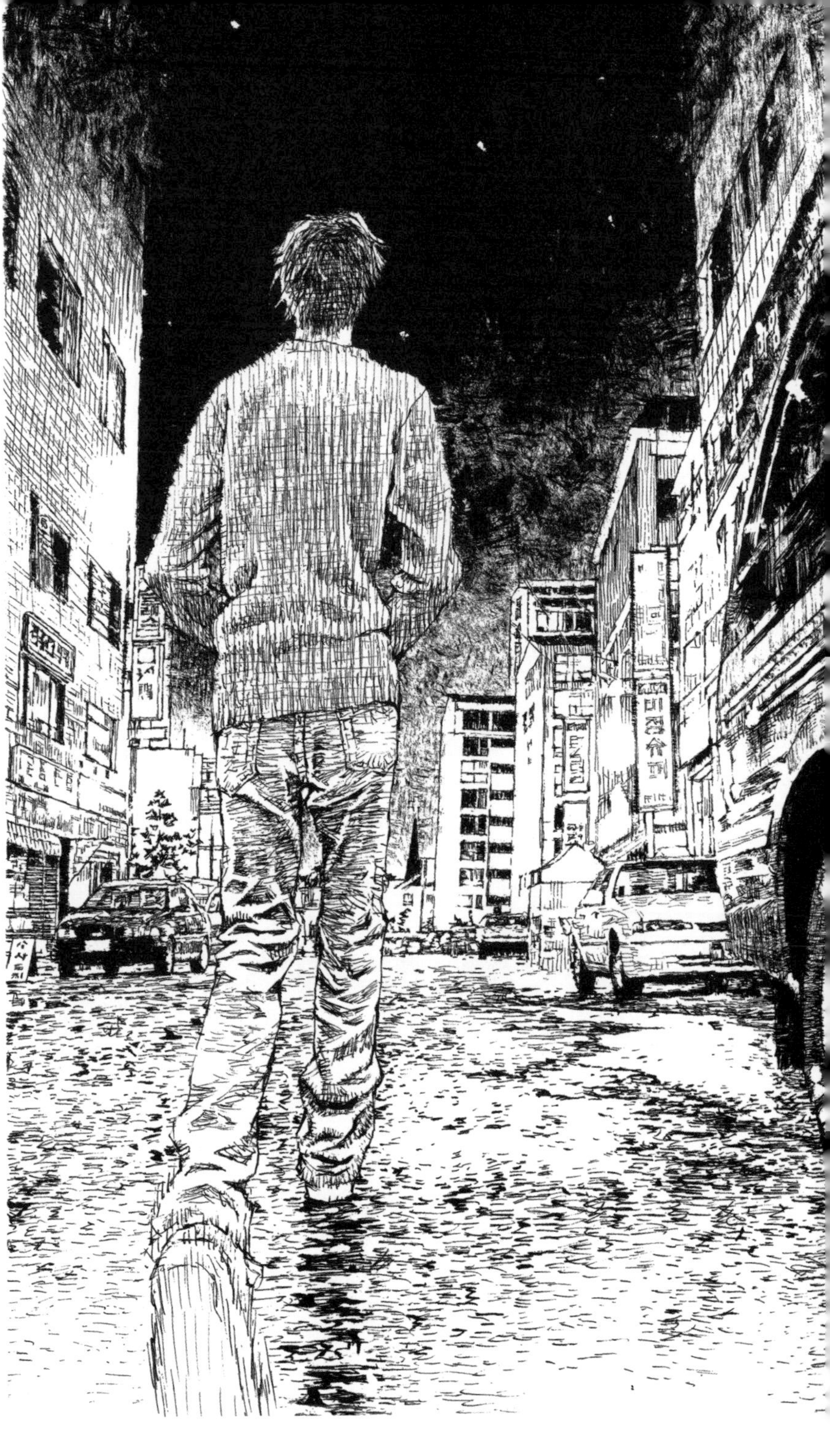

SONG FOR YOU

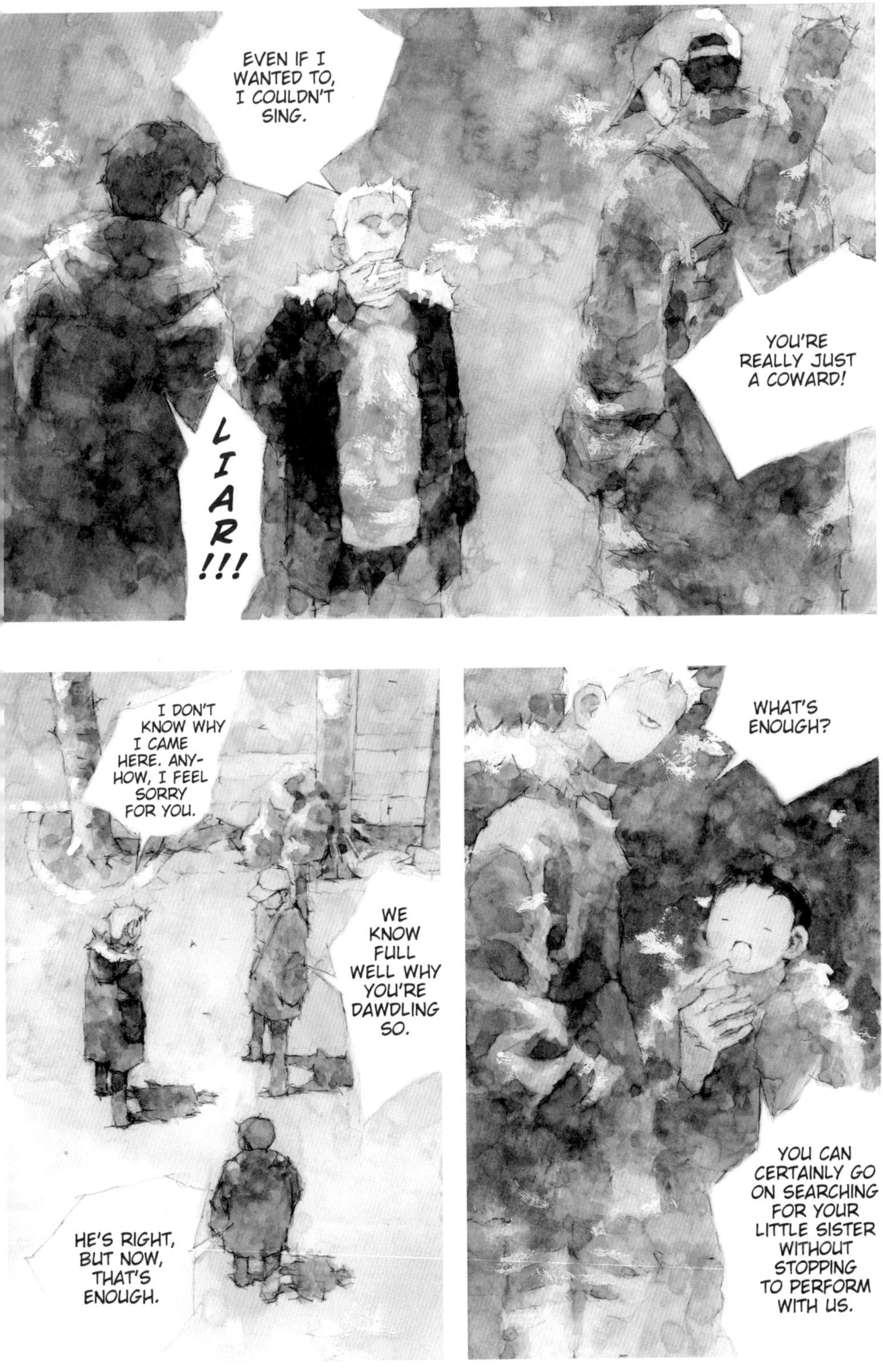
EVEN IF I WANTED TO, I COULDN'T SING.
LIAR!!!
YOU'RE REALLY JUST A COWARD!
I DON'T KNOW WHY I CAME HERE. ANY-HOW, I FEEL SORRY FOR YOU.
WE KNOW FULL WELL WHY YOU'RE DAWDLING SO.
HE'S RIGHT, BUT NOW, THAT'S ENOUGH.
WHAT'S ENOUGH?
YOU CAN CERTAINLY GO ON SEARCHING FOR YOUR LITTLE SISTER WITHOUT STOPPING TO PERFORM WITH US.

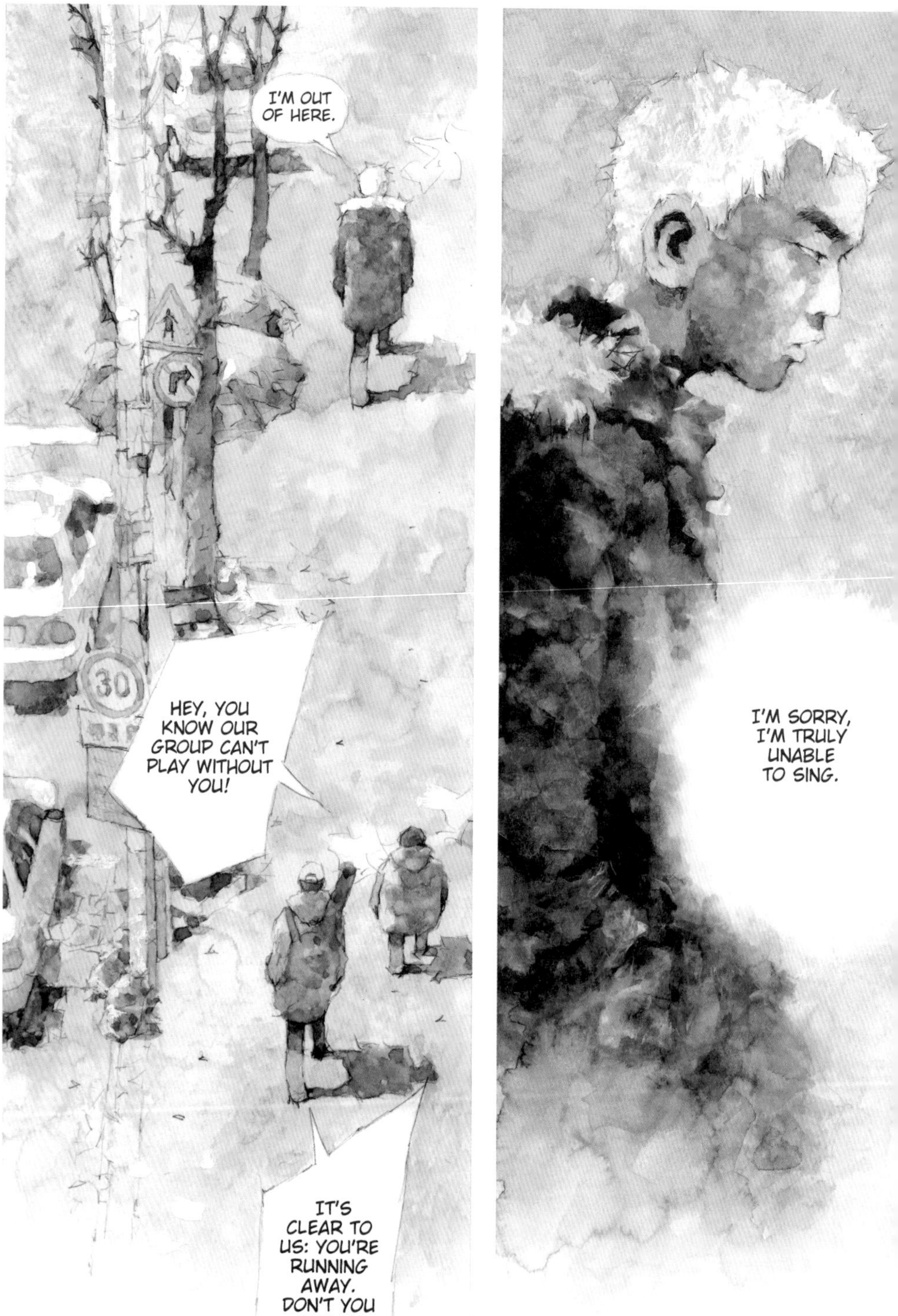
I'M OUT OF HERE.
HEY, YOU KNOW OUR GROUP CAN'T PLAY WITHOUT YOU!
IT'S CLEAR TO US: YOU'RE RUNNING AWAY. DON'T YOU GET IT?
I'M SORRY, I'M TRULY UNABLE TO SING.

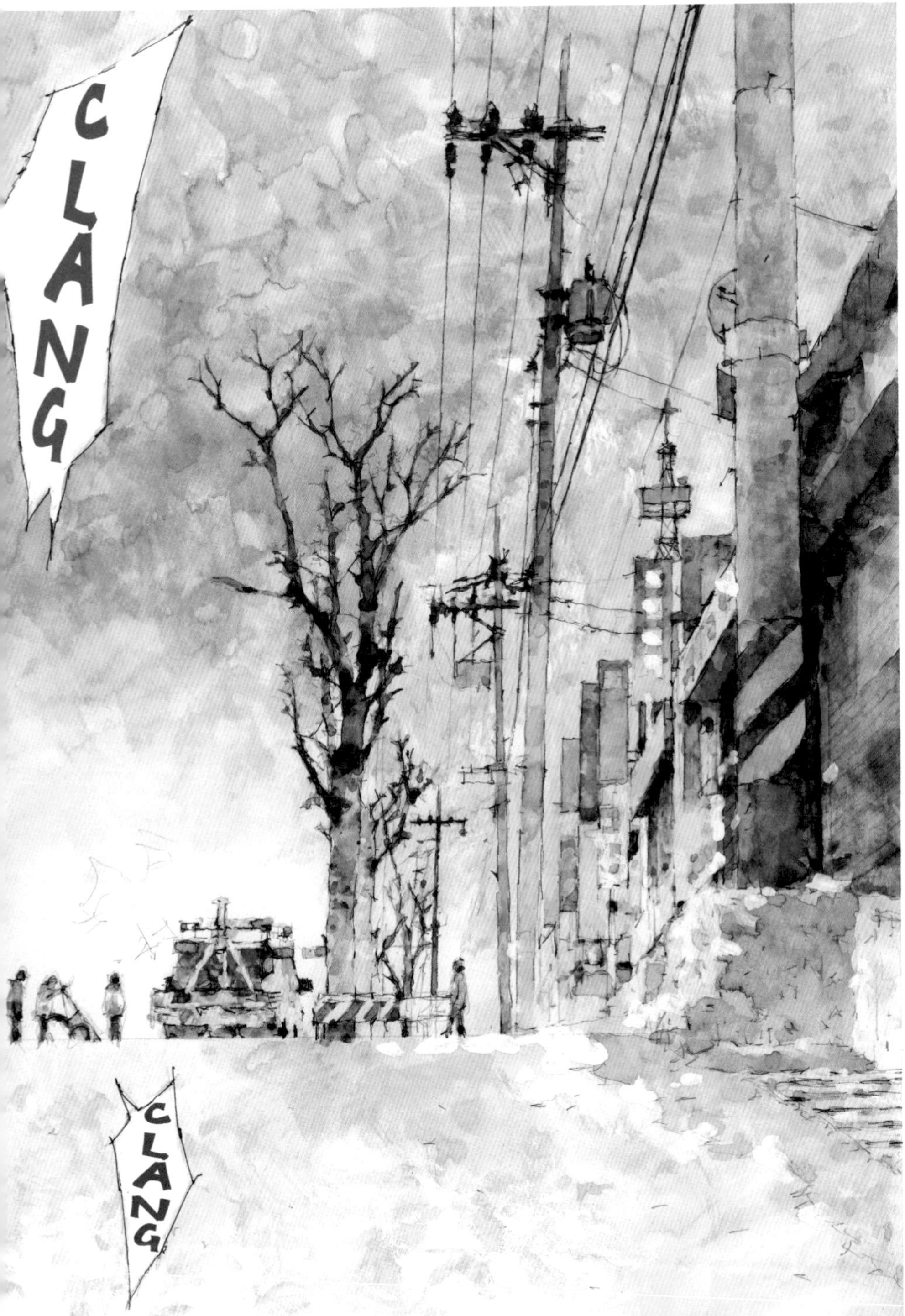
CLANG
CLANG

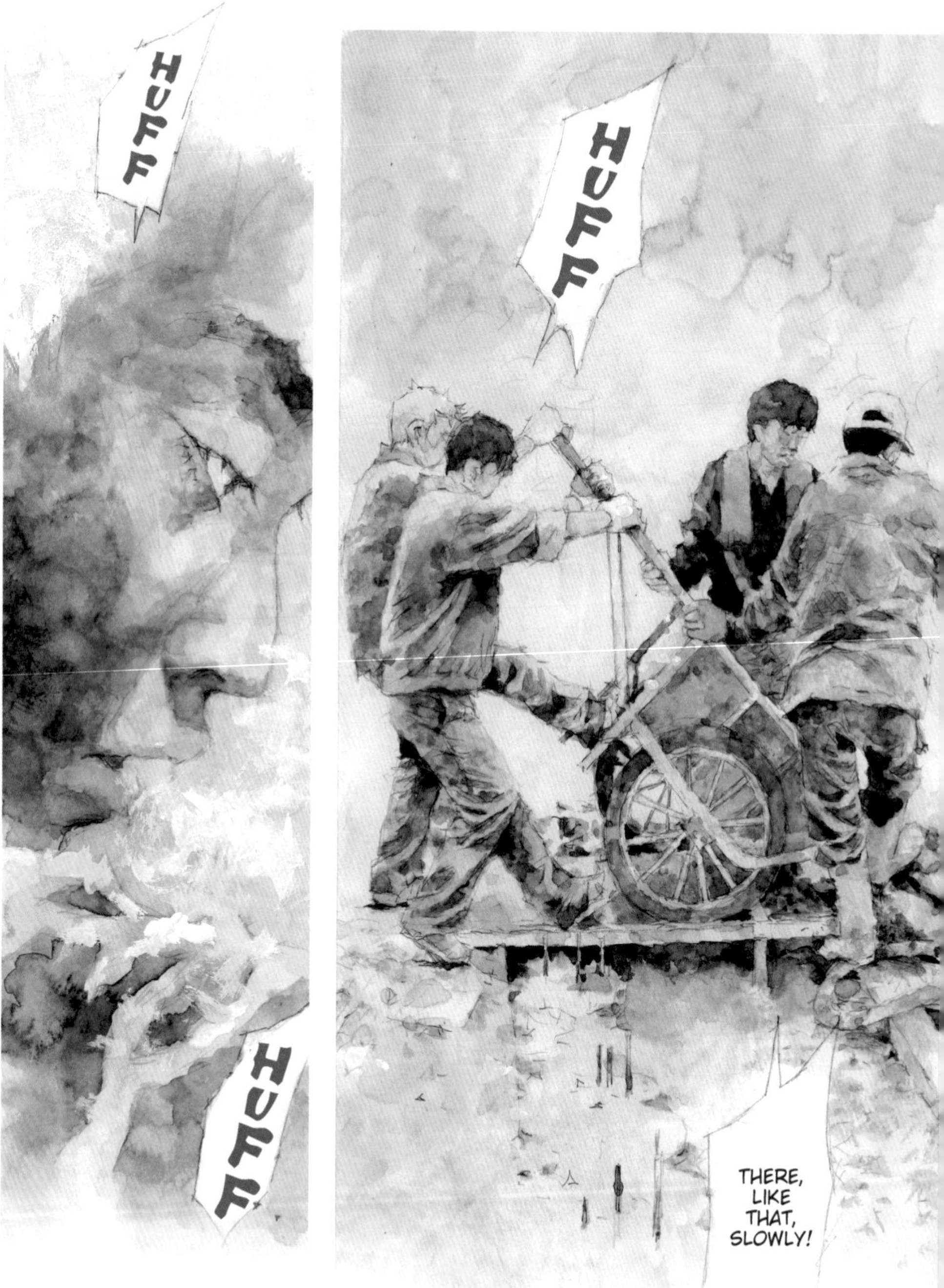
HUFF
HUFF
HUFF
THERE, LIKE THAT, SLOWLY!

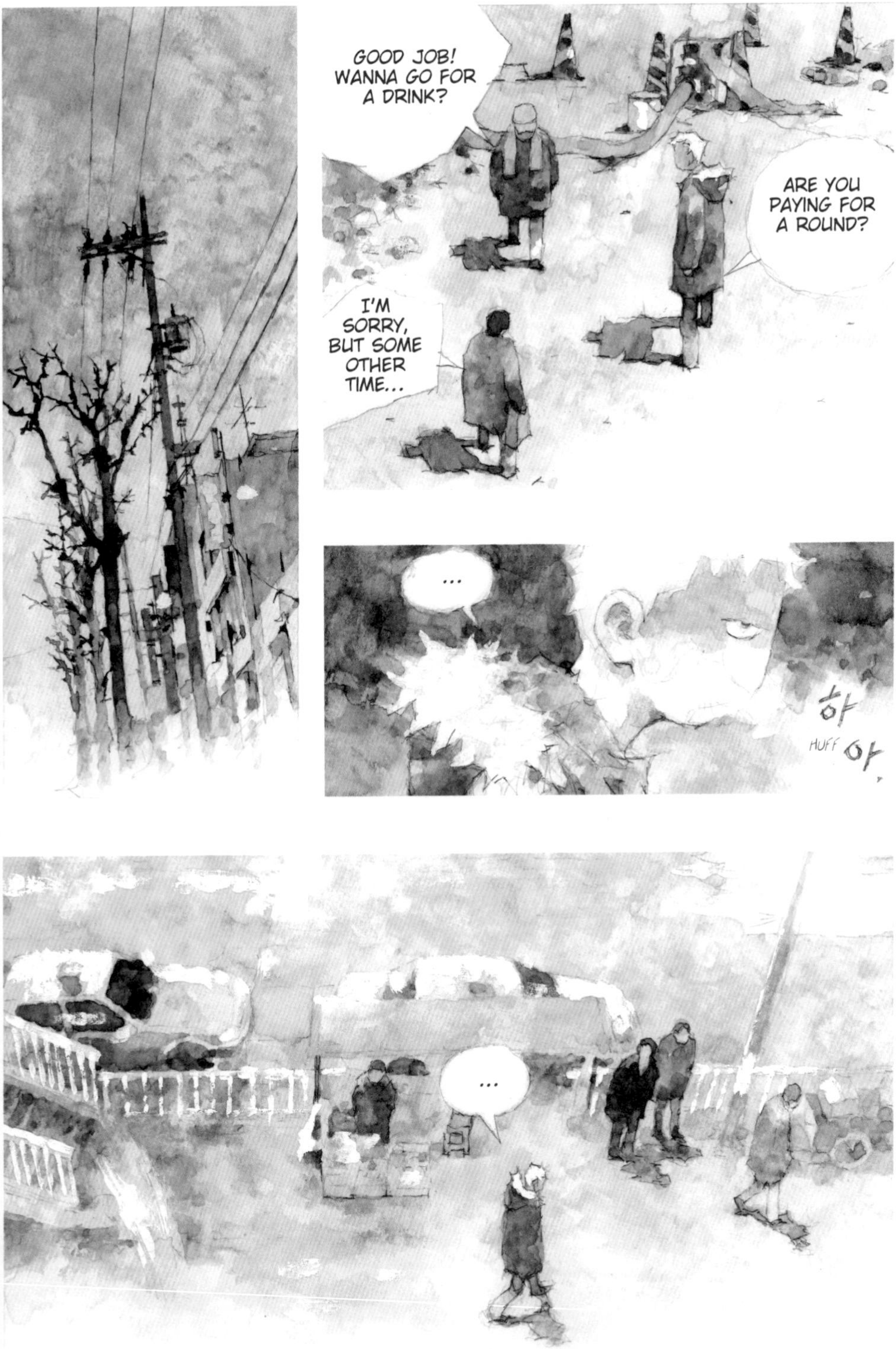
GOOD JOB! WANNA GO FOR A DRINK?
ARE YOU PAYING FOR A ROUND?
I'M SORRY, BUT SOME OTHER TIME...
...
하
HUFF 아
...

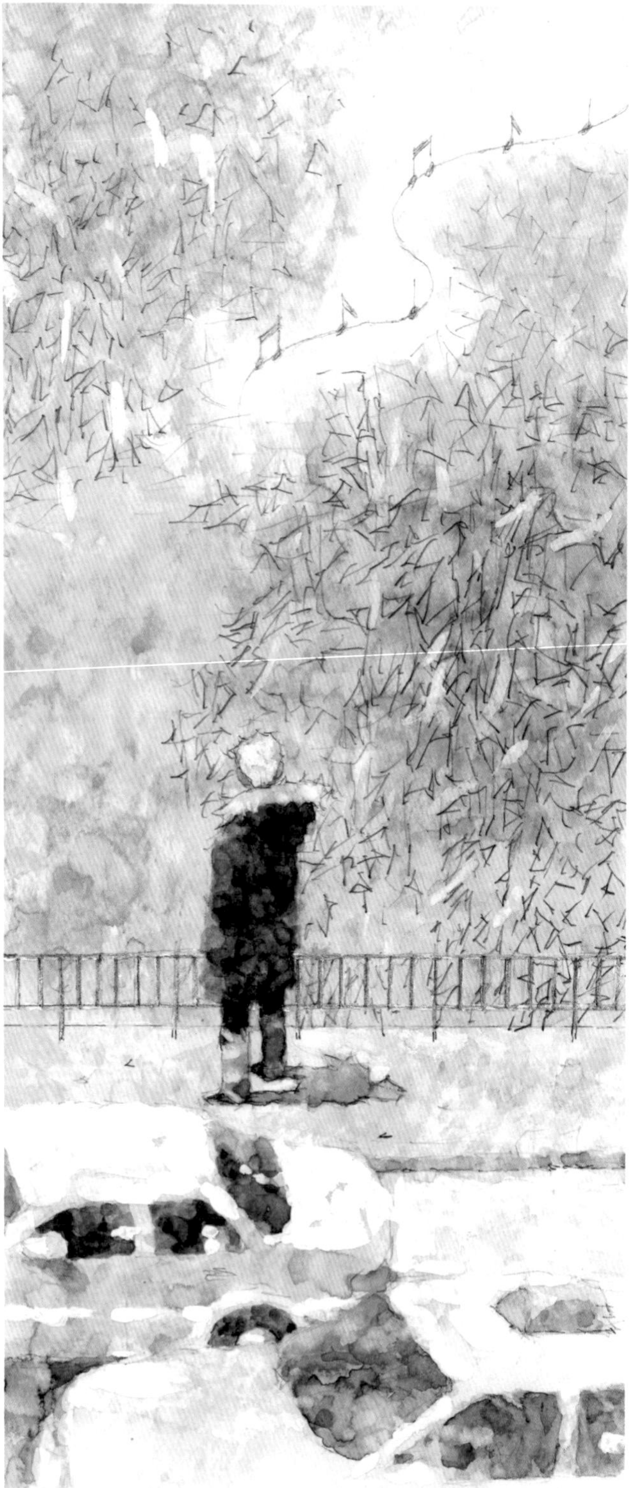

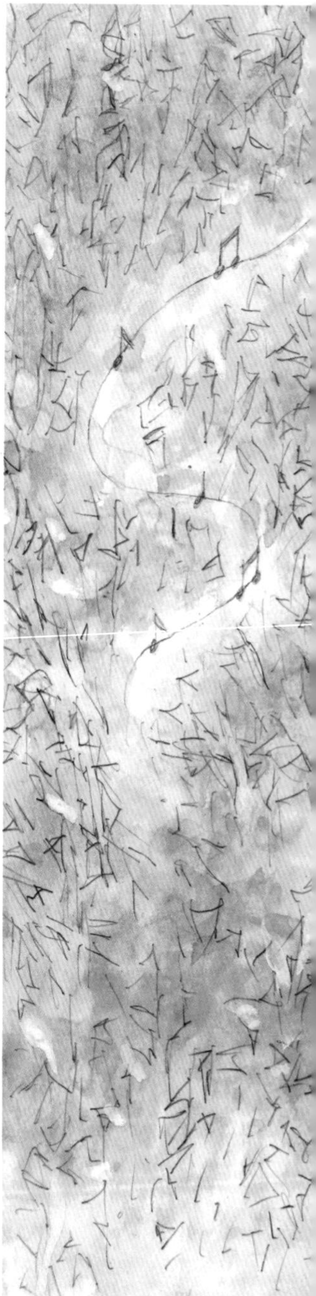

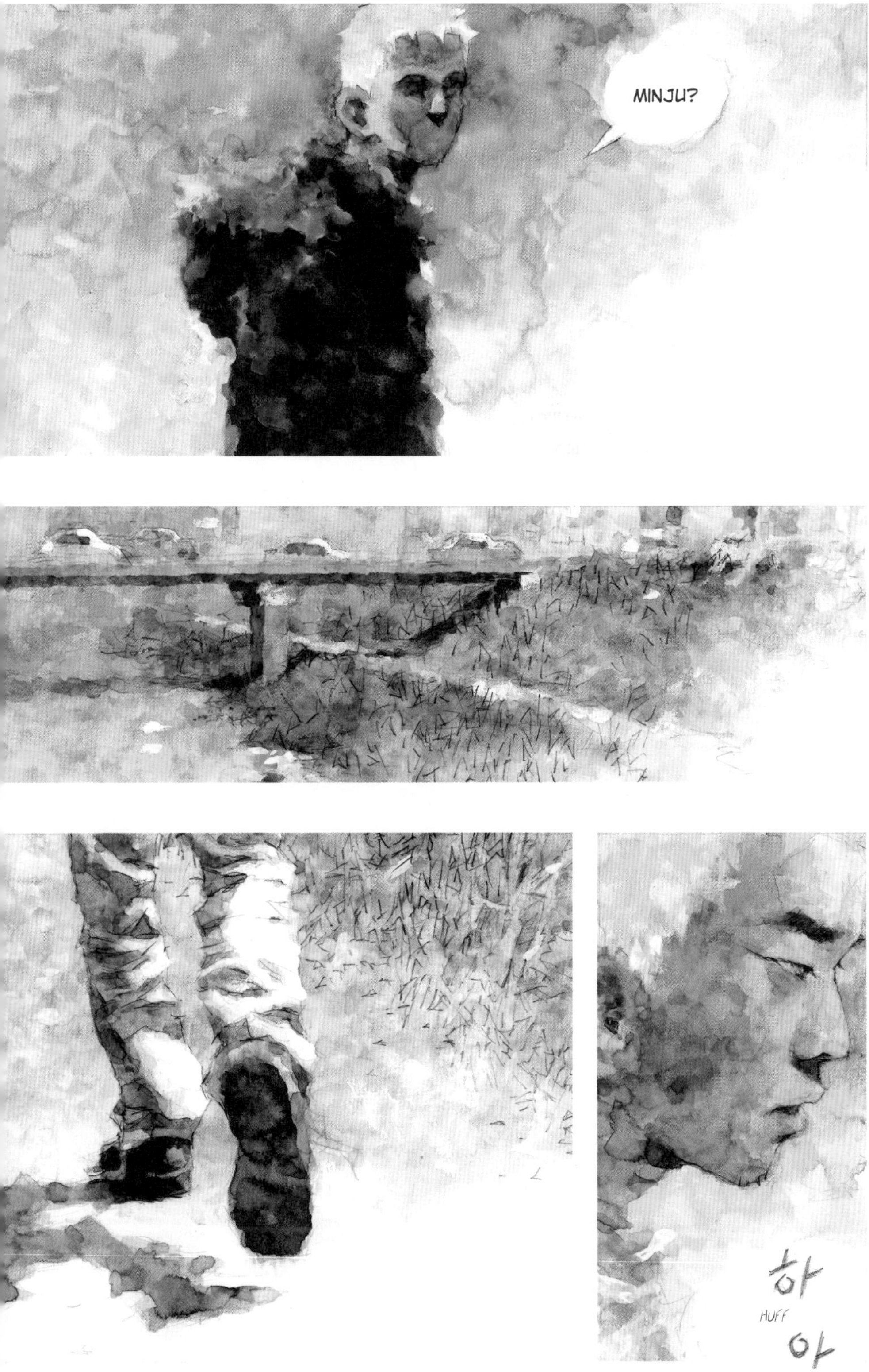
MINJU?
하
HUFF
아

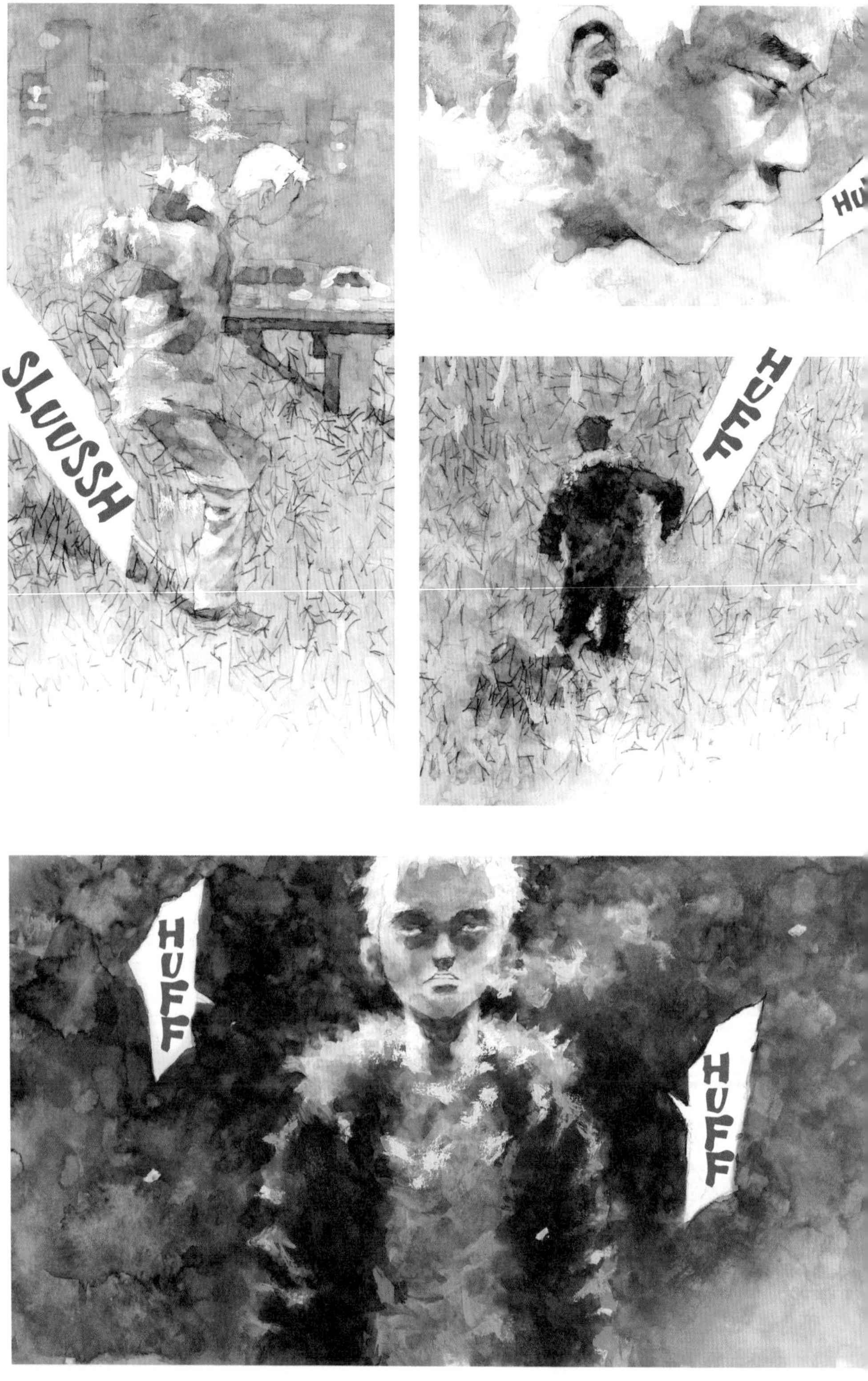
SLUUSSH
HU
HUFF
HUFF
HUFF

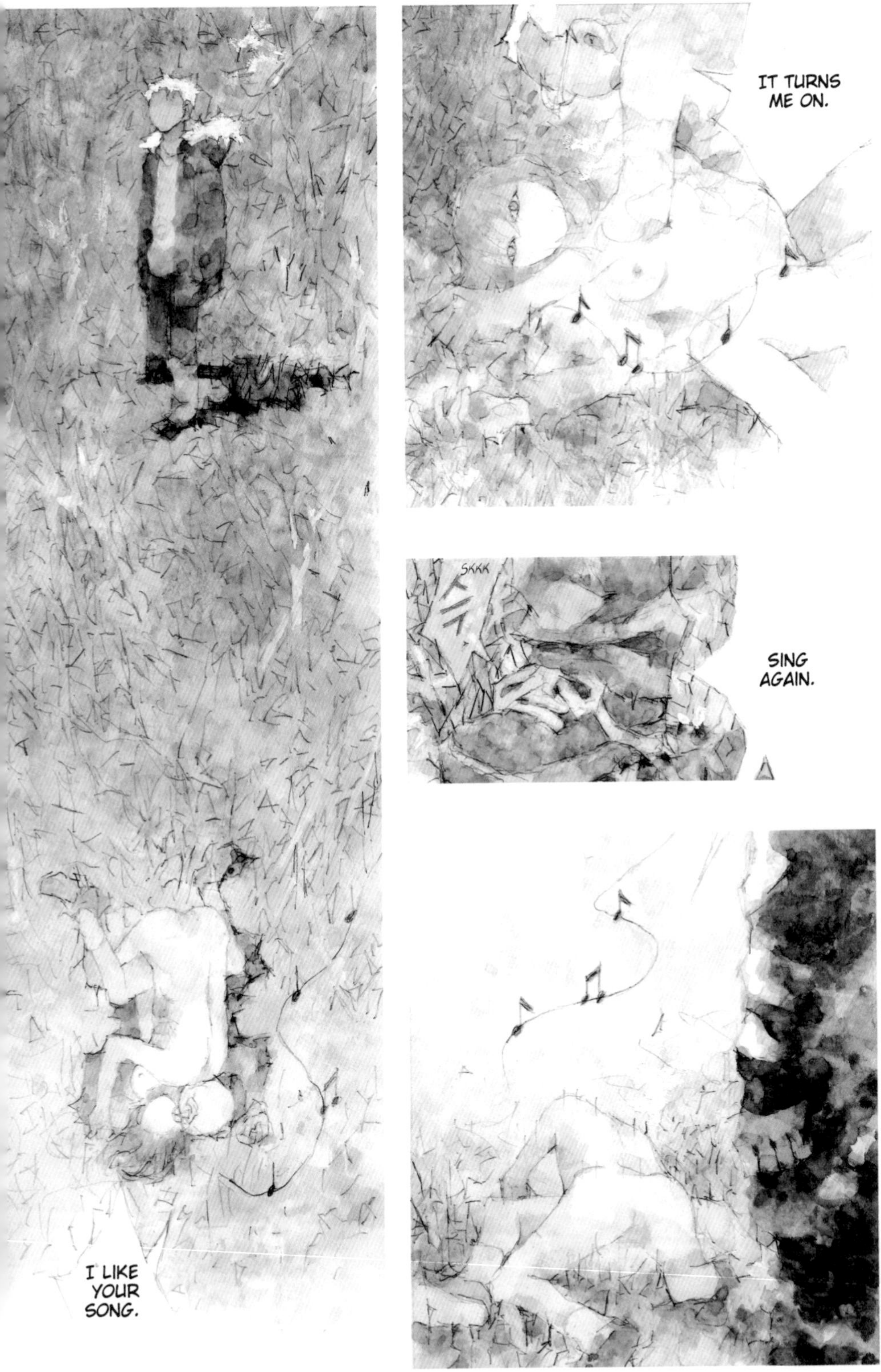
I LIKE YOUR SONG.
IT TURNS ME ON.
SKKK
SING AGAIN.

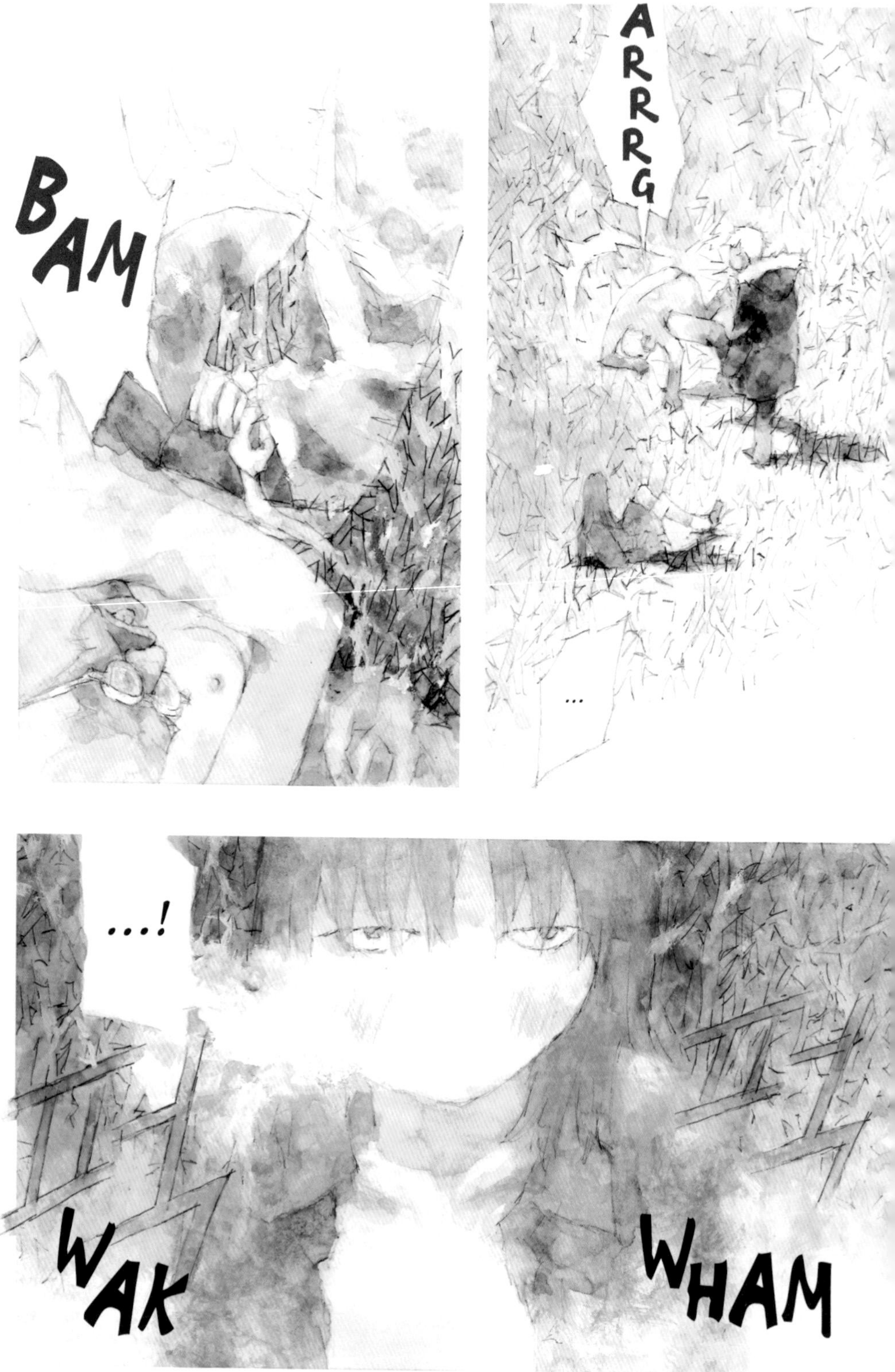
ARRRG
...
BAM
...!
WHAM
WAK

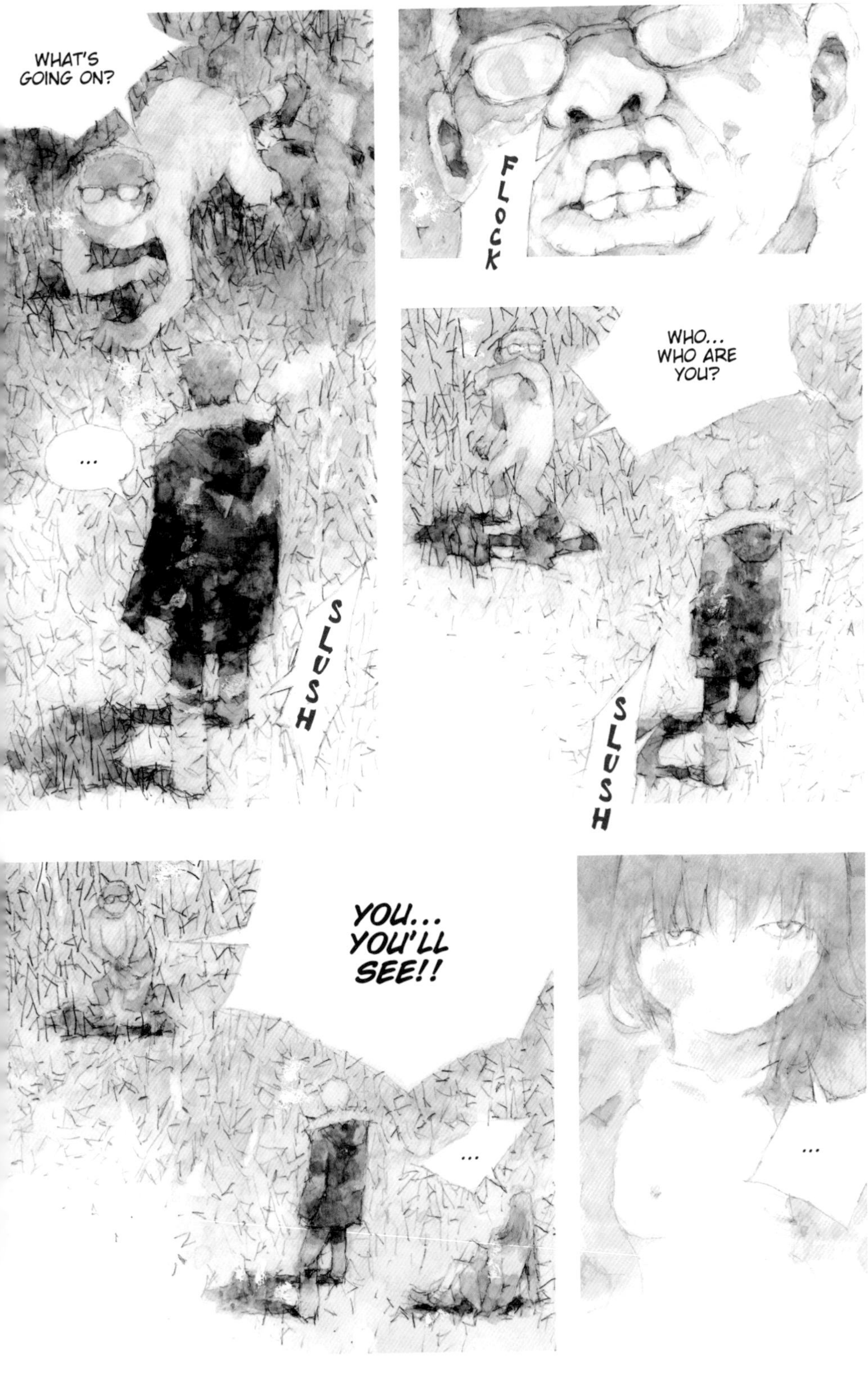
WHAT'S GOING ON?
...
SLUSH
FLOCK
WHO... WHO ARE YOU?
SLUSH
YOU... YOU'LL SEE!!
...
...

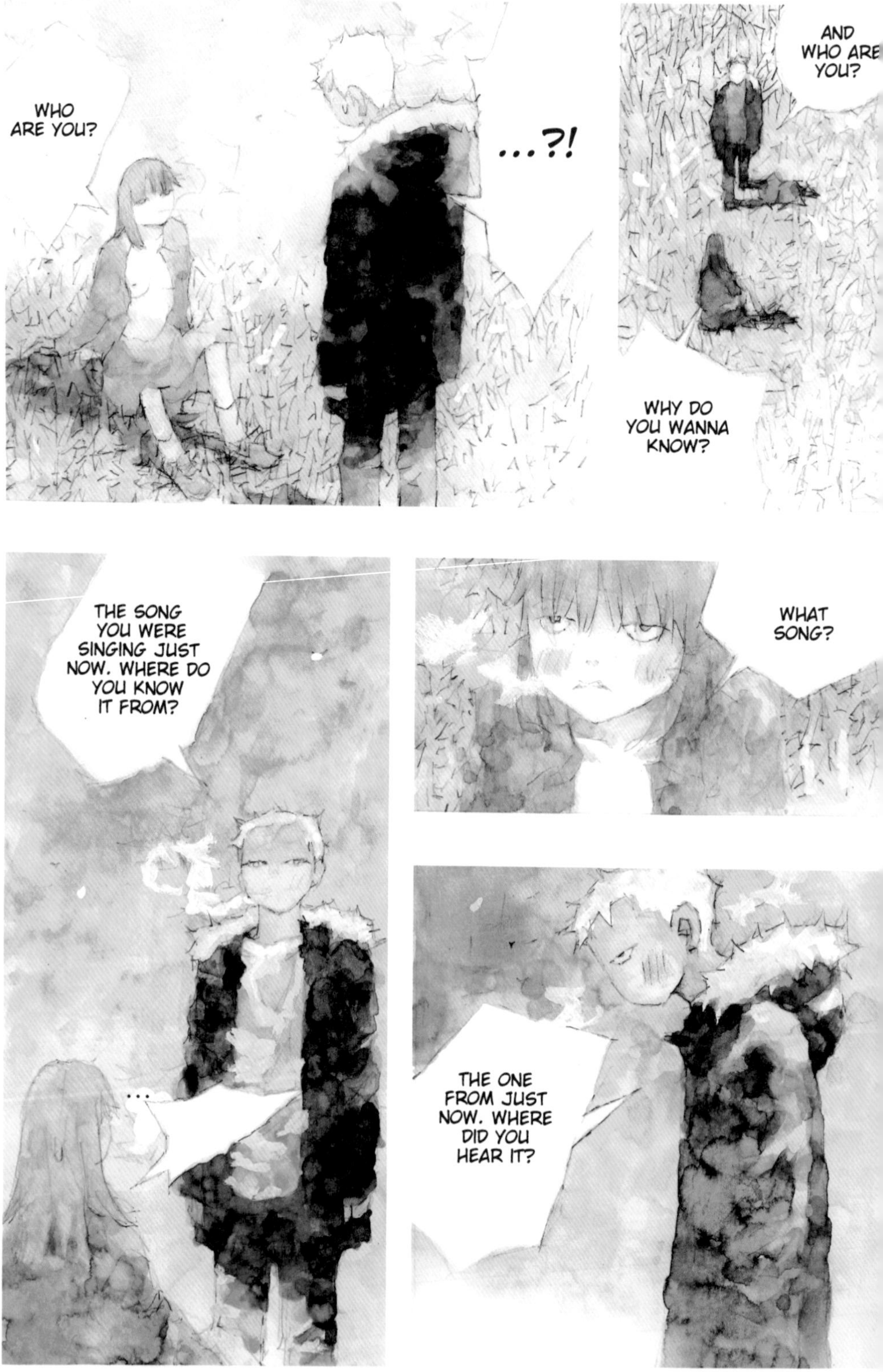
WHO ARE YOU?
...?!
AND WHO ARE YOU?
WHY DO YOU WANNA KNOW?
THE SONG YOU WERE SINGING JUST NOW. WHERE DO YOU KNOW IT FROM?
...
WHAT SONG?
THE ONE FROM JUST NOW. WHERE DID YOU HEAR IT?

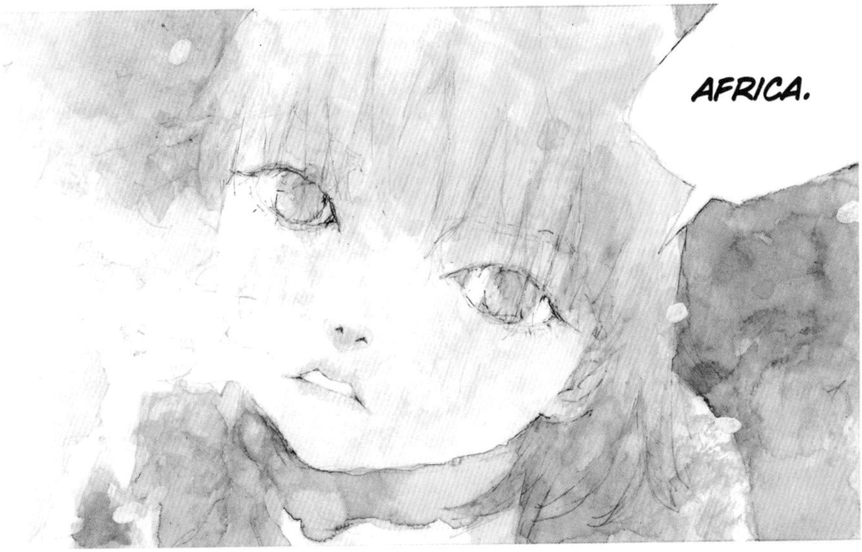
AFRICA.

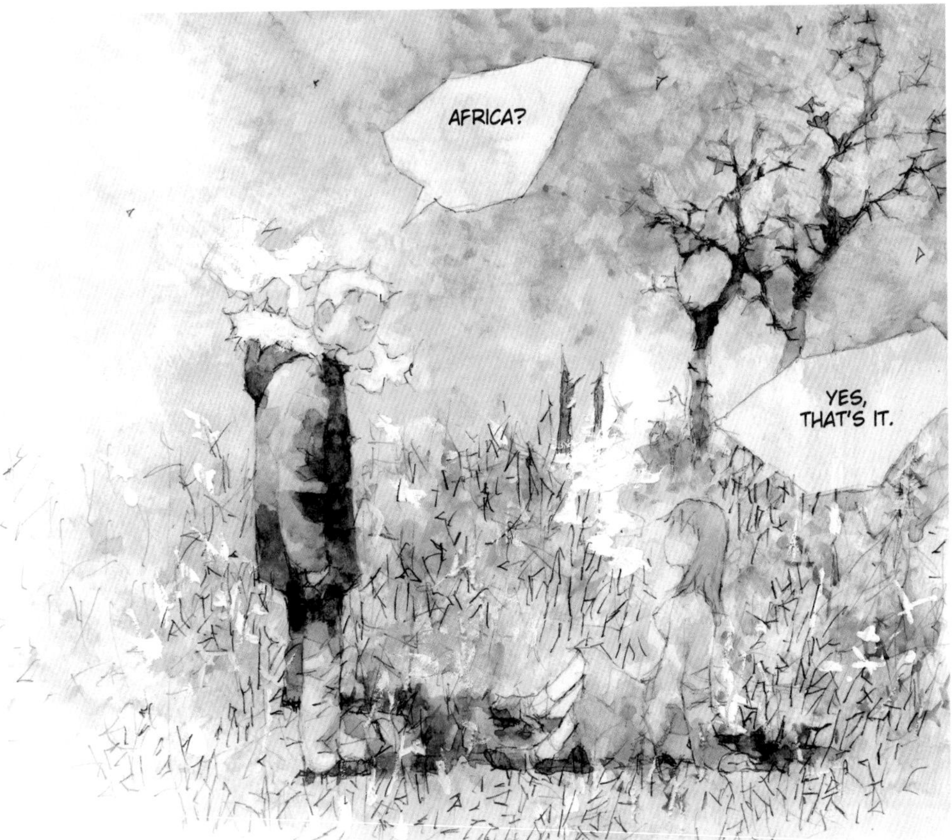
AFRICA?
YES, THAT'S IT.

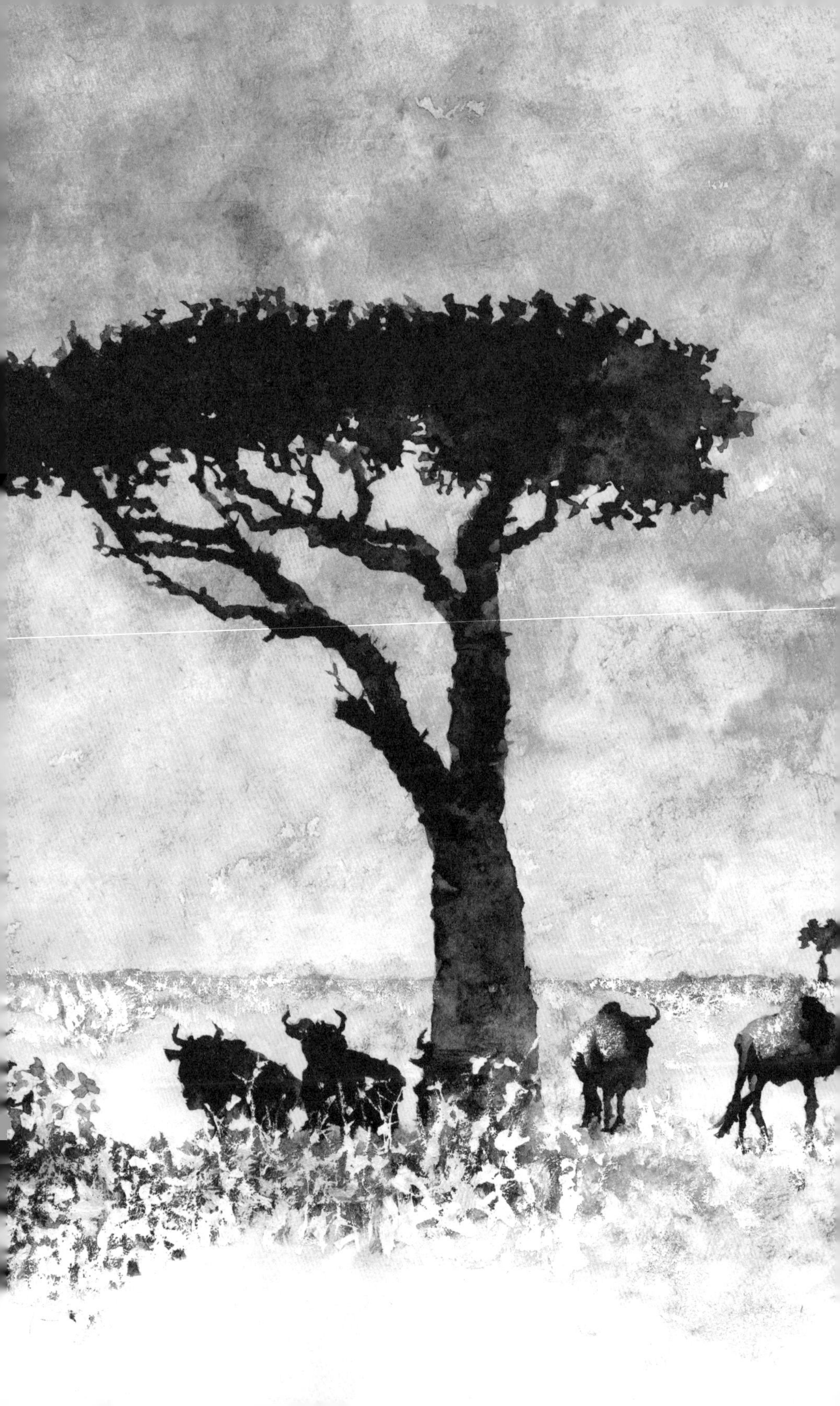

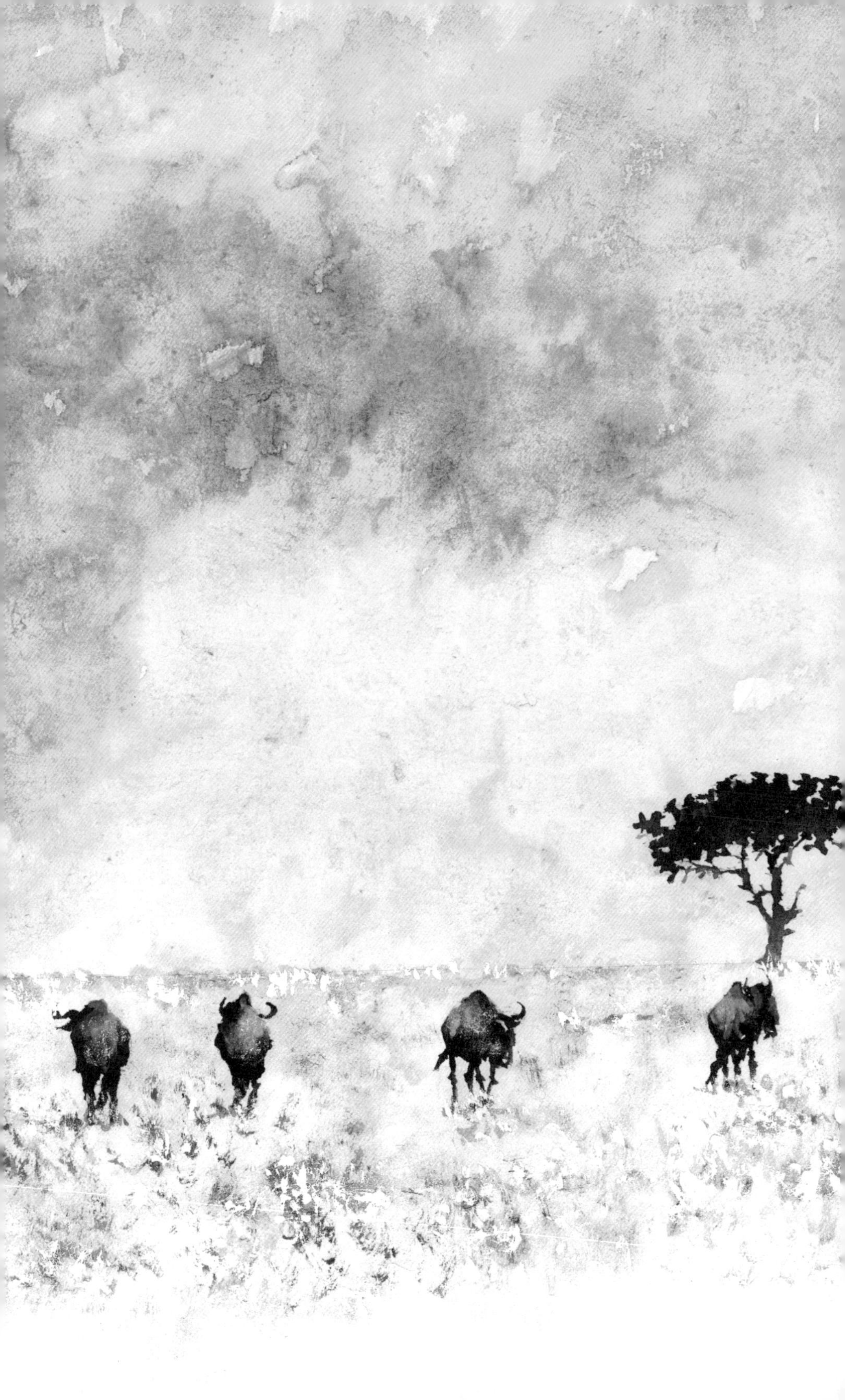

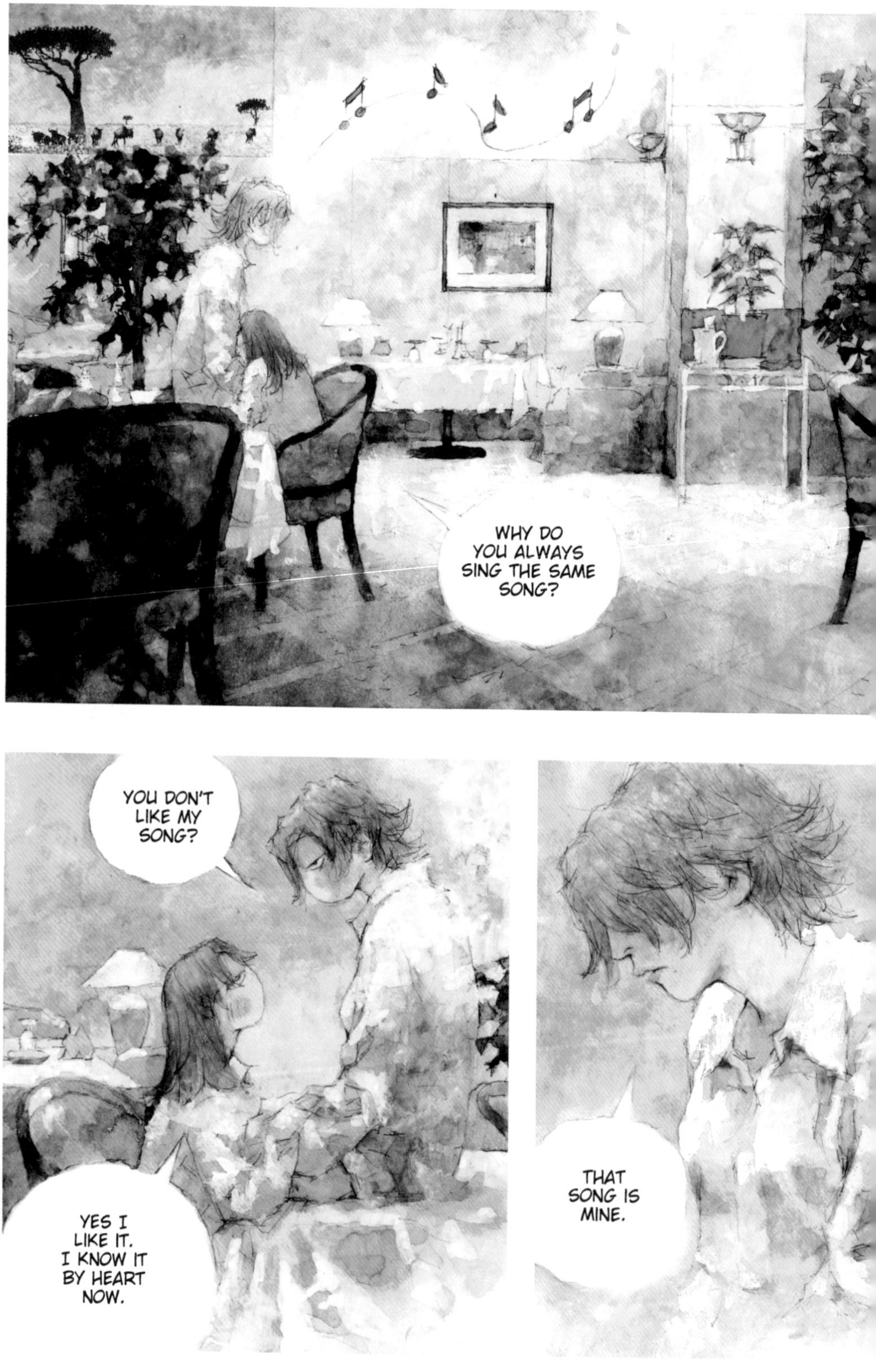
WHY DO YOU ALWAYS SING THE SAME SONG?
YOU DON'T LIKE MY SONG?
YES I LIKE IT. I KNOW IT BY HEART NOW.
THAT SONG IS MINE.

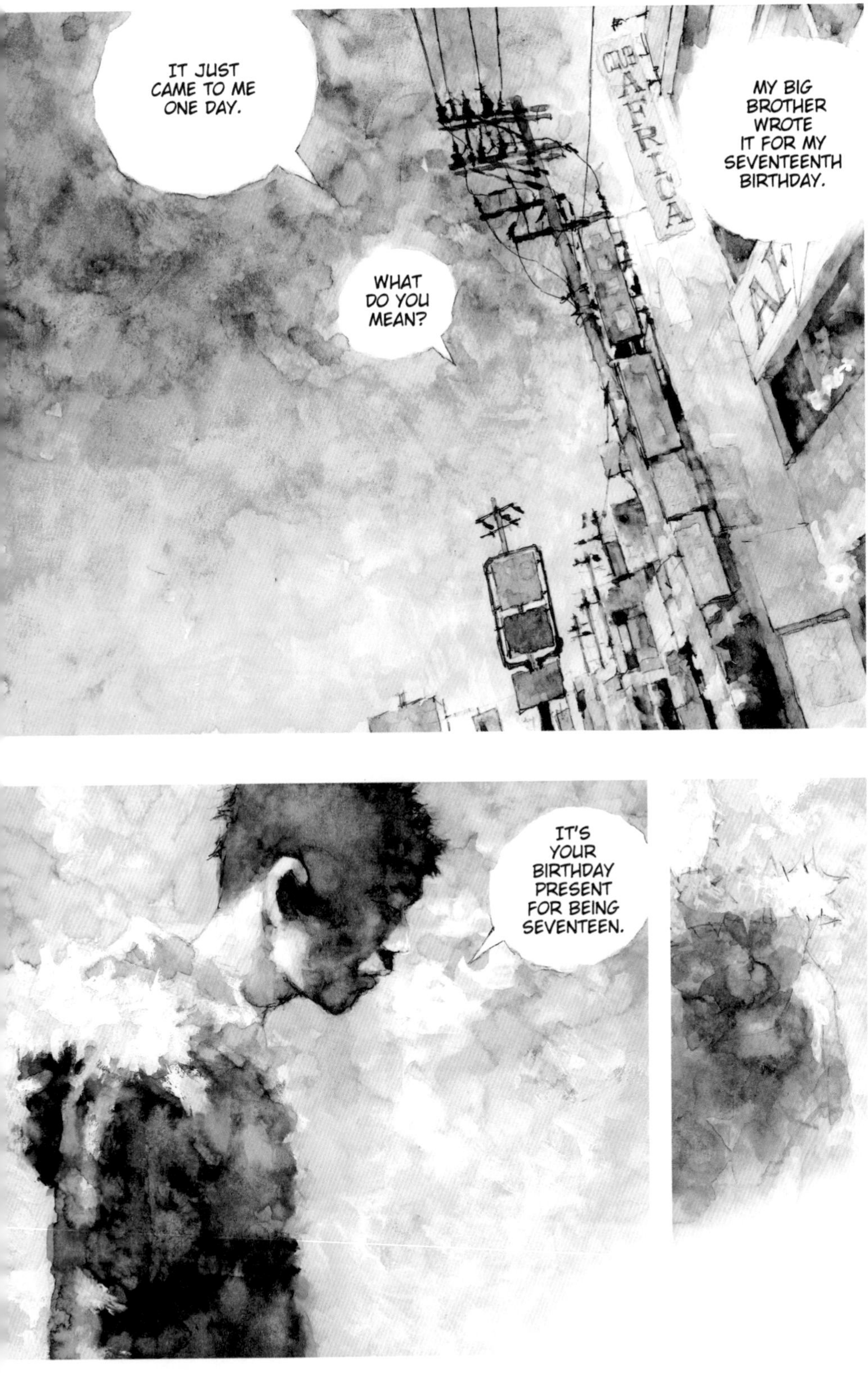
IT JUST CAME TO ME ONE DAY.
WHAT DO YOU MEAN?
AFRICA
MY BIG BROTHER WROTE IT FOR MY SEVENTEENTH BIRTHDAY.
IT'S YOUR BIRTHDAY PRESENT FOR BEING SEVENTEEN.

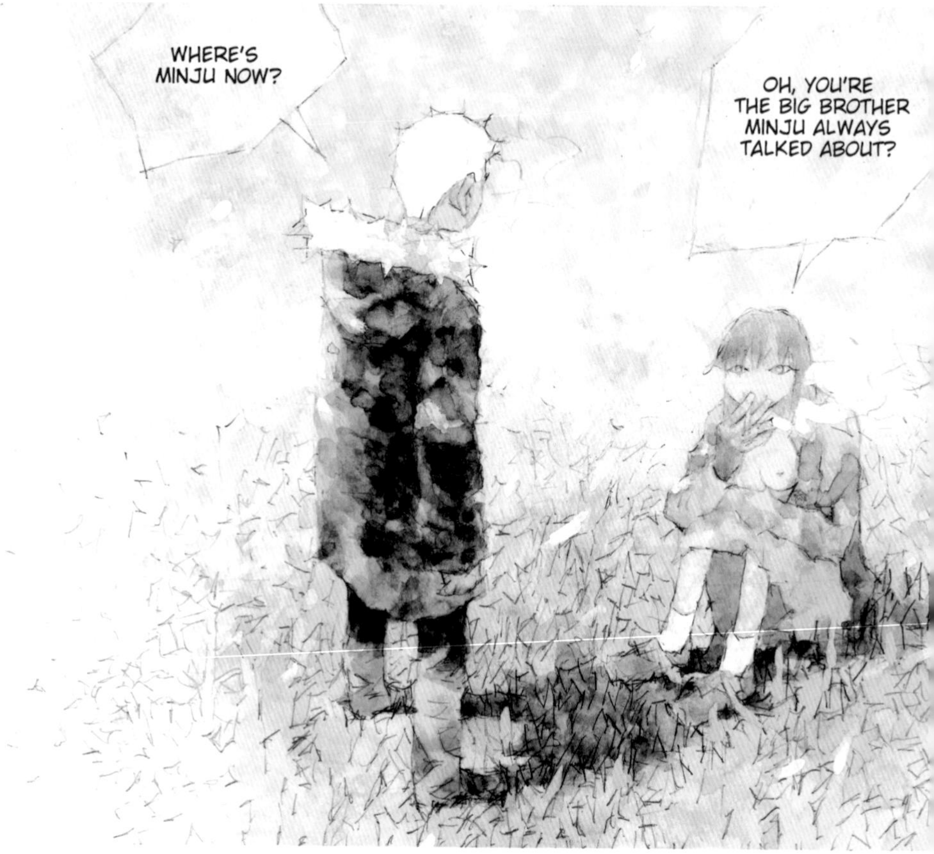
WHERE'S MINJU NOW?
OH, YOU'RE THE BIG BROTHER MINJU ALWAYS TALKED ABOUT?

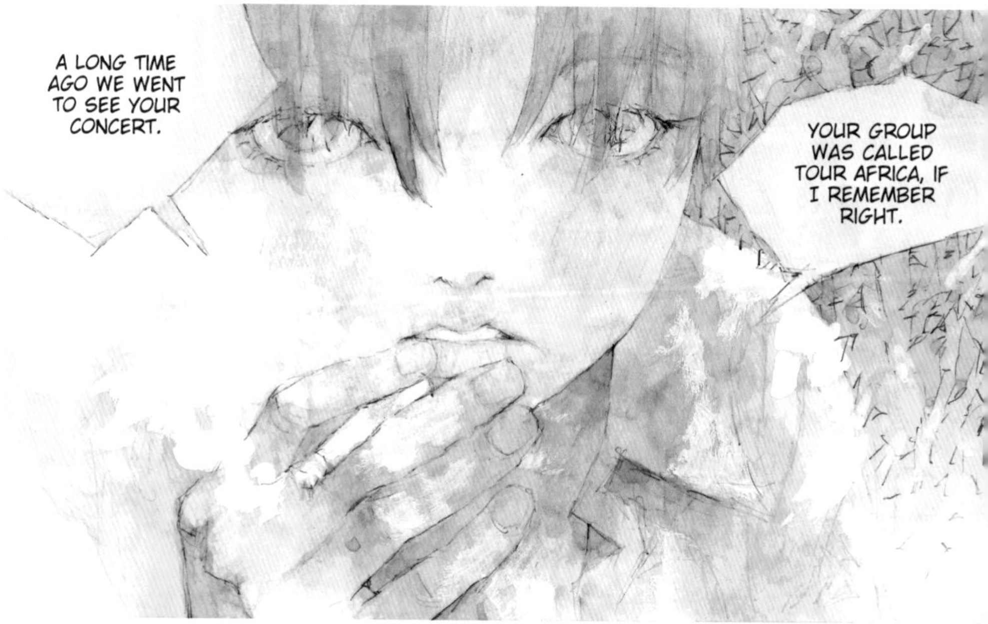
A LONG TIME AGO WE WENT TO SEE YOUR CONCERT.
YOUR GROUP WAS CALLED TOUR AFRICA, IF I REMEMBER RIGHT.

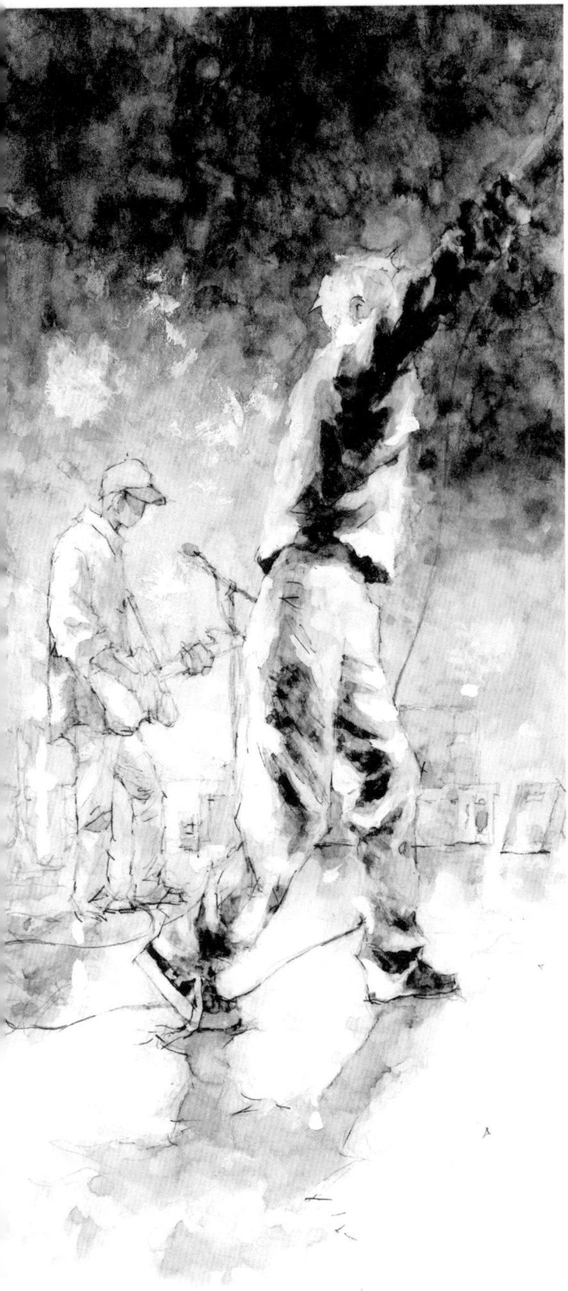

I DON'T REALLY RECALL
THE SONGS,

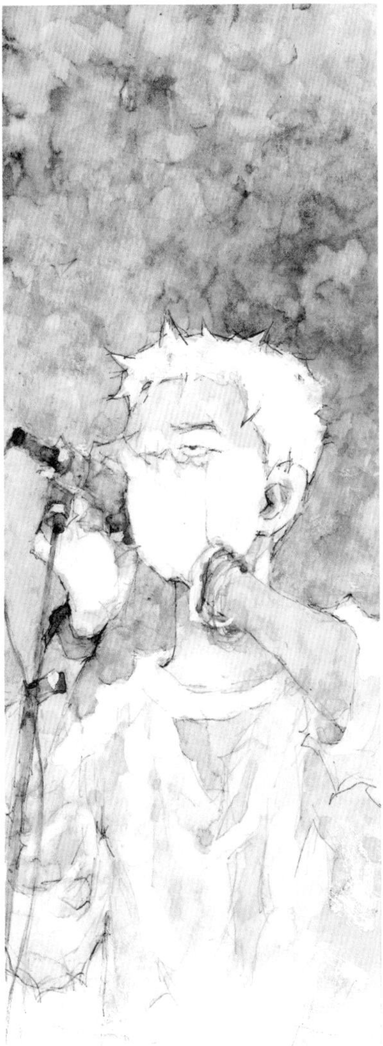

BUT I CAN STILL SEE
MINJU'S FACE. SHE ONLY
HAD EYES FOR YOU.

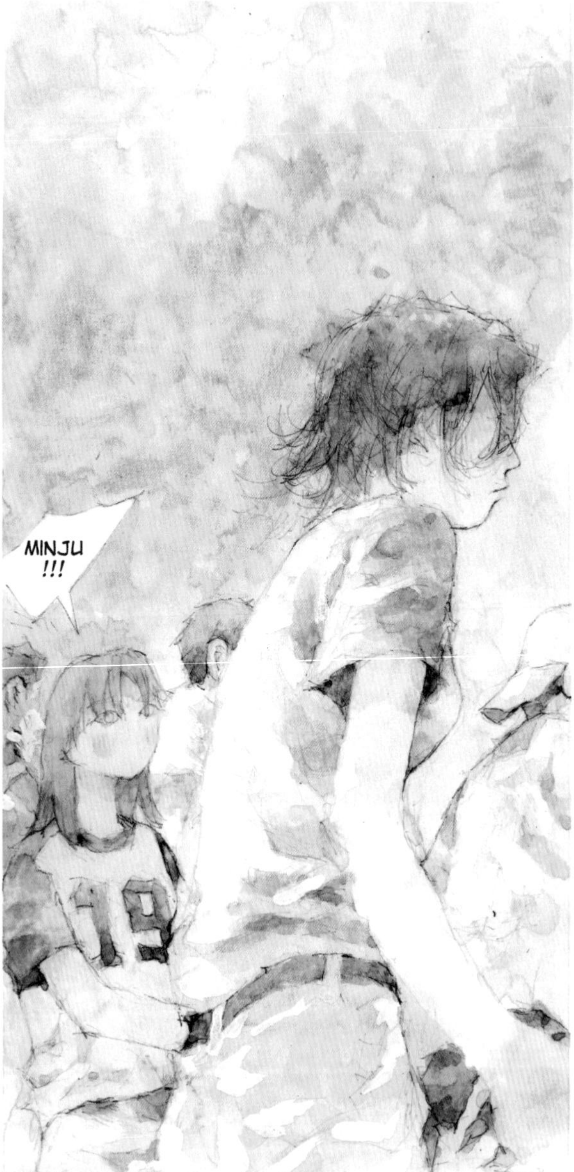
MINJU
!!!

THE POOR THING...
SHE HAD TEARS
IN HER EYES.

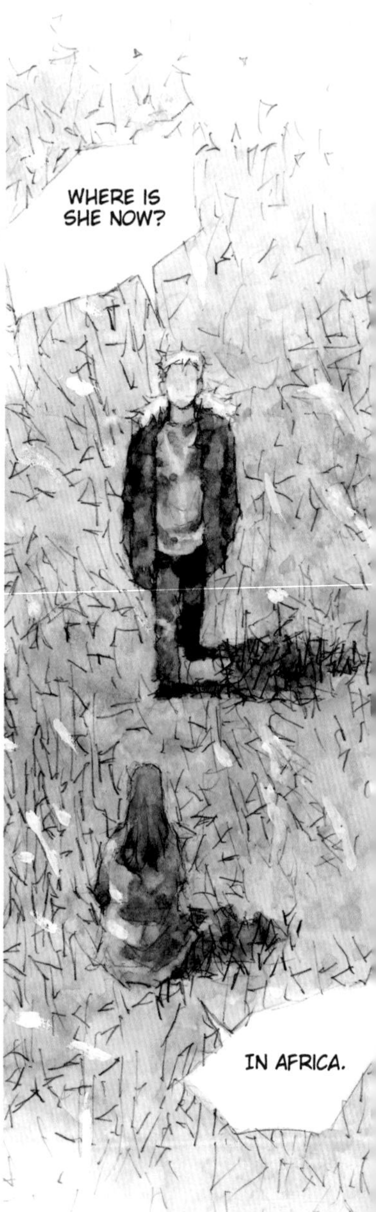
WHERE IS
SHE NOW?
IN AFRICA.

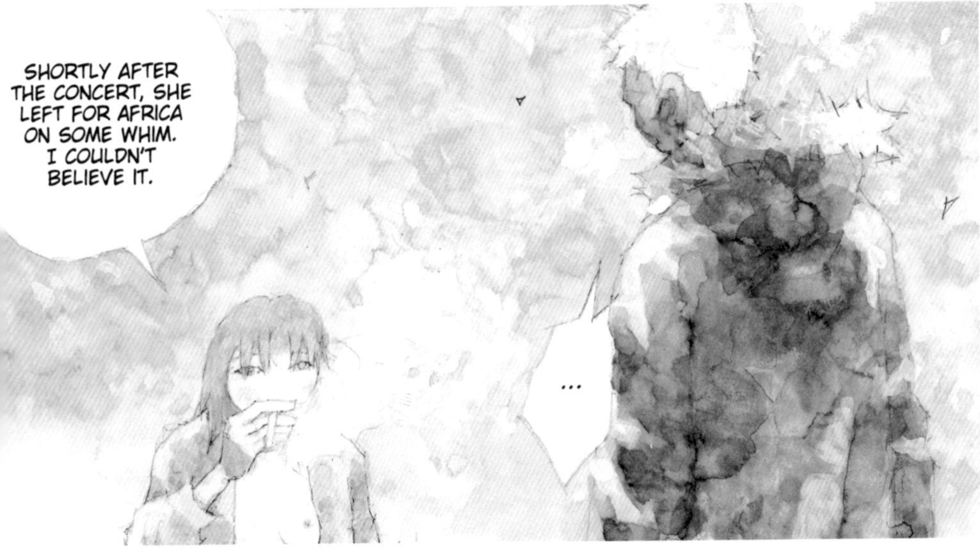
SHORTLY AFTER THE CONCERT, SHE LEFT FOR AFRICA ON SOME WHIM. I COULDN'T BELIEVE IT.
...

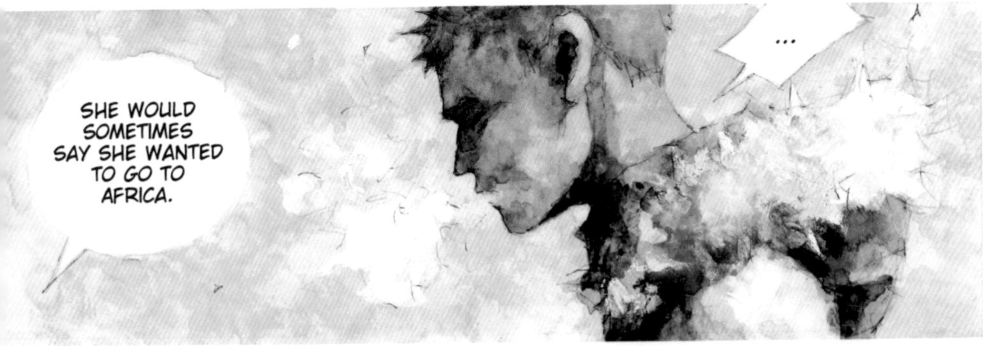
SHE WOULD SOMETIMES SAY SHE WANTED TO GO TO AFRICA.
...

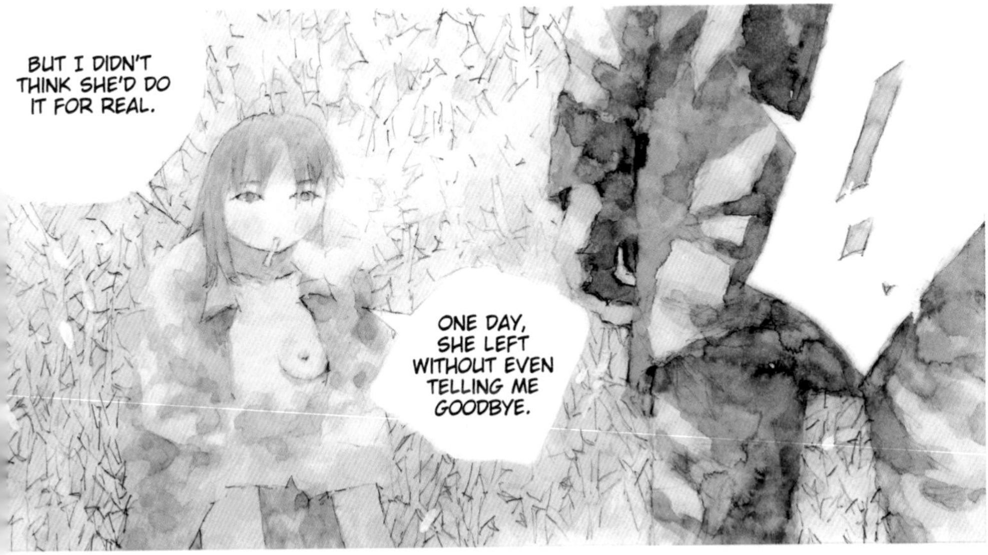
BUT I DIDN'T THINK SHE'D DO IT FOR REAL.
ONE DAY, SHE LEFT WITHOUT EVEN TELLING ME GOODBYE.

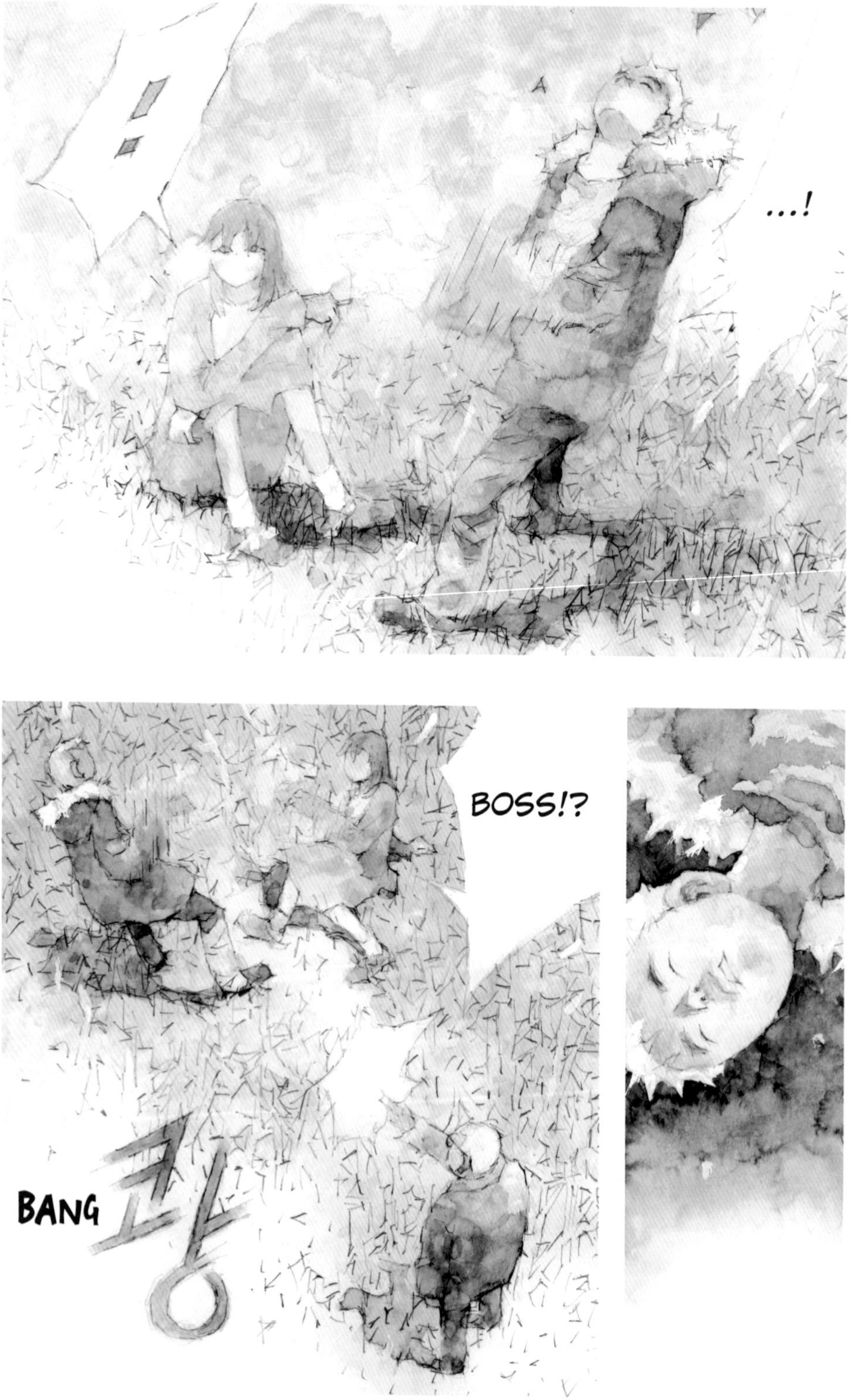
...!
BOSS!?
BANG

YOU
SEE
THAT?

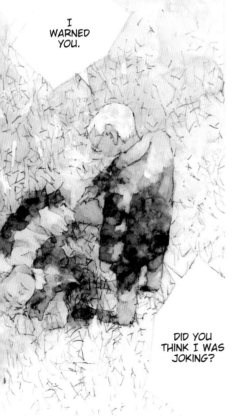

I
WARNED
YOU.

DID YOU
THINK I WAS
JOKING?

WHERE DID
YOU FIND
THAT GUN?

SHUT
UP!!!

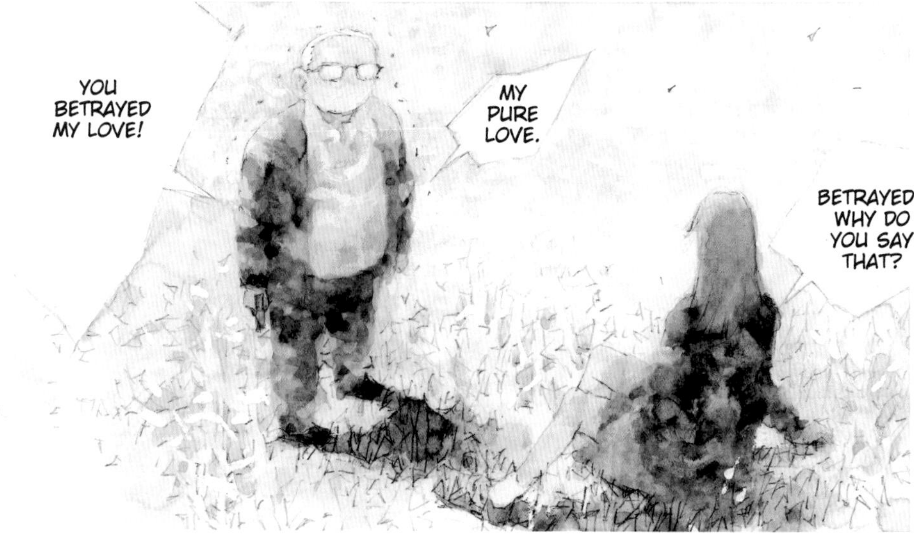
YOU BETRAYED MY LOVE!
MY PURE LOVE.
BETRAYED? WHY DO YOU SAY THAT?

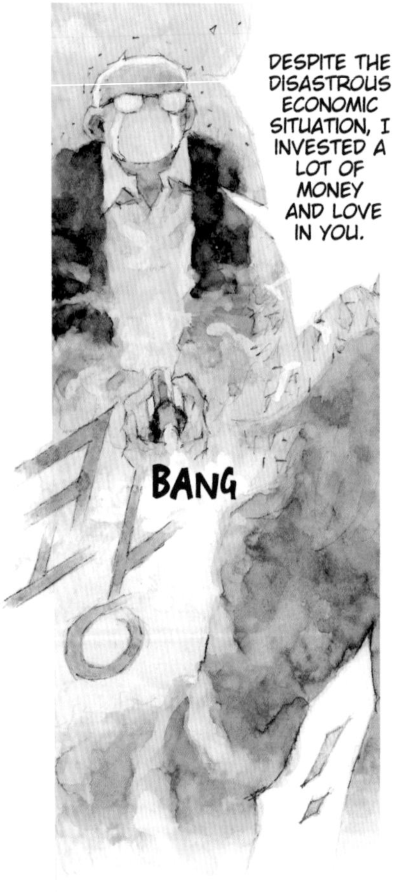
DESPITE THE DISASTROUS ECONOMIC SITUATION, I INVESTED A LOT OF MONEY AND LOVE IN YOU.
BANG

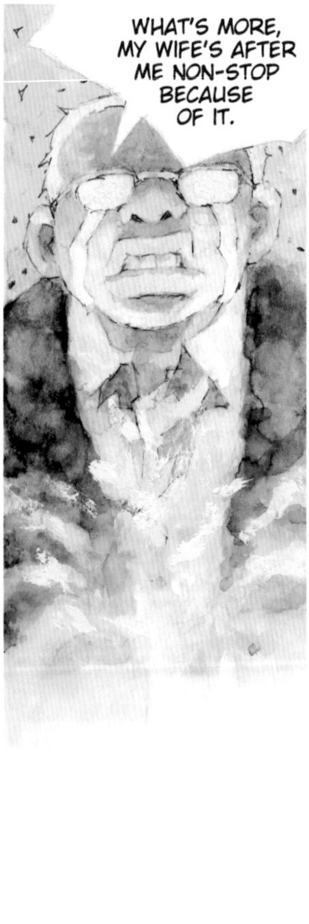
WHAT'S MORE, MY WIFE'S AFTER ME NON-STOP BECAUSE OF IT.

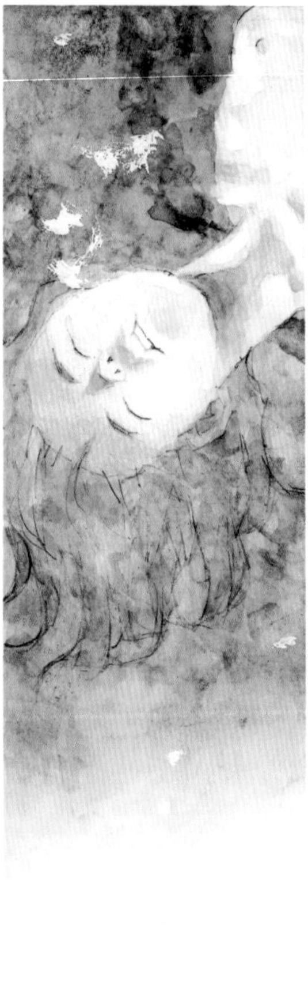

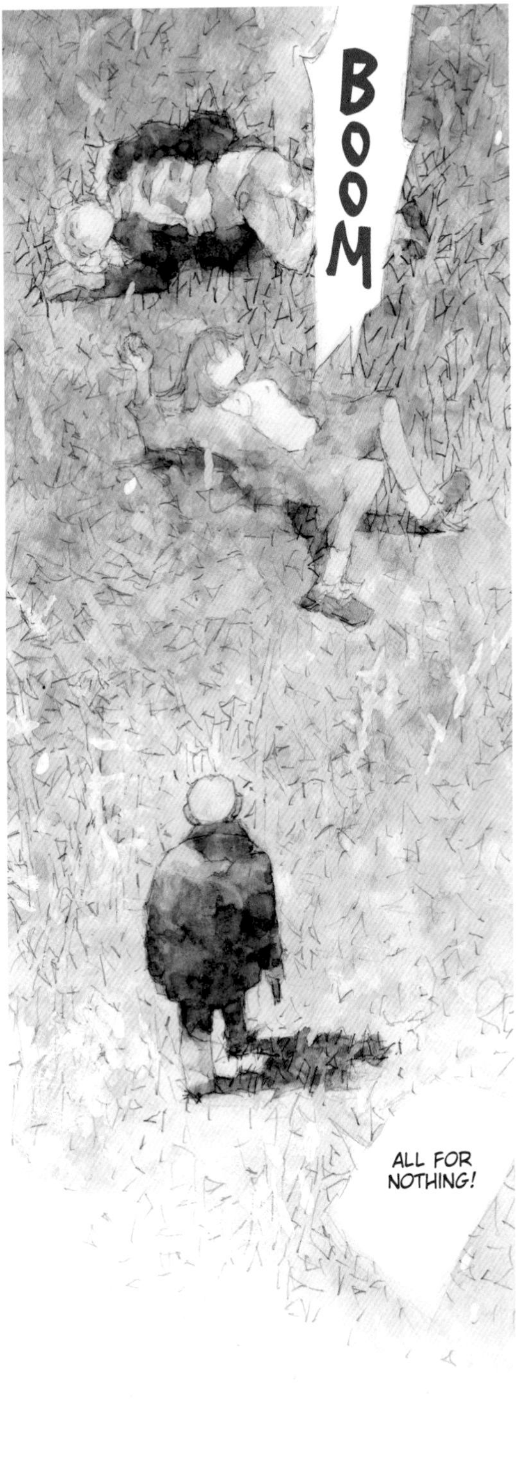
BOOM
ALL FOR NOTHING!

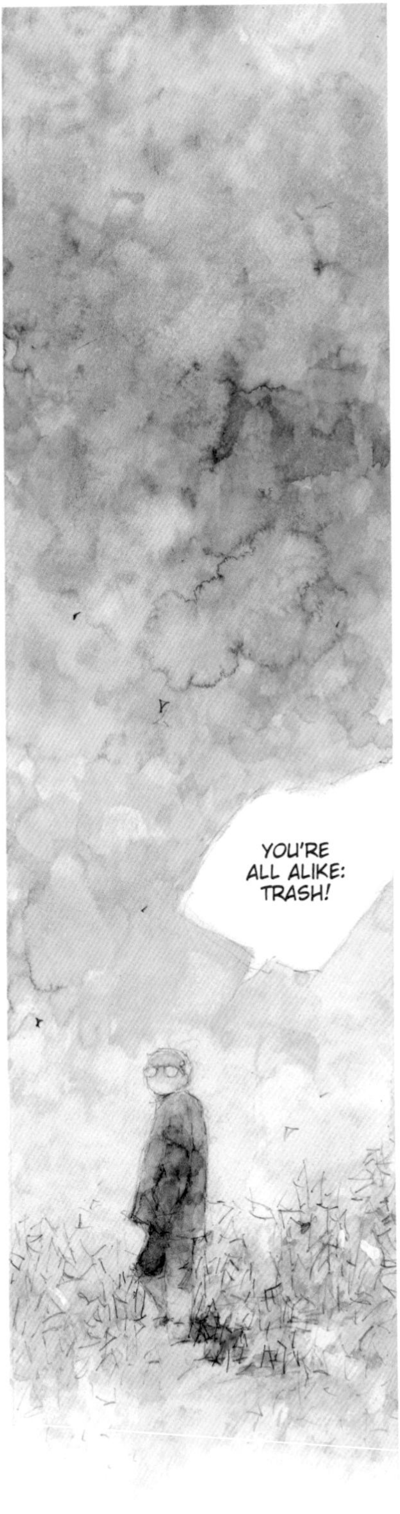
YOU'RE ALL ALIKE: TRASH!

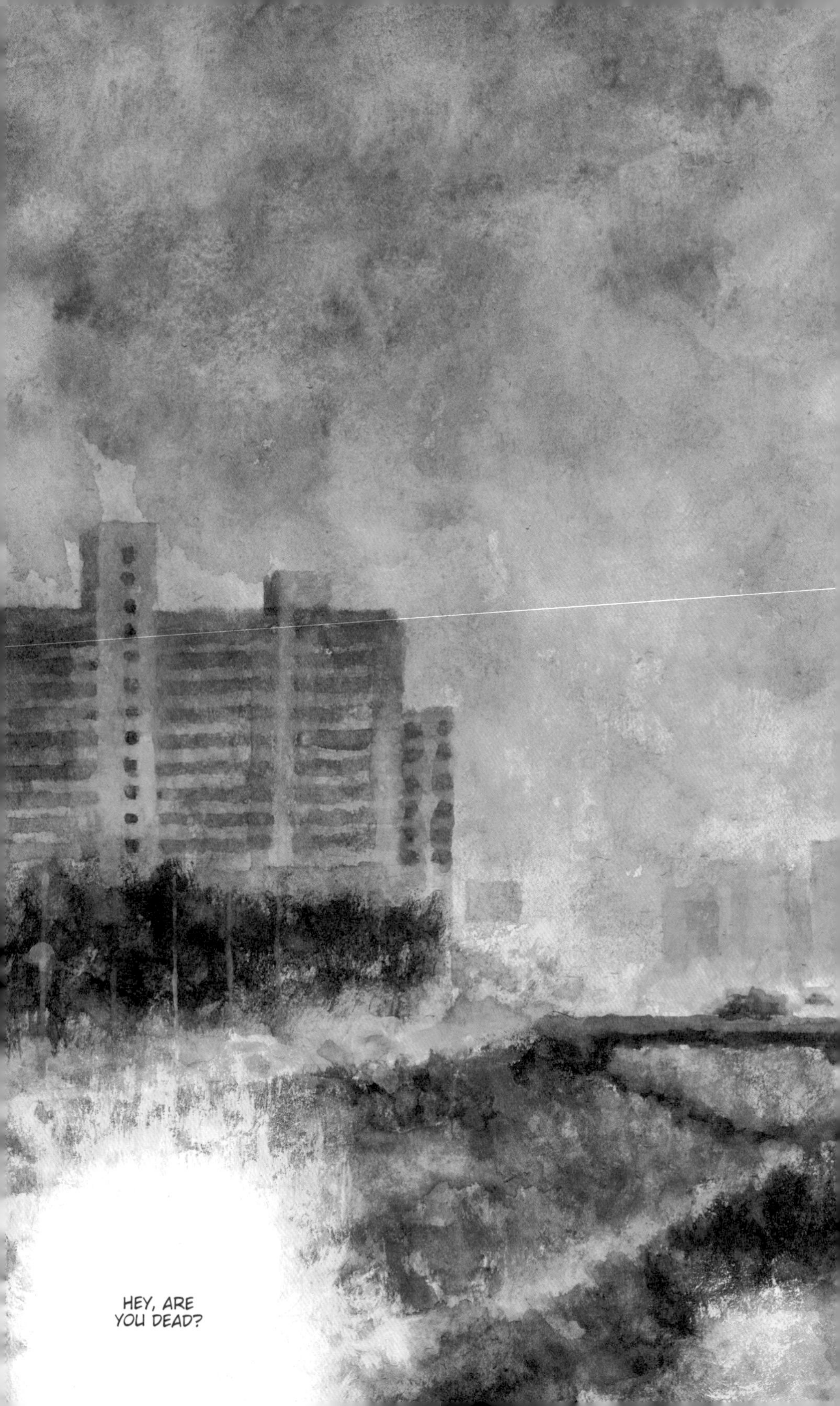
HEY, ARE
YOU DEAD?

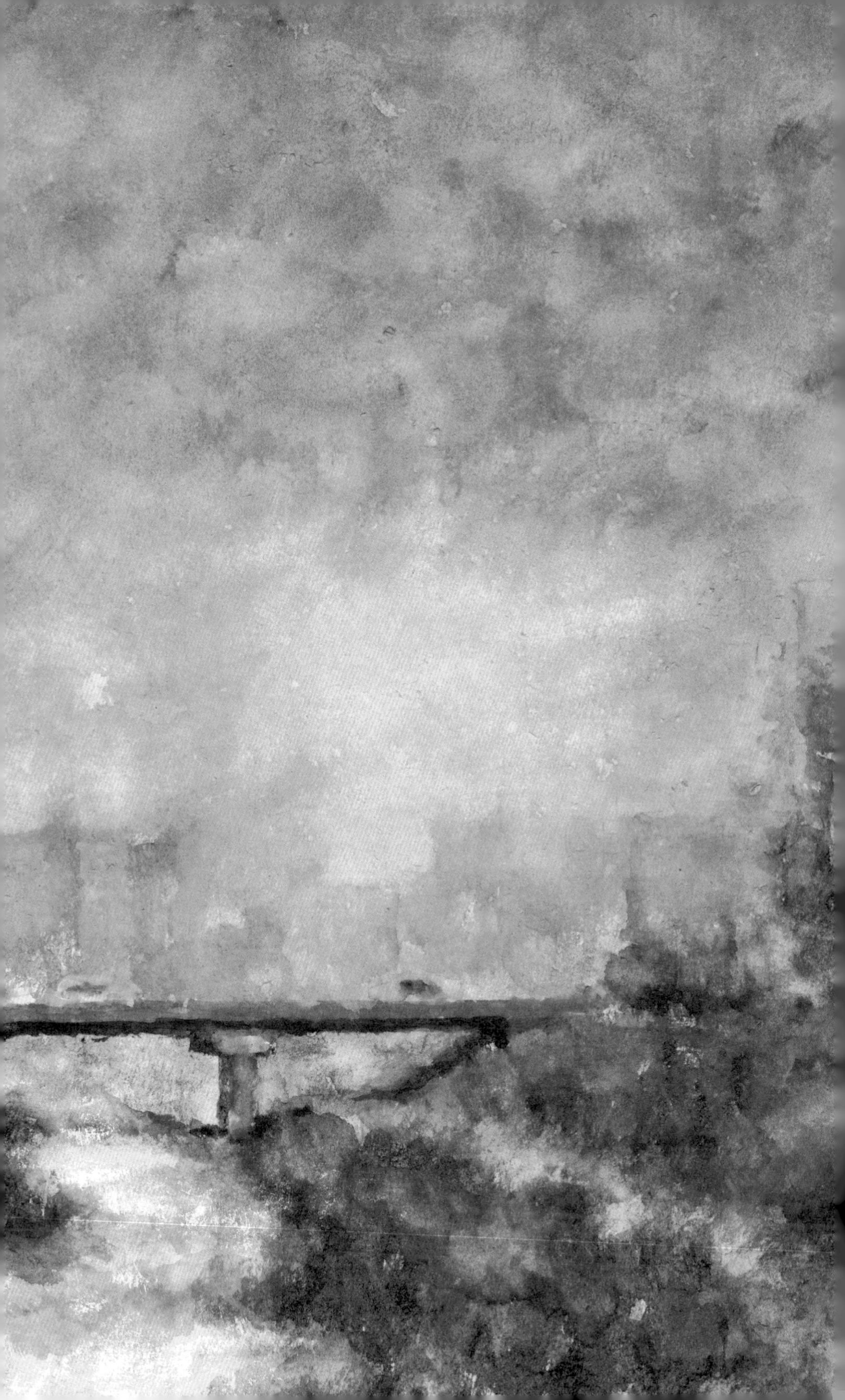

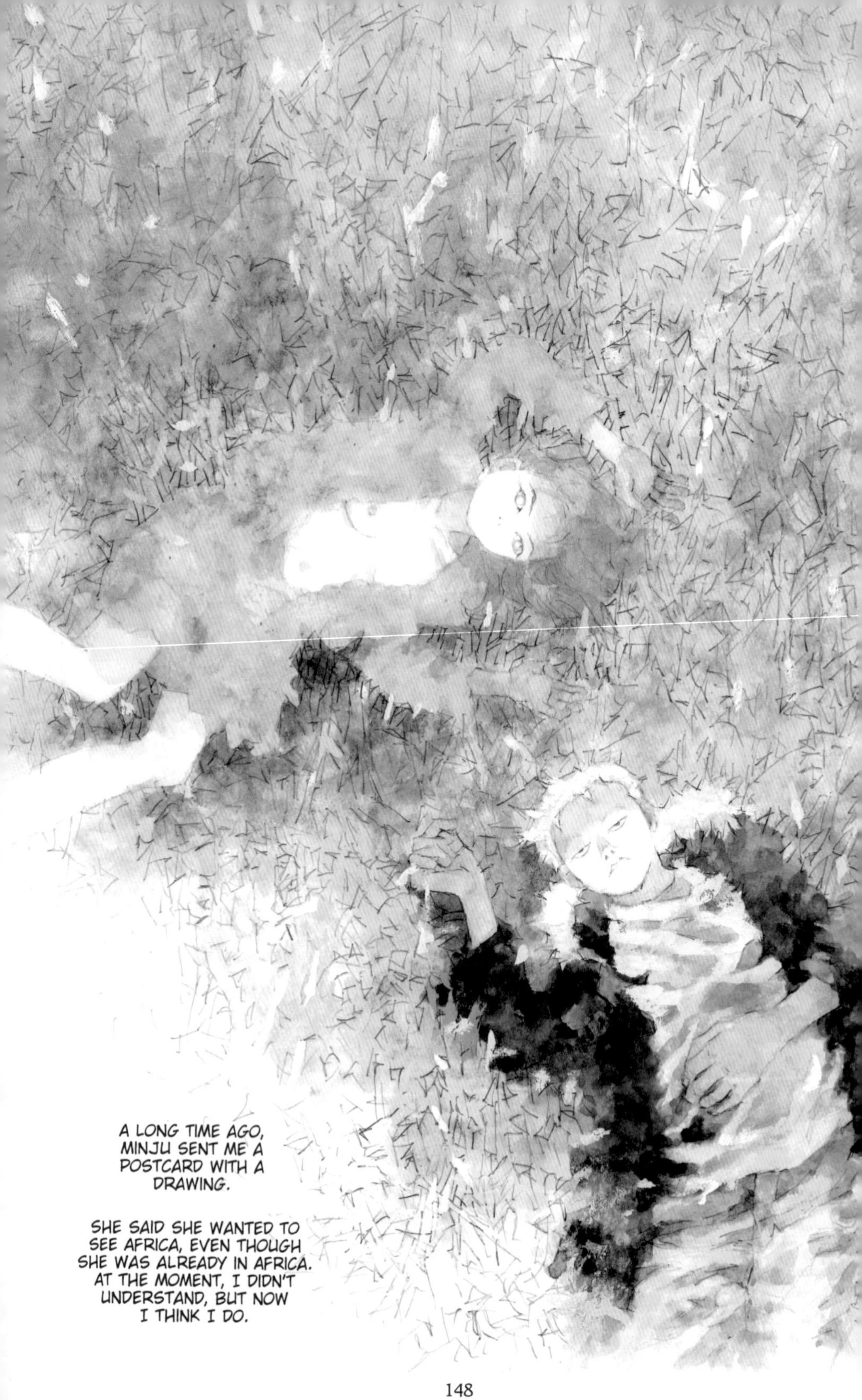
A LONG TIME AGO, MINJU SENT ME A POSTCARD WITH A DRAWING.
SHE SAID SHE WANTED TO SEE AFRICA, EVEN THOUGH SHE WAS ALREADY IN AFRICA. AT THE MOMENT, I DIDN'T UNDERSTAND, BUT NOW I THINK I DO.

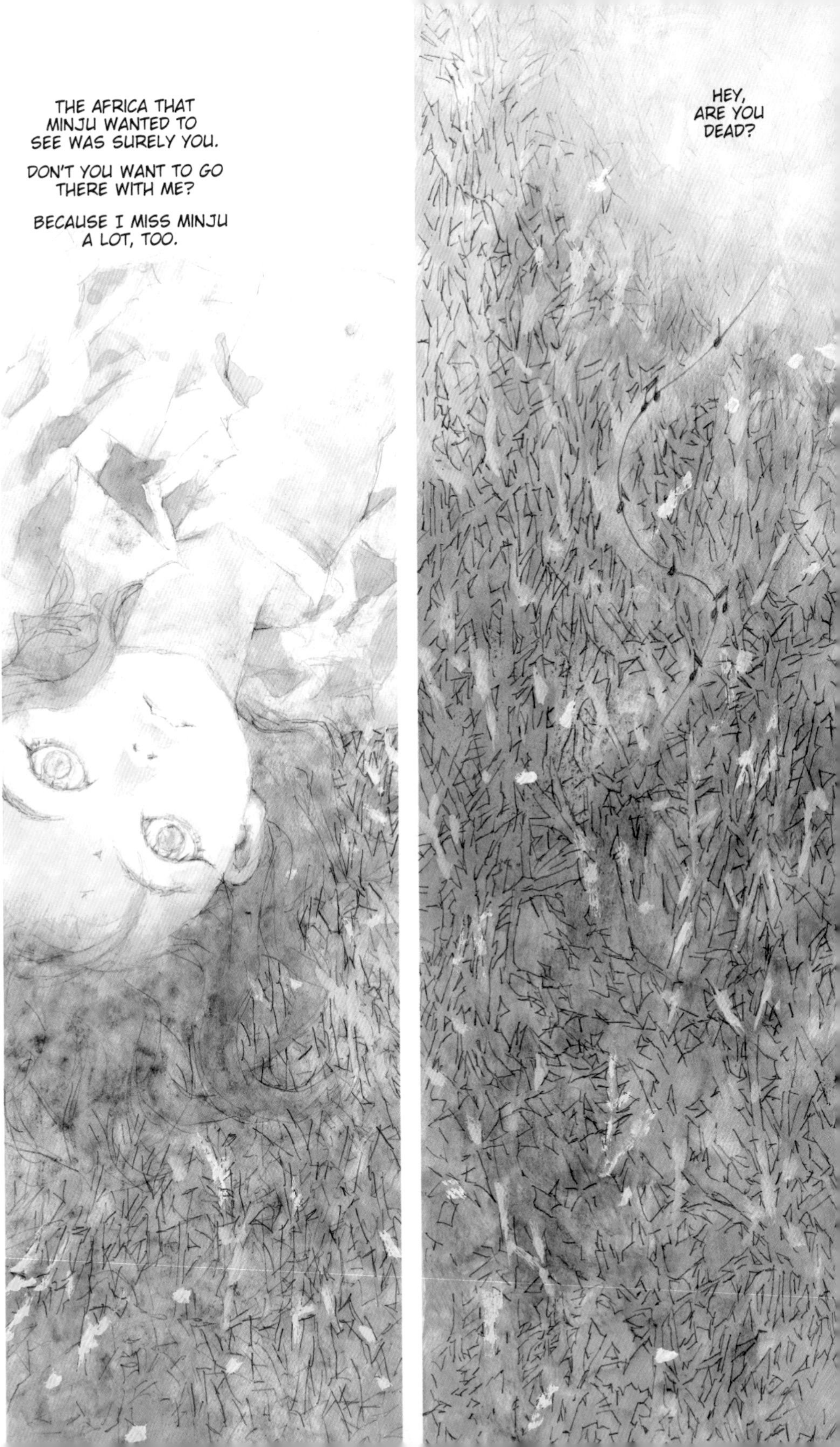
HEY, ARE YOU DEAD?
THE AFRICA THAT MINJU WANTED TO SEE WAS SURELY YOU.
DON'T YOU WANT TO GO THERE WITH ME?
BECAUSE I MISS MINJU A LOT, TOO.

I'M DREAMING OF AFRICA.

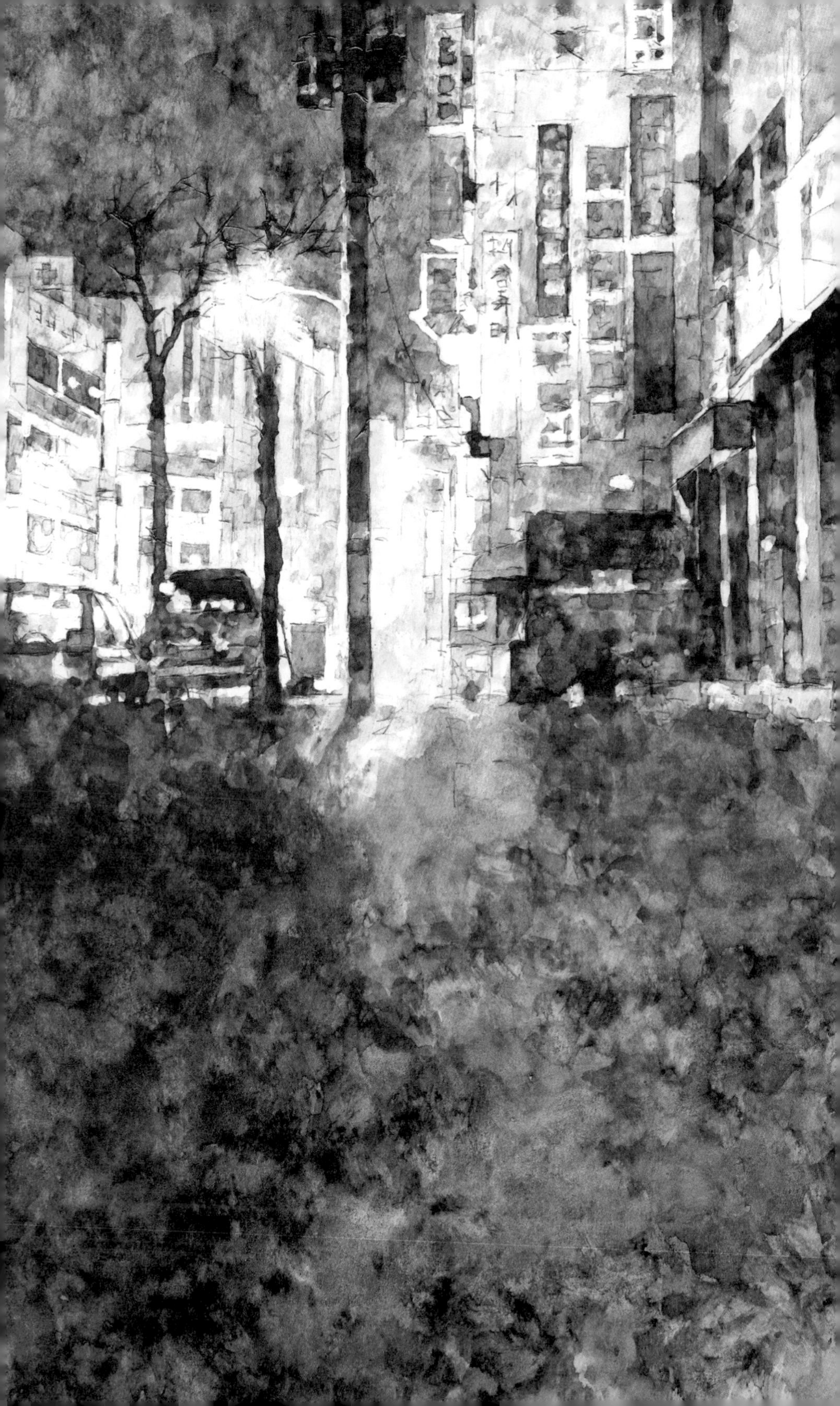

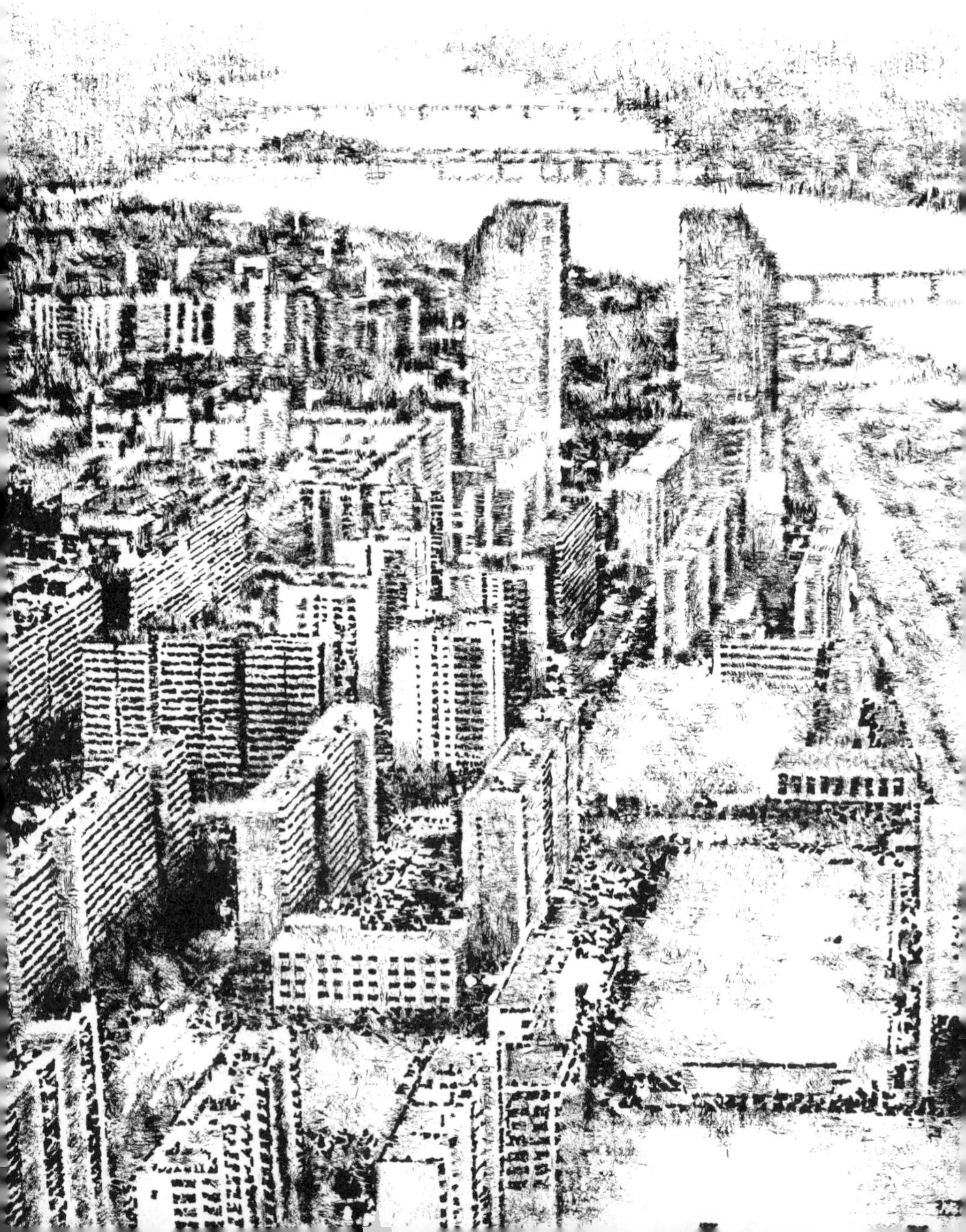

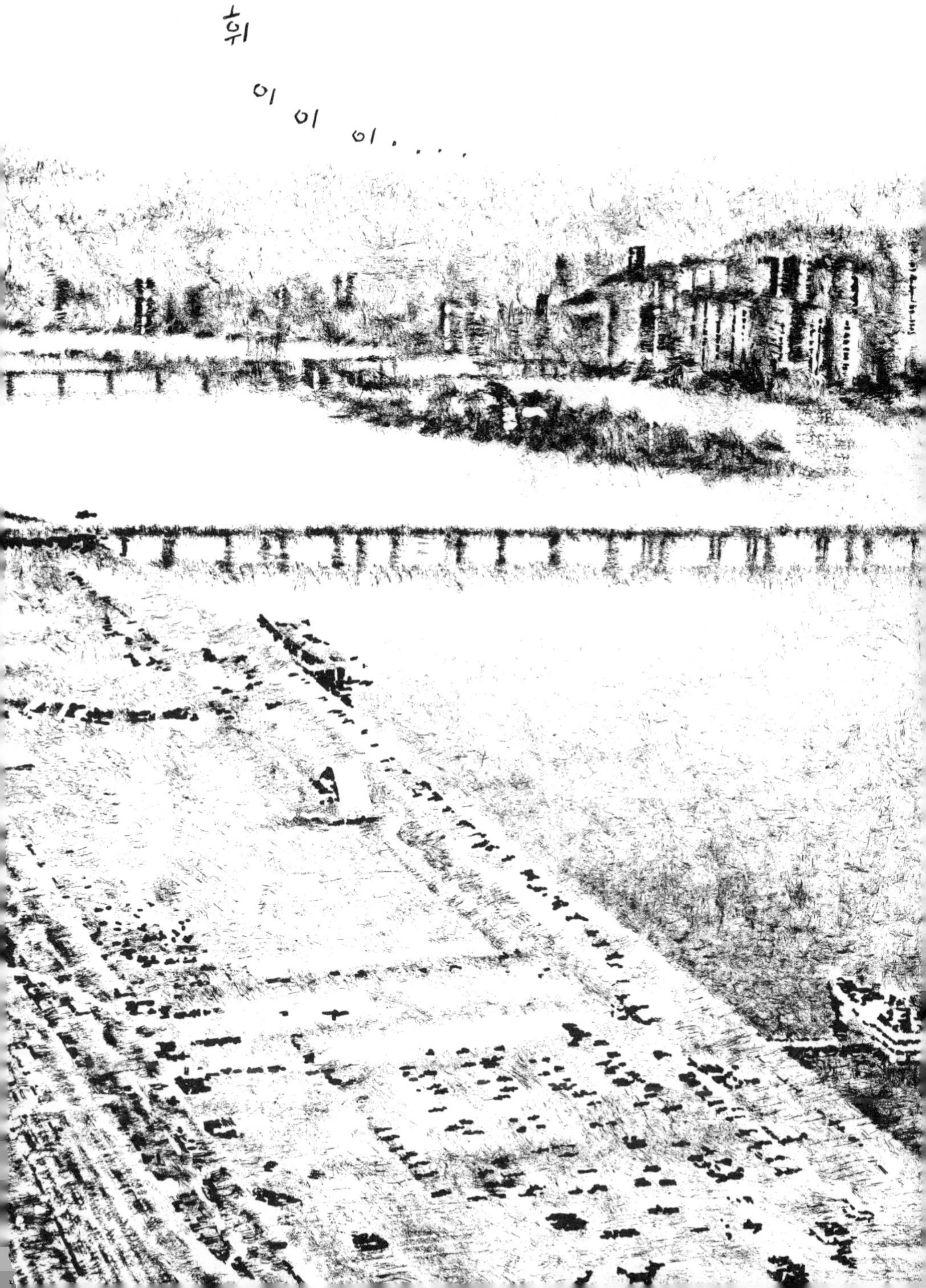
휘 이 이 이. . . .

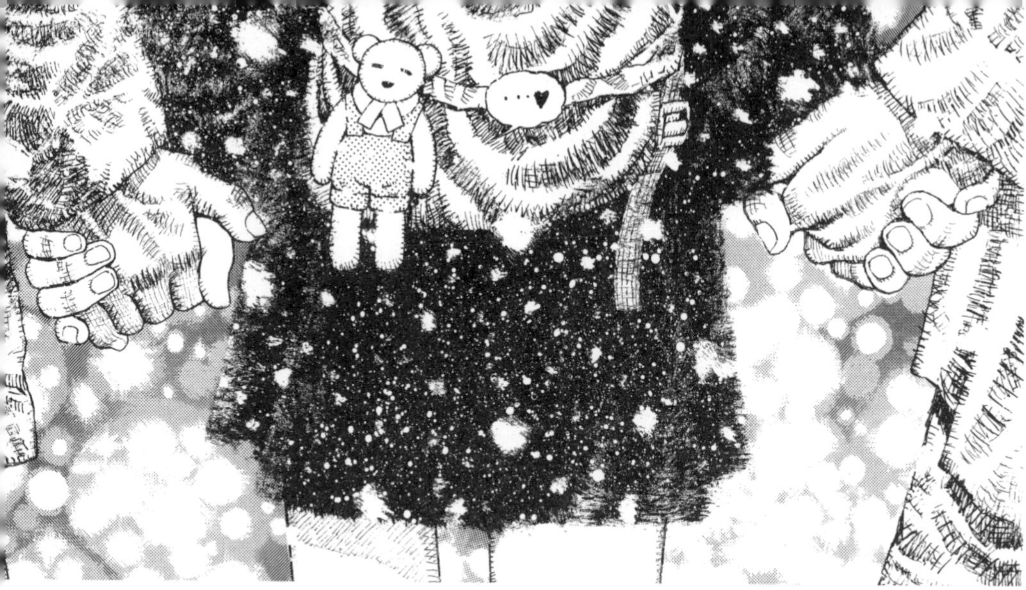

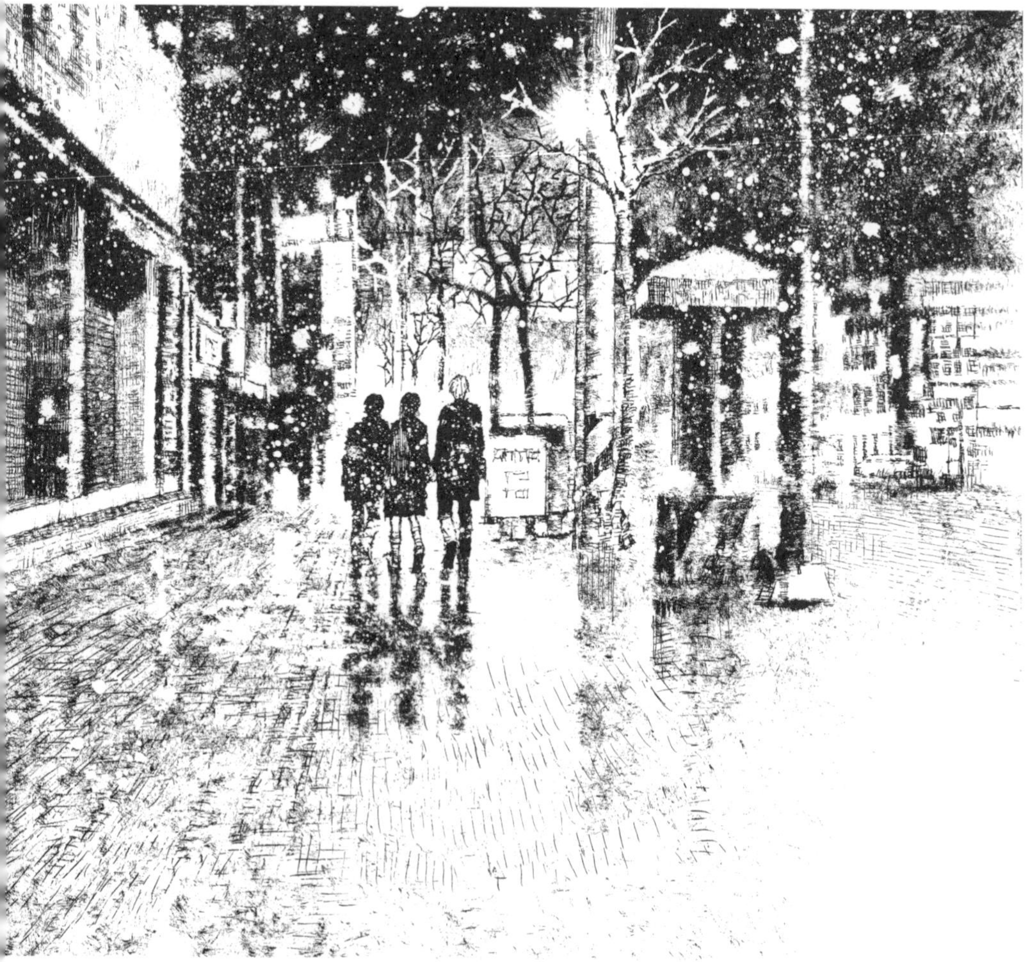

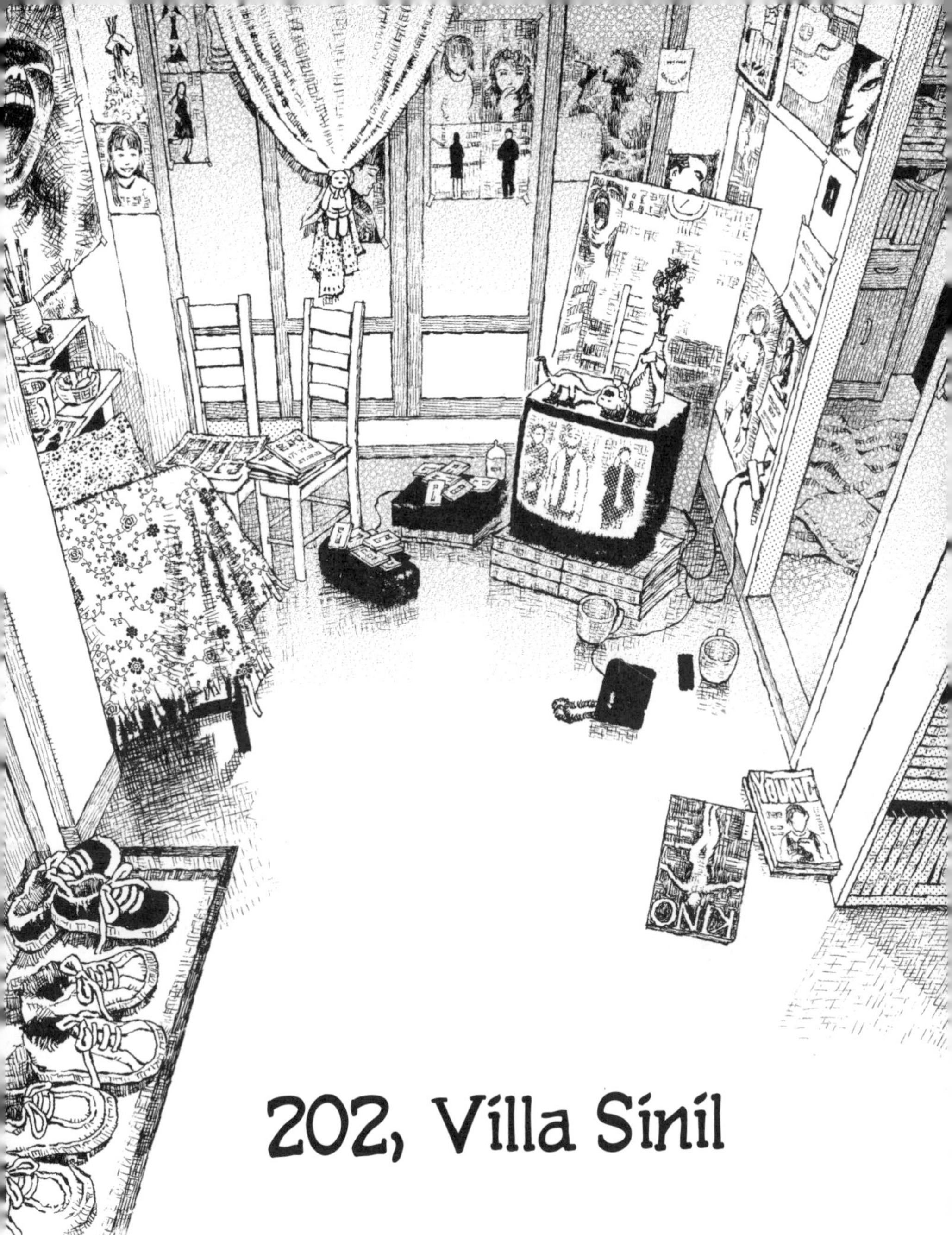
YOUNG
KINO

202, Villa Sinil

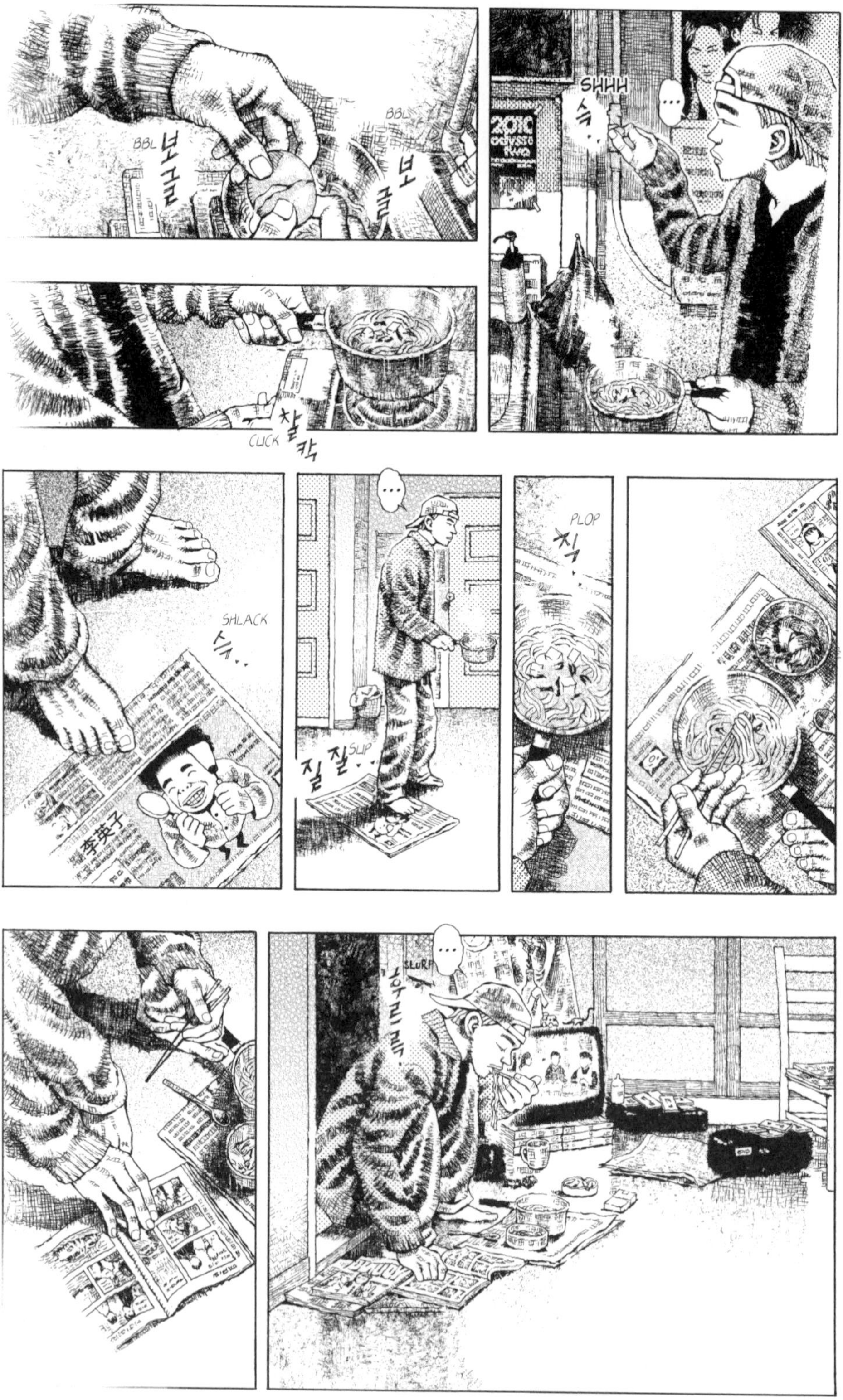
BBL 보글
BBL 보글
SHHH 슥..
...
CLICK 찰칵
SHLACK
...
SLIP 질질..
PLOP
...
SLURP 후루룩..

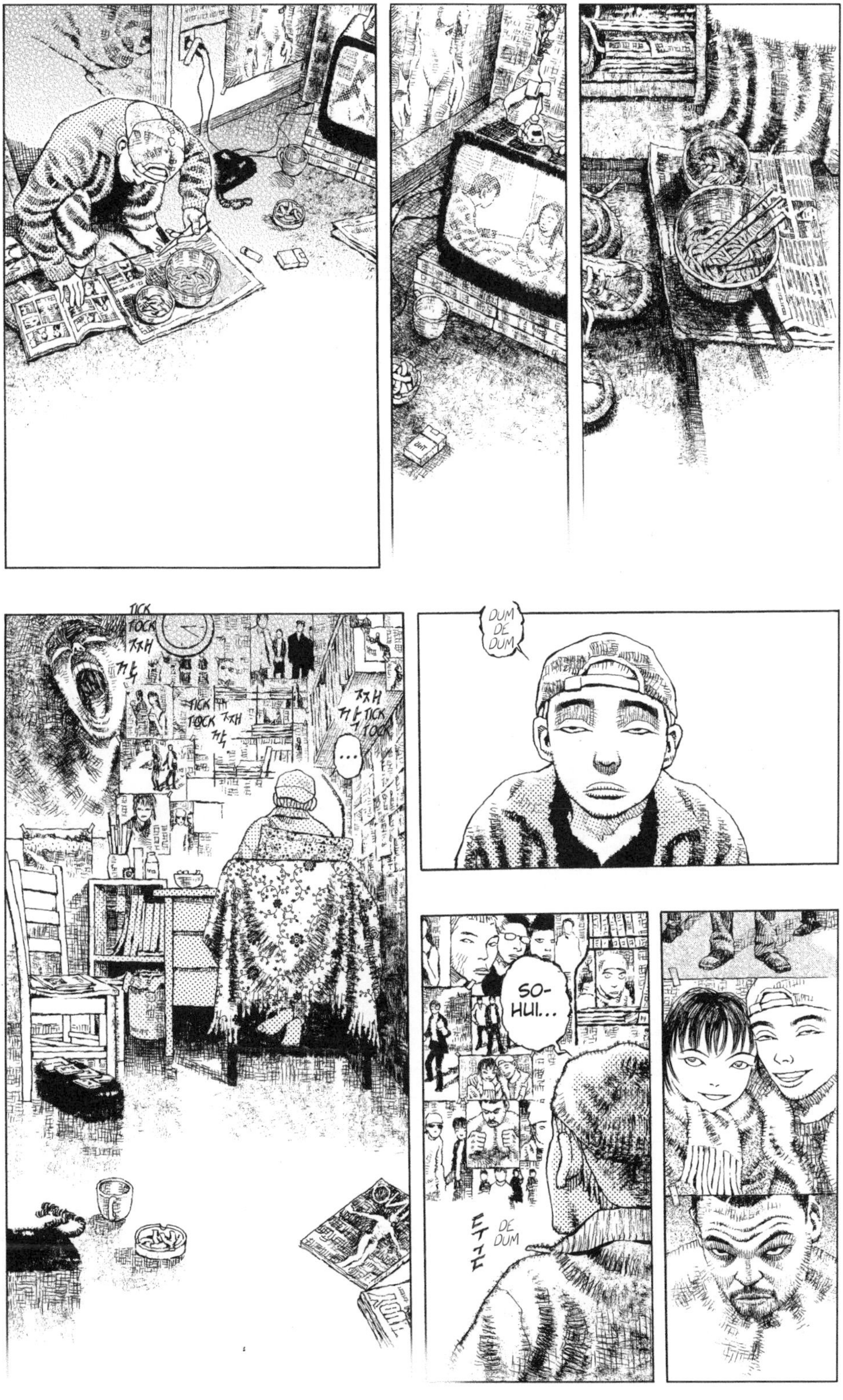
TICK
TOCK
TICK
TOCK
TICK
TOCK
...
DUM
DE
DUM
SO-
HUI...
DE
DUM

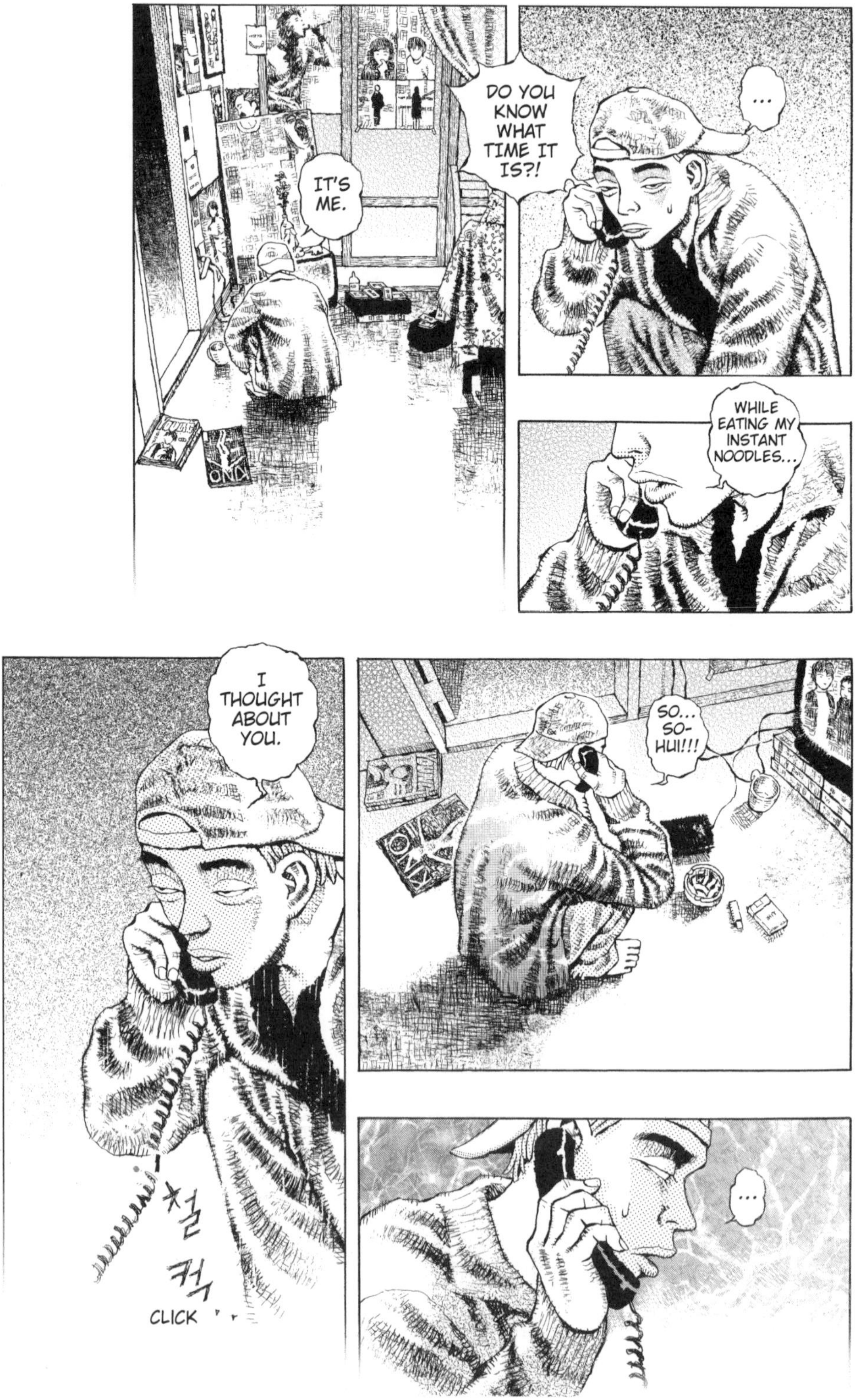
IT'S ME.
DO YOU KNOW WHAT TIME IT IS?!
...
WHILE EATING MY INSTANT NOODLES...
I THOUGHT ABOUT YOU.
철컥
CLICK
SO... SO-HUI!!!
...

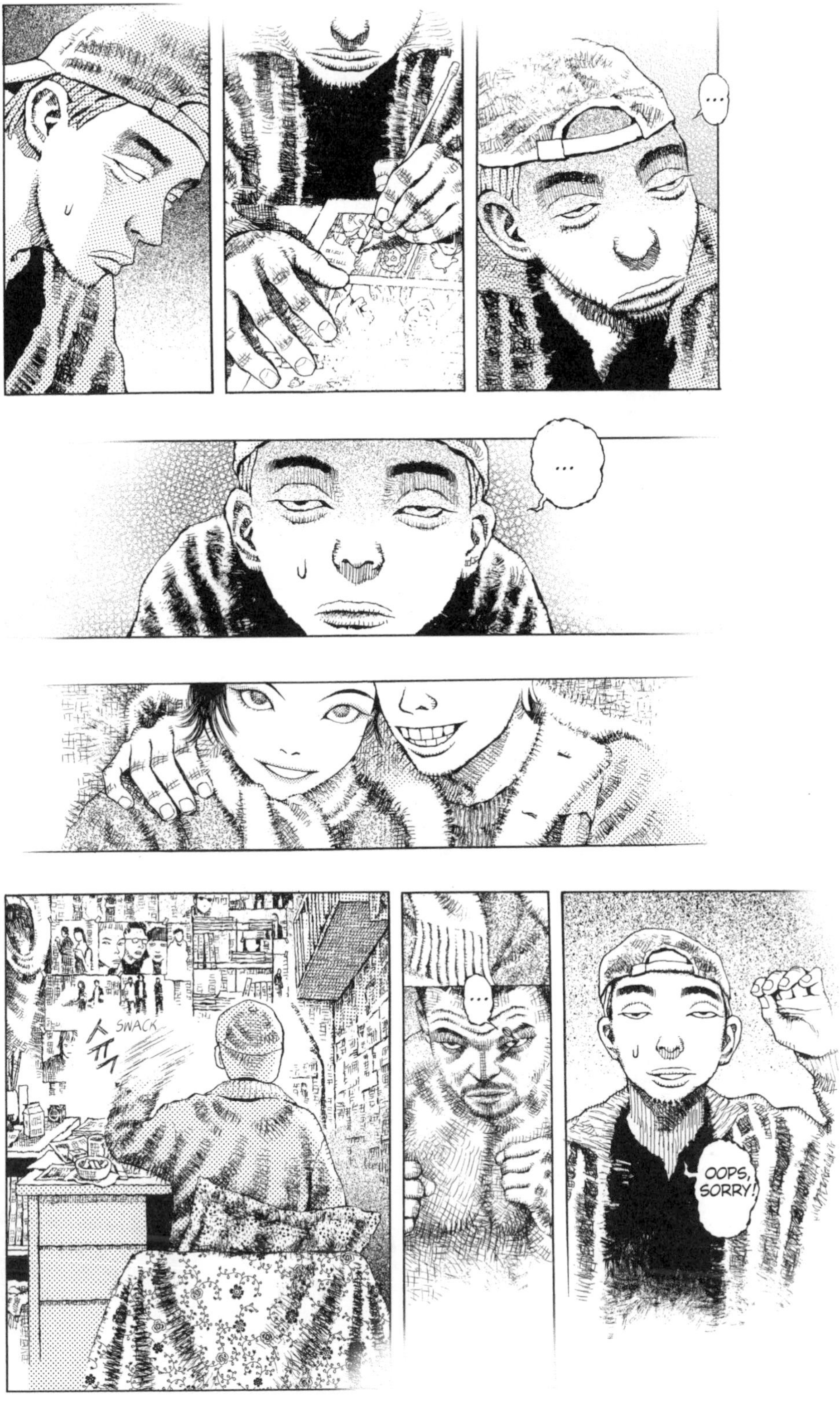
...
...
SWACK
...
OOPS, SORRY!

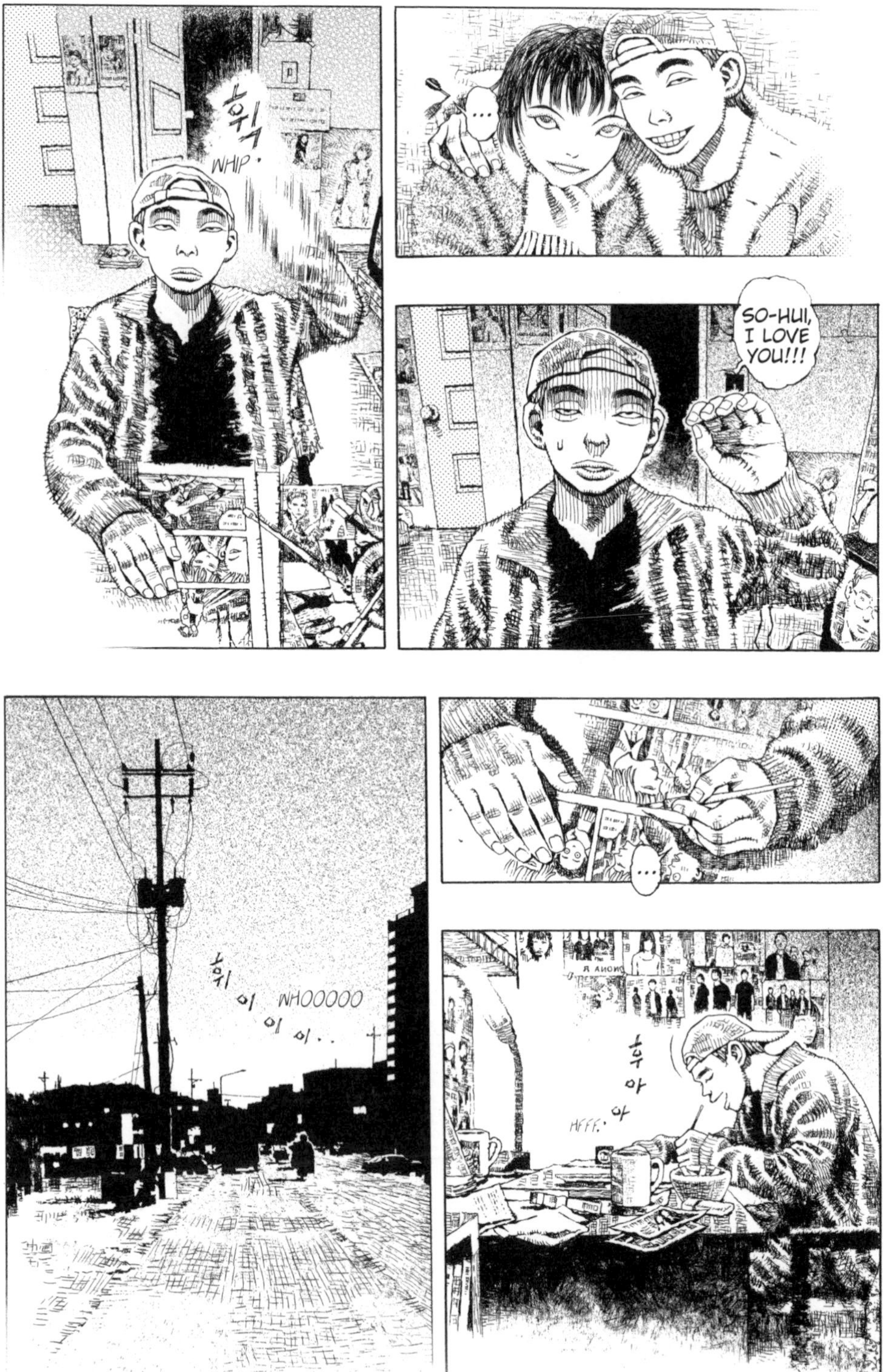
휙
WHIP.
...
SO-HUI, I LOVE YOU!!!
휘이 이 이 이..
WHOOOOO
...
후아 아
HFFF.

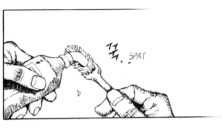

SCRATCH
SCRATCH

SPRT

RUB
RUB

WE'VE JUST LEARNED THAT THE COMEDIAN JO YEONG-JA...

...

RUB
RUB

...WAS BURNED ON HER FACE. THE CIRCUMSTANCES OF THE ACCIDENT ARE STILL UNKNOWN.

MISS JO, WHO'S BEEN CALLED A TIME DELAY BOMB IN THE WORLD OF COMIC SHOWS...

...WILL BE FORCED TO SUSPEND HER PERFORMANCES FOR SOME TIME.

...

RUB

SWEET! I DIDN'T LIKE HER ANYHOW!

AND NOW FOR INTERNATIONAL NEWS...

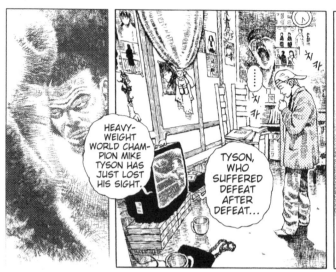

HEAVY-WEIGHT WORLD CHAMPION MIKE TYSON HAS JUST LOST HIS SIGHT.

TYSON, WHO SUFFERED DEFEAT AFTER DEFEAT...

WHAT?

I DON'T BELIEVE IT!

RUB

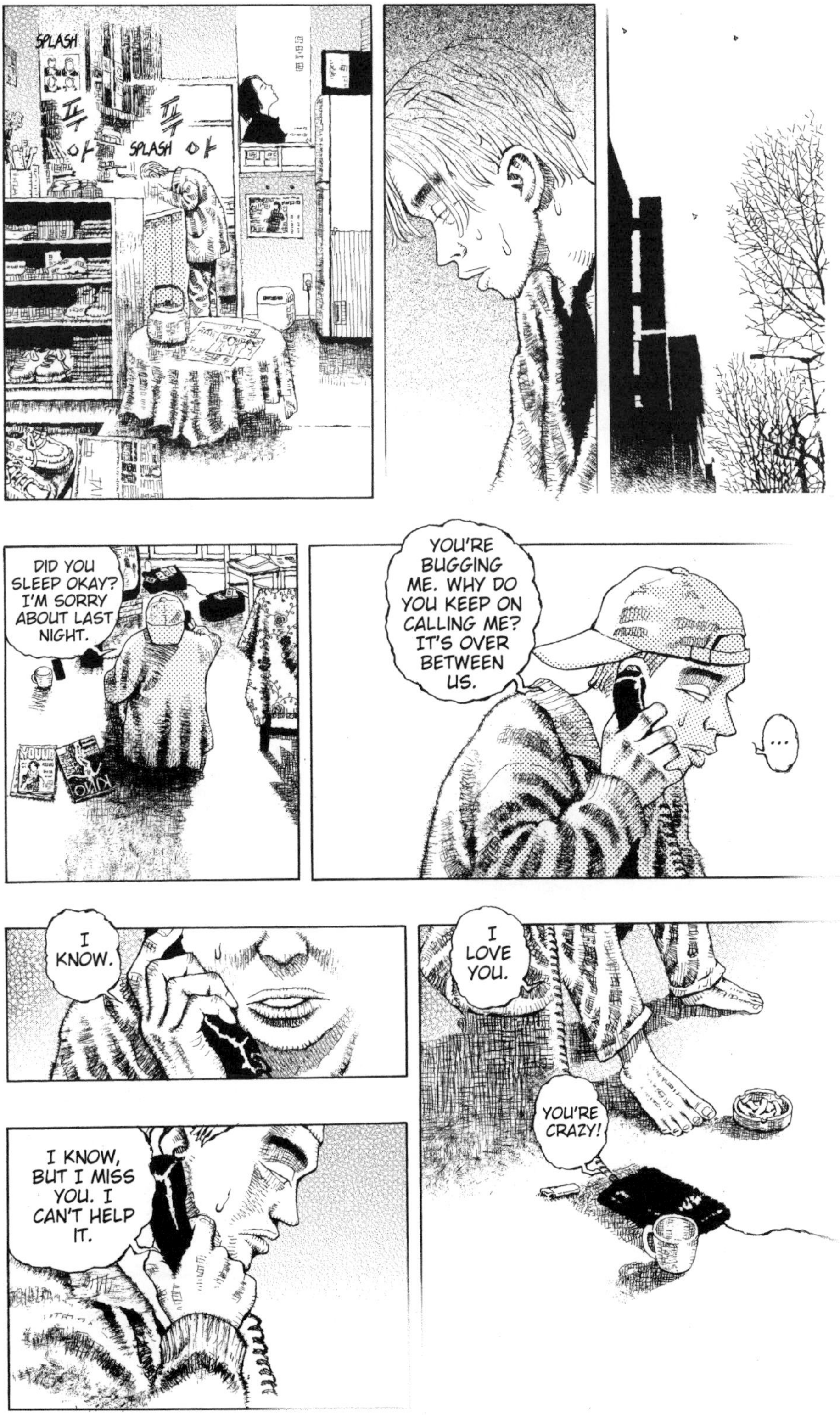
SPLASH
SPLASH
DID YOU SLEEP OKAY? I'M SORRY ABOUT LAST NIGHT.
YOU'RE BUGGING ME. WHY DO YOU KEEP ON CALLING ME? IT'S OVER BETWEEN US.
...
I KNOW.
I KNOW, BUT I MISS YOU. I CAN'T HELP IT.
I LOVE YOU.
YOU'RE CRAZY!

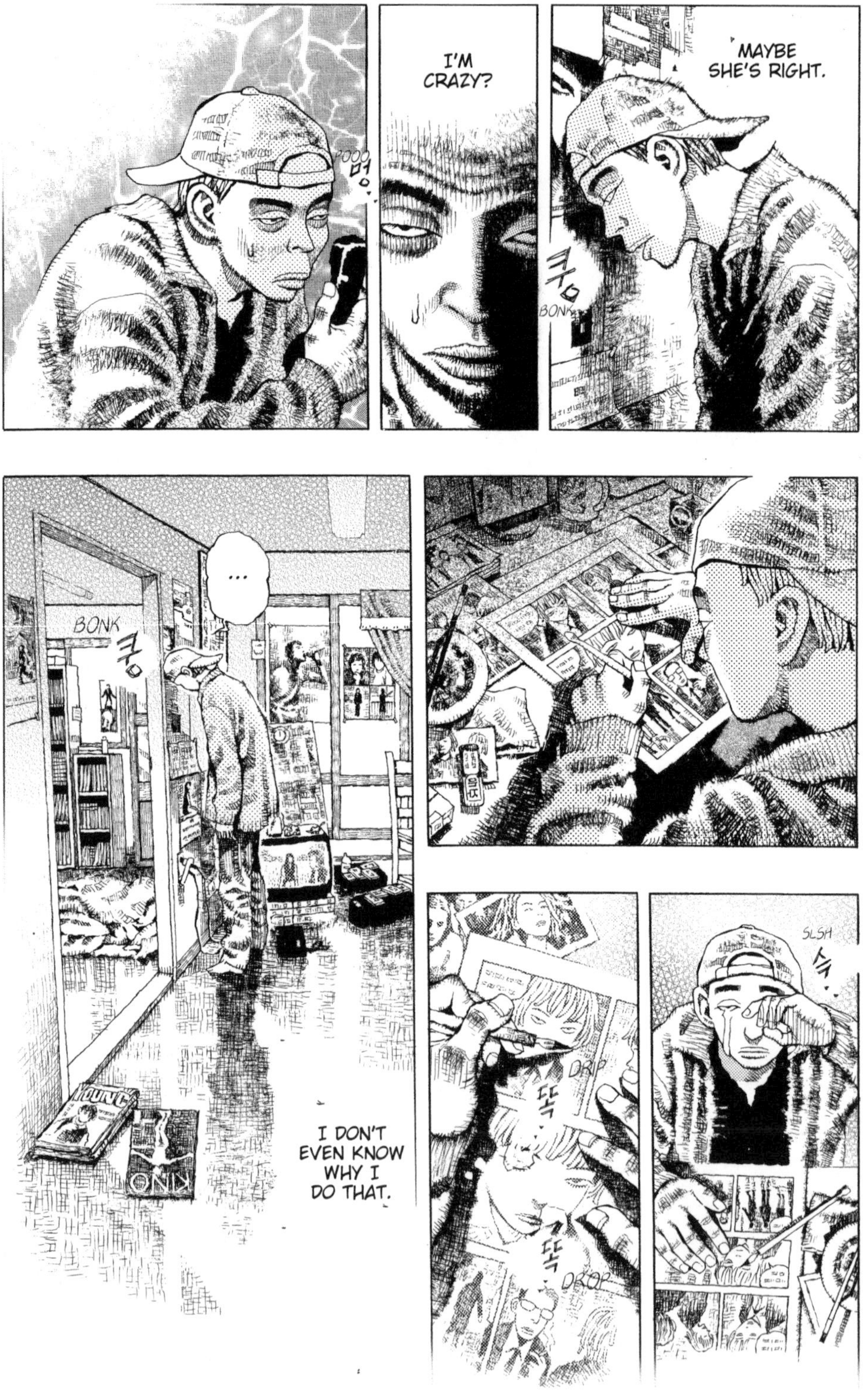
POOO
멍...
I'M CRAZY?
MAYBE SHE'S RIGHT.
쿵
BONK
...
BONK
쿵
SLSH
쓱...
DRIP
뚝
뚝
DROP
I DON'T EVEN KNOW WHY I DO THAT.

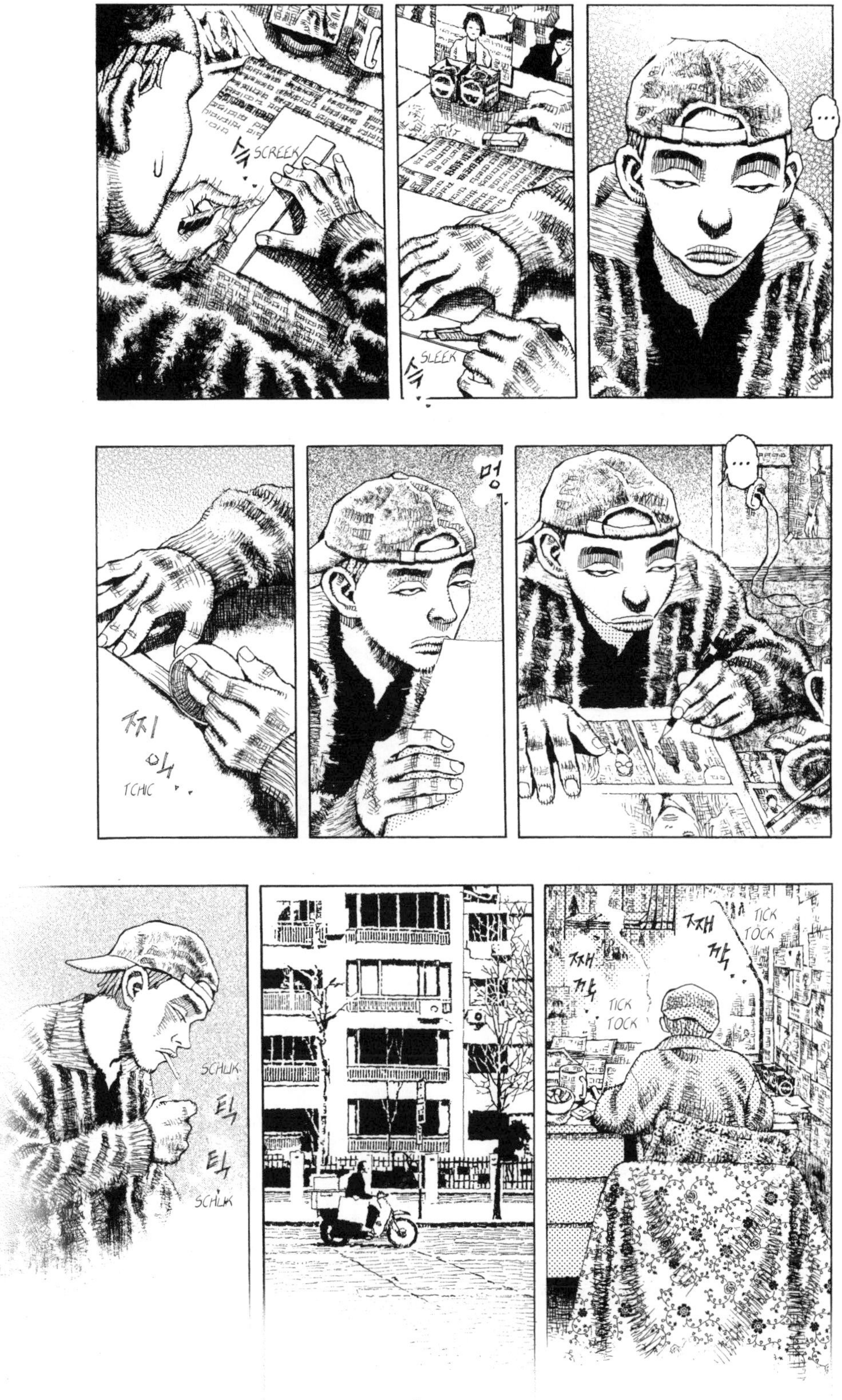

슥
SCREEK
SLEEK
슥
...
지이
TCHIC
멍
...
SCHLIK
틱
틱
SCHLIK
째깍
TICK
TOCK
째깍
TICK
TOCK

SLEEEK
SLEEEK
...
SPECIAL BULLETI
TWO LONGTIME MEMBERS OF THE NATIONAL ASSEMBLY HAVE JUST BEEN SAVAGELY MURDERED...
...IN TWO DIFFERENT LOCATIONS.
...
THE TWO ASSEMBLY-MEN WERE STABBED TO DEATH.
...
...
WHIP
CLUMP

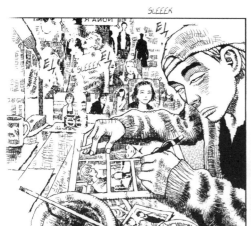

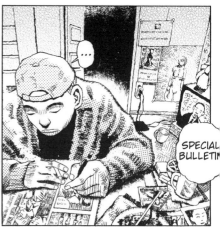

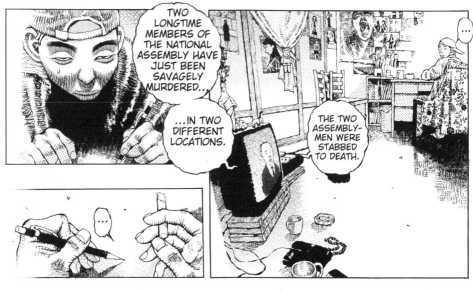

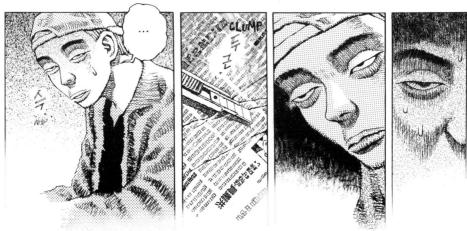

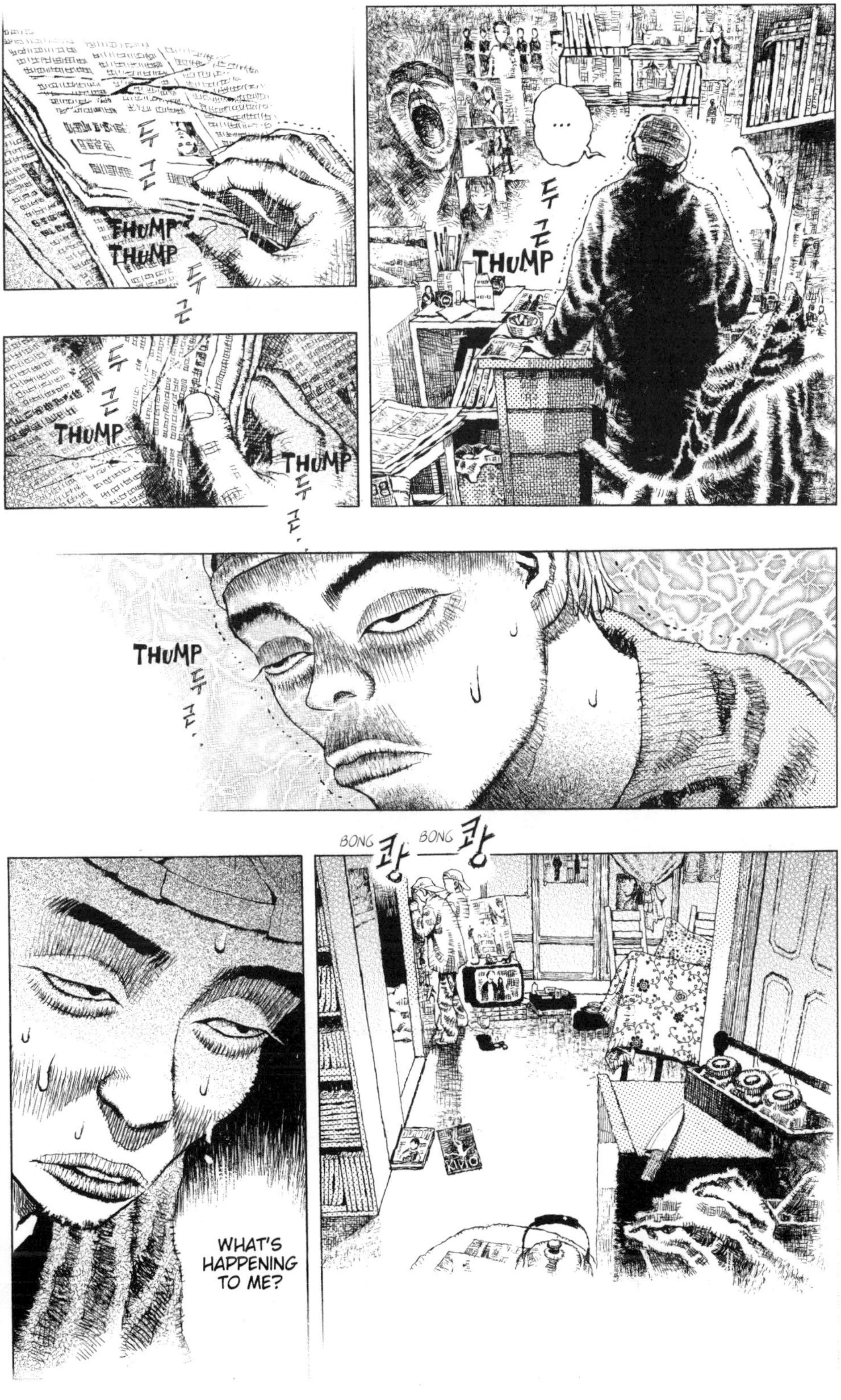
두근
THUMP
THUMP
두근
두근
THUMP
THUMP
두근
...
두근
THUMP
THUMP
두근
WHAT'S HAPPENING TO ME?
BONG
쾅
BONG
쾅

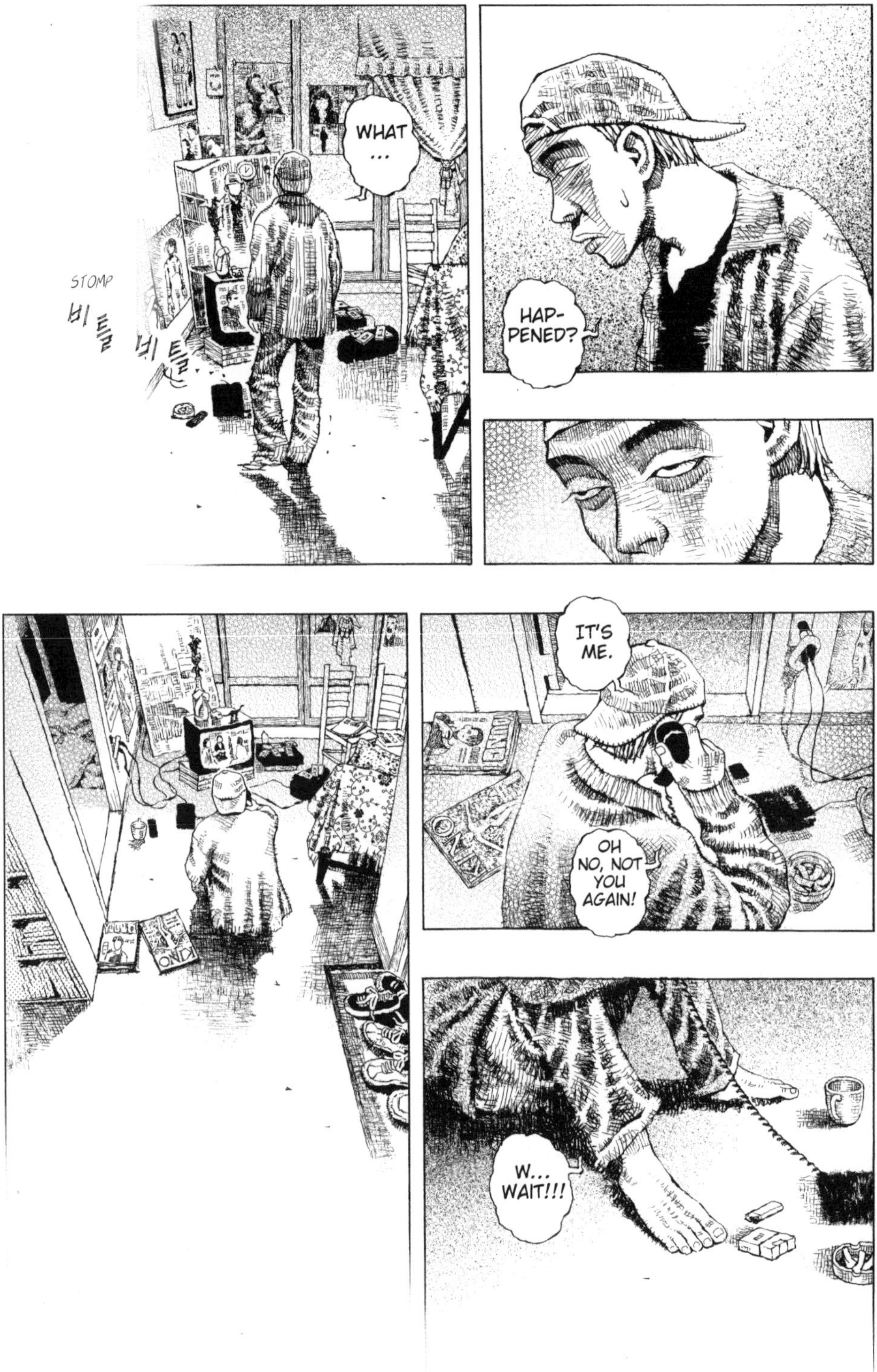

WHAT ...
STOMP
비틀 비틀
HAP-PENED?
IT'S ME.
OH NO, NOT YOU AGAIN!
W... WAIT!!!

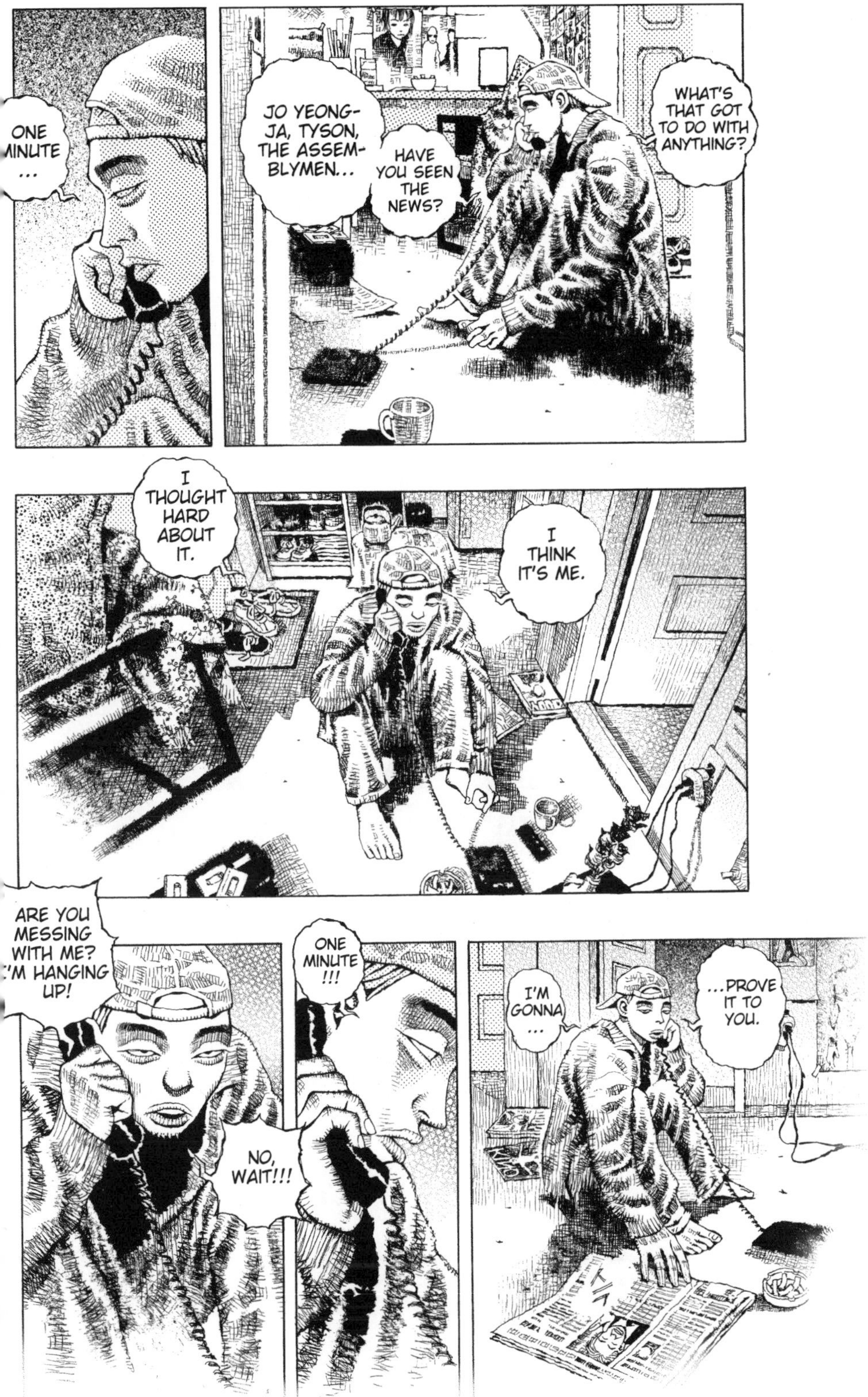
ONE MINUTE ...
JO YEONG-JA, TYSON, THE ASSEMBLYMEN...
HAVE YOU SEEN THE NEWS?
WHAT'S THAT GOT TO DO WITH ANYTHING?
I THOUGHT HARD ABOUT IT.
I THINK IT'S ME.
ARE YOU MESSING WITH ME? I'M HANGING UP!
ONE MINUTE !!!
NO, WAIT!!!
I'M GONNA ...
...PROVE IT TO YOU.

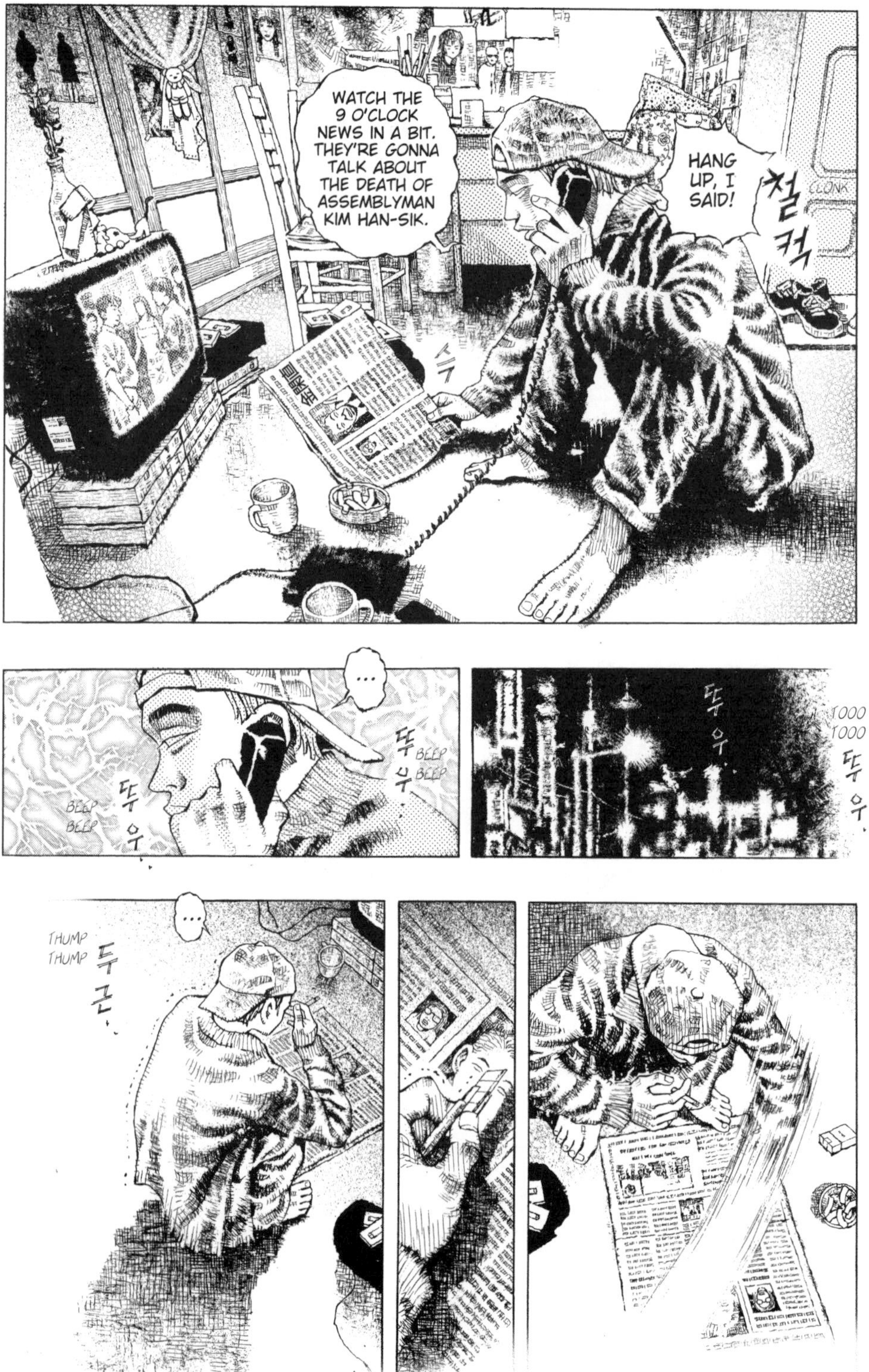

WATCH THE 9 O'CLOCK NEWS IN A BIT. THEY'RE GONNA TALK ABOUT THE DEATH OF ASSEMBLYMAN KIM HAN-SIK.
HANG UP, I SAID!
철컥
CLONK
...
뚜우
BEEP BEEP
뚜우
BEEP BEEP
뚜우
TOOO TOOO
뚜우
...
THUMP THUMP
두근

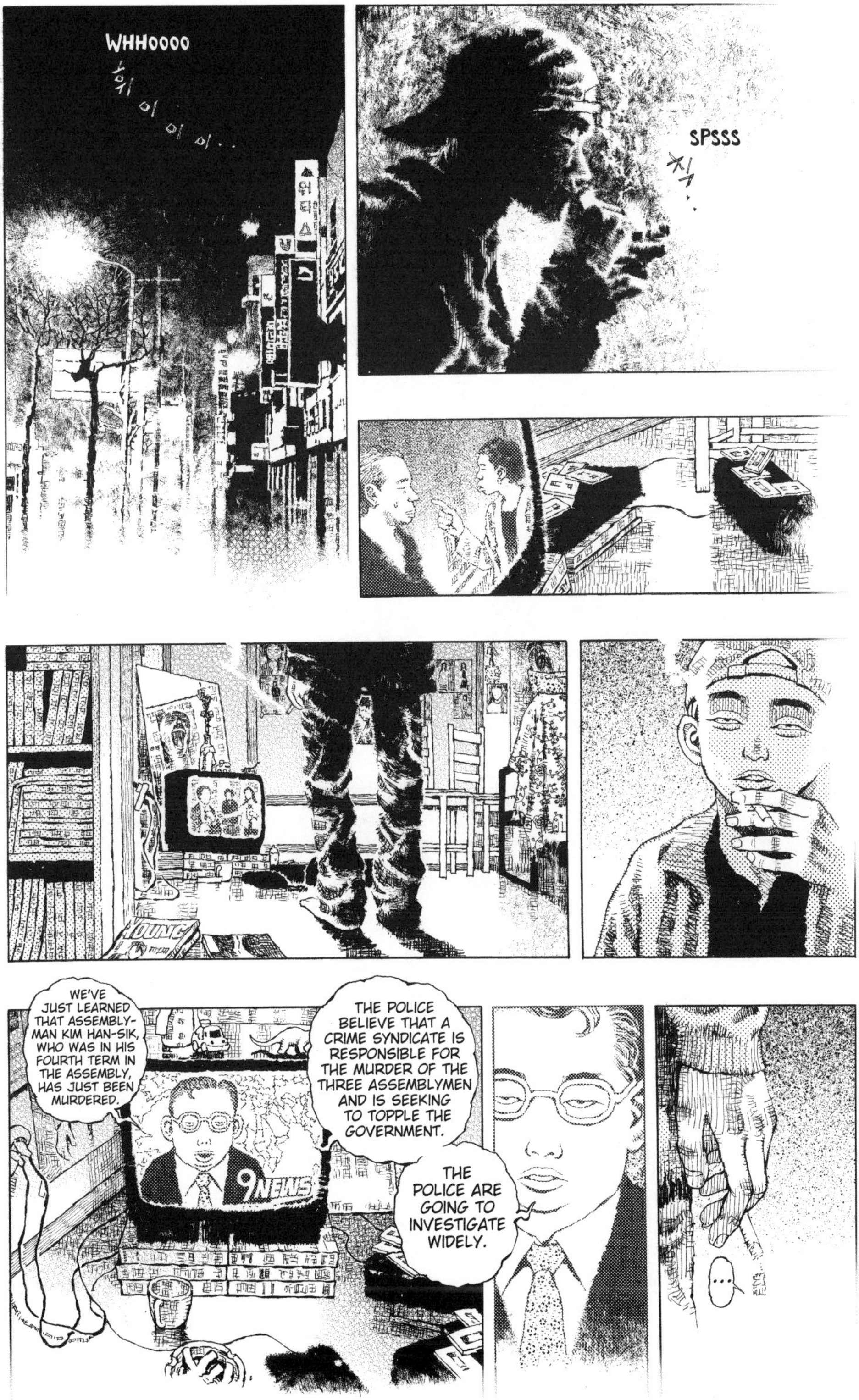
WHHOOOO
SPSSS
YOUNG
WE'VE JUST LEARNED THAT ASSEMBLY-MAN KIM HAN-SIK, WHO WAS IN HIS FOURTH TERM IN THE ASSEMBLY, HAS JUST BEEN MURDERED.
THE POLICE BELIEVE THAT A CRIME SYNDICATE IS RESPONSIBLE FOR THE MURDER OF THE THREE ASSEMBLYMEN AND IS SEEKING TO TOPPLE THE GOVERNMENT.
9NEWS
THE POLICE ARE GOING TO INVESTIGATE WIDELY.
...

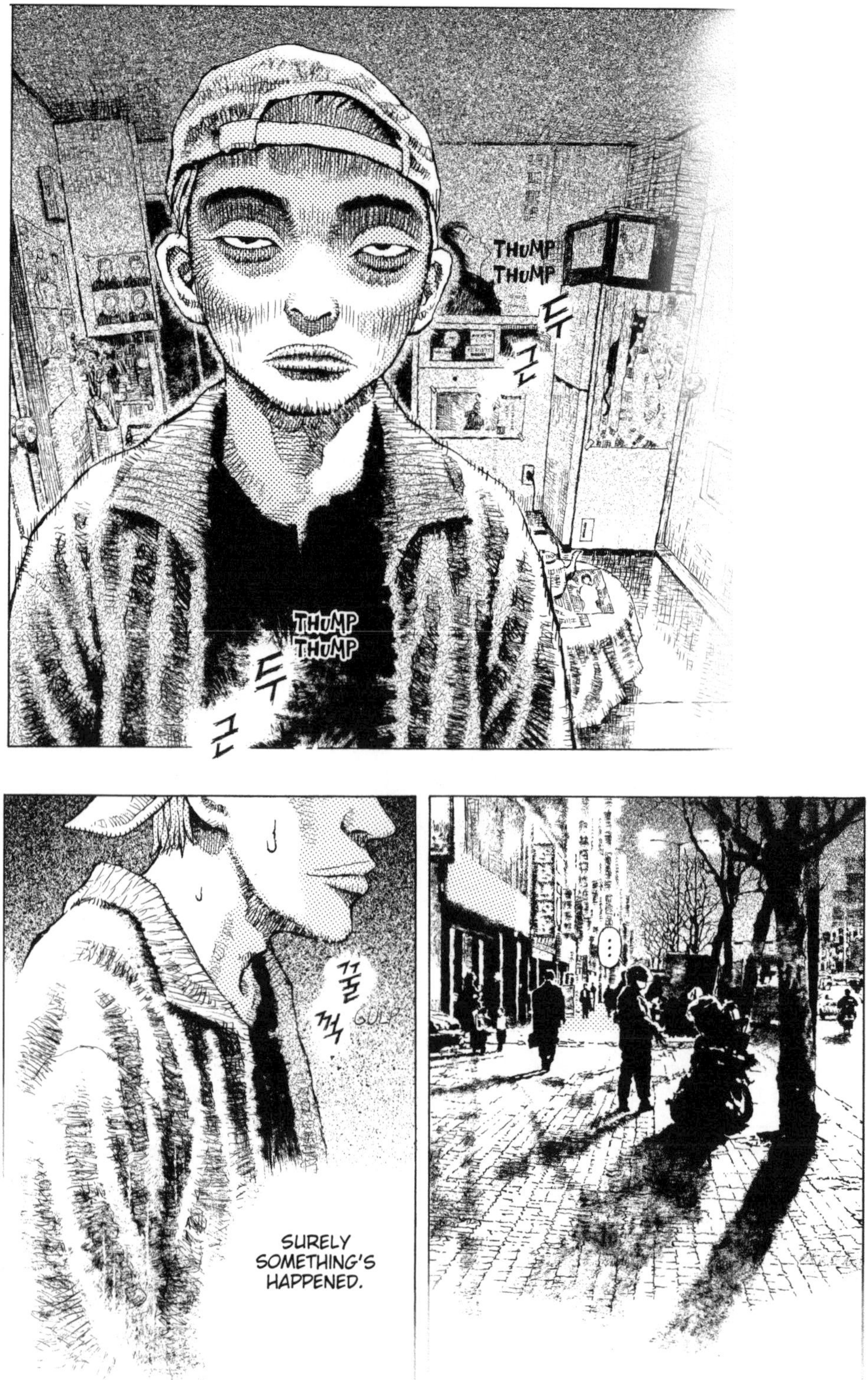

THUMP THUMP
두근
THUMP THUMP
두근
꿀꺽
GULP
SURELY SOMETHING'S HAPPENED.
...

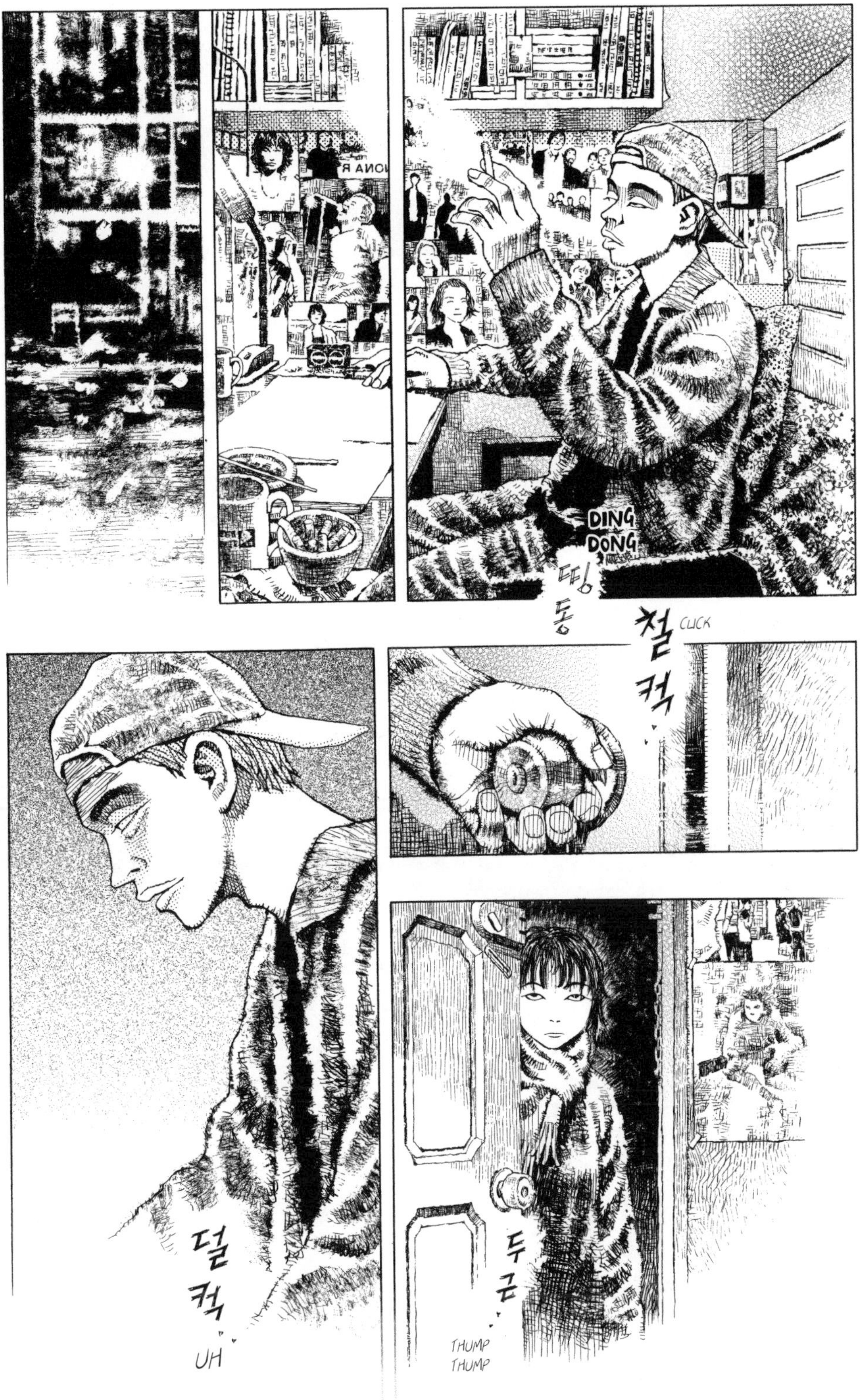
DING DONG
띵 동
철컥
CLICK
덜컥
UH
두근
THUMP THUMP

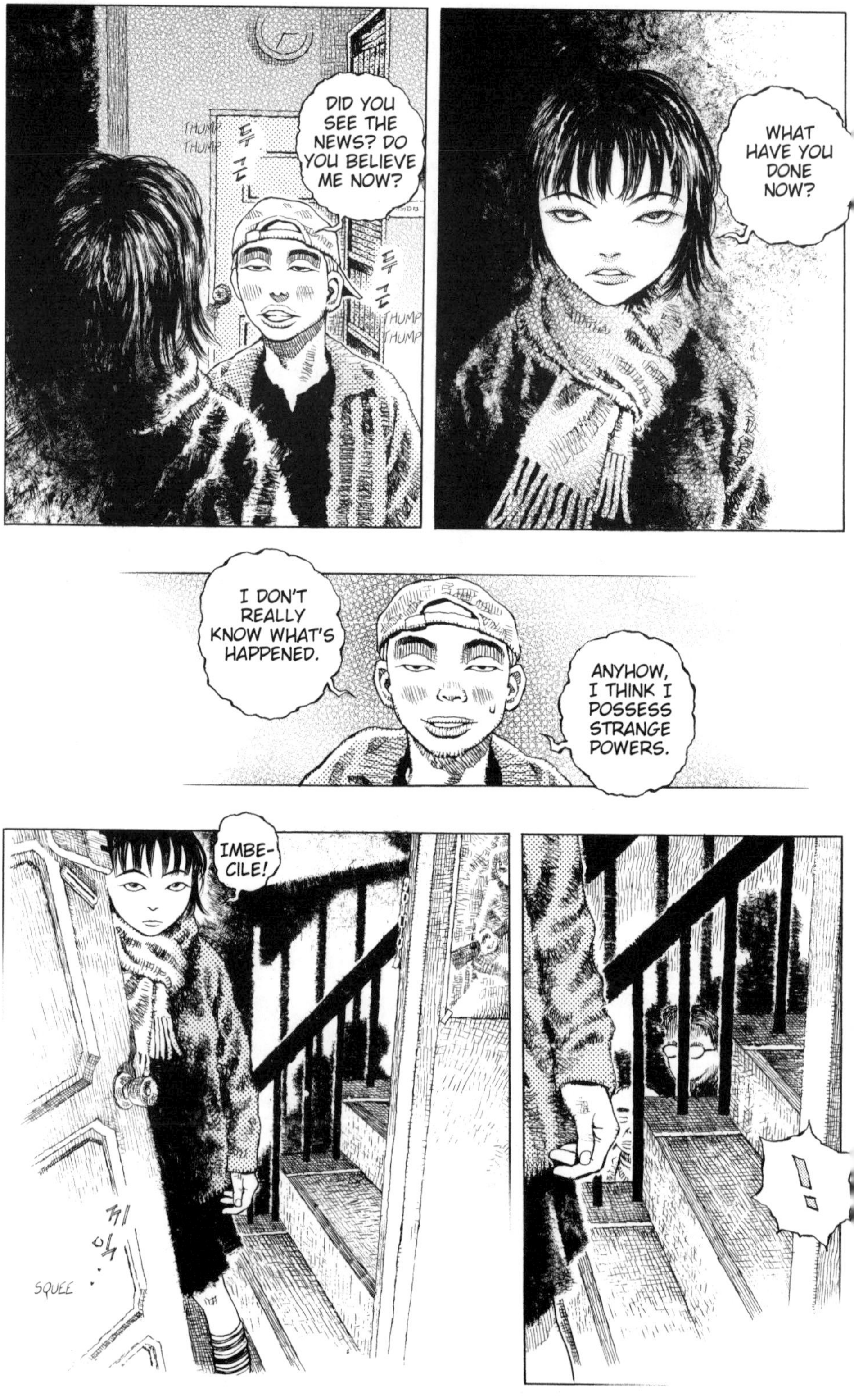
DID YOU SEE THE NEWS? DO YOU BELIEVE ME NOW?
THUMP THUMP
THUMP THUMP
WHAT HAVE YOU DONE NOW?
I DON'T REALLY KNOW WHAT'S HAPPENED.
ANYHOW, I THINK I POSSESS STRANGE POWERS.
IMBE-CILE!
SQUEE
!

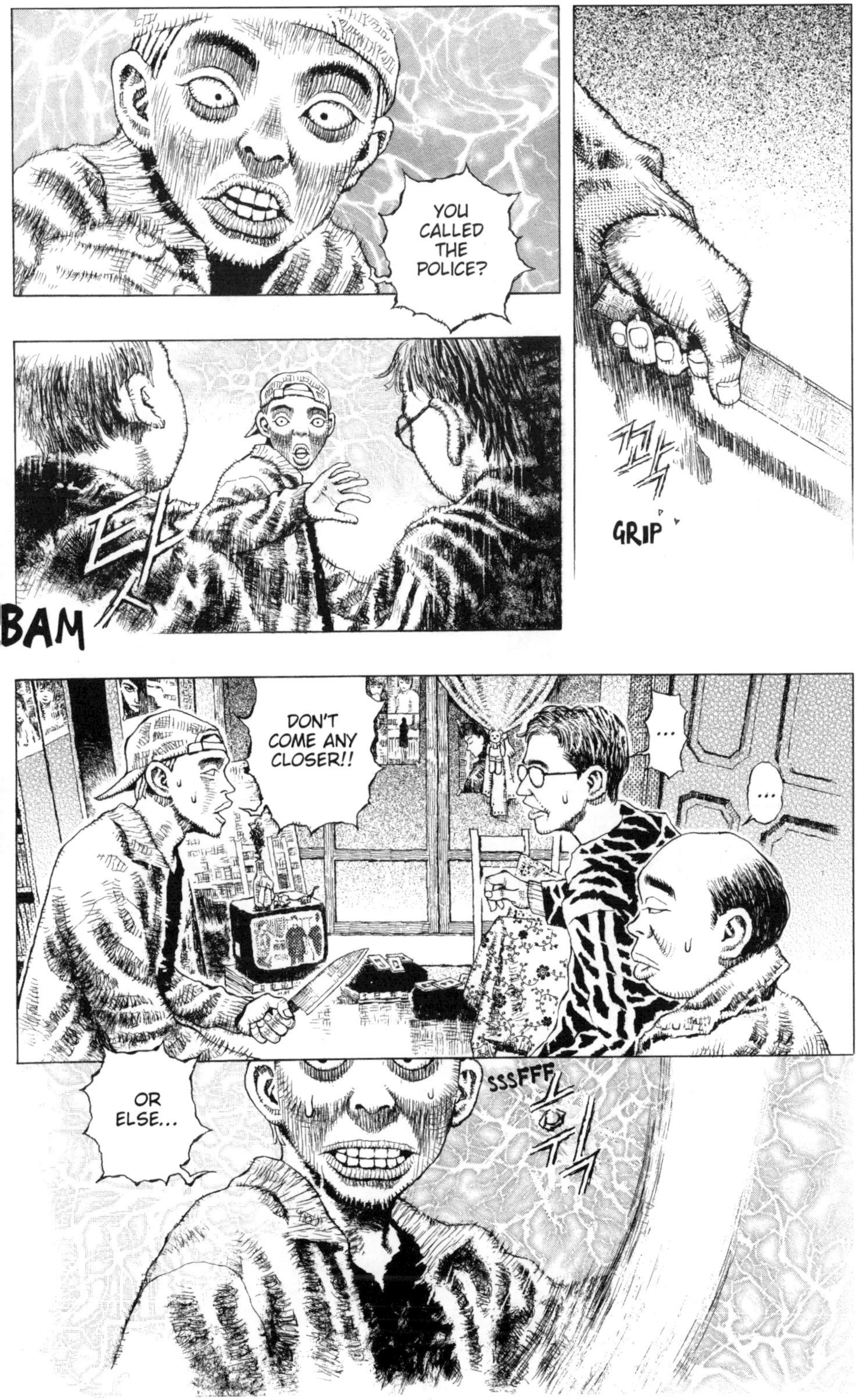
YOU CALLED THE POLICE?
GRIP
BAM
DON'T COME ANY CLOSER!!
...
...
OR ELSE...
SSSFFF

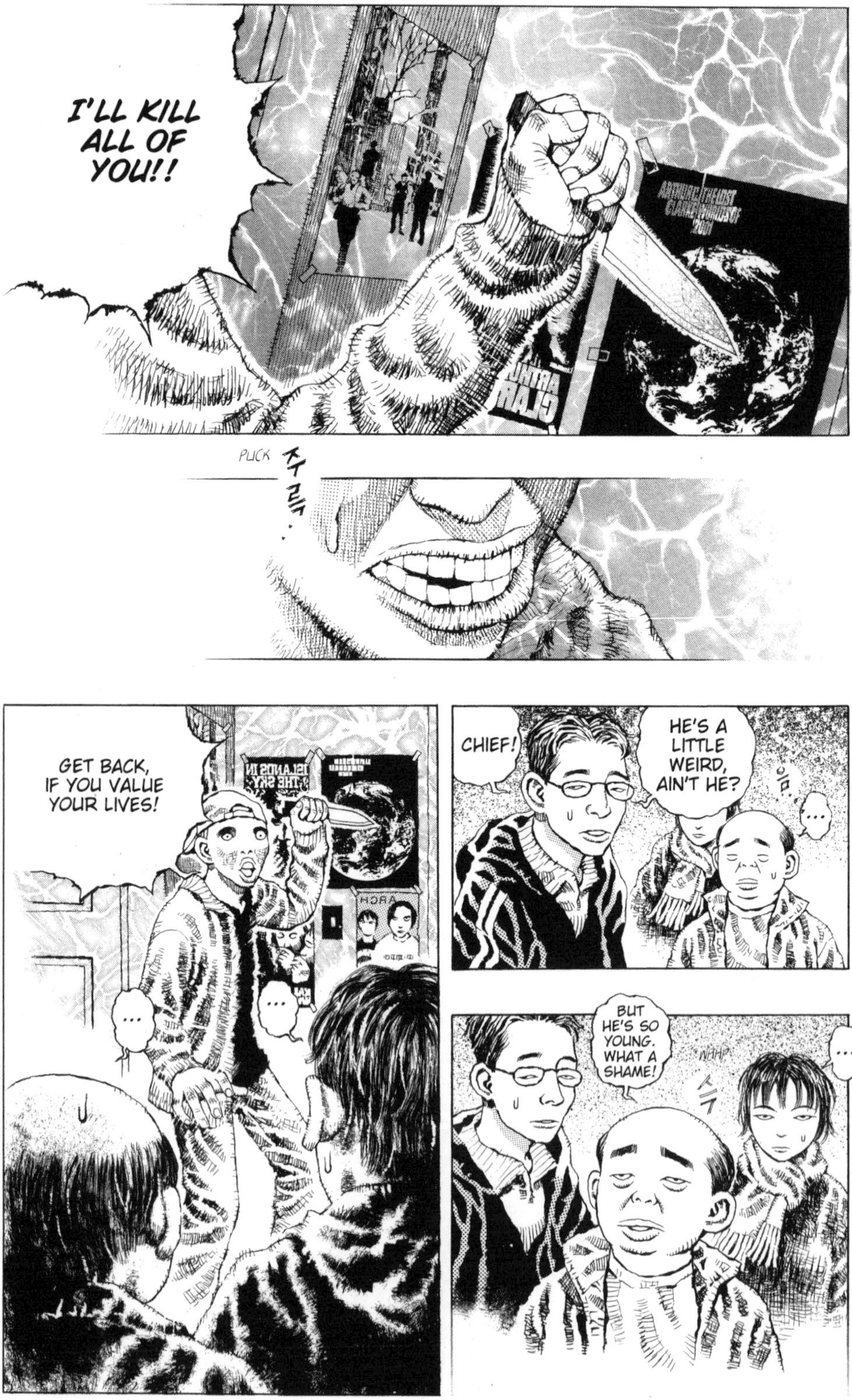
I'LL KILL ALL OF YOU!!
PUCK
GET BACK, IF YOU VALUE YOUR LIVES!
...
...
CHIEF!
HE'S A LITTLE WEIRD, AIN'T HE?
...
BUT HE'S SO YOUNG. WHAT A SHAME!
WHAP
...

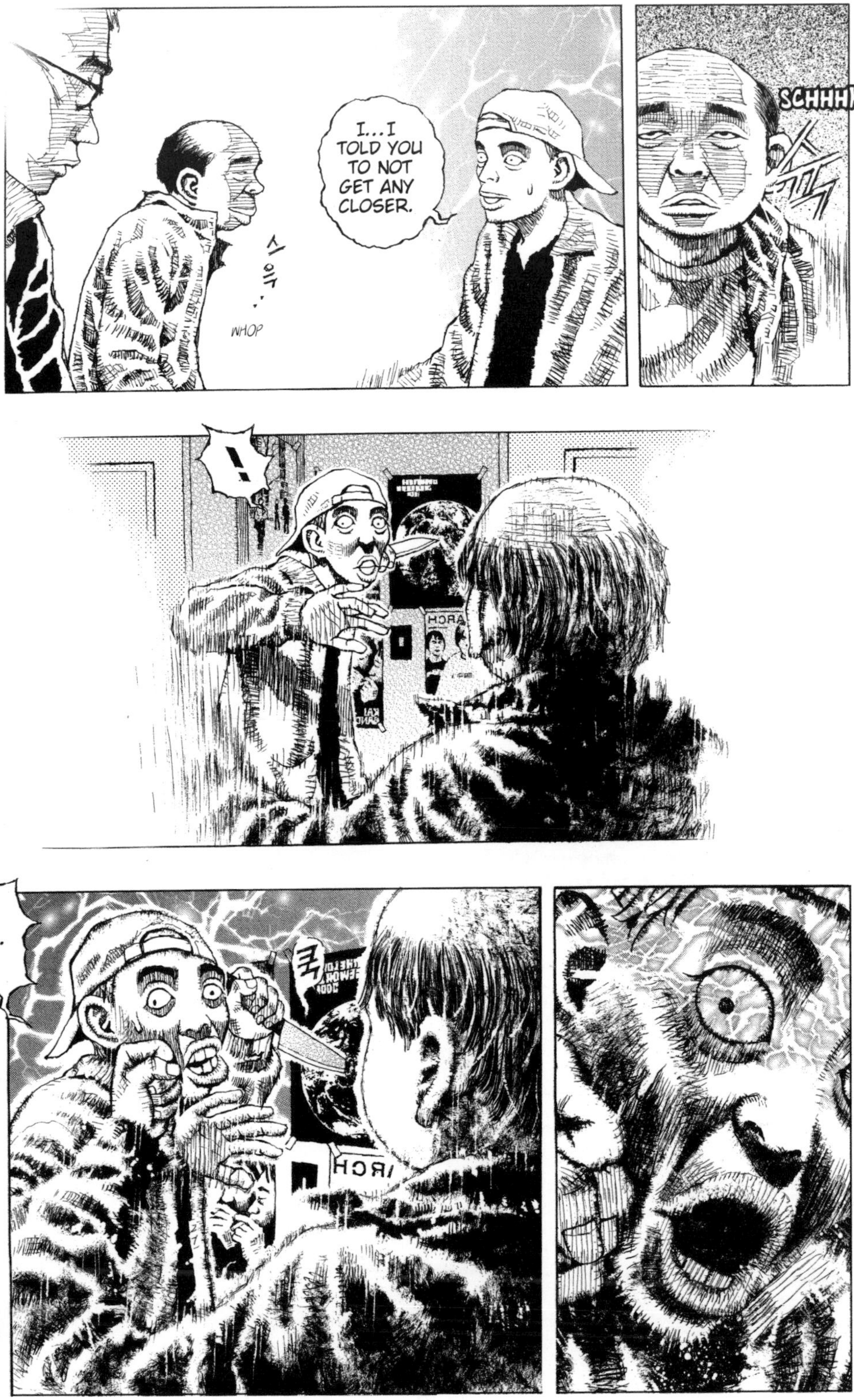
I...I TOLD YOU TO NOT GET ANY CLOSER.
스윽..
WHOP
SCHHHK
!
콕

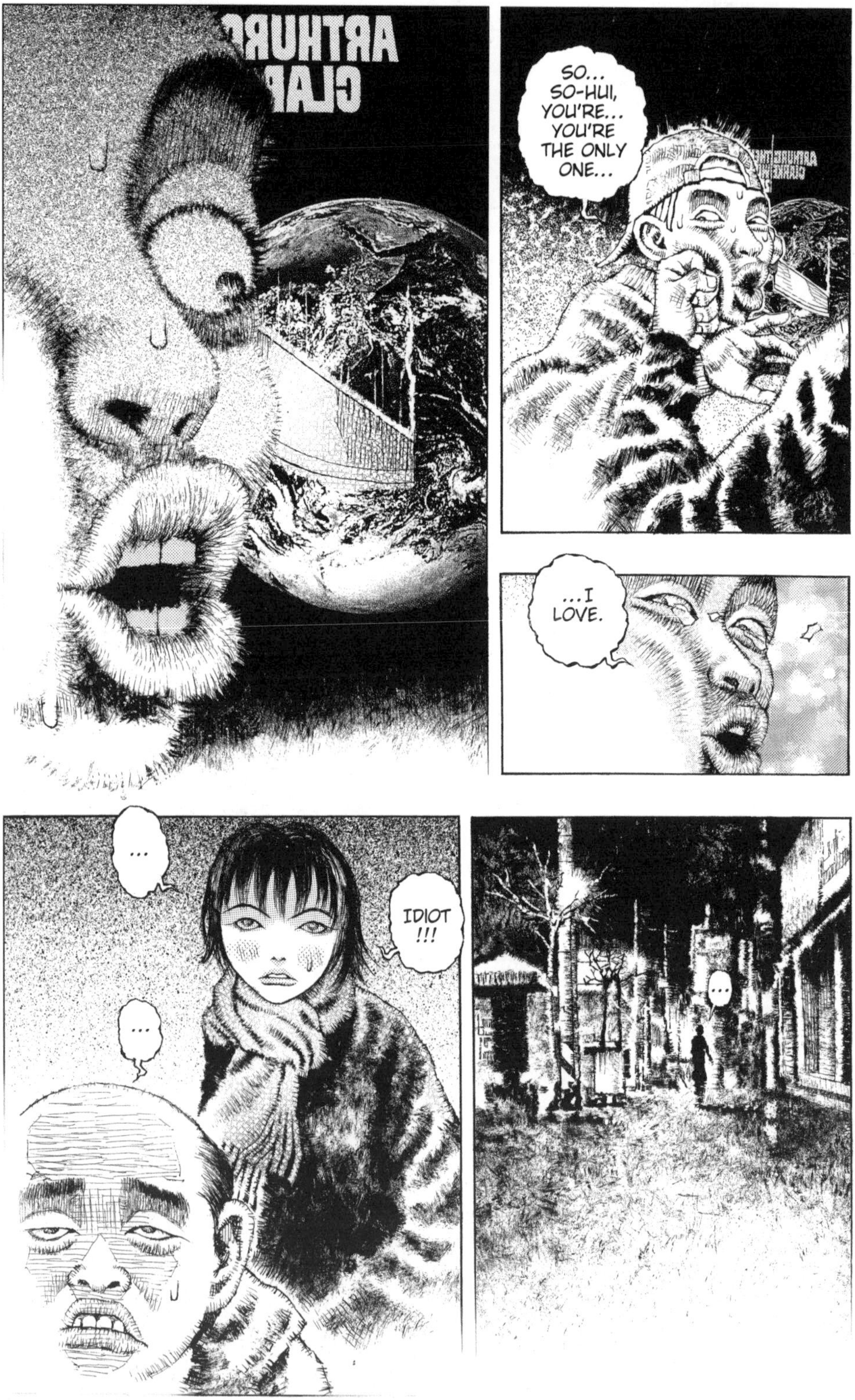
SO... SO-HUI, YOU'RE... YOU'RE THE ONLY ONE...
...I LOVE.
...
IDIOT !!!
...
...

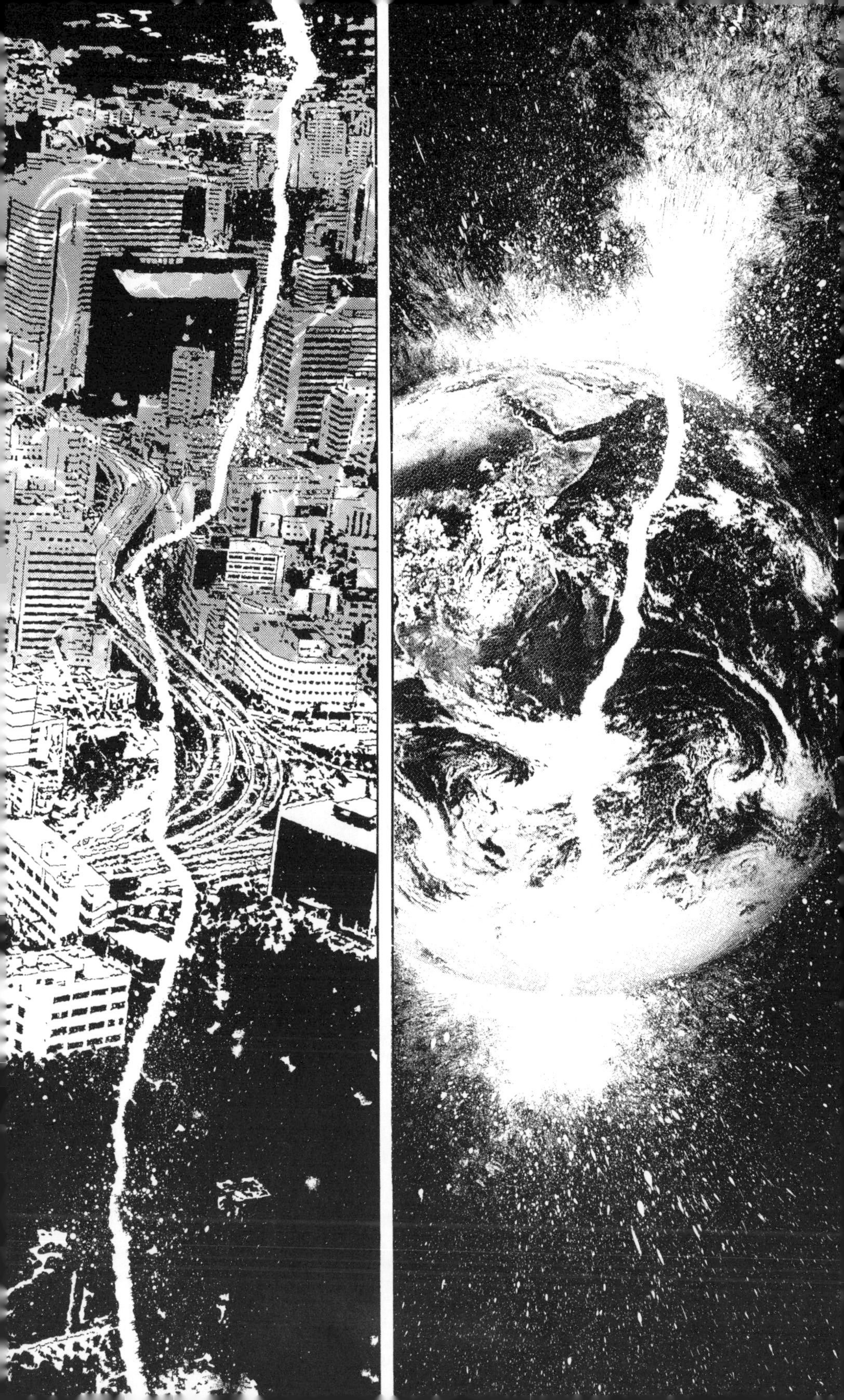

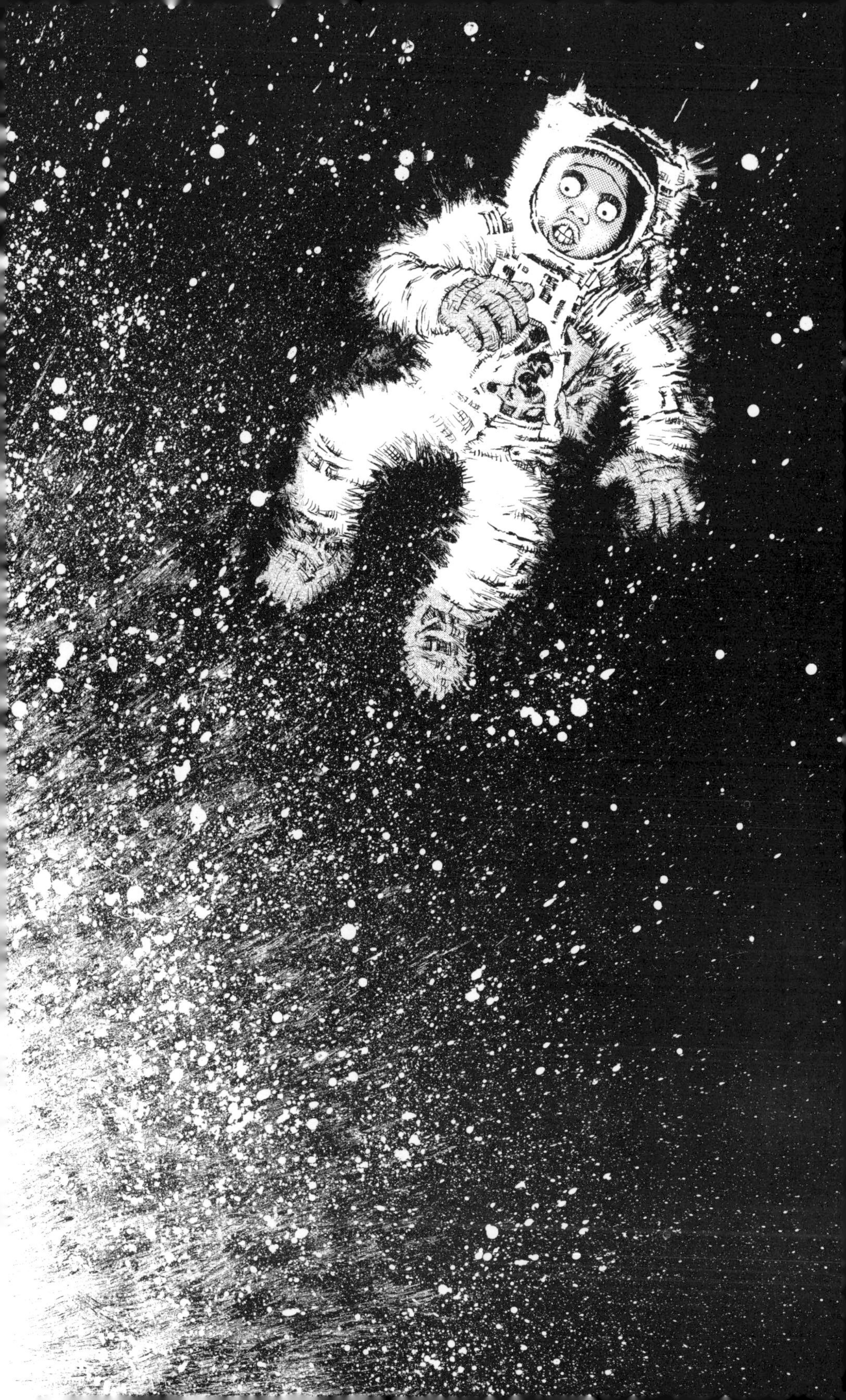

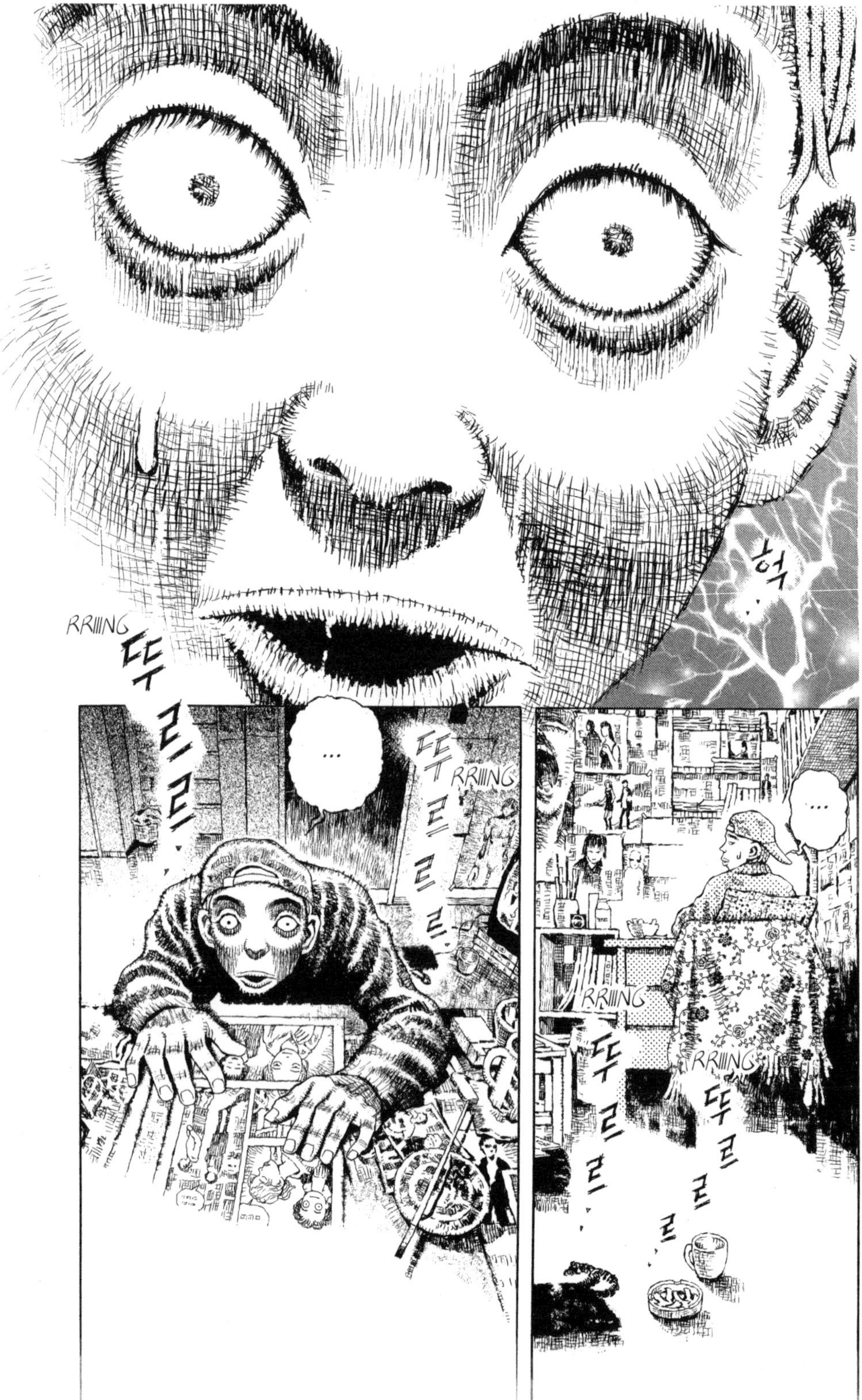
헉.
RRIIING
뚜르르.
...
RRIIING
뚜르르르.
...
RRIIING
뚜르르.
RRIIING
뚜르르르.

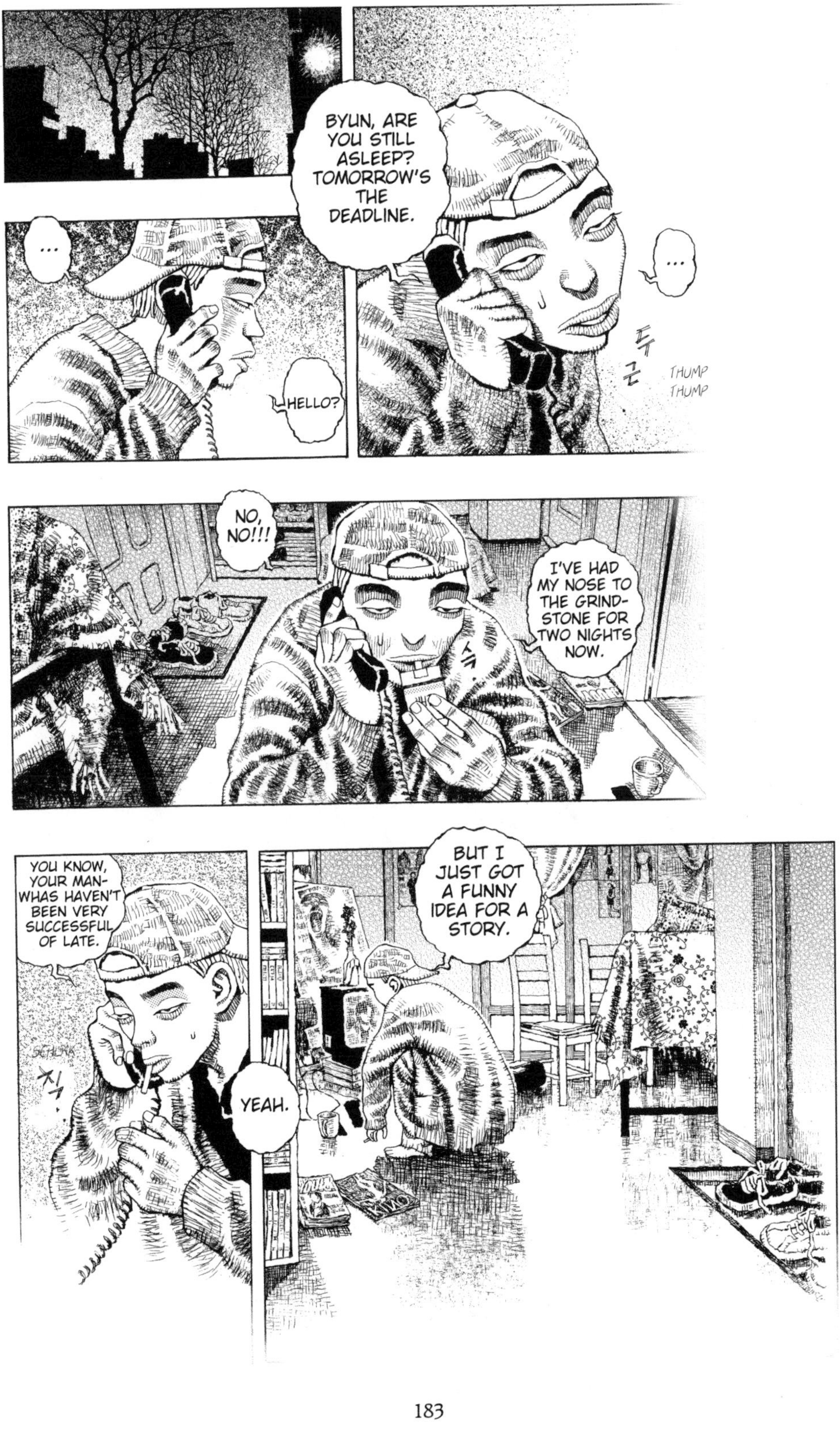
BYUN, ARE YOU STILL ASLEEP? TOMORROW'S THE DEADLINE.
...
HELLO?
...
THUMP THUMP
NO, NO!!!
I'VE HAD MY NOSE TO THE GRIND-STONE FOR TWO NIGHTS NOW.
YOU KNOW, YOUR MAN-WHAS HAVEN'T BEEN VERY SUCCESSFUL OF LATE.
BUT I JUST GOT A FUNNY IDEA FOR A STORY.
YEAH.

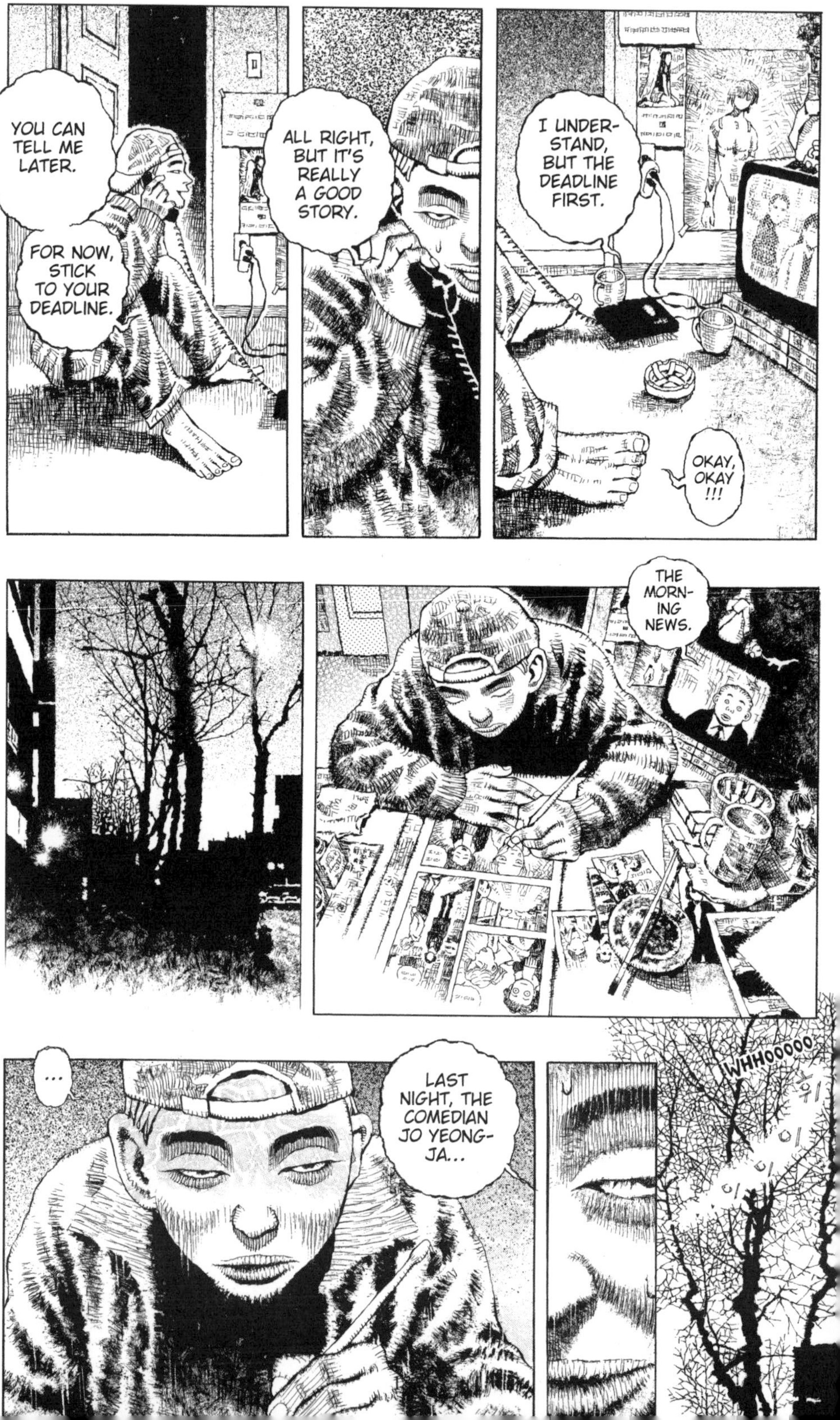
YOU CAN TELL ME LATER.
FOR NOW, STICK TO YOUR DEADLINE.
ALL RIGHT, BUT IT'S REALLY A GOOD STORY.
I UNDER-STAND, BUT THE DEADLINE FIRST.
OKAY, OKAY !!!
THE MORN-ING NEWS.
...
LAST NIGHT, THE COMEDIAN JO YEONG-JA...
WHHOOOOO

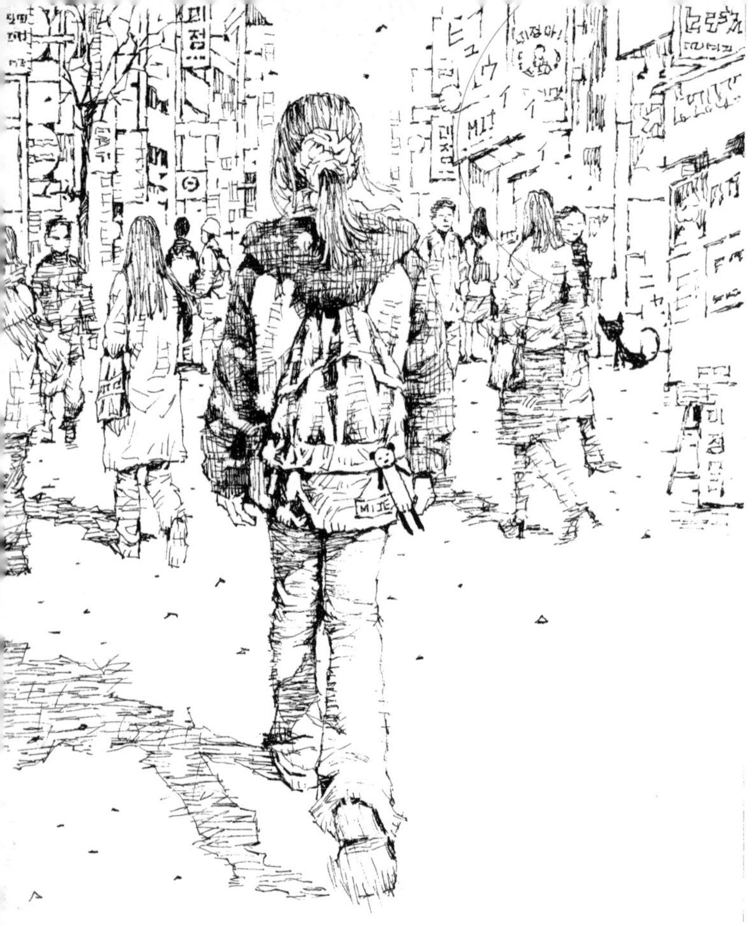
MIJE

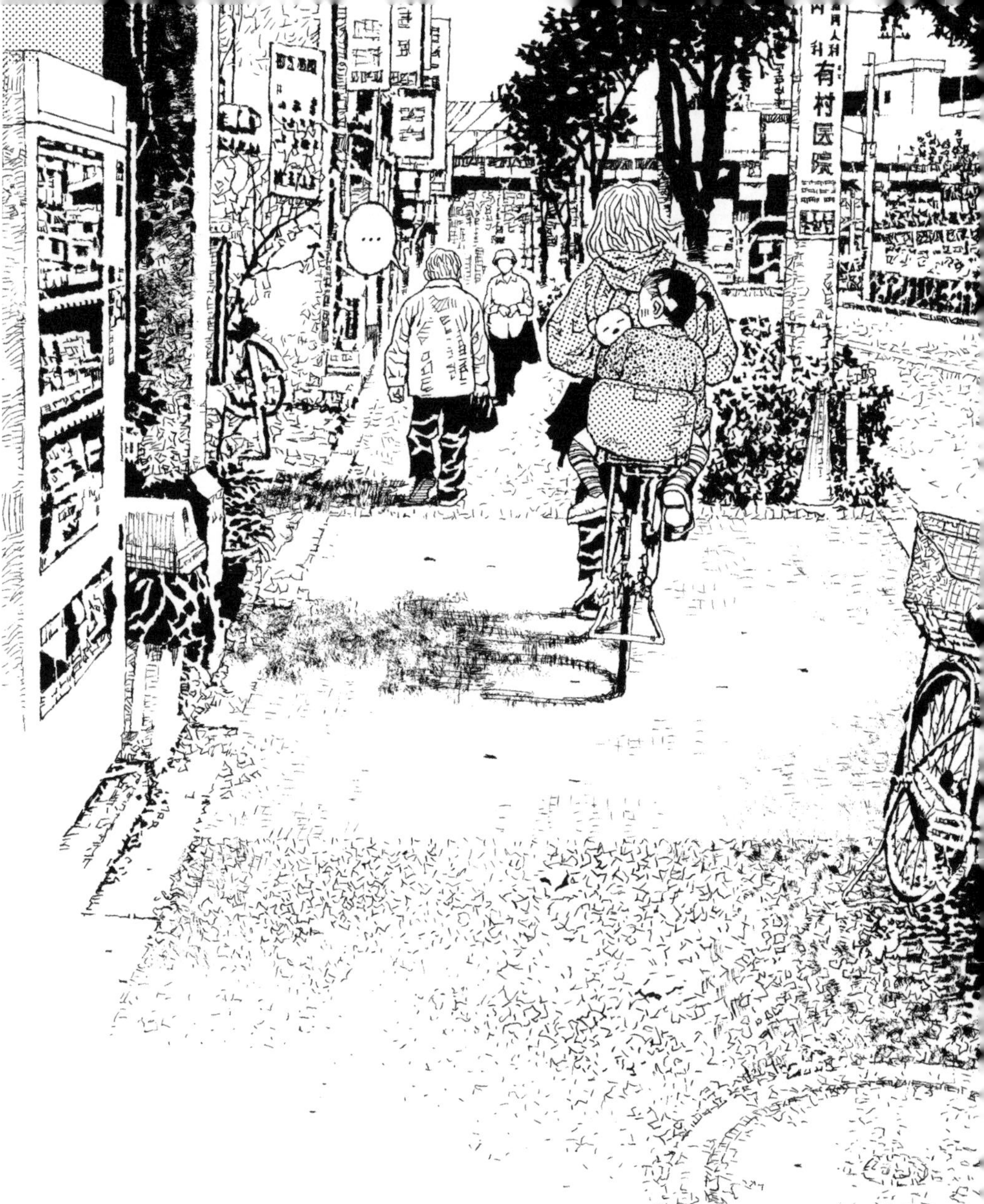
...
有村医院

Courage, grandpa!

Tokyo, 2001

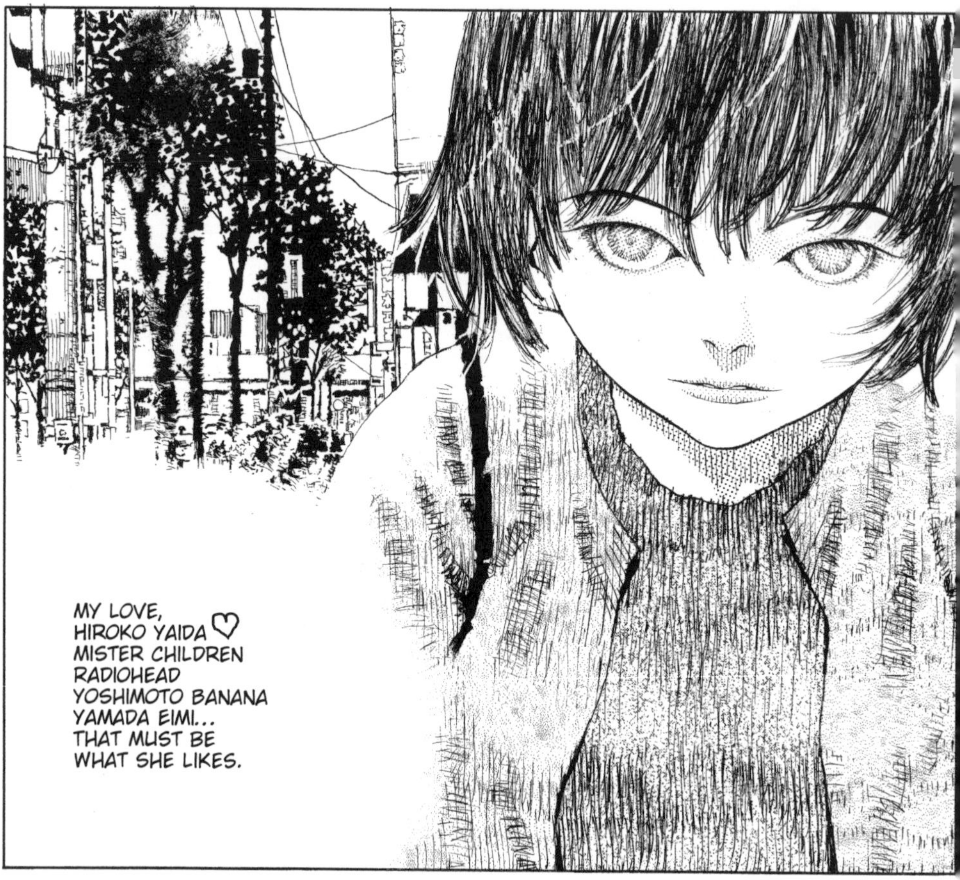
MY LOVE,
HIROKO YAIDA ♡
MISTER CHILDREN
RADIOHEAD
YOSHIMOTO BANANA
YAMADA EIMI...
THAT MUST BE
WHAT SHE LIKES.

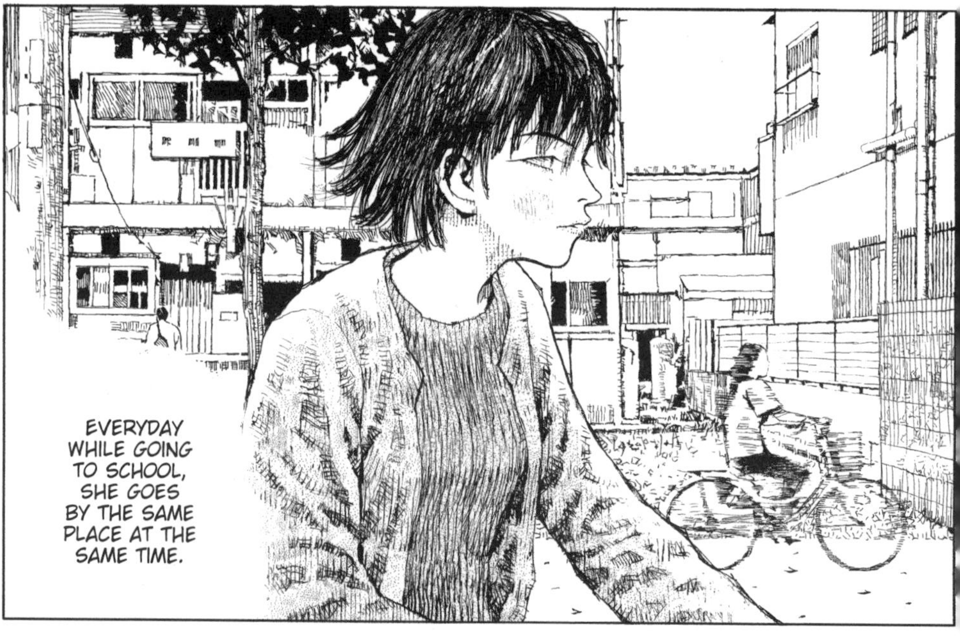
EVERYDAY
WHILE GOING
TO SCHOOL,
SHE GOES
BY THE SAME
PLACE AT THE
SAME TIME.

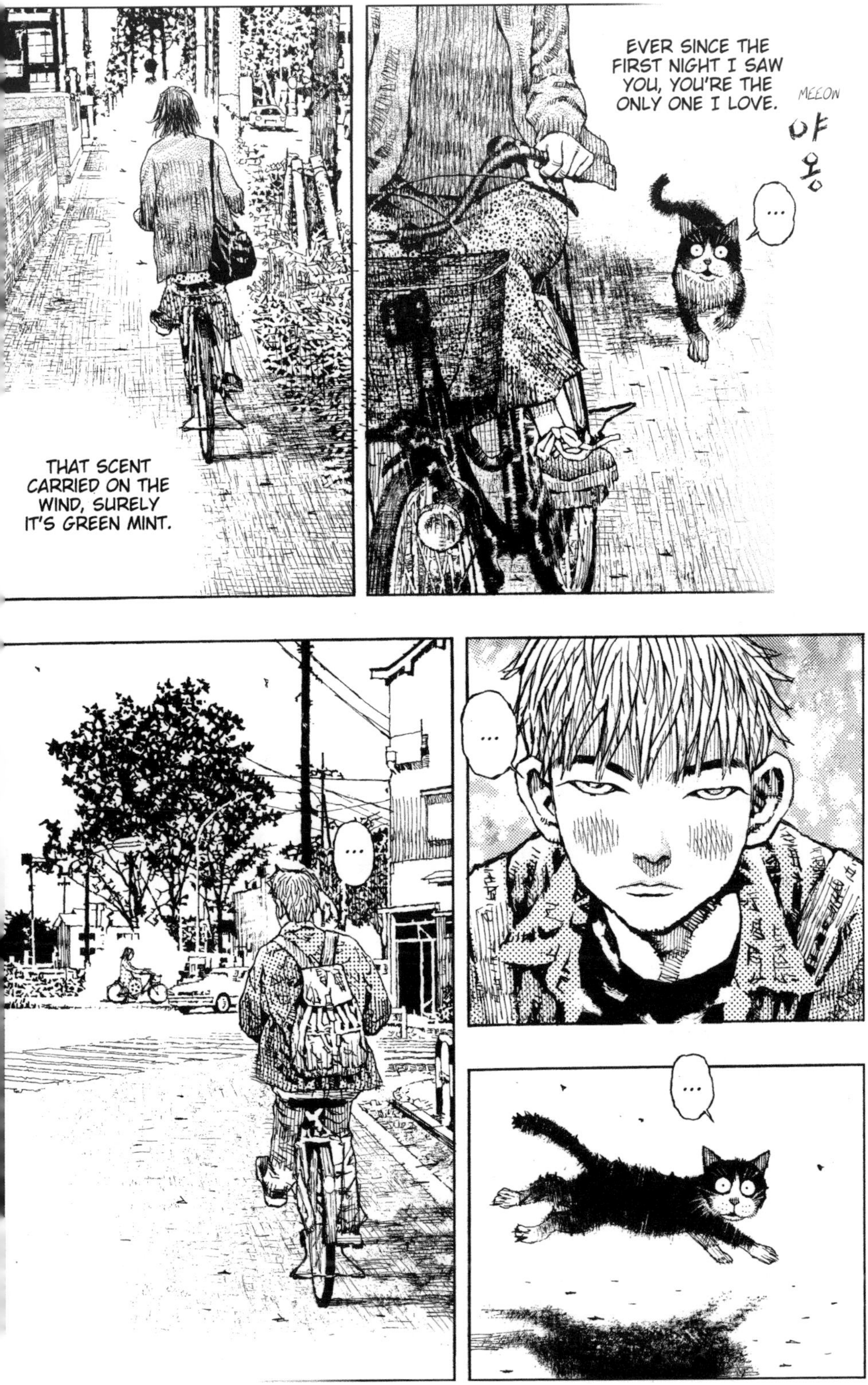
THAT SCENT CARRIED ON THE WIND, SURELY IT'S GREEN MINT.
EVER SINCE THE FIRST NIGHT I SAW YOU, YOU'RE THE ONLY ONE I LOVE.
MEEOW
야옹
...
...
...
...

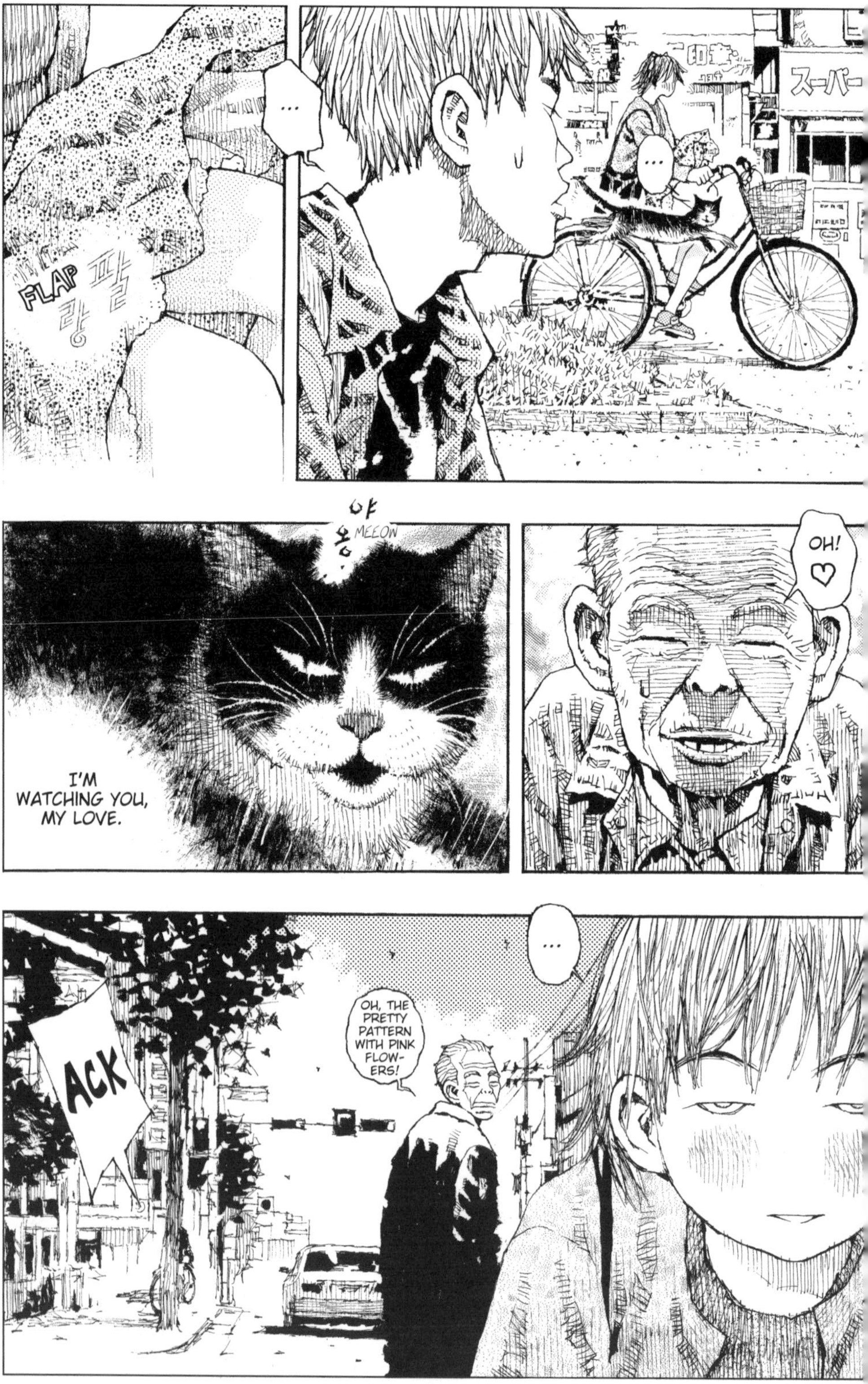
FLAP
팔랑
...
...
スーパー
야옹
MEEOW
I'M WATCHING YOU, MY LOVE.
OH! ♥
ACK
OH, THE PRETTY PATTERN WITH PINK FLOW-ERS!
...

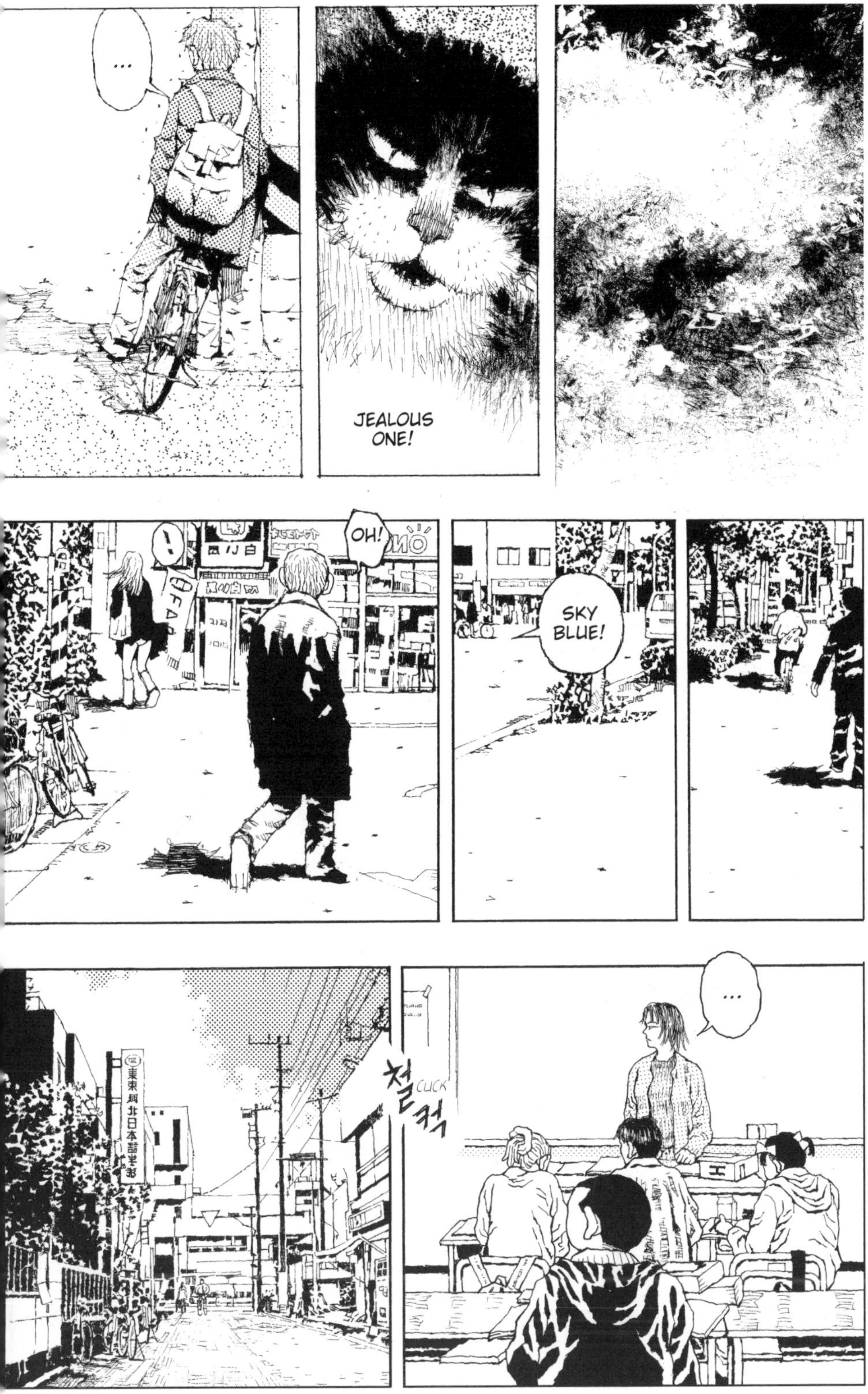
...
JEALOUS ONE!
!
OH!
SKY BLUE!
철컥
CLICK
...

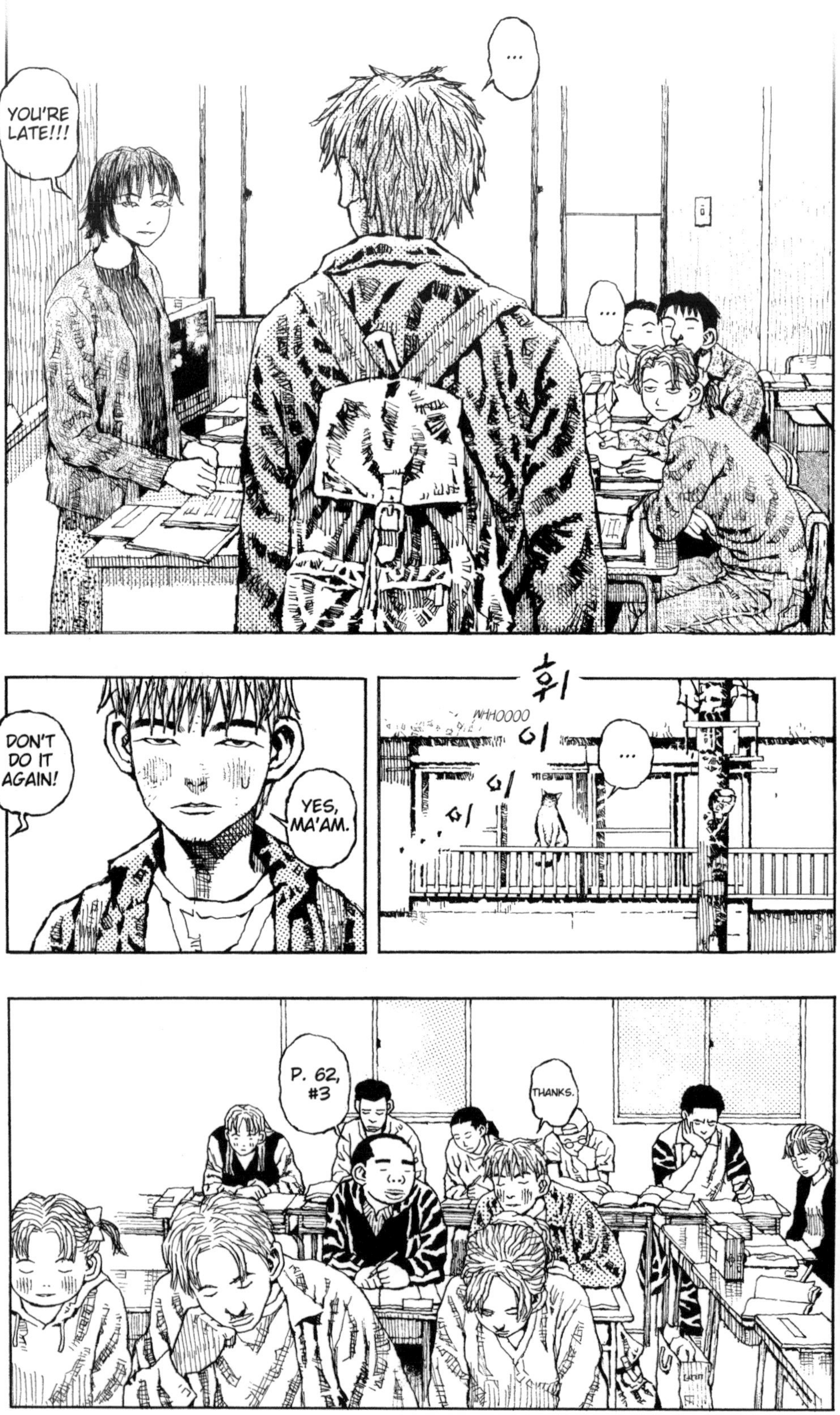
...
YOU'RE LATE!!!
...
DON'T DO IT AGAIN!
YES, MA'AM.
휘
이
이
이
WHHOOOO
...
P. 62, #3
THANKS.

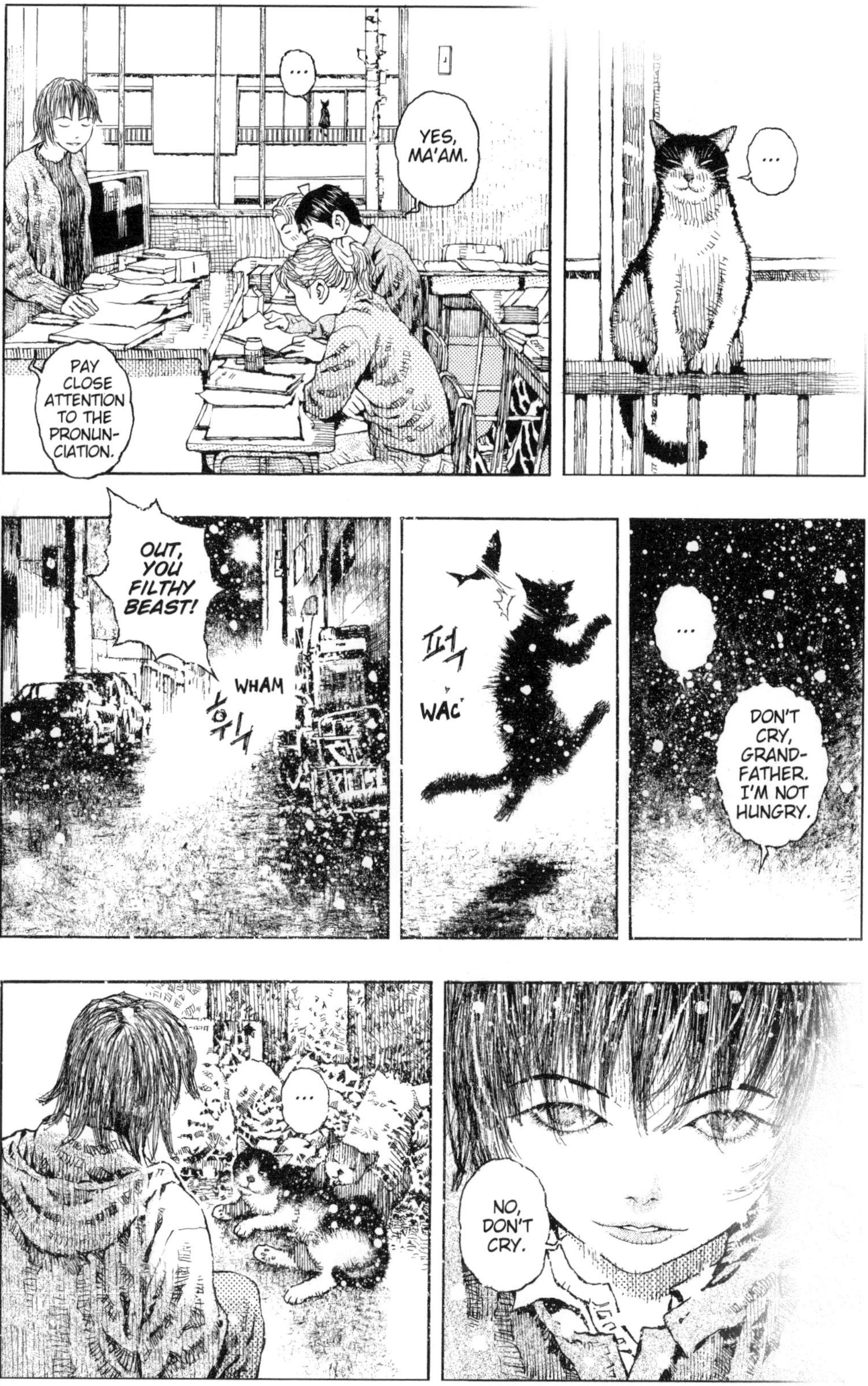
PAY CLOSE ATTENTION TO THE PRONUN-CIATION.
...
YES, MA'AM.
...
OUT, YOU FILTHY BEAST!
WHAM
WAC
...
DON'T CRY, GRAND-FATHER. I'M NOT HUNGRY.
...
NO, DON'T CRY.

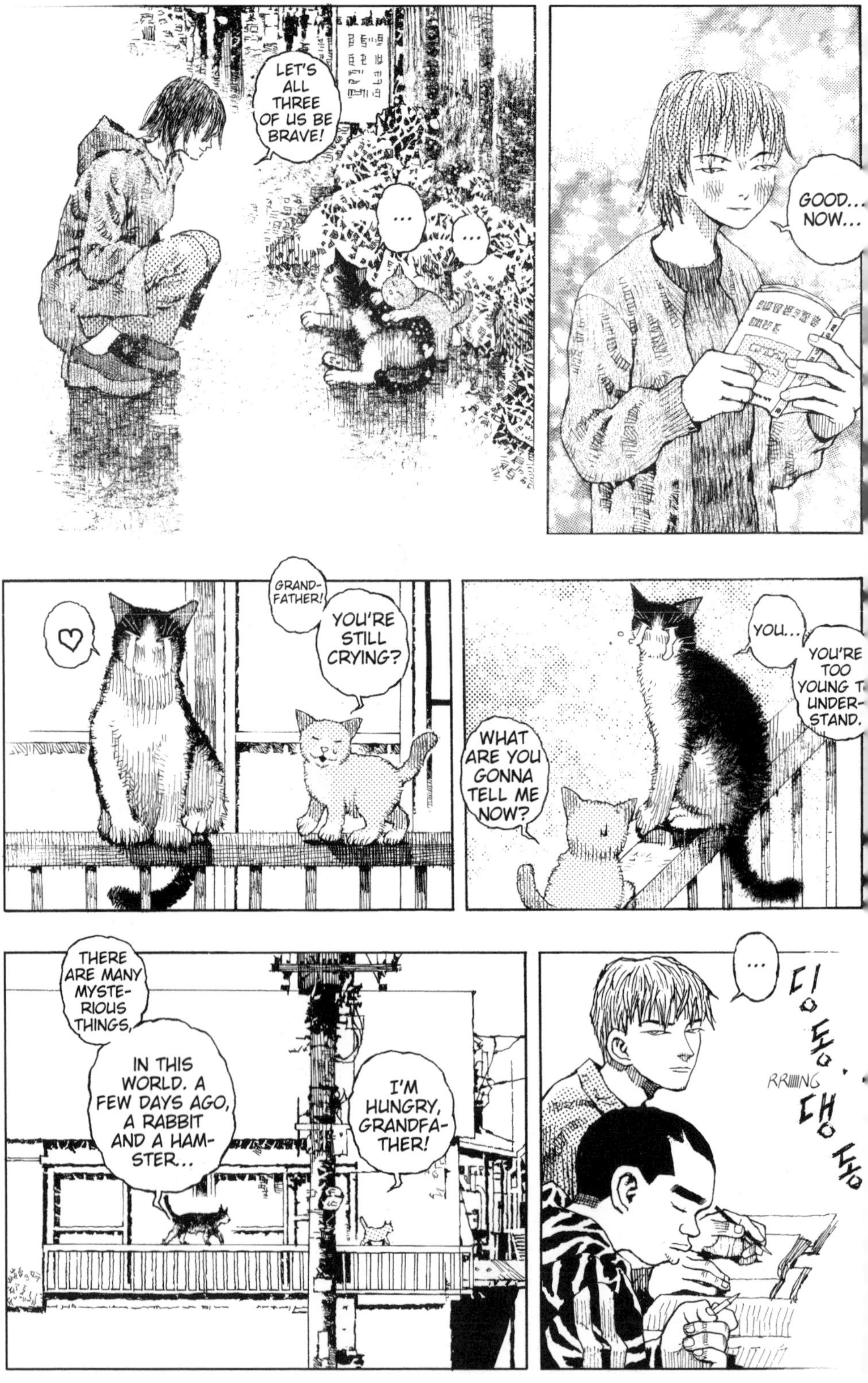

LET'S ALL THREE OF US BE BRAVE!
...
...
GOOD... NOW...
GRAND-FATHER!
YOU'RE STILL CRYING?
YOU...
YOU'RE TOO YOUNG T UNDER-STAND.
WHAT ARE YOU GONNA TELL ME NOW?
THERE ARE MANY MYSTE-RIOUS THINGS,
IN THIS WORLD. A FEW DAYS AGO, A RABBIT AND A HAM-STER...
I'M HUNGRY, GRANDFA-THER!
...
딩동 댕동
RRIIING

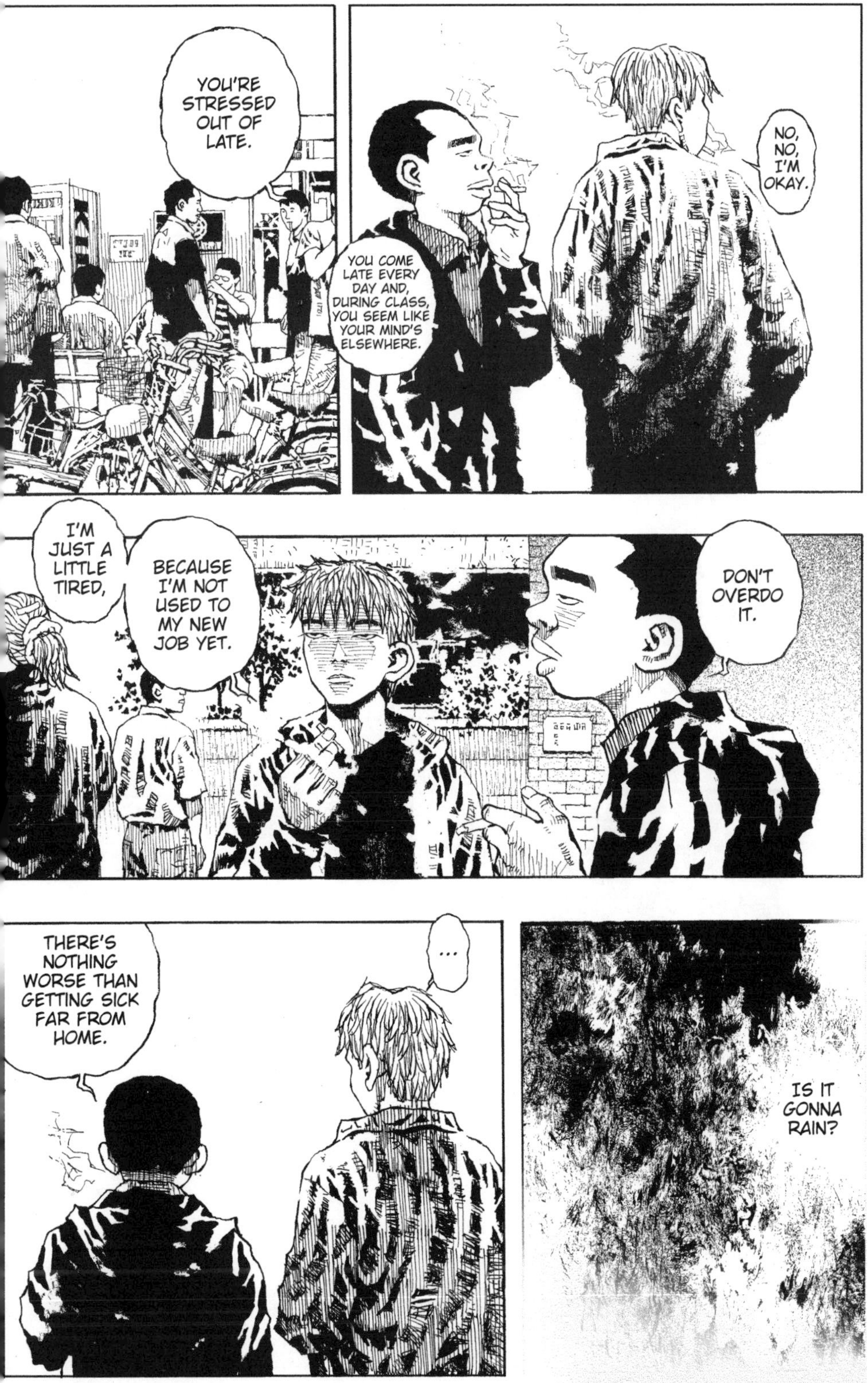
YOU'RE STRESSED OUT OF LATE.
YOU COME LATE EVERY DAY AND, DURING CLASS, YOU SEEM LIKE YOUR MIND'S ELSEWHERE.
NO, NO, I'M OKAY.
I'M JUST A LITTLE TIRED,
BECAUSE I'M NOT USED TO MY NEW JOB YET.
DON'T OVERDO IT.
THERE'S NOTHING WORSE THAN GETTING SICK FAR FROM HOME.
...
IS IT GONNA RAIN?

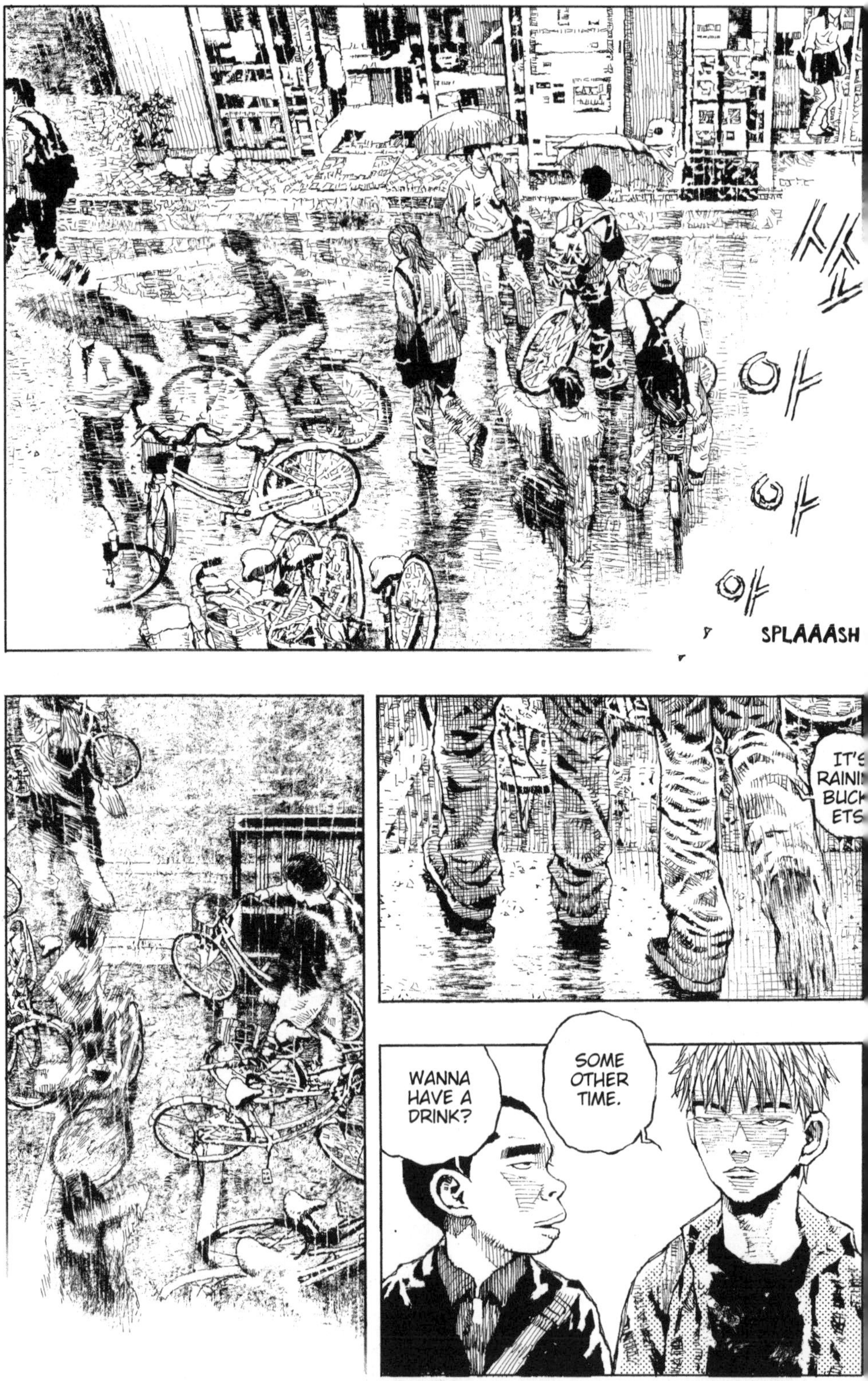
SPLAAASH
IT'S RAINING BUCKETS
WANNA HAVE A DRINK?
SOME OTHER TIME.

IT'S A DOWN-POUR.

...

U 'T E AN REL- ?

NO.

...

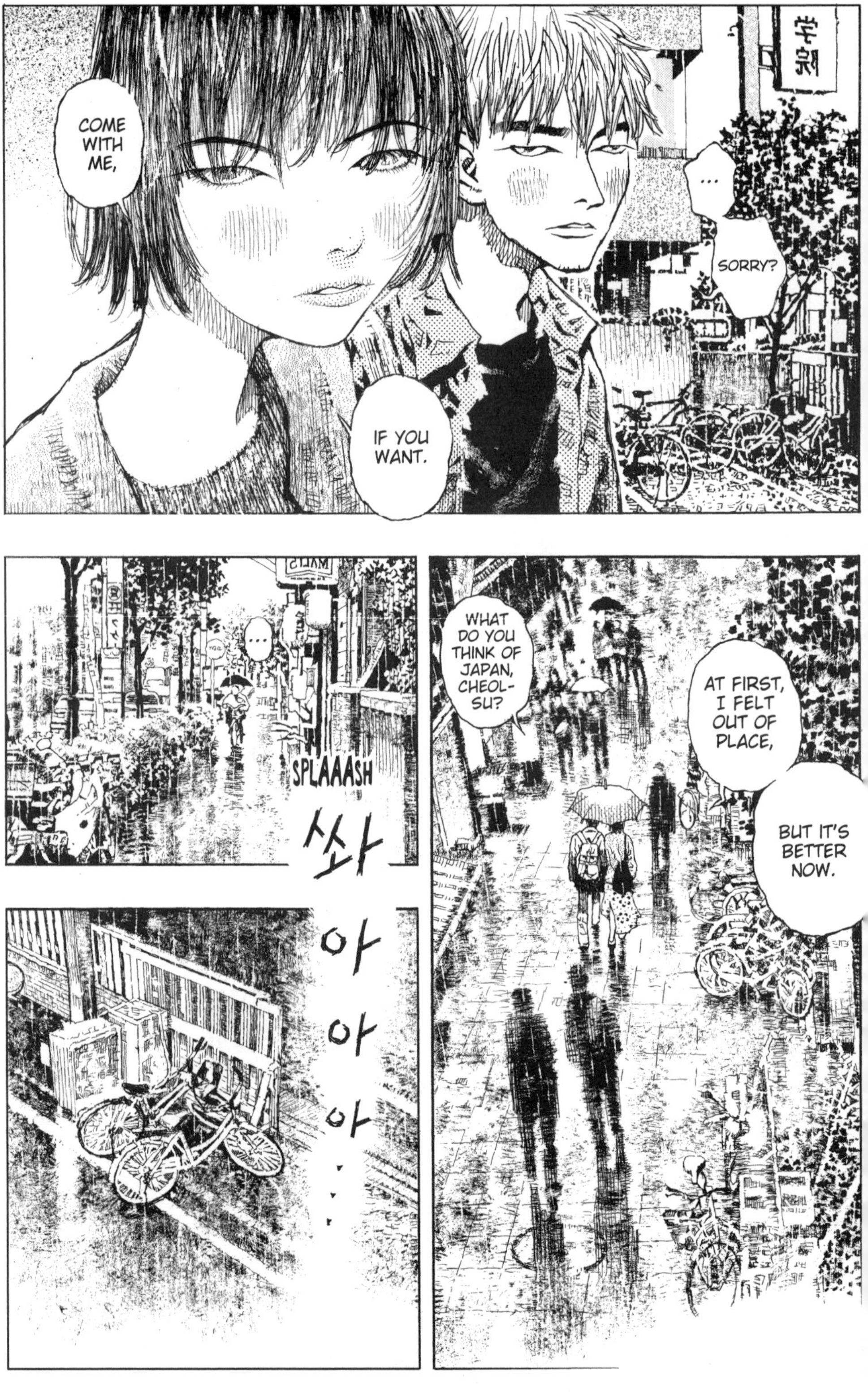

COME WITH ME,
...
SORRY?
IF YOU WANT.
...
SPLAAASH
쏴아아아...
WHAT DO YOU THINK OF JAPAN, CHEOL-SU?
AT FIRST, I FELT OUT OF PLACE,
BUT IT'S BETTER NOW.

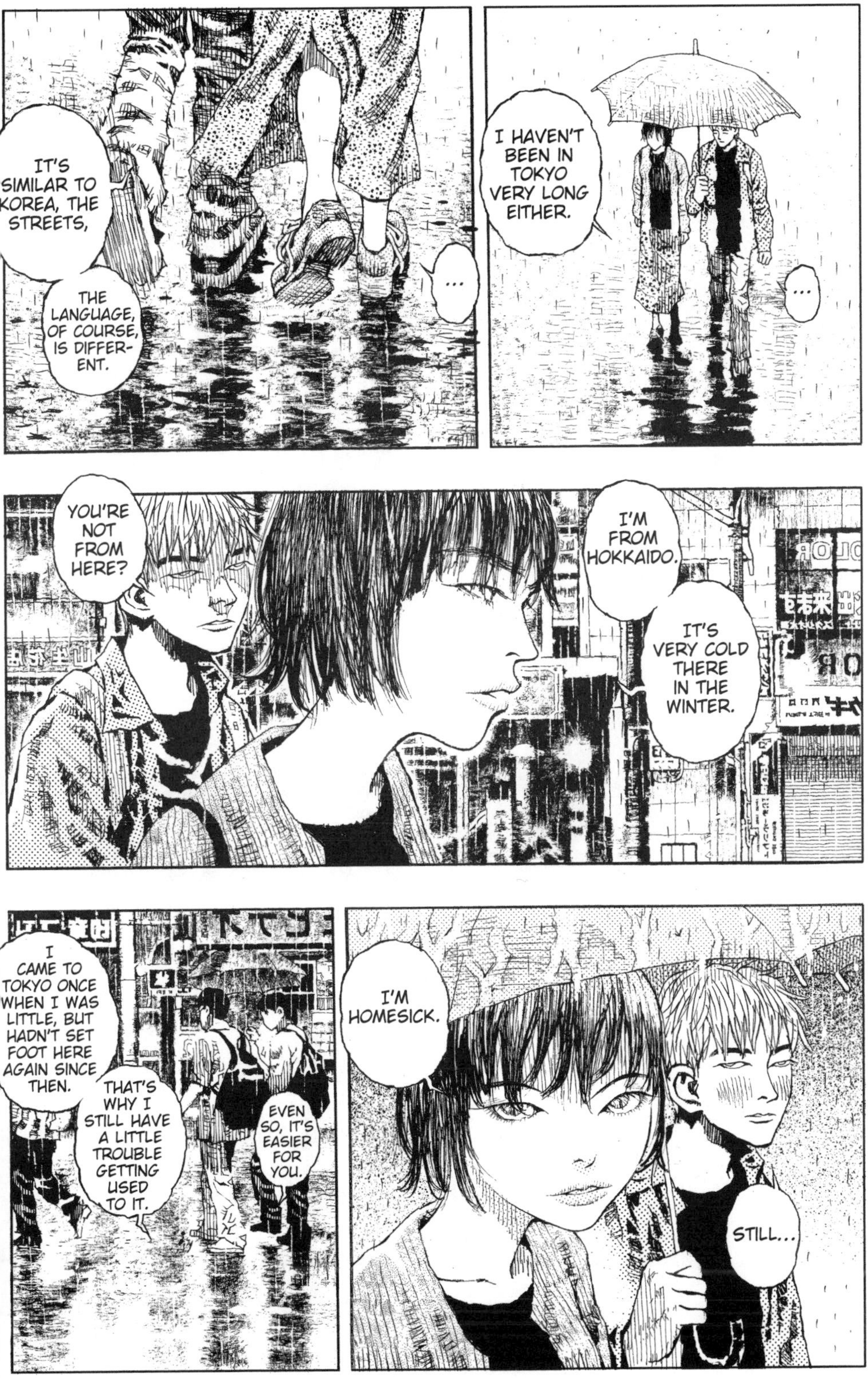
IT'S SIMILAR TO KOREA, THE STREETS,
THE LANGUAGE, OF COURSE, IS DIFFERENT.
...
I HAVEN'T BEEN IN TOKYO VERY LONG EITHER.
...
YOU'RE NOT FROM HERE?
I'M FROM HOKKAIDO.
IT'S VERY COLD THERE IN THE WINTER.
I CAME TO TOKYO ONCE WHEN I WAS LITTLE, BUT HADN'T SET FOOT HERE AGAIN SINCE THEN.
THAT'S WHY I STILL HAVE A LITTLE TROUBLE GETTING USED TO IT.
EVEN SO, IT'S EASIER FOR YOU.
I'M HOMESICK.
STILL...

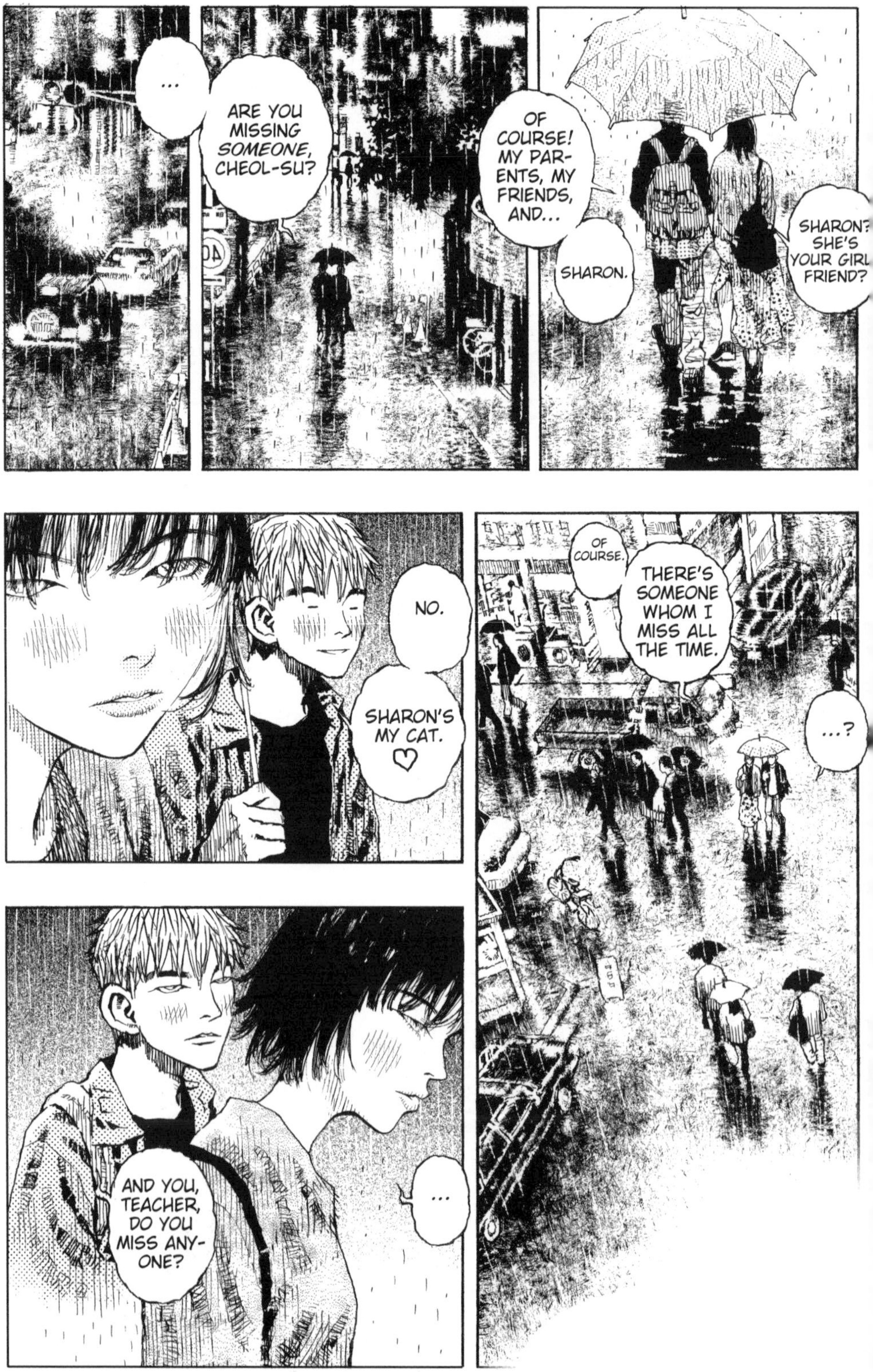
...
ARE YOU MISSING SOMEONE, CHEOL-SU?
OF COURSE! MY PARENTS, MY FRIENDS, AND...
SHARON.
SHARON? SHE'S YOUR GIRLFRIEND?
NO.
SHARON'S MY CAT. ♡
AND YOU, TEACHER, DO YOU MISS ANYONE?
...
OF COURSE.
THERE'S SOMEONE WHOM I MISS ALL THE TIME.
...?

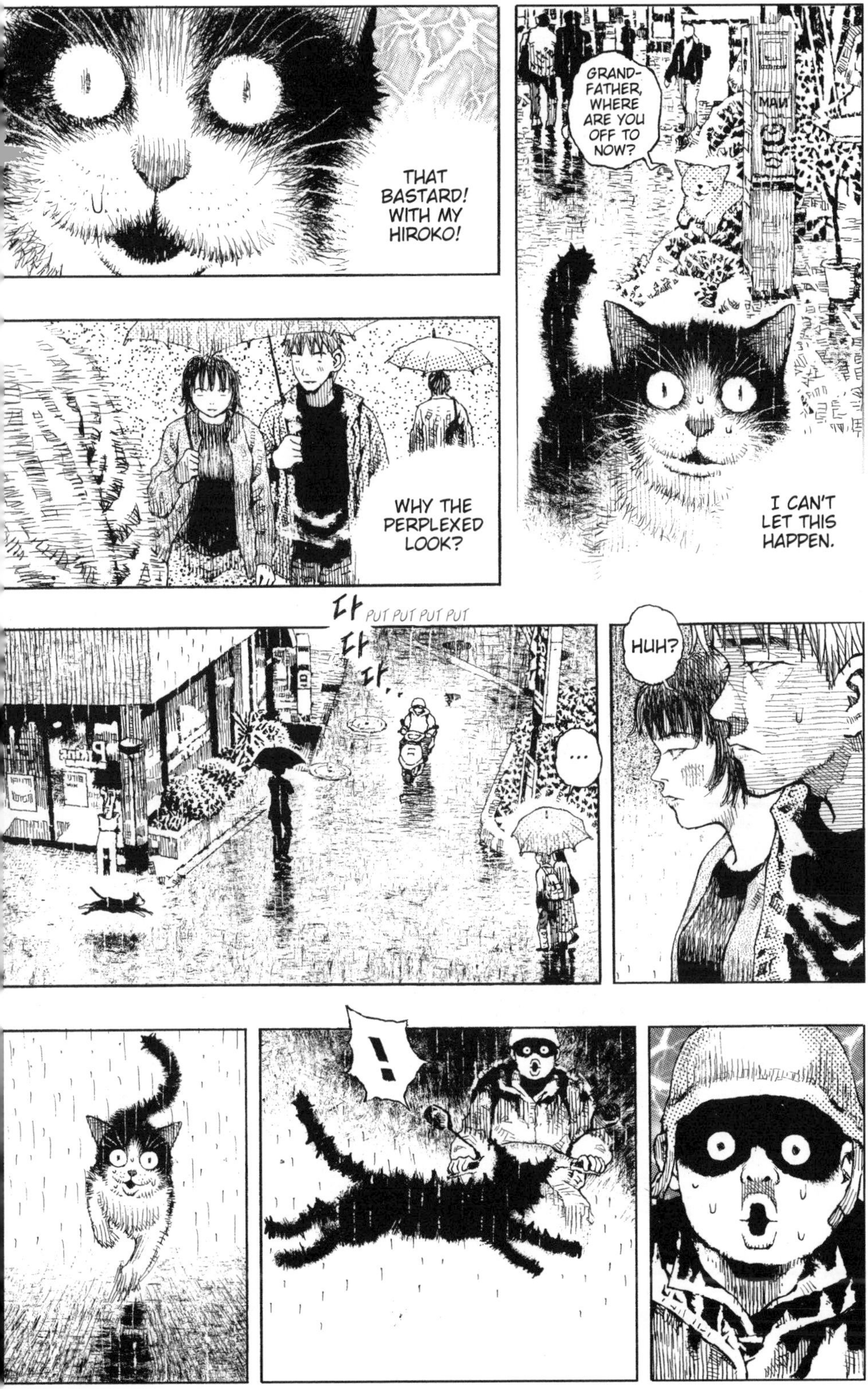
THAT BASTARD! WITH MY HIROKO!
GRAND-FATHER, WHERE ARE YOU OFF TO NOW?
MAN
WHY THE PERPLEXED LOOK?
I CAN'T LET THIS HAPPEN.
다 다 다 PUT PUT PUT PUT
...
HUH?
!

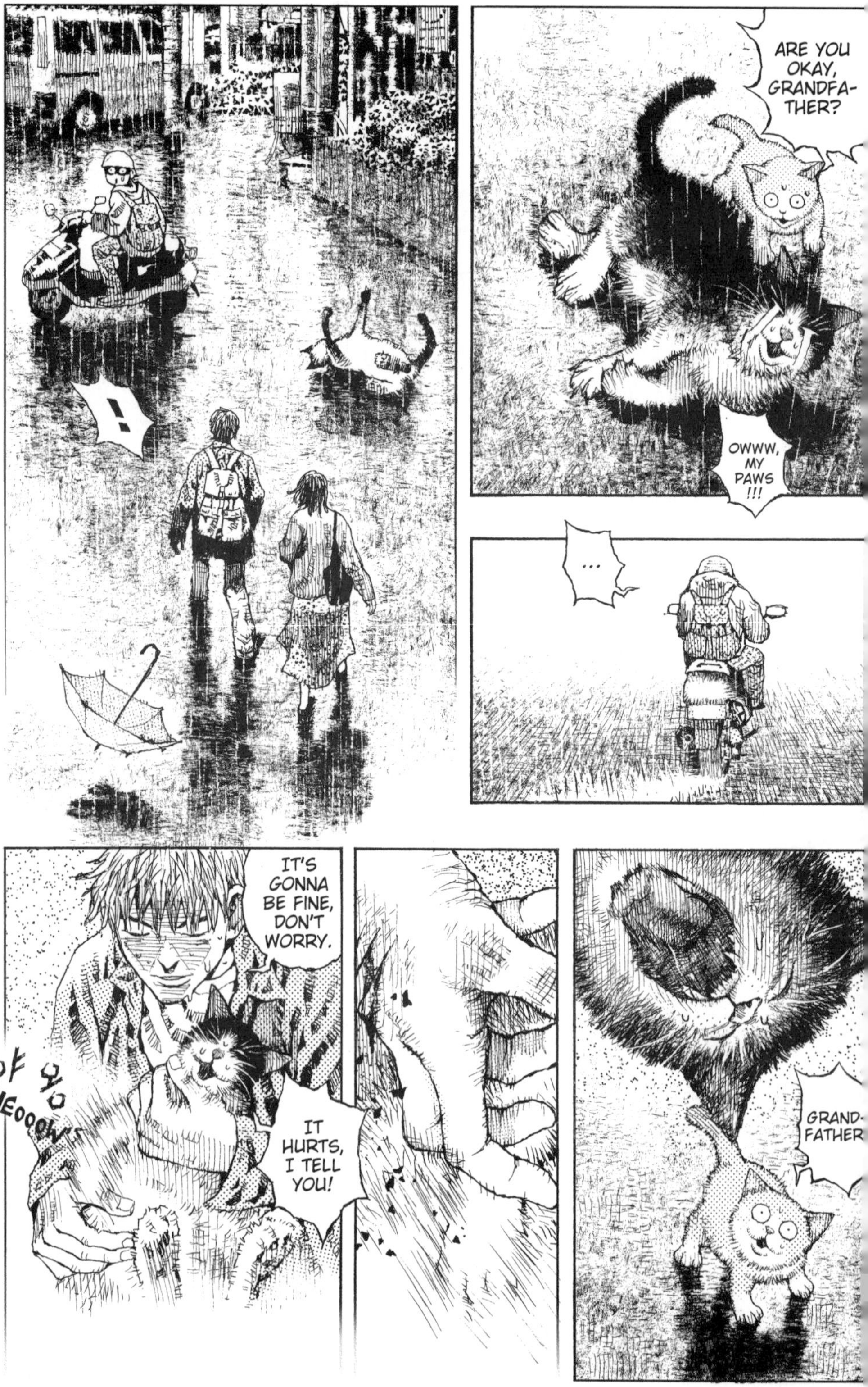
!
ARE YOU OKAY, GRANDFA-THER?
OWWW, MY PAWS!!!
...
IT'S GONNA BE FINE, DON'T WORRY.
MEOOOW
IT HURTS, I TELL YOU!
GRAND-FATHER

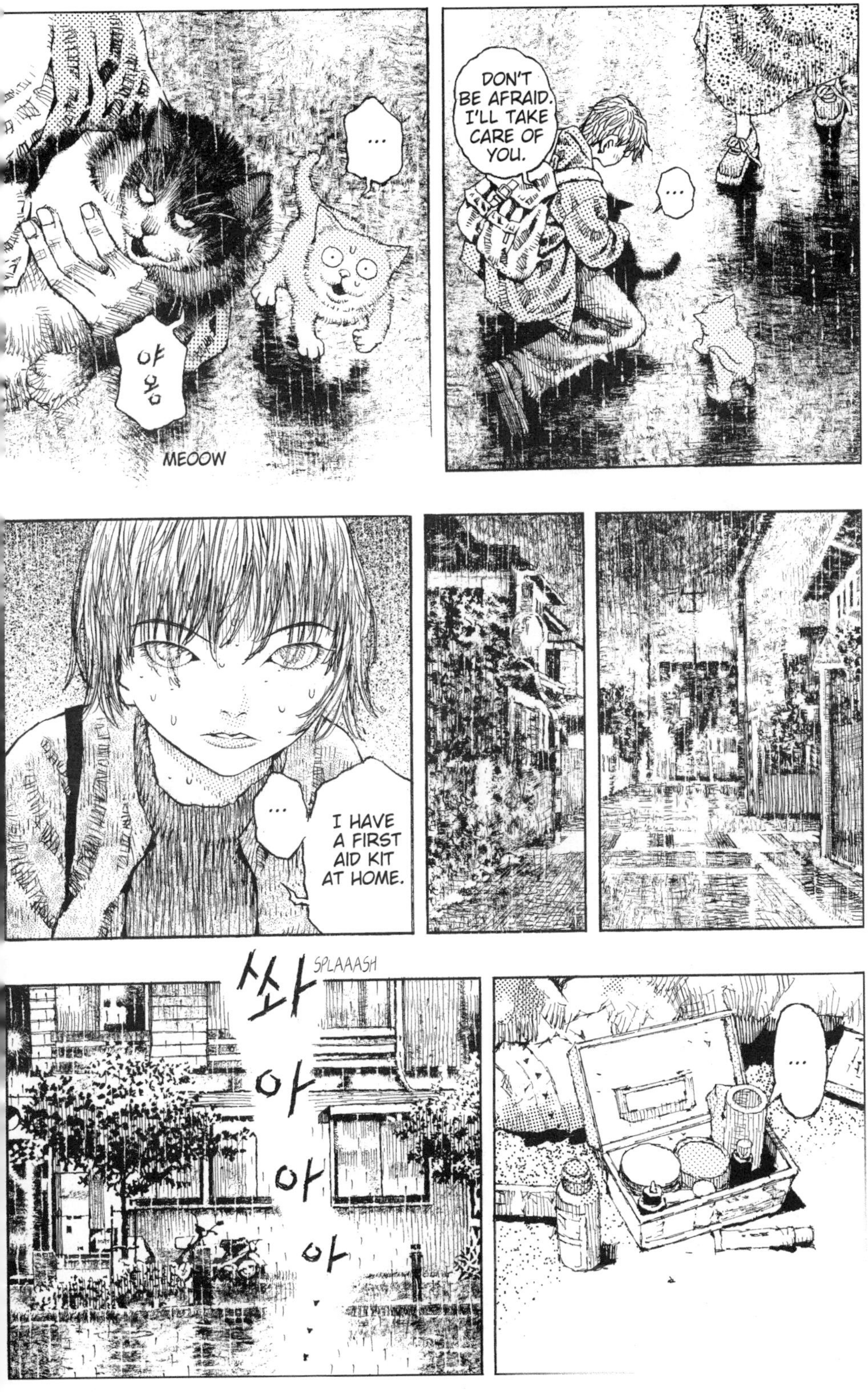

...
야옹
MEOOW
DON'T BE AFRAID. I'LL TAKE CARE OF YOU.
...
...
I HAVE A FIRST AID KIT AT HOME.
쏴아아아...
SPLAAASH
...

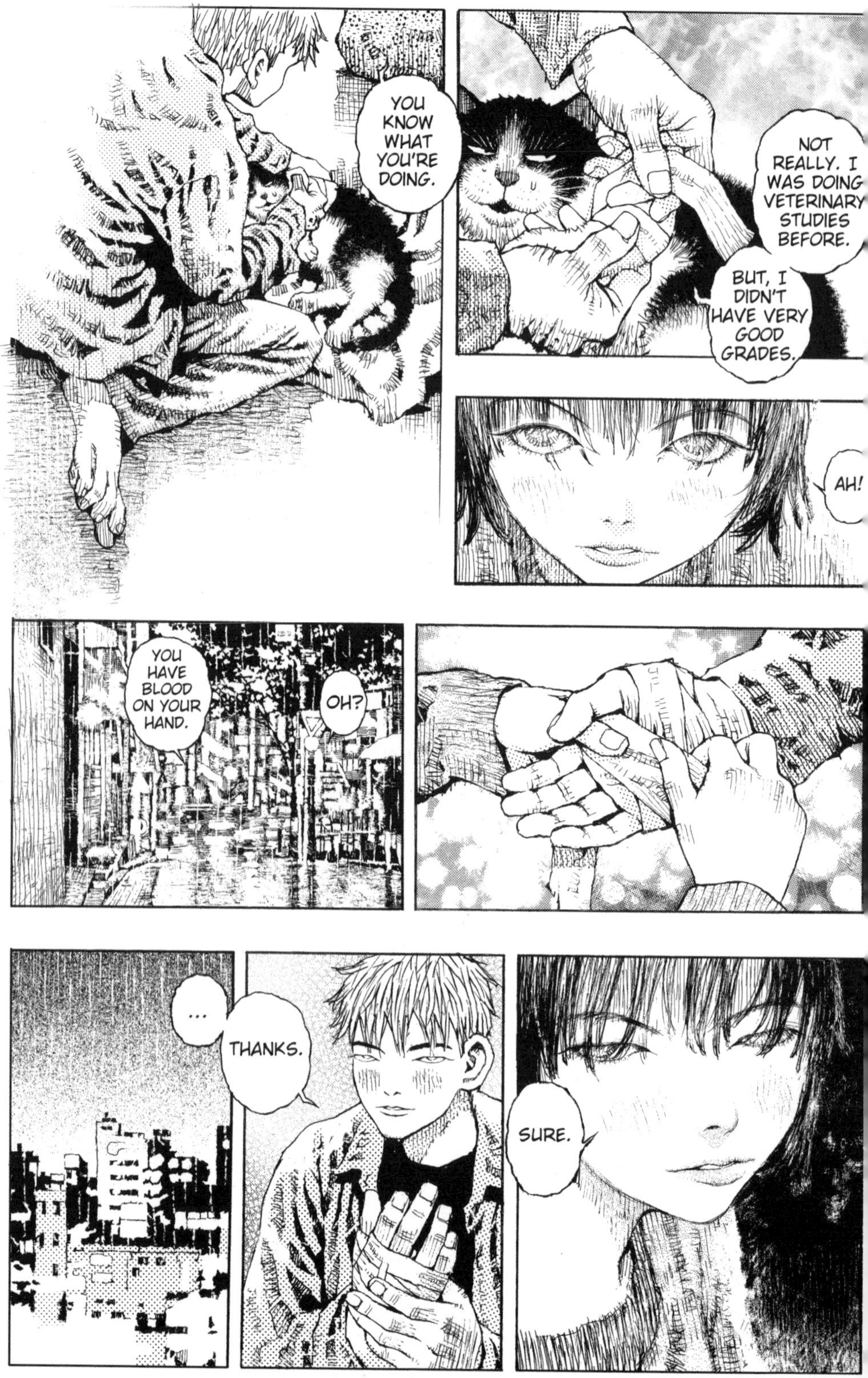
YOU KNOW WHAT YOU'RE DOING.
NOT REALLY. I WAS DOING VETERINARY STUDIES BEFORE.
BUT, I DIDN'T HAVE VERY GOOD GRADES.
AH!
YOU HAVE BLOOD ON YOUR HAND.
OH?
...
THANKS.
SURE.

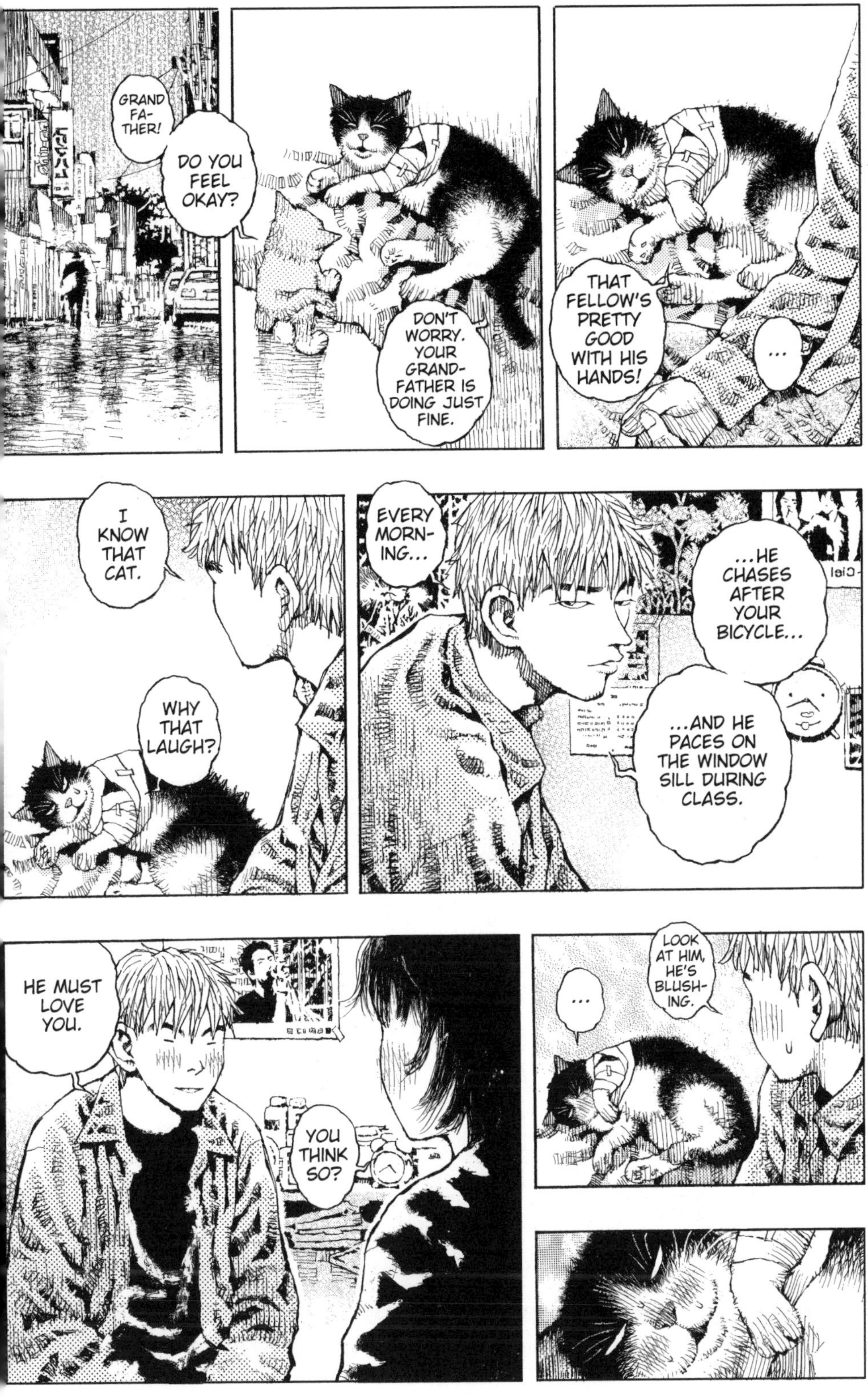
GRAND FA- THER!
DO YOU FEEL OKAY?
DON'T WORRY. YOUR GRAND- FATHER IS DOING JUST FINE.
THAT FELLOW'S PRETTY GOOD WITH HIS HANDS!
...
I KNOW THAT CAT.
WHY THAT LAUGH?
EVERY MORN- ING...
...HE CHASES AFTER YOUR BICYCLE...
...AND HE PACES ON THE WINDOW SILL DURING CLASS.
HE MUST LOVE YOU.
YOU THINK SO?
...
LOOK AT HIM, HE'S BLUSH- ING.

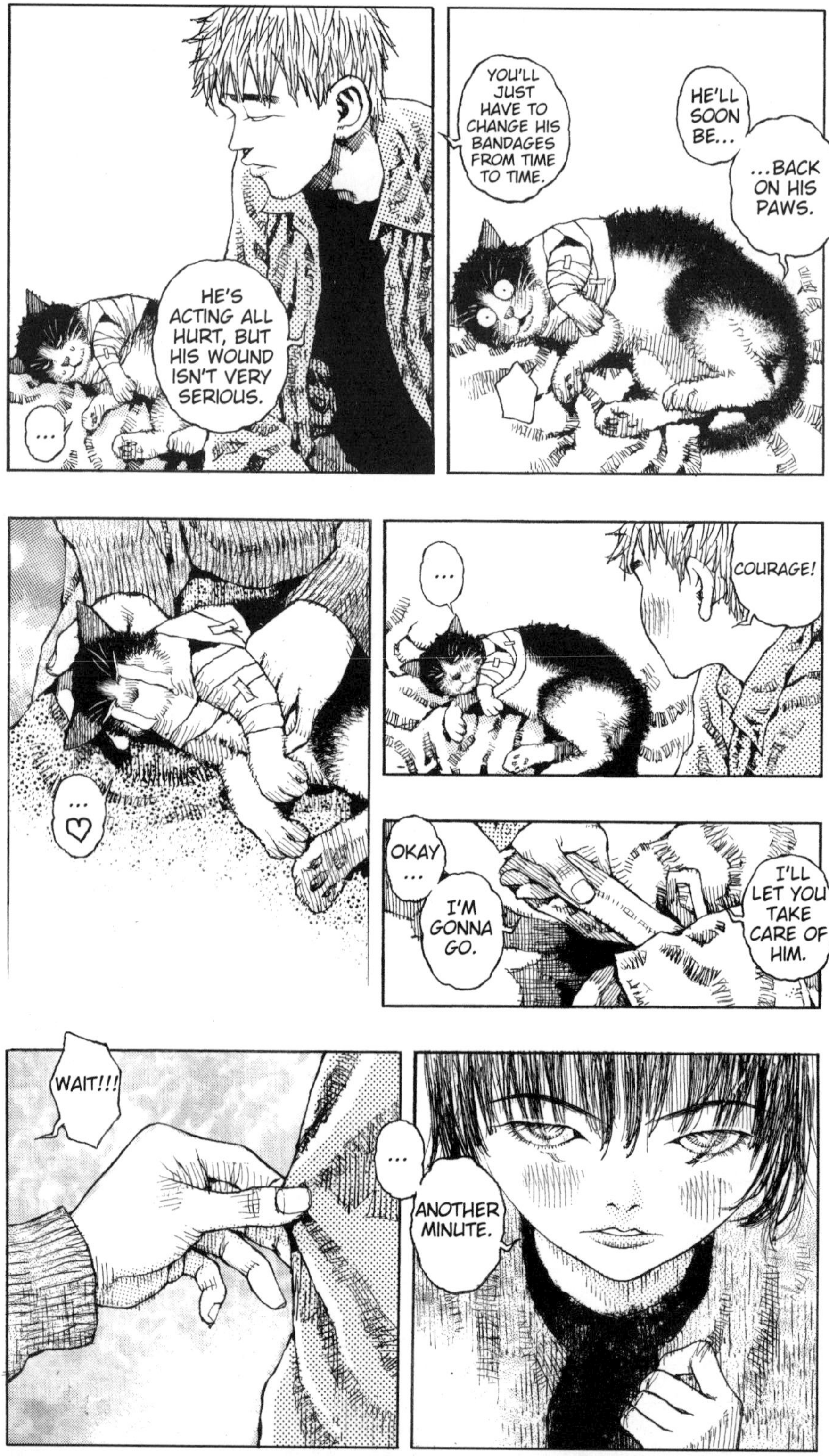
HE'S ACTING ALL HURT, BUT HIS WOUND ISN'T VERY SERIOUS.
...
YOU'LL JUST HAVE TO CHANGE HIS BANDAGES FROM TIME TO TIME.
HE'LL SOON BE...
...BACK ON HIS PAWS.
... ♡
...
COURAGE!
OKAY ...
I'M GONNA GO.
I'LL LET YOU TAKE CARE OF HIM.
WAIT!!!
...
ANOTHER MINUTE.

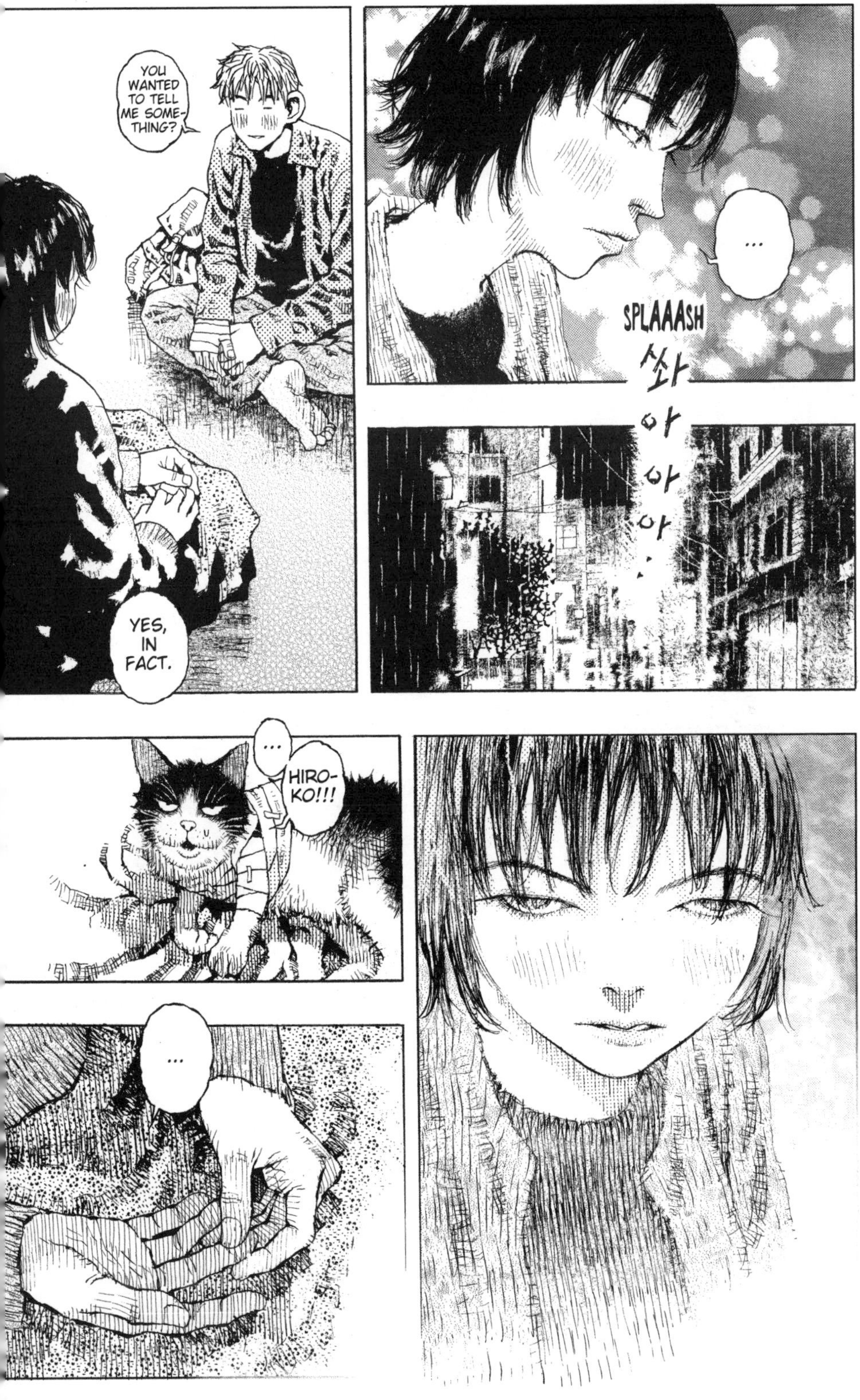

...
SPLAAASH
쏴아아아...
YOU WANTED TO TELL ME SOME-THING?
YES, IN FACT.
...
HIRO-KO!!!
...

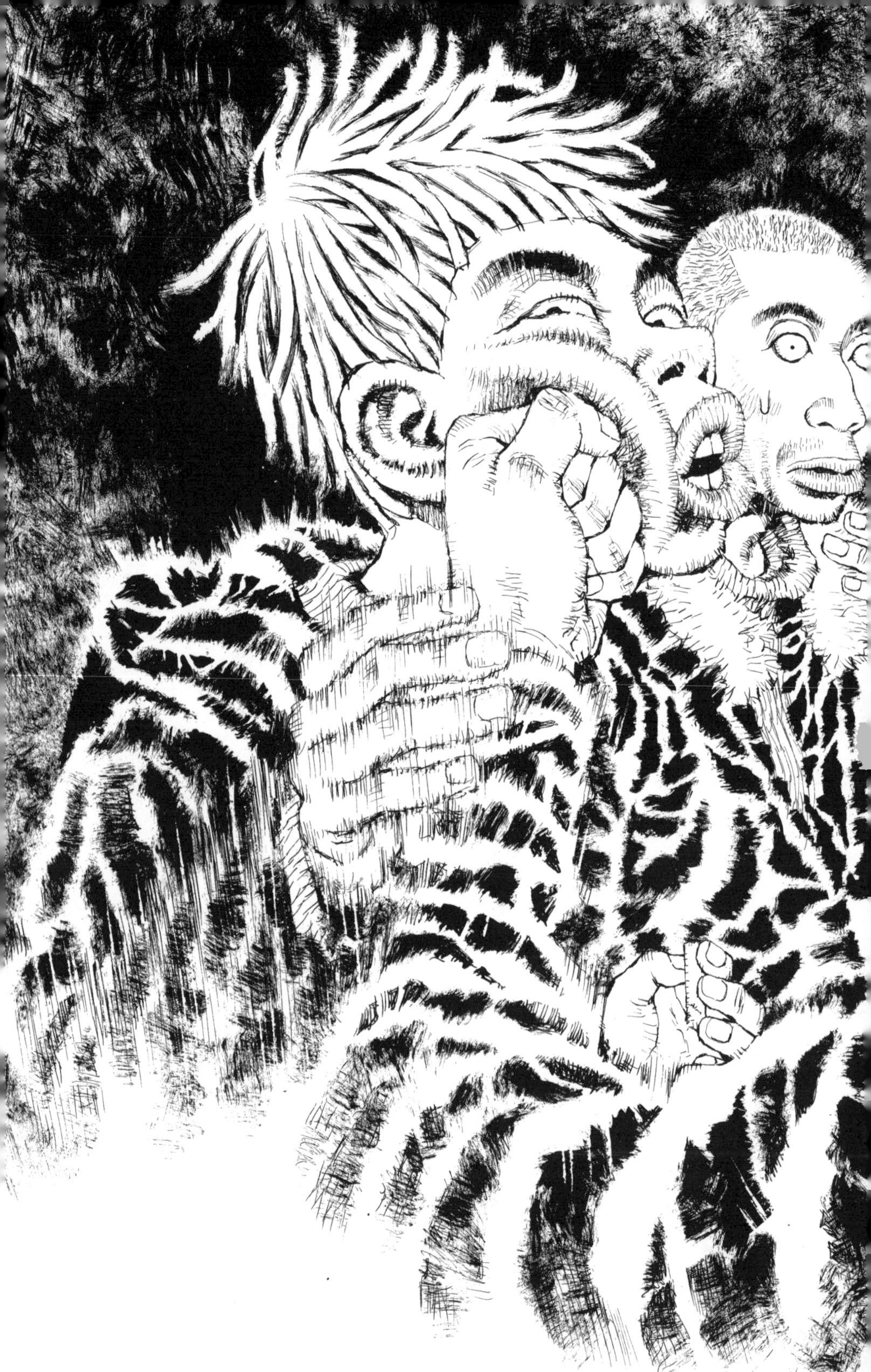

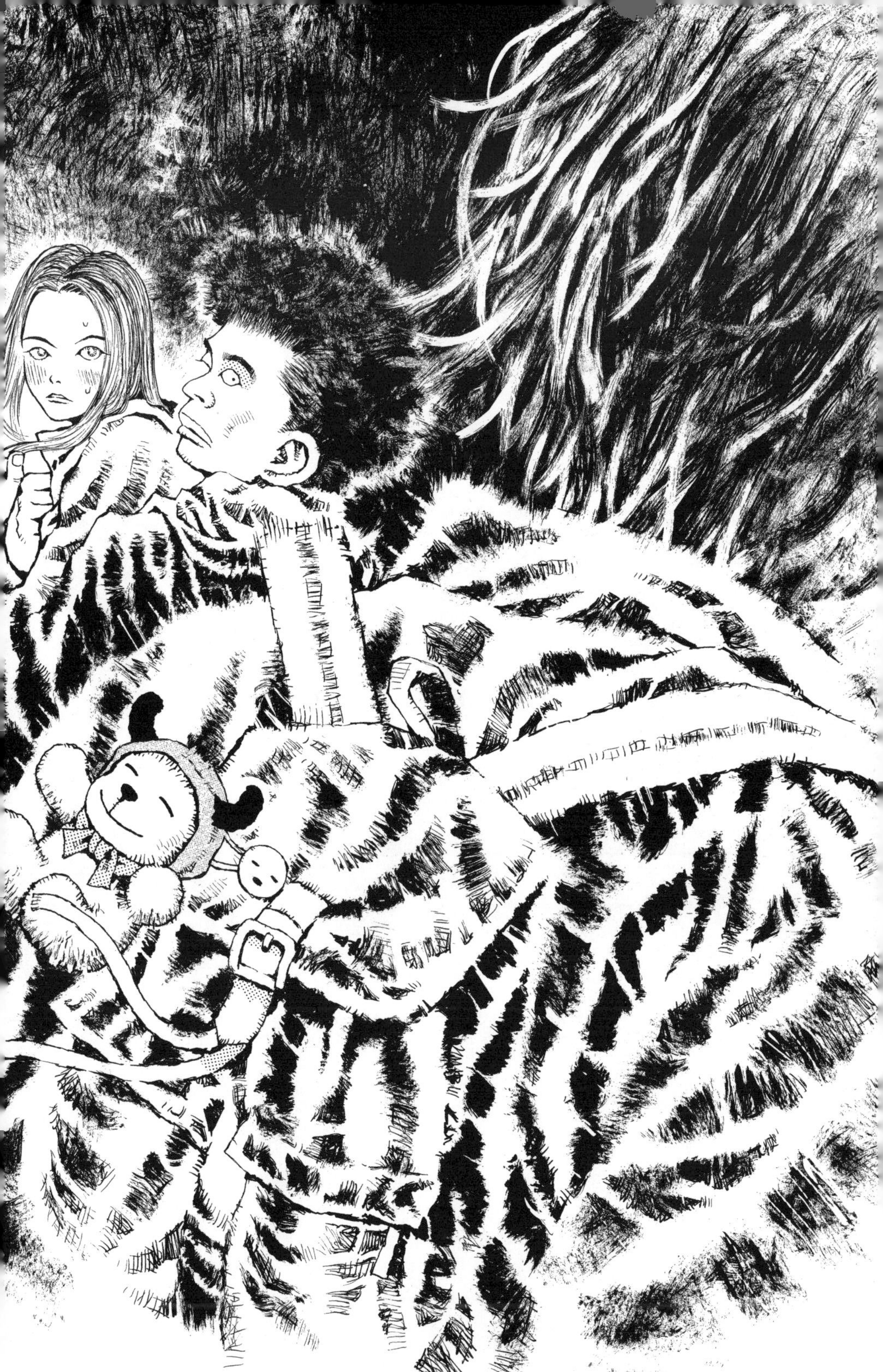

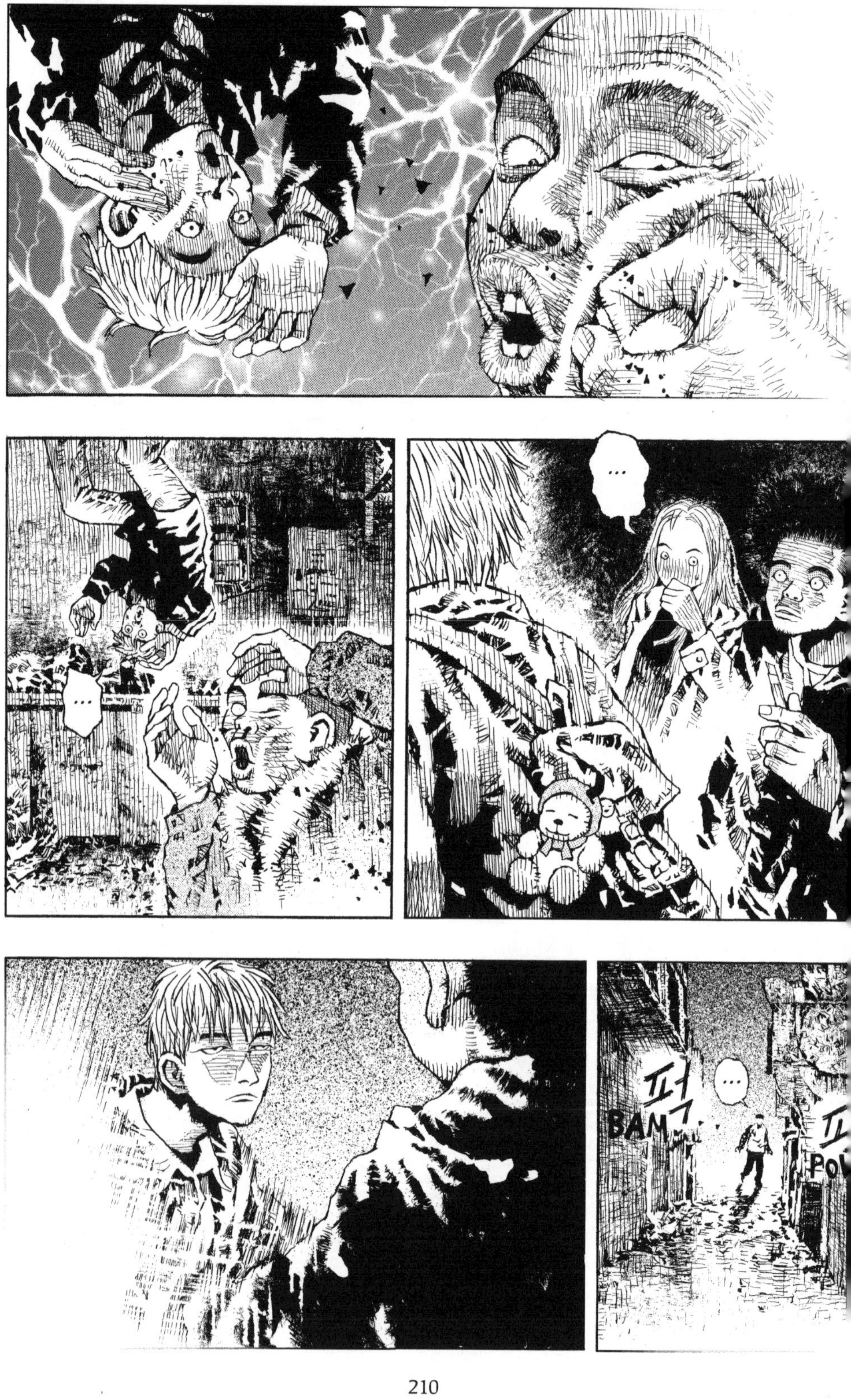
...
...
...
퍼억
BAM

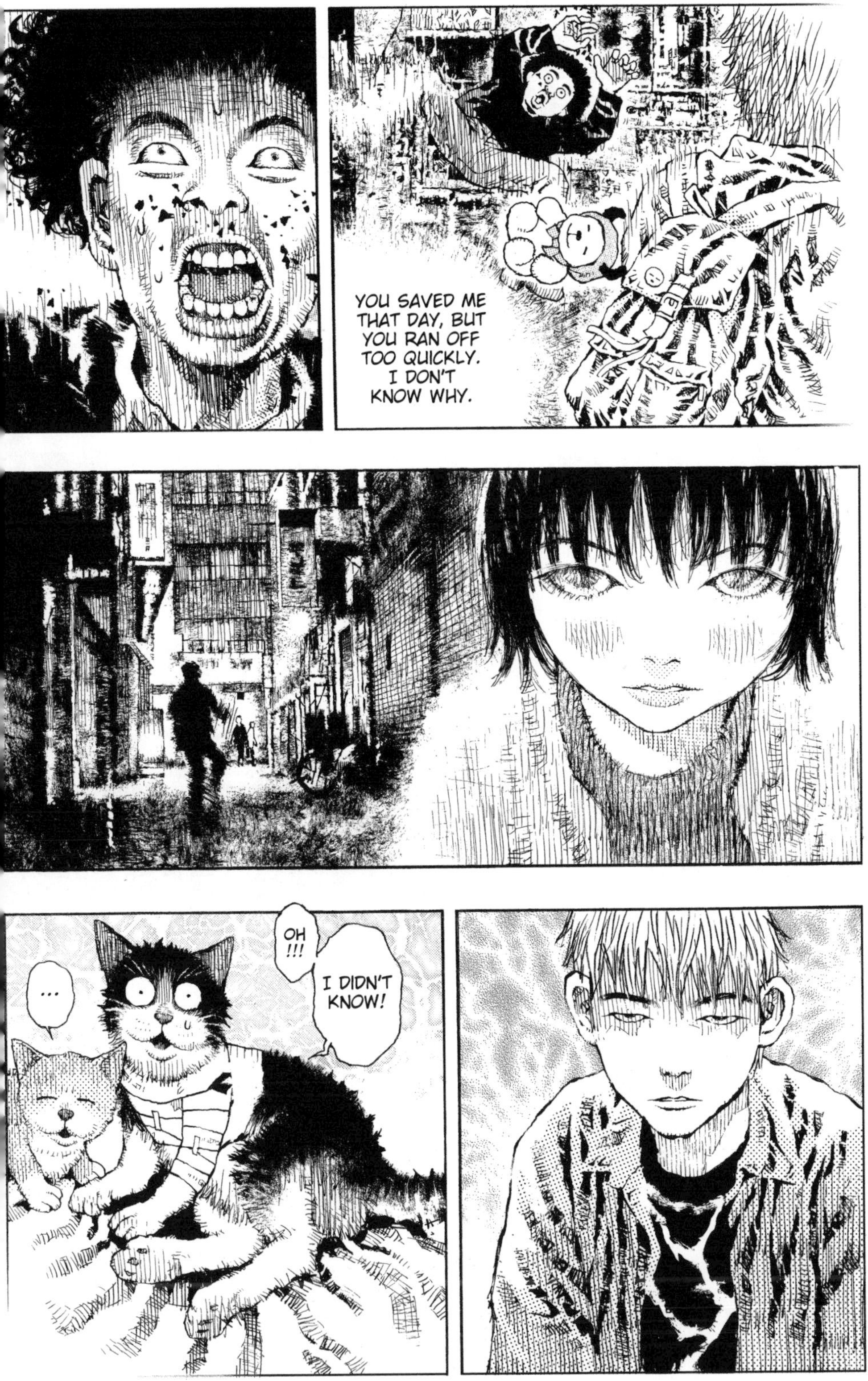
YOU SAVED ME THAT DAY, BUT YOU RAN OFF TOO QUICKLY. I DON'T KNOW WHY.
...
OH !!!
I DIDN'T KNOW!

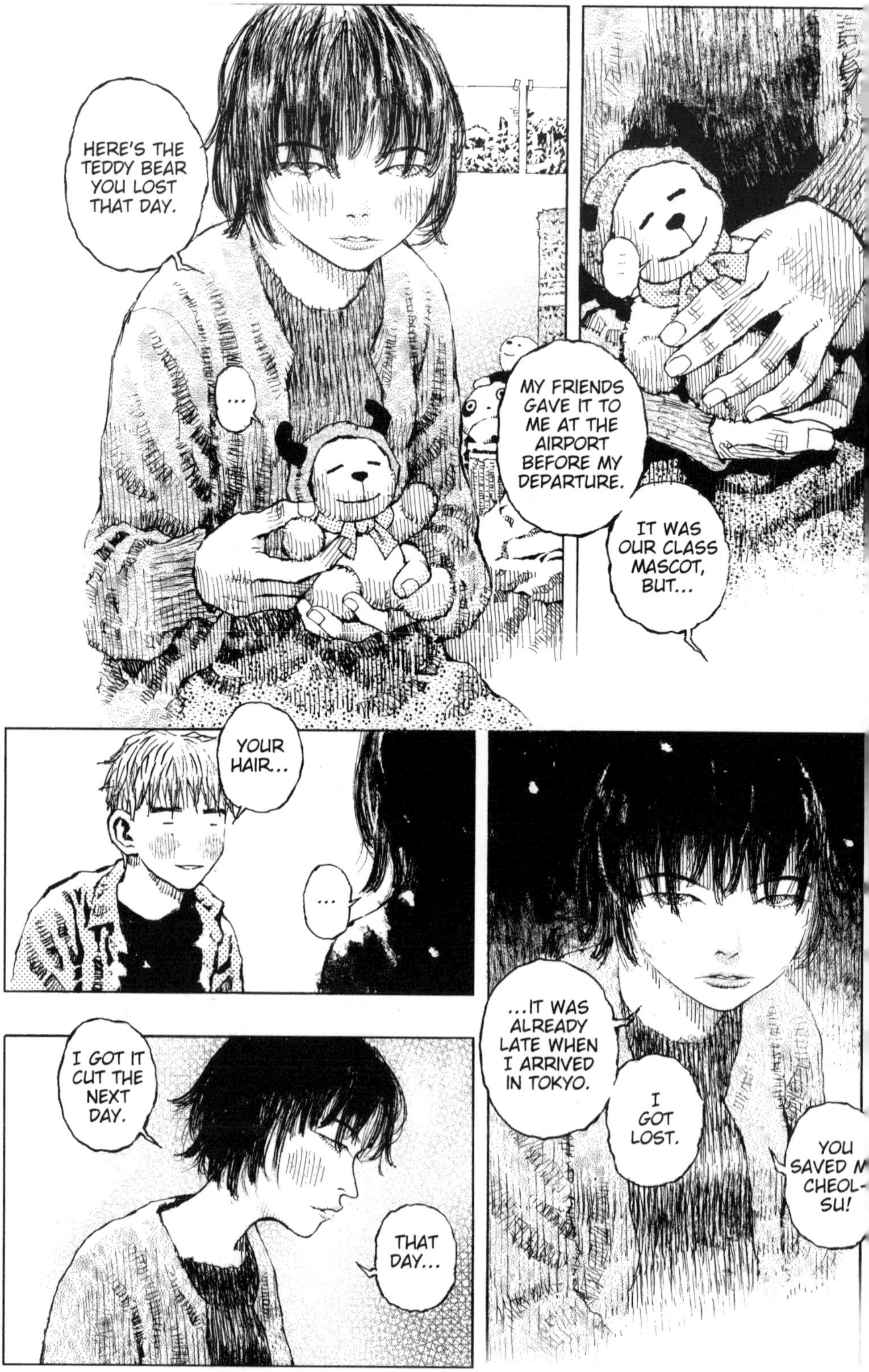
HERE'S THE TEDDY BEAR YOU LOST THAT DAY.
...
MY FRIENDS GAVE IT TO ME AT THE AIRPORT BEFORE MY DEPARTURE.
IT WAS OUR CLASS MASCOT, BUT...
YOUR HAIR...
...
I GOT IT CUT THE NEXT DAY.
THAT DAY...
...IT WAS ALREADY LATE WHEN I ARRIVED IN TOKYO.
I GOT LOST.
YOU SAVED M
CHEOL-SU!

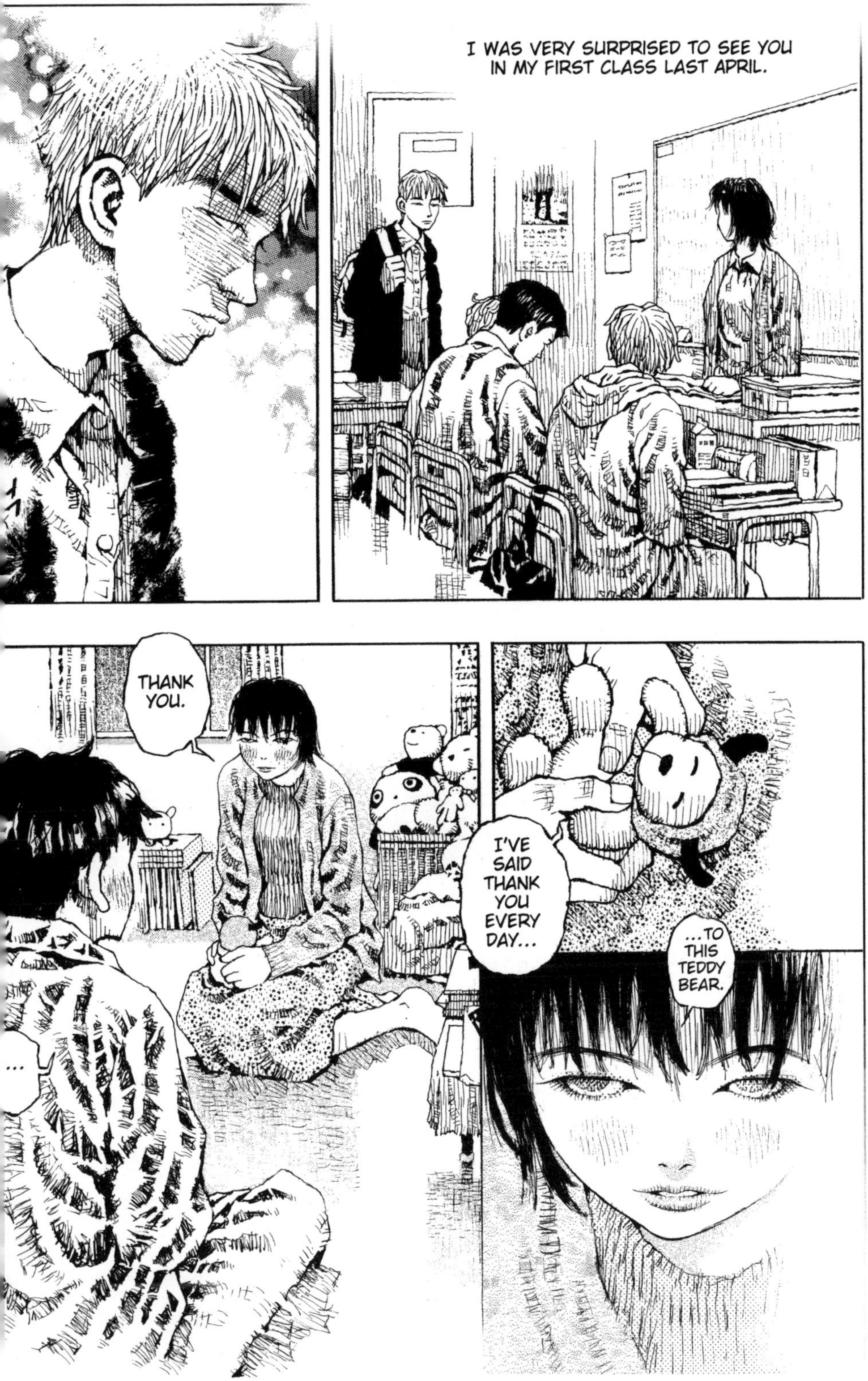
I WAS VERY SURPRISED TO SEE YOU IN MY FIRST CLASS LAST APRIL.
THANK YOU.
...
I'VE SAID THANK YOU EVERY DAY...
...TO THIS TEDDY BEAR.

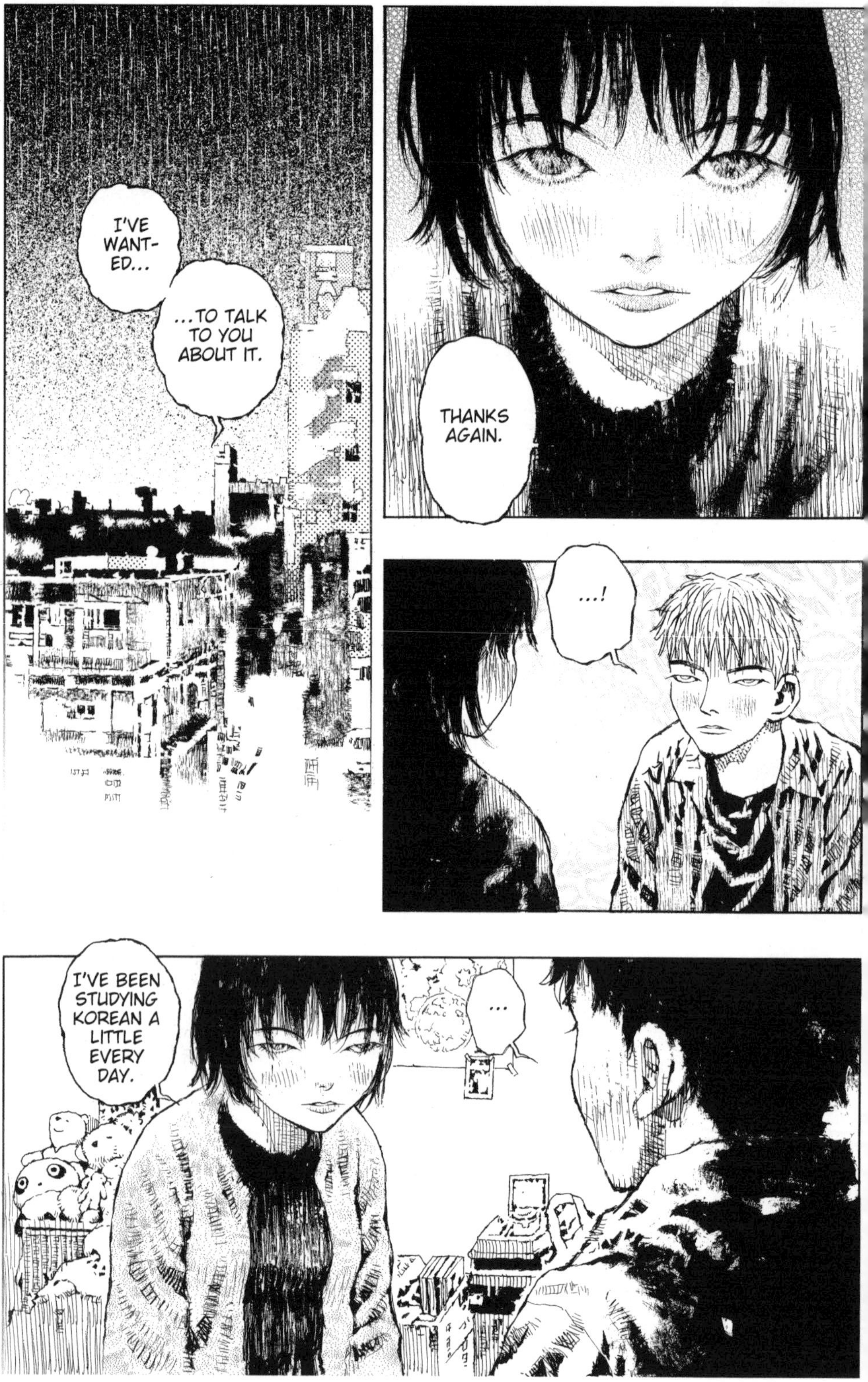
I'VE WANT-ED...
...TO TALK TO YOU ABOUT IT.
THANKS AGAIN.
...!
I'VE BEEN STUDYING KOREAN A LITTLE EVERY DAY.
...

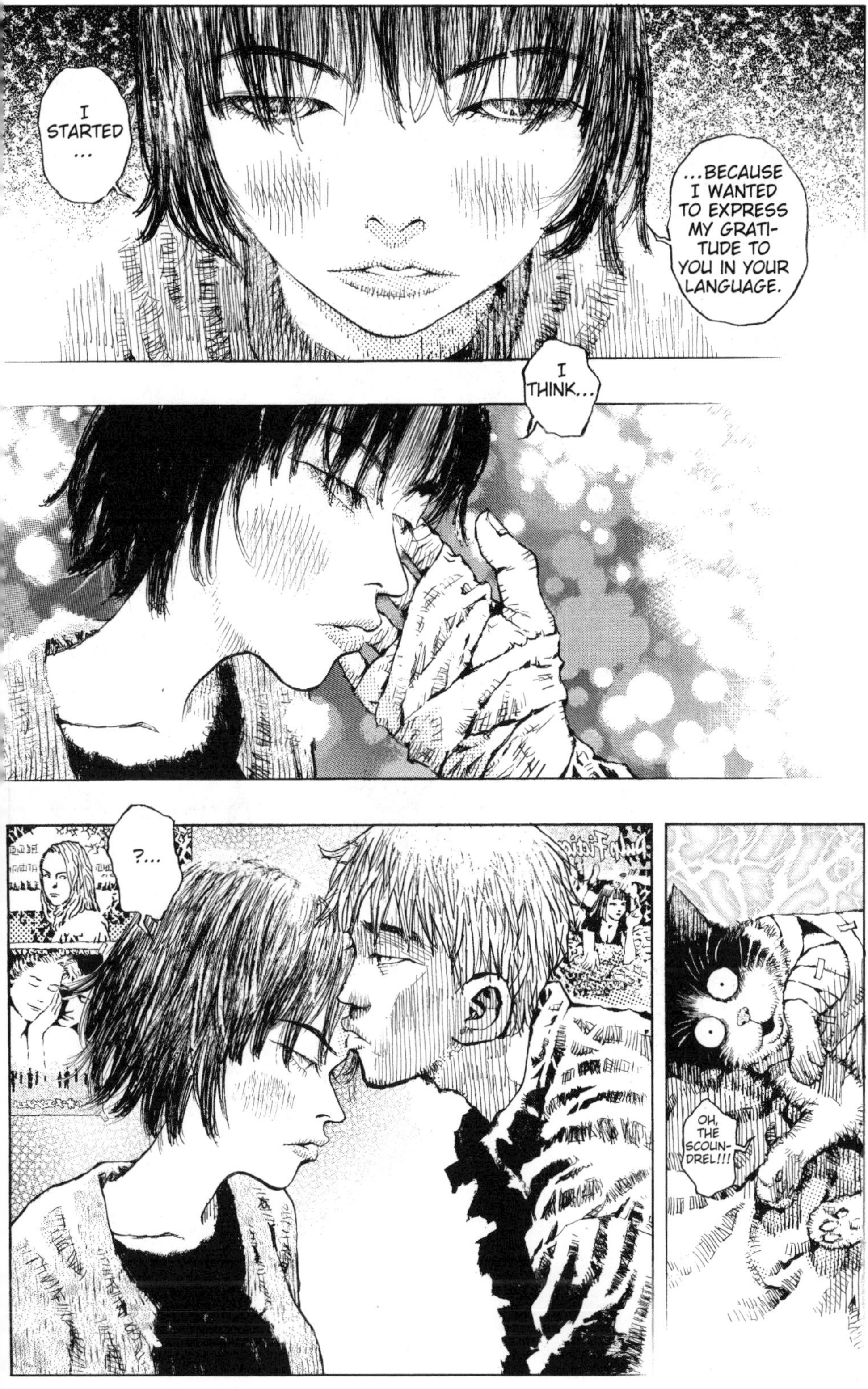
I STARTED ...
...BECAUSE I WANTED TO EXPRESS MY GRATITUDE TO YOU IN YOUR LANGUAGE.
I THINK...
?...
OH, THE SCOUNDREL!!!

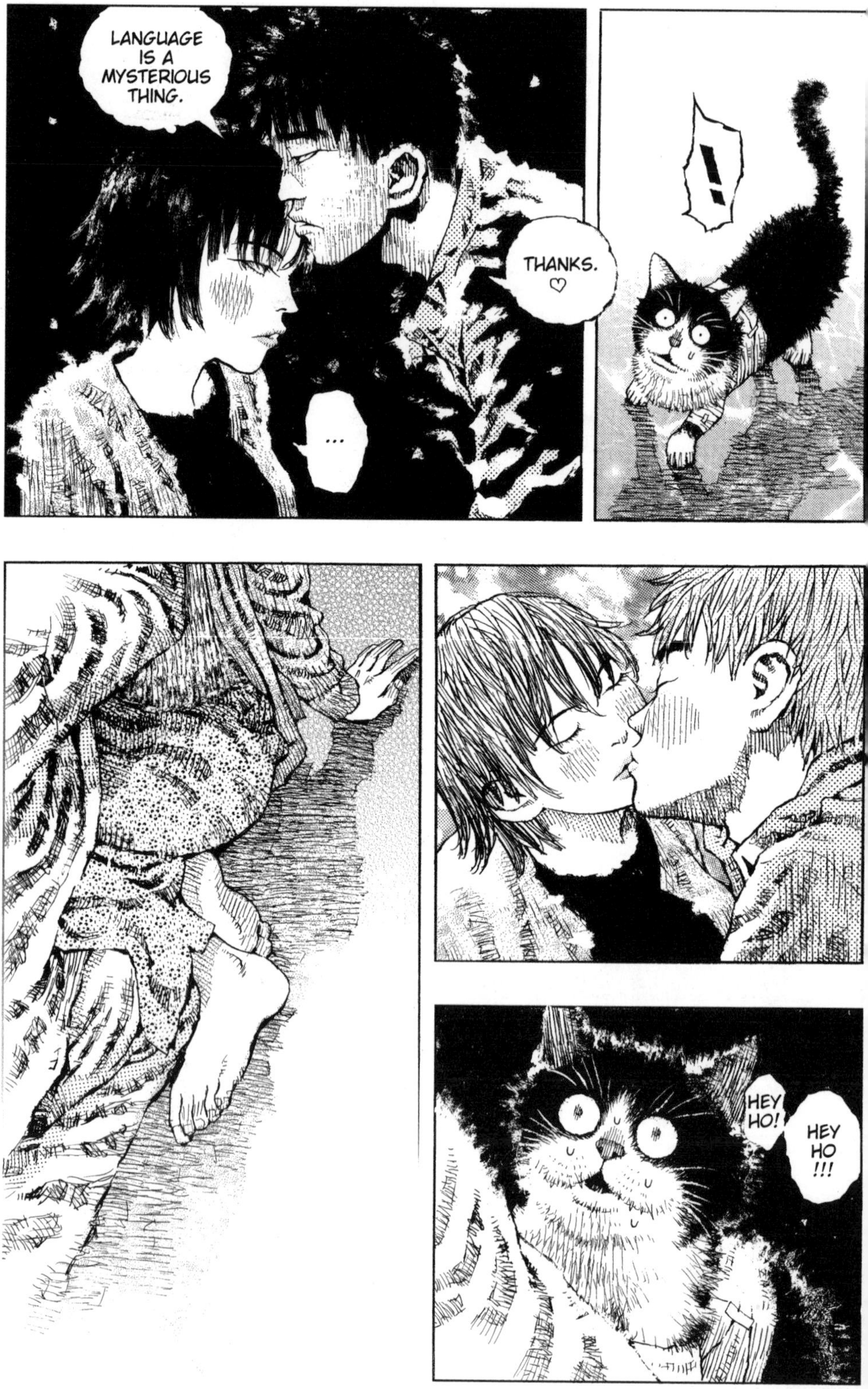
LANGUAGE IS A MYSTERIOUS THING.
!
THANKS. ♡
...
HEY HO!
HEY HO !!!

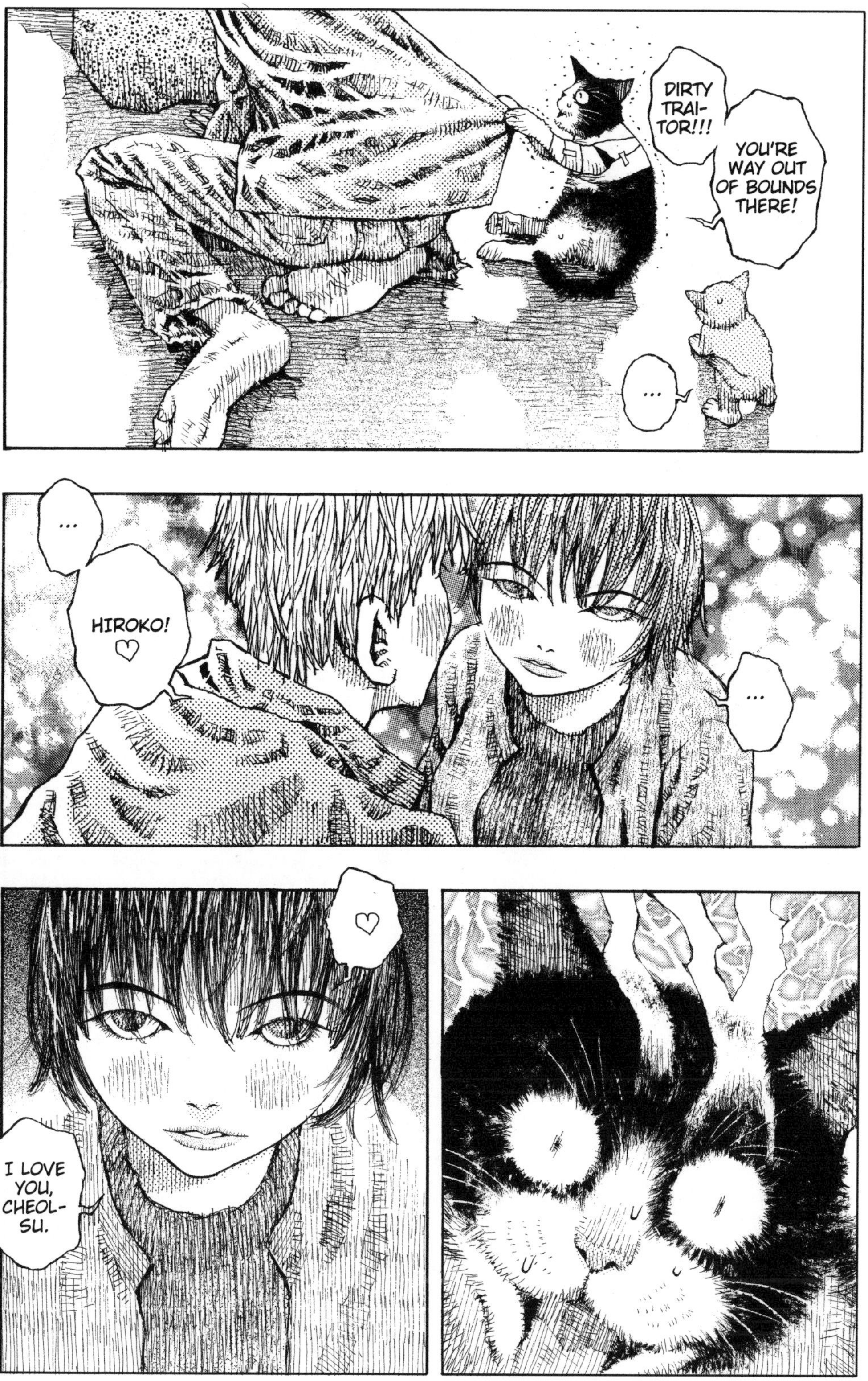
DIRTY TRAI-TOR!!!
YOU'RE WAY OUT OF BOUNDS THERE!
...
...
HIROKO! ♡
...
♡
I LOVE YOU, CHEOL-SU.

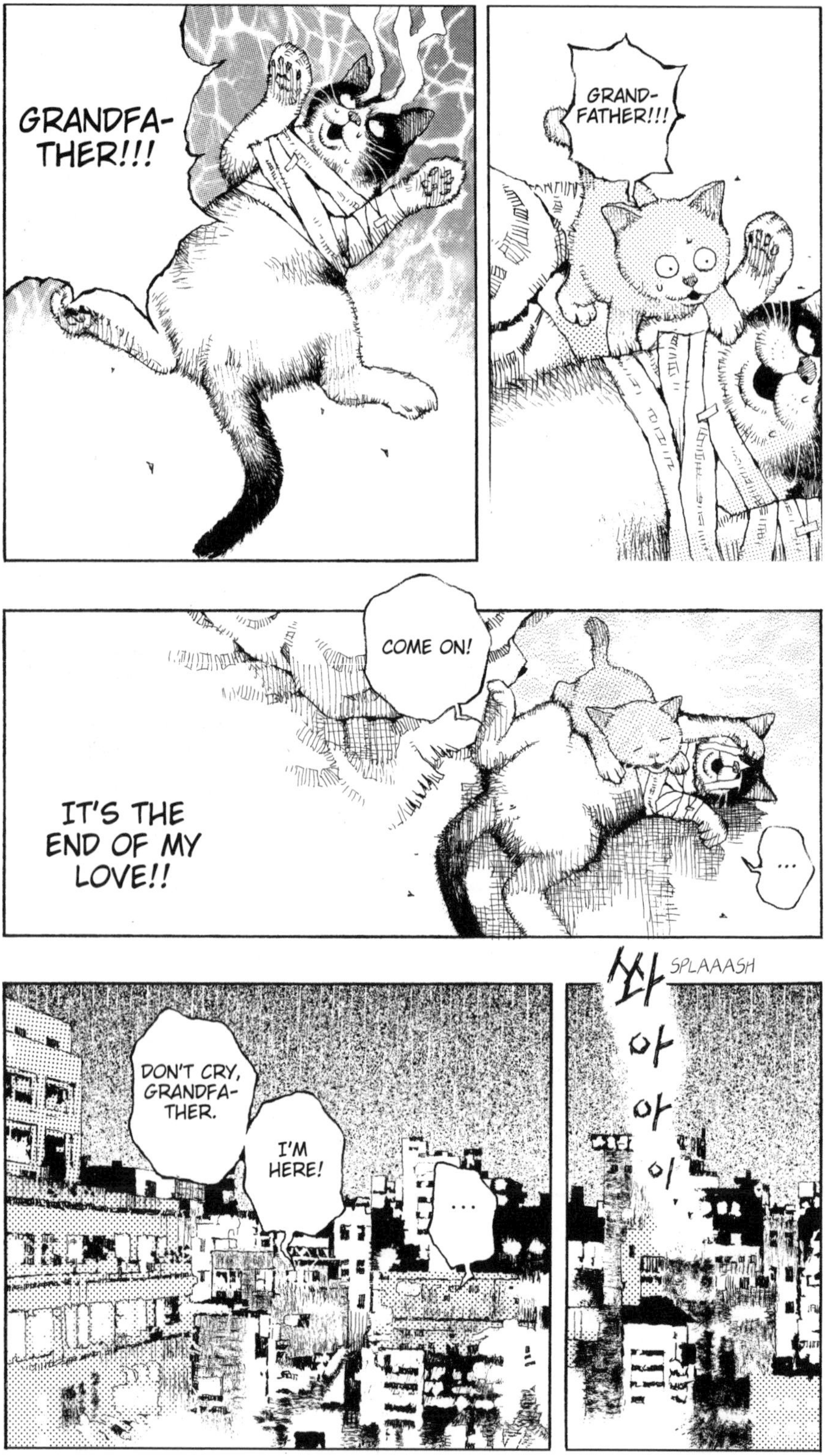
GRANDFA-
THER!!!
GRAND-
FATHER!!!
COME ON!
IT'S THE
END OF MY
LOVE!!
...
DON'T CRY,
GRANDFA-
THER.
I'M
HERE!
...
쏴아아이
SPLAAASH

A short tall tale
Inspired By Yang Seung-Cheon

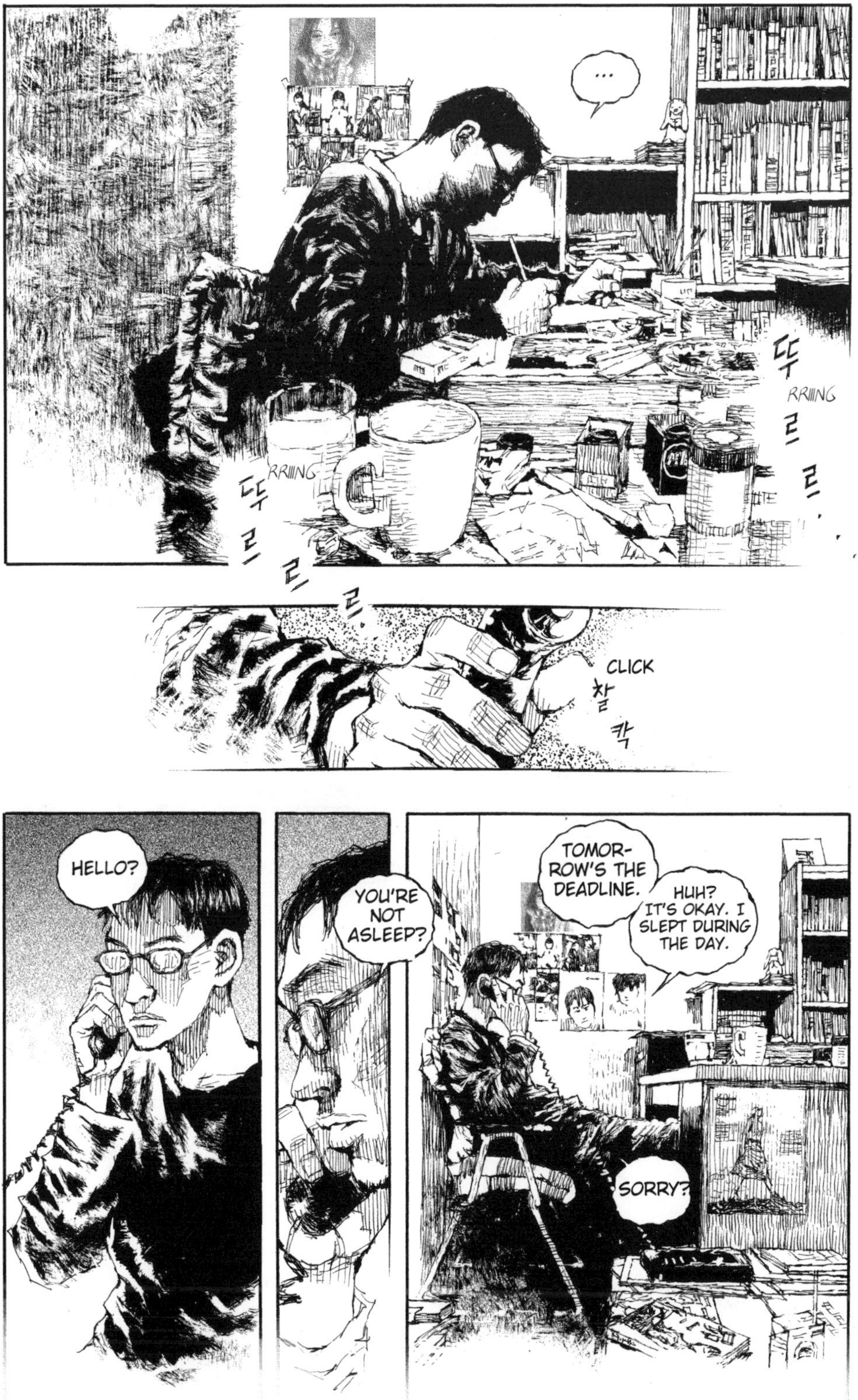
...
뚜르르...
RRIIING
RRIIING
뚜르르르.
CLICK
찰칵
HELLO?
YOU'RE NOT ASLEEP?
TOMOR-ROW'S THE DEADLINE.
HUH? IT'S OKAY. I SLEPT DURING THE DAY.
SORRY?

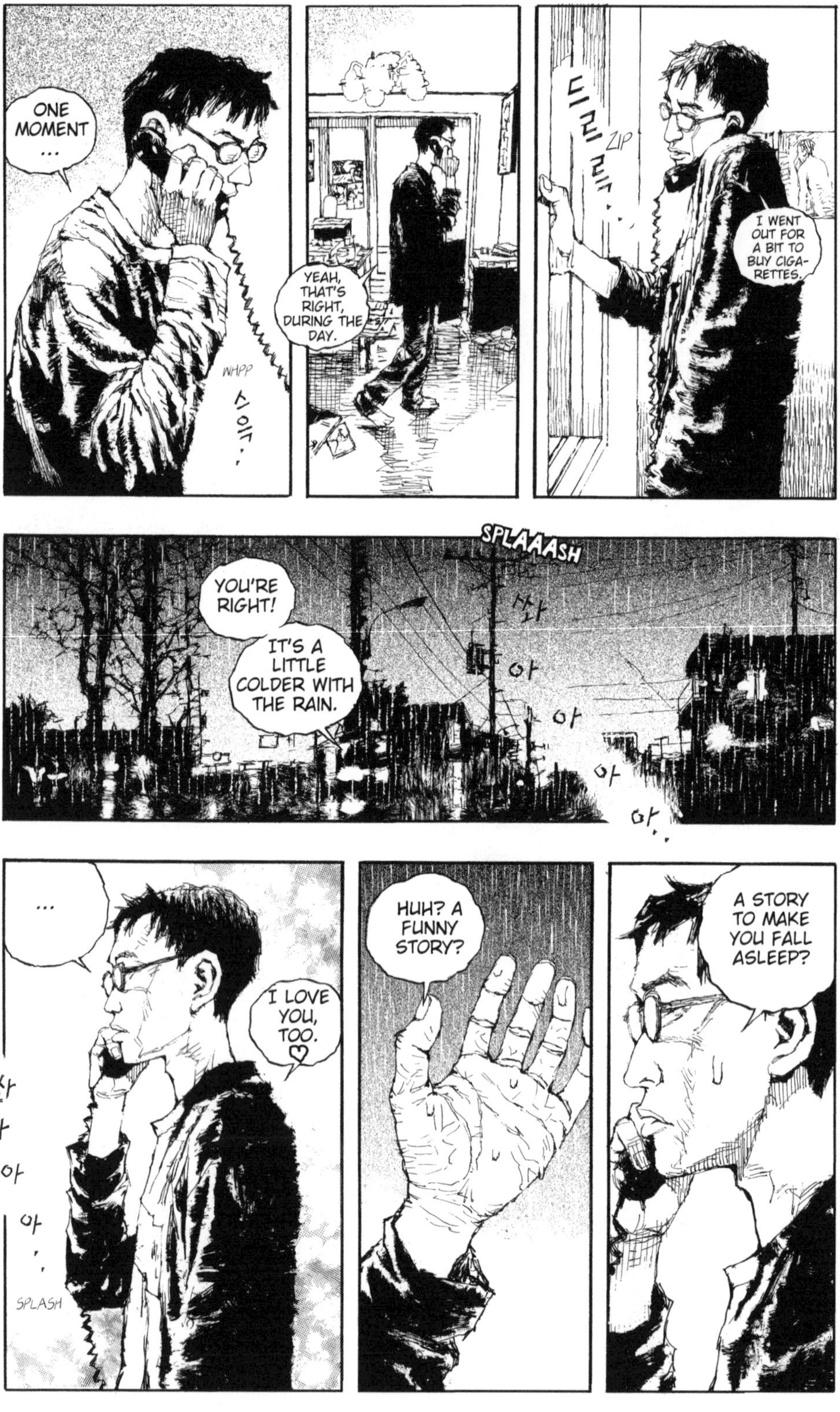
ONE MOMENT ...
WHPP
시익..
YEAH, THAT'S RIGHT, DURING THE DAY.
ZIP
드르륵..
I WENT OUT FOR A BIT TO BUY CIGA- RETTES.
SPLAAASH
YOU'RE RIGHT!
IT'S A LITTLE COLDER WITH THE RAIN.
쏴아아아아..
...
I LOVE YOU, TOO.
쏴아아아..
SPLASH
HUH? A FUNNY STORY?
A STORY TO MAKE YOU FALL ASLEEP?

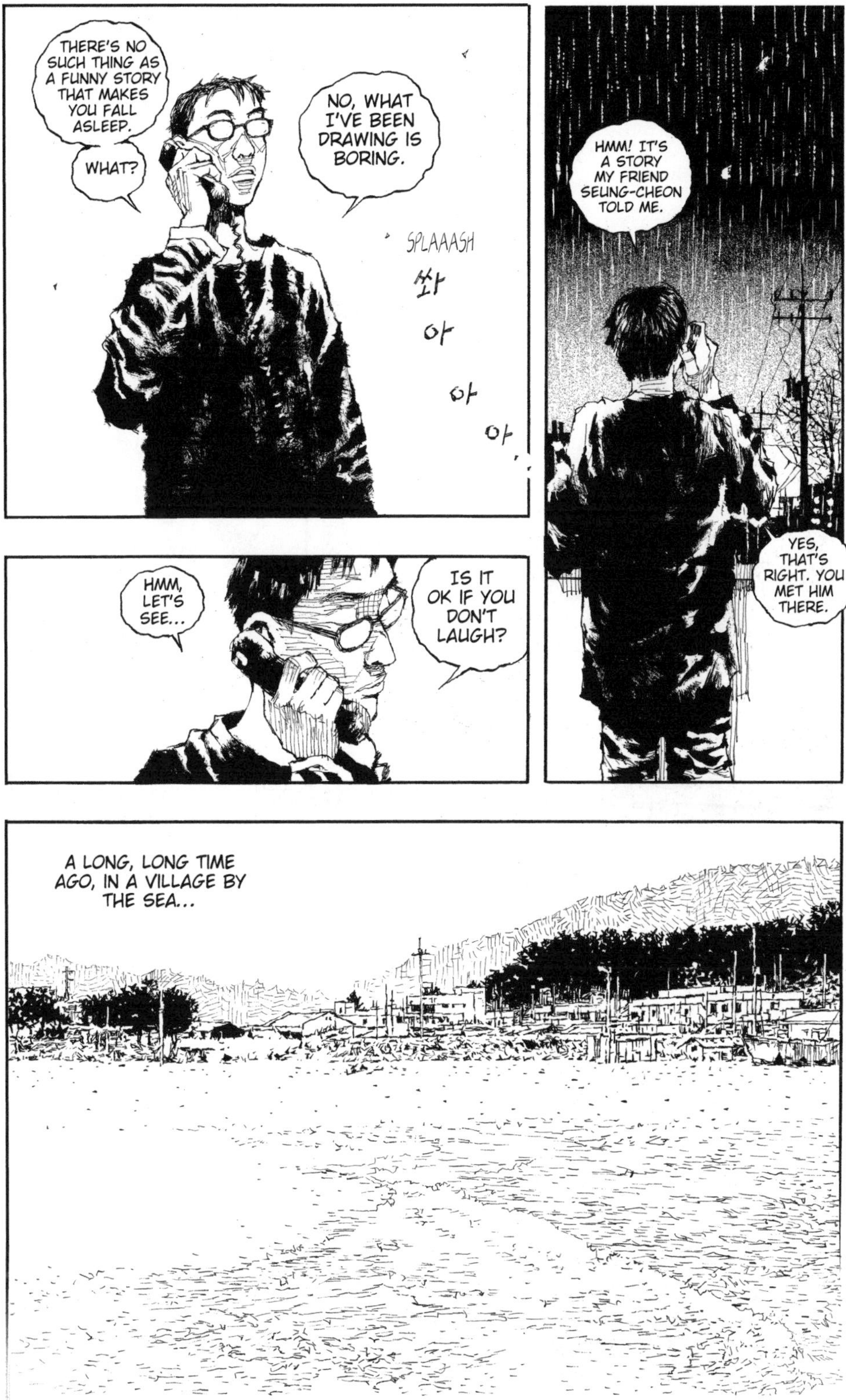
THERE'S NO SUCH THING AS A FUNNY STORY THAT MAKES YOU FALL ASLEEP.
WHAT?
NO, WHAT I'VE BEEN DRAWING IS BORING.
SPLAAASH
쏴
아
아
아
HMM! IT'S A STORY MY FRIEND SEUNG-CHEON TOLD ME.
YES, THAT'S RIGHT. YOU MET HIM THERE.
HMM, LET'S SEE...
IS IT OK IF YOU DON'T LAUGH?
A LONG, LONG TIME AGO, IN A VILLAGE BY THE SEA...

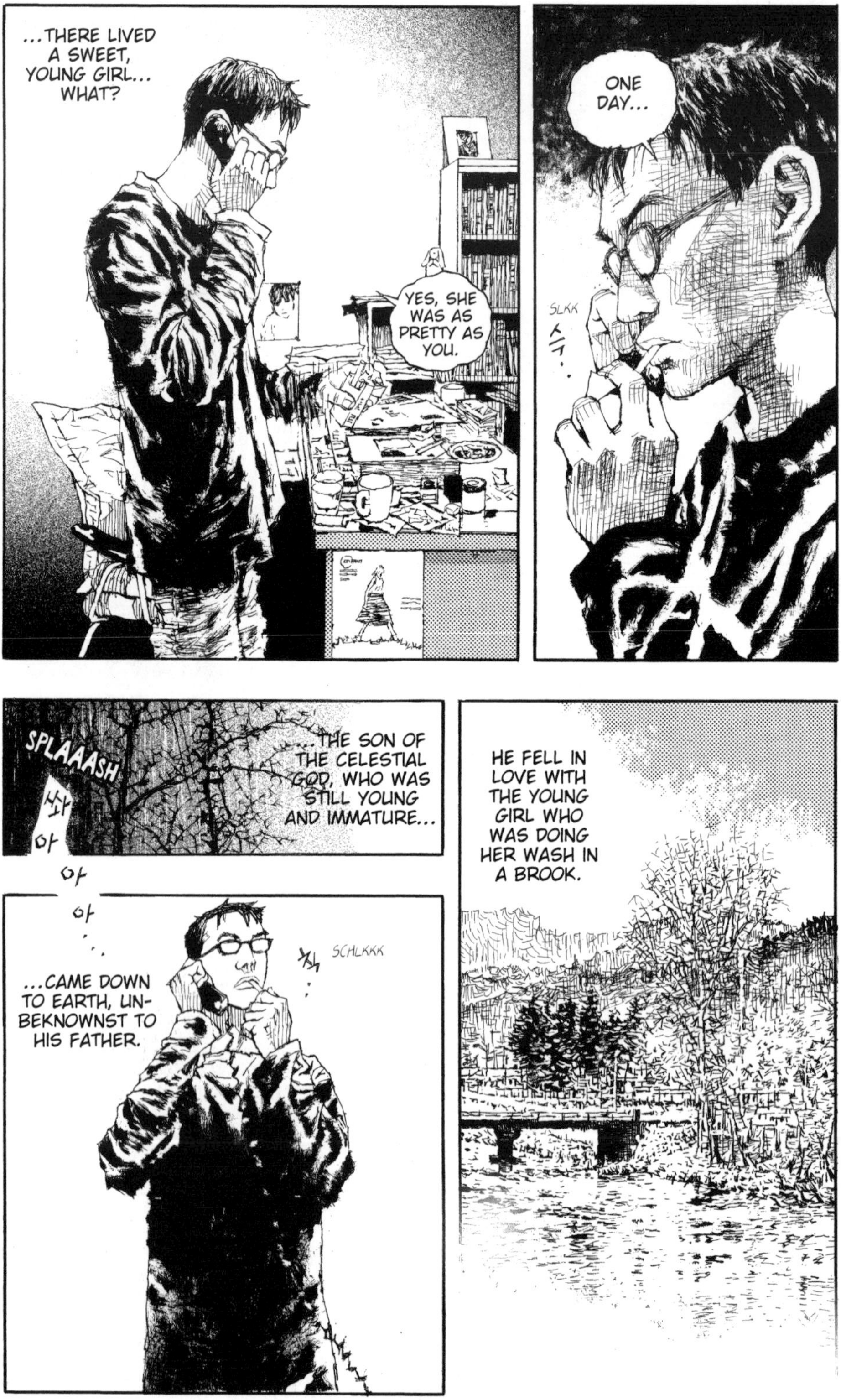

...THERE LIVED A SWEET, YOUNG GIRL... WHAT?
YES, SHE WAS AS PRETTY AS YOU.
ONE DAY...
SLKK
SPLAAASH
싸아아아...
...THE SON OF THE CELESTIAL GOD, WHO WAS STILL YOUNG AND IMMATURE...
...CAME DOWN TO EARTH, UNBEKNOWNST TO HIS FATHER.
SCHLKKK
HE FELL IN LOVE WITH THE YOUNG GIRL WHO WAS DOING HER WASH IN A BROOK.

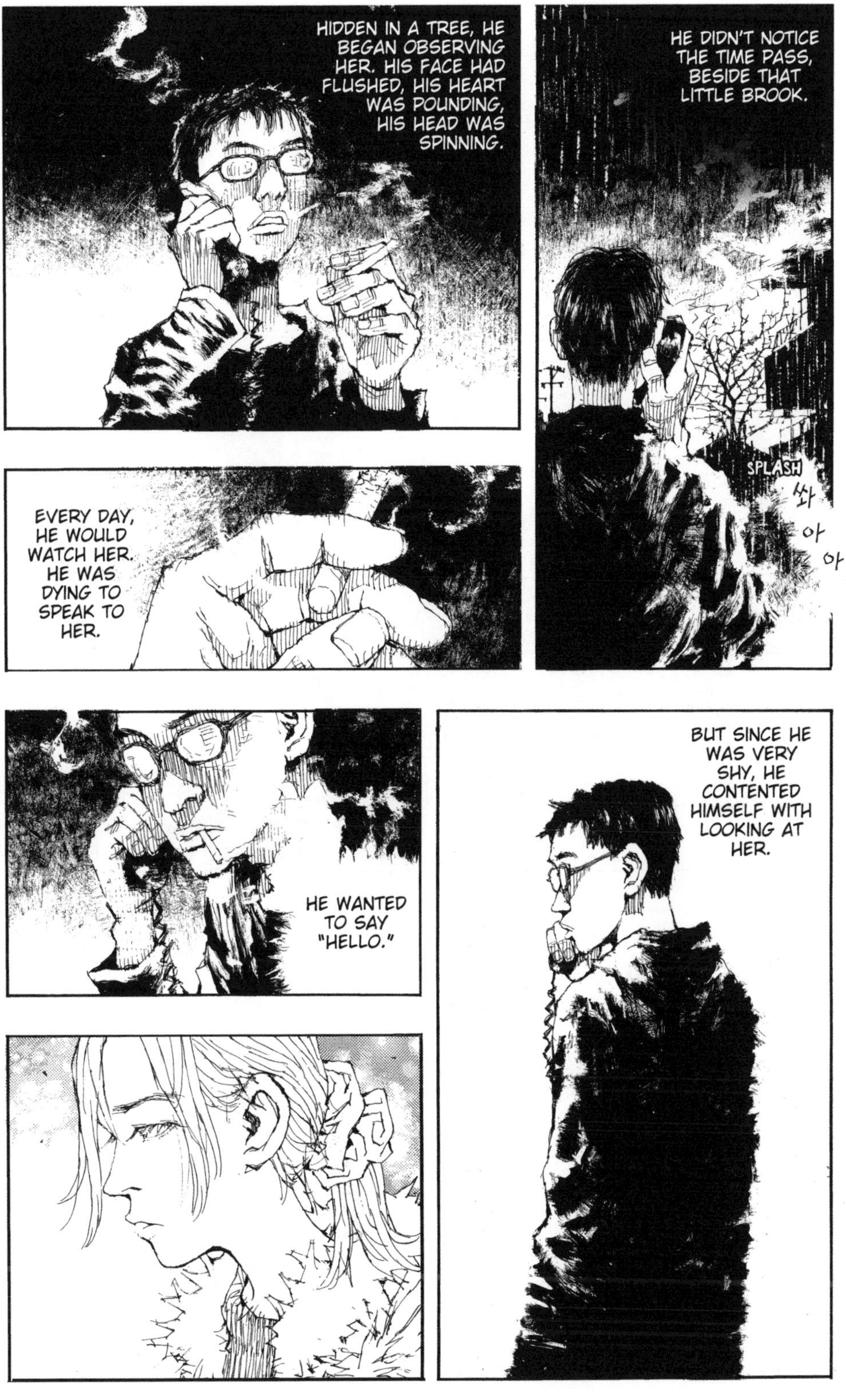
HIDDEN IN A TREE, HE BEGAN OBSERVING HER. HIS FACE HAD FLUSHED, HIS HEART WAS POUNDING, HIS HEAD WAS SPINNING.
HE DIDN'T NOTICE THE TIME PASS, BESIDE THAT LITTLE BROOK.
SPLASH
쏴
아
아
EVERY DAY, HE WOULD WATCH HER. HE WAS DYING TO SPEAK TO HER.
HE WANTED TO SAY "HELLO."
BUT SINCE HE WAS VERY SHY, HE CONTENTED HIMSELF WITH LOOKING AT HER.

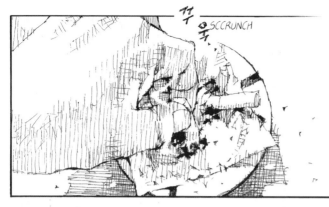
SCCRUNCH

AFTER SEVERAL DAYS SPENT IN THE THROES OF PASSION, HE DECIDED TO CALL UPON HAPPINESS AND FLU, WHO BOTH WERE LEADING IDLE LIVES. WITH ALL SINCERITY, HE CONFIDED IN THEM.

"HELP ME!!" HE BESEACHED THEM.

FLU AND HAPPINESS, WHO HAD NOTHING TO DO ALL DAY LONG IN THE SWEET, CELESTIAL KINGDOM, COMPLAINED ABOUT HAVING TO COME DOWN TO EARTH, FOR IT WAS COLD THERE.

THEY ARGUED THAT HIS LOVE WAS IMPOSSIBLE.

BUT, AT HIS IMPLORING LOOK, THEY GAVE IN, OUT OF PITY.

SO THEY CAME DOWN TO THE FRIGID EARTH, BUT ONCE THEY'D SPIED THE YOUNG GIRL, THEY FELL HOPELESSLY IN LOVE.

AS THOUGH STRUCK BY LIGHTNING, THEY FORGOT ABOUT THE CELESTIAL GOD'S SON.

226

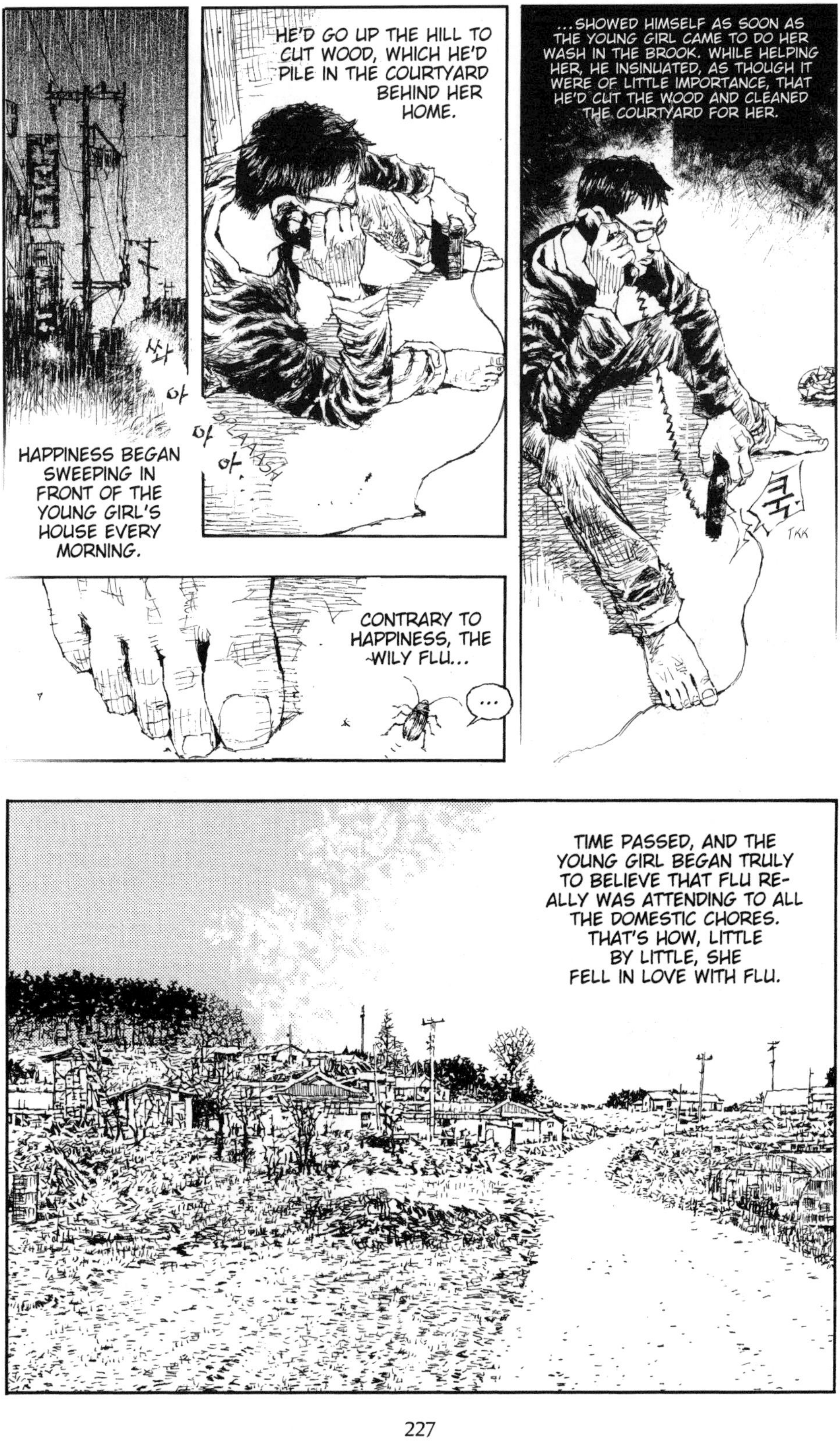

HAPPINESS BEGAN SWEEPING IN FRONT OF THE YOUNG GIRL'S HOUSE EVERY MORNING.
쏴 아 아 아
SPLAAAASH
HE'D GO UP THE HILL TO CUT WOOD, WHICH HE'D PILE IN THE COURTYARD BEHIND HER HOME.
CONTRARY TO HAPPINESS, THE WILY FLU...
...
...SHOWED HIMSELF AS SOON AS THE YOUNG GIRL CAME TO DO HER WASH IN THE BROOK. WHILE HELPING HER, HE INSINUATED, AS THOUGH IT WERE OF LITTLE IMPORTANCE, THAT HE'D CUT THE WOOD AND CLEANED THE COURTYARD FOR HER.
콕
TKK
TIME PASSED, AND THE YOUNG GIRL BEGAN TRULY TO BELIEVE THAT FLU REALLY WAS ATTENDING TO ALL THE DOMESTIC CHORES. THAT'S HOW, LITTLE BY LITTLE, SHE FELL IN LOVE WITH FLU.

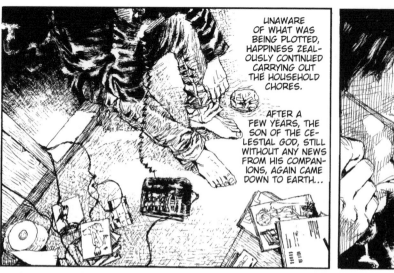

UNAWARE OF WHAT WAS BEING PLOTTED, HAPPINESS ZEALOUSLY CONTINUED CARRYING OUT THE HOUSEHOLD CHORES.

AFTER A FEW YEARS, THE SON OF THE CELESTIAL GOD, STILL WITHOUT ANY NEWS FROM HIS COMPANIONS, AGAIN CAME DOWN TO EARTH...

...TO SEE WHAT WAS HAPPENING.

IN THE MEANTIME, THE YOUNG GIRL HAD GROWN UP, HER FACE WAS OF A LILY-LIKE COMPLEXION AND HER LIPS ROSY RED.

COUGH

IMMEDIATELY UPON SEEING HER AGAIN, THE SON OF THE CELESTIAL GOD, FORGETTING WHO HE WAS, DECIDED TO CONFESS HIS LOVE TO HER, BUT...

COUGH

RIGHT AT THAT VERY MOMENT, FLU CAME UP, AND THE YOUNG GIRL REELED WITH EMOTION.

HUH? FRIGHTENED BY THE SUDDEN APPEARANCE OF THE SON OF THE CELESTIAL GOD, FLU TOOK TO HIS HEELS.

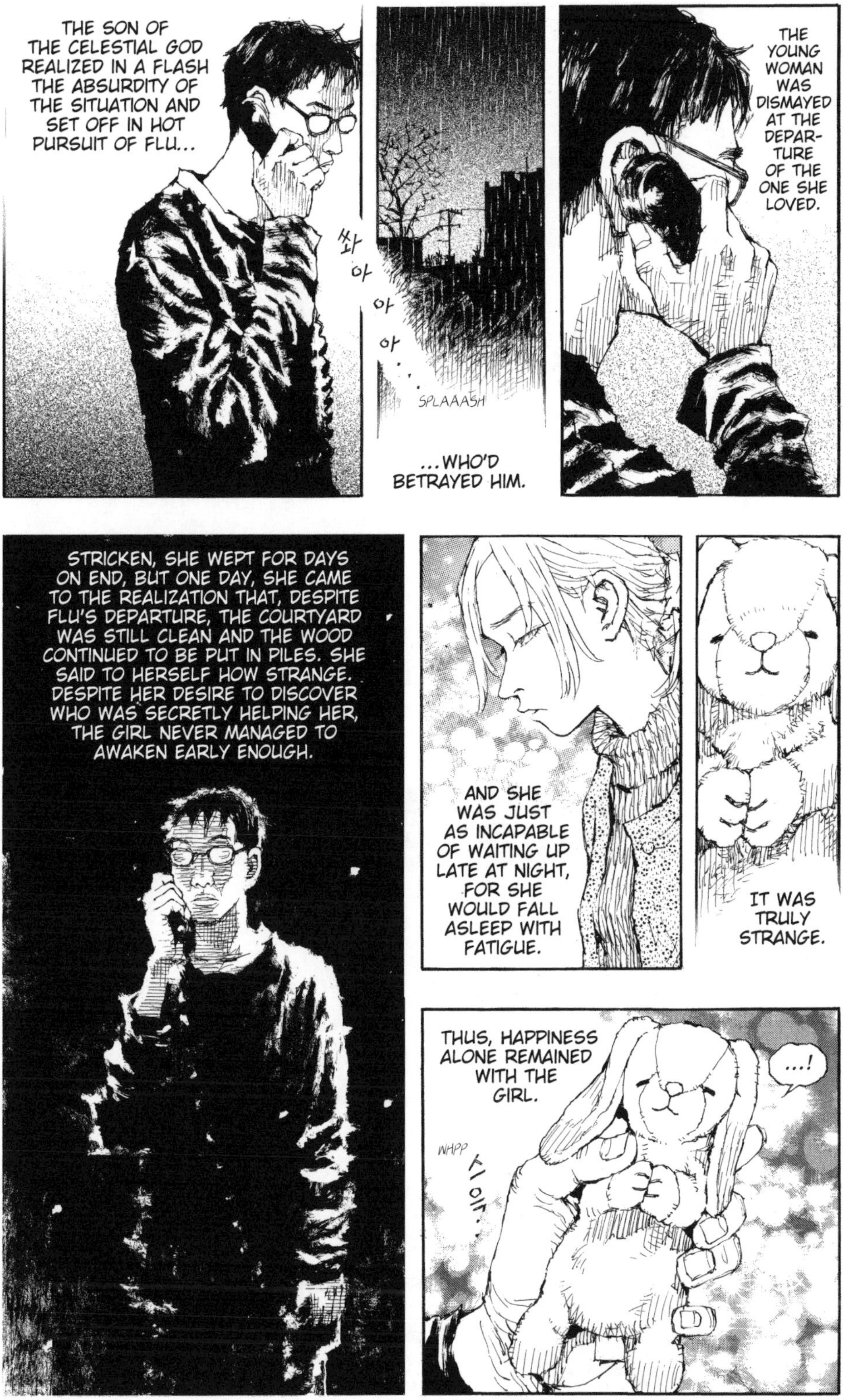
THE SON OF THE CELESTIAL GOD REALIZED IN A FLASH THE ABSURDITY OF THE SITUATION AND SET OFF IN HOT PURSUIT OF FLU...
쏴아아아...
SPLAAASH
...WHO'D BETRAYED HIM.
THE YOUNG WOMAN WAS DISMAYED AT THE DEPARTURE OF THE ONE SHE LOVED.
STRICKEN, SHE WEPT FOR DAYS ON END, BUT ONE DAY, SHE CAME TO THE REALIZATION THAT, DESPITE FLU'S DEPARTURE, THE COURTYARD WAS STILL CLEAN AND THE WOOD CONTINUED TO BE PUT IN PILES. SHE SAID TO HERSELF HOW STRANGE. DESPITE HER DESIRE TO DISCOVER WHO WAS SECRETLY HELPING HER, THE GIRL NEVER MANAGED TO AWAKEN EARLY ENOUGH.
AND SHE WAS JUST AS INCAPABLE OF WAITING UP LATE AT NIGHT, FOR SHE WOULD FALL ASLEEP WITH FATIGUE.
IT WAS TRULY STRANGE.
THUS, HAPPINESS ALONE REMAINED WITH THE GIRL.
...!
WHPP

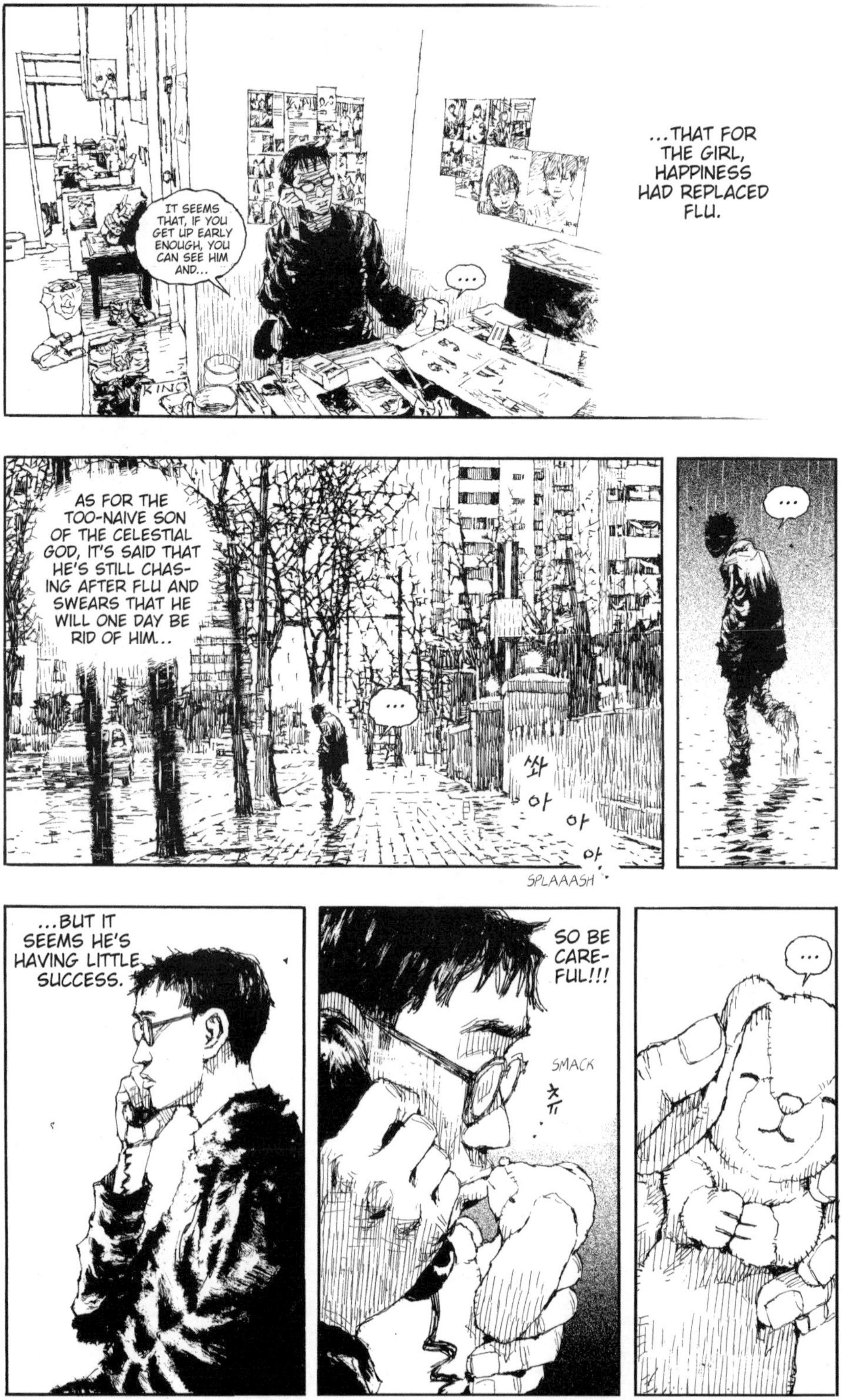

IT SEEMS THAT, IF YOU GET UP EARLY ENOUGH, YOU CAN SEE HIM AND...
...
...THAT FOR THE GIRL, HAPPINESS HAD REPLACED FLU.
AS FOR THE TOO-NAIVE SON OF THE CELESTIAL GOD, IT'S STILL SAID THAT HE'S STILL CHASING AFTER FLU AND SWEARS THAT HE WILL ONE DAY BE RID OF HIM...
...
쏴아아아
SPLAAASH
...
...BUT IT SEEMS HE'S HAVING LITTLE SUCCESS.
SO BE CAREFUL!!!
SMACK
...

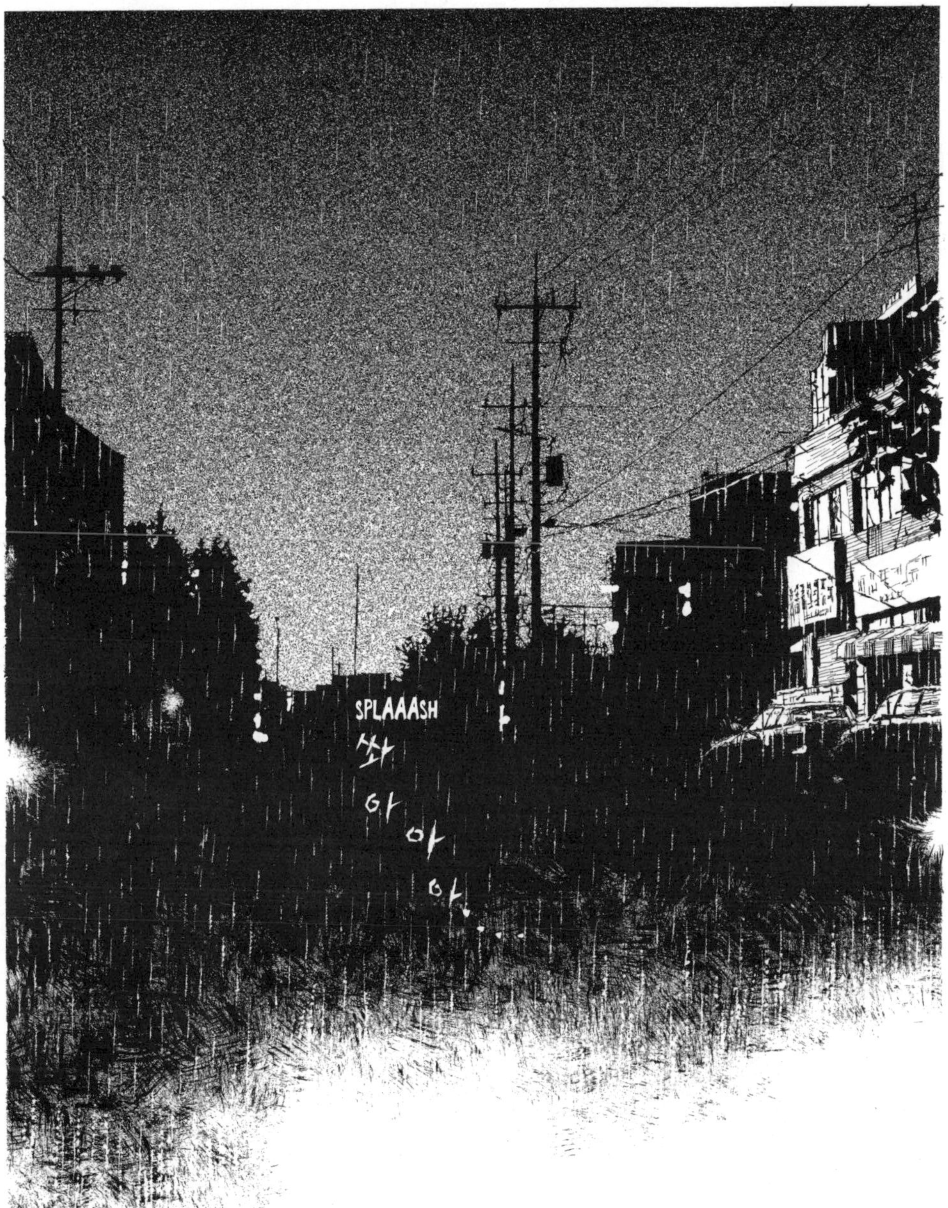
SPLAAASH
쏴

THAT NASTY FLU
WILL SURELY
COME VISIT YOU.

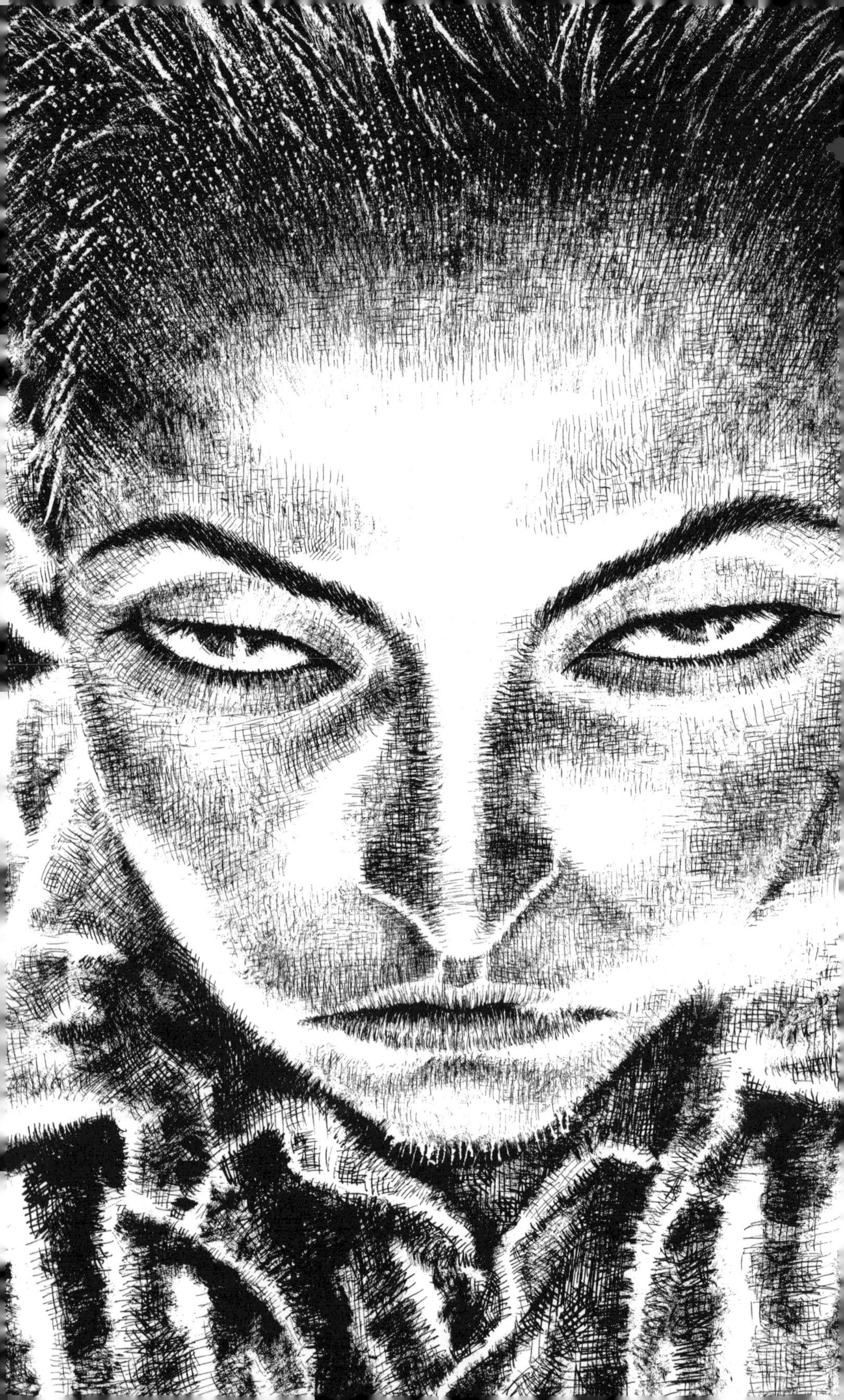

I'VE BEEN DRAWING *MANWHAS* FOR SOME TIME NOW, BUT I FEEL LIKE I'M GOING IN CIRCLES. I SEE NO PROGRESS, EXCEPT FOR THAT OF WORRIES.

MY SECOND COLLECTION OF STORIES, *MIJEONG*, TOTALLY REFLECTS MY CURRENT STATE OF MIND: ETERNALLY HESITANT, I FEEL LIKE I'M STUCK IN AN IMPASSE.

I WOULD LIKE TO THANK THE SEOUL ANIMATION CENTER AND KILCHATKI PUBLISHING, WHO HAVE HELPED MY MODEST EFFORTS SEE THE LIGHT OF DAY.

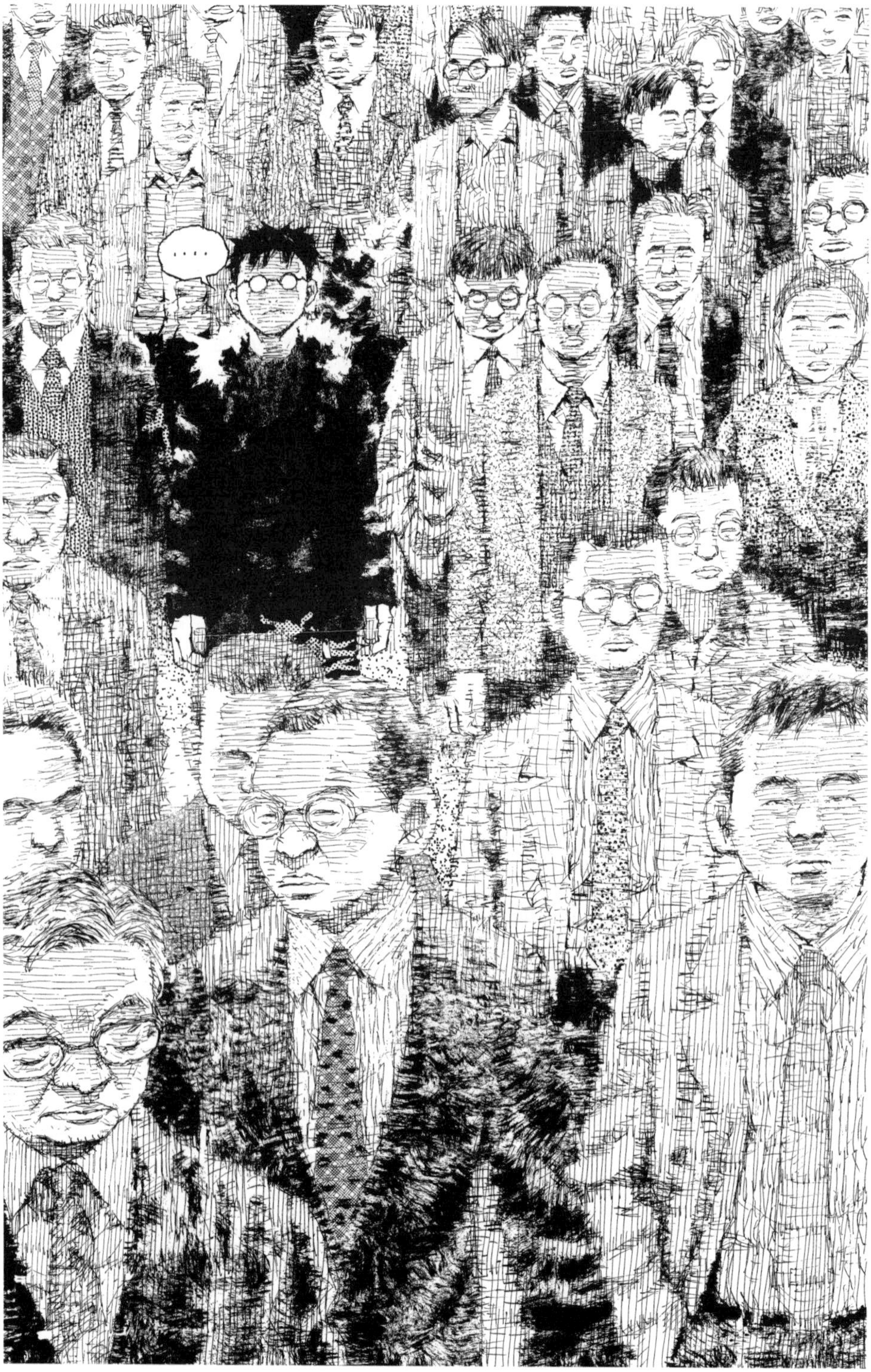
....

MIJEONG-A delightful manwha Byun Byung Jun-style

Kim Nak-ho, comics specialist,
editor of a webzine devoted to graphic novels,
Dugo Boja ("What We Shall See").

It's a rather delicate task to pen a review destined to be placed at the back of a book. It's a little like giving a speech about newlyweds on the occasion of a wedding. Furthermore, it's not very easy to write a commentary on a collection whose tales are so different from one another. Nor can I ruin the readers' pleasure by droning on about the author. So I'm in quite a fix. It would be interesting, however, to show the evidence of the author's creative potential and to observe how his talent will evolve. In general, a collection of stories includes diverse tales that foreshadow a project of even greater scope. One might compare them to the B side of a record. One discovers on it the author's ideas in an unrefined state, as well as the signs of his evolution.

After the publication of Princess Anna, which met with critical praise, Byun Byung Jun devoted himself to depicting the city. But he doesn't content himself with making a backdrop of it or of giving it a conventional, elegant, and sophisticated image. He is more interested in the situations and feelings of the city-dwellers. A Manwha is a comic book that tells a story, but the city described by Byun Byung Jun is a story in and of itself.

With Byun Byung Jun, the familiar city awakens emotions in us, all the while conserving its realism. Sometimes there emanates an atmosphere of solitude and cold, other times a renewal of hope. In the city of Byun Byung Jun live human beings who are suffering. Some of them attempt to treat their wounds; others strive simply to survive.

Byun Byung Jun's characters belong, above all else, to their past. The author shows first their present life, harmoniously melting into the background, then introduces, little by little, their past. The author adds nothing further to the initial drama. The sole goal of the unfolding of the story is putting an end to what happened in the past. Full-page drawings in an expressionist style—the mark of Byun Byung Jun—give the reader the impression of entering fully into the décor of the story. The pictorial style of the author obliges the reader to remain an observer and does not invite to identify with the characters. The narrative sometimes takes on a joking tone, other times, it becomes "indirect," referring to distant or absent characters.

Created in the first years of the new century, the stories assembled in Mijeong are the fruit of the pictorial experiments of Byun Byung Jun. His first collection, First Love, had diverse environments for its canvas—the city and its coldness, the countryside and its warm atmosphere—and he touched upon several themes in it, whereas Mijeong has for its sole décor the city, but he experiments with diverse pictorial styles to portray it. The collection treats upon two subjects principally: the wanderings of men in search of a meaning to their lives and the wounds from which the young suffer. The first theme fascinates us all the more as we discover therein the traces of an emotional self-portrait of the author.

"Mijeong," the eponymous tale for the collection, took inspiration from the film Wings of Desire, in which one of the heroes ventures into the coldness of the city in search of "something else." Byun Byung Jun, in his own fashion, treats upon this same theme in this work where his two preferred subjects appear. The story was published in Manwha Quarterly in Spring 2003, but the author was still working on it in January of the same year, when he was at comic book festival in Angoulême, France, where he'd been invited to present his work.

The second tale, "Yeon-Du, 17 years old," was created during the summer of 2003, to be published in Japan. In it, the author tells the story of a deeply wounded young girl, a theme already broached in Princess Anna, but which he develops here with perfect mastery. With simplicity and dexterity, he depicts the tragic ambience of urban life and finishes the story on a hopeful note.

Next comes "Utility," created in collaboration with Yun In-Wan, a well-known writer in the world of manwha for teenagers. The story doesn't entirely meet our expectations, but this small dark comedy, which takes place against a backdrop of infantile cruelty and city darkness, lets us glimpse another potential of the author. "Utility" was published as a supplement to the Japanese magazine Big Comic Spirits in April 2002.

"A Song for You," a tale all in pastel colors, is more recent. It dates from Autumn 2003. The characters in it are less harsh, and one can observe a significant progress in the representation of space.

As for the black humor present in "202, Villa Simil", it's a genre which the author hadn't made use of in a long time, which proves that his talent in this domain remains vigorous. He created this work in Spring 2000, during his studies in Japan. The delirious imagination used in this self-portrait sets up an amusing comedy. "202, Villa Simil" received a prize for promising young authors at the competition organized by Big Comic Spirits of Shôgakukan and appeared in that magazine in December 2001.

We find the same tone in the following piece, "Courage, Grandfather!" Here, no hallucinations, but rather the recourse to a melodramatic element with, at the story's center, a beautiful young woman.

Yang Seung-Chan wrote the scenario for the last tale in the collection, "A Short Tall Tale". The hero, impassive, tells his girlfriend over the phone a little tale that's both funny and melancholic. The reader is caught up in the universe of the story in which two characters evolve, the ingenious incarnations of Flu and Happiness. However, the setting encourages the reader to lend his attention to the relationship between the hero and his invisible girlfriend, rather than to the story being told. And, once again, the protagonist is an artist of manhwa, trapped in a dark, little room, an image of the author himself. Thus the fictive self-portrait present in "Mijeong" and the one, closer to reality, of the last tale, create a coherence between the beginning and the end of the book, uniting the whole.

Since this collection perfectly reflects Byun Byung Jun's progress, certain defects are still perceptible, which he should correct: a lack of plot twists that might captivate the reader, the quasi-repetition of images from one square to the next, defects which the author has not yet remedied since the appearance of Princess Anna. One can discern, however, that, in his own way, he's striving to surmount them and to move beyond them.

Here then is the delightful collection of tales that Byun Byung Jun has presented to us in the first years of the new century. One senses in it the budding of a masterpiece in which his privileged themes, already present in this collection, will all melt together: the sophistication of urban life, wounded youth, the black humor of unexpected situations, etc.

A few years ago, Byun Byung Jun was hailed as the "heir" to Pak Heung-Yong. People had noticed that the urban life and landscapes depicted in First Love and Princess Anna strongly resembled those in the manwha authored by Pak Heung-Yong, published in the Eighties. By coincidence, one of the latter's collections was titled "White Page," and the Korean word Mijeong has not only the original meaning of "pure beauty" derived from Chinese and is often used a woman's name but also means "something as yet undefined." Perhaps the author was attempting to personify thus the heroine of whom we all dream. One could also suppose that he chose it as a symbol for a new departure. It will therefore be interesting to see in which direction the next work by Byun Byung Jun evolves and what its title will be.

Byun Byung-Jun started in manhwa in 1995 and, armed with both passion and talent, is one of its most promising rising stars. His works, mostly lyrical short stories for which he draws the backgrounds based on his own photographs, has garnered him many awards both in Korea and in Japan where he studied comics for a few years.

Run, Bong-Gu, Run!
Byun Byung-Jun
a little manhwa
graphic novel

BUJA'S DIARY
SEYEONG O

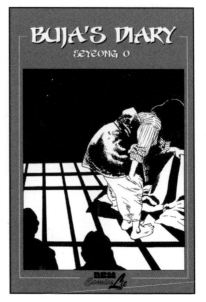